Fighting Words

Contradictions of Modernity

The modern era has been uniquely productive of theory. Some theory claimed uniformity despite human differences or unilinear progress in the face of catastrophic changes. Other theory was informed more deeply by the complexities of history and recognition of cultural specificity. This series seeks to further the latter approach by publishing books that explore the problems of theorizing the modern in its manifold and sometimes contradictory forms and that examine the specific locations of theory within the modern.

Edited by Craig Calhoun

New York University

Fighting Words

Black Women and the Search for Justice

Patricia Hill Collins

Contradictions of Modernity, Volume 7

 University of Minnesota Press

Minneapolis

London

Published by the University of Minnesota Press
111 Third Avenue South, Suite 290
Minneapolis, MN 55401–2520
http://www.upress.umn.edu

Printed in the United States of America on acid-free paper

Library of Congress Cataloging-in-Publication Data

Collins, Patricia Hill, 1948–
    Fighting words : Black women and the search for justice / Patricia Hill Collins.
        p.   cm. — (Contradictions of modernity ; v. 7)
    Includes bibliographical references (p. 283) and index.
    ISBN 0-8166-2376-7 (hardcover : alk. paper). — ISBN 0-8166-2377-5 (pbk. : alk paper)
    1. Afro-American women—Political activity.   2. Afro-American women—Social conditions.   3. Feminism—United States.   4. Social sciences—Philosophy.   5. Critical theory.   I. Title.   II. Series.
E185.86.C5817   1998
305.48′896073—dc21   98-17051

The University of Minnesota is an equal-opportunity educator and employer.

10 09 08 07 06 05 04 03 02 01 00 99   10 9 8 7 6 5 4 3 2

Contents

Acknowledgments

Many people participated in all phases of this project, and many thanks are in order. Because I worked on *Fighting Words* from 1991 to 1997, I accumulated a long list of people who contributed to the completion of this project. I thank the students in my African-American studies and women's studies seminars at the University of Cincinnati for their patience and incisive comments on various ideas in this volume. My gratitude also goes out to the students, colleagues, and new friends I met while a Presidential Professor at the University of Michigan in the Center for African and AfroAmerican Studies and Women's Studies in fall 1994.

For the institutional support needed to work on this manuscript during the 1995–1997 academic years, I thank Joseph Caruso, dean of the College of Arts and Sciences at the University of Cincinnati; John Brackett, head of the Department of African-American Studies; and Robin Sheets, director of the Women's Studies Program. The Charles Phelps Taft Fund at the University of Cincinnati made two important contributions to this project. First, the faculty development grant that funded a quarter of release time in 1995 greatly assisted me. Also, the research budget that accompanied my being named Charles Phelps Taft Professor of Sociology in 1996 funded part of the expenses incurred in final manuscript preparation. I also remain grateful for the numerous invitations that I received to lecture on college campuses and at professional meetings. These trips enabled me to work through the ideas in this volume with diverse audiences. Although the list of colleagues and new friends that I met during these visits is too long to list, I appreciate all of the ideas that people shared with me.

Student research assistance was invaluable for this project. Susan Freeman, Jennifer Ridenaur, and Diane Pisacreta, the women's studies graduate students who researched many of the topics covered in *Fighting Words,* each contributed much to its completion. Melinda Spong Guenes and Tina Beyene both deserve special recognition for their diligence in working with final versions of the manuscript. Both contributed important ideas as well as much-needed copyediting and research expertise. Valerie Ruffin's assistance with indexing and proofreading was invaluable. Special thanks go to Patrice L. Dickerson at the University of Michigan for assistance with the data reported in chapter 3 and to Shanda Calhoun for ideas about cover art.

Reviewer comments on the manuscript were invaluable. Special appreciation goes out to Craig Calhoun for his diplomatic yet insightful comments on an earlier version of this manuscript. I also found the suggestions of Charles Lemert and Barbara Christian, the two external reviewers for this manuscript, immensely helpful. I also thank my colleague and friend Margaret L. Andersen for casting a conceptual and editorial eye on the final manuscript. I am also very grateful to Lisa Freeman, the former director of the University of Minnesota Press and the editor of this project through its many years of preparation. I also acknowledge the efforts of Micah Kleit, Tammy Zambo, and the wonderful staff at the University of Minnesota Press for making the production stages of this project so positive.

A segment of chapter 2 was originally published in the *Black Scholar* (26, 1, March 1996: 9–17) under the title "What's in a Name? Womanism, Black Feminism, and Beyond." An earlier version of chapter 4 appeared in *Current Perspectives in Social Theory* (17 [1997] 3–37) under the title "How Much Difference Is Too Much? Black Feminist Thought and the Politics of Postmodern Social Theory."

Finally, I acknowledge the support of my husband, Roger; my daughter, Valerie; my father, Albert Hill; and my aunt, Marjorie Edwards.

Introduction

The Politics of Critical Social Theory

In the early 1970s, I was assigned to teach a curriculum unit entitled "The Community" to a class of African-American second graders. The community in my students' textbook consisted of single-family homes nestled in plush green grass, populated by all sorts of friendly White people they had never met and probably would never meet. Phrases like "Let's visit our men at the firehouse," "Cross only at the corner," and "The policeman is your friend" peppered the text, all designed to reassure my second graders that children were loved, cared for, and safe in their communities.

My students lived in quite a different community. Most resided in a nearby racially segregated public housing project. Their neighborhood experienced all of the social problems that typically accompany poverty and political powerlessness. As I read to them from the pages of their text and saw their blank, bored, and occasionally angry expressions, I realized that I was lying to them. Worse yet, we all knew that the book and I were lying. So I asked them to tell me about their community as they experienced it. One little boy tentatively raised his hand. To my shock, he shared a story of how, because the housing commission had left the doors open, his best friend had fallen down an elevator chute the day before. His friend had been killed.

At that moment, I faced an important choice. I could teach the status quo or I could teach for a change. I did not see how I could lie to my students, no matter how pure my intentions to prepare them for an imagined third-grade entrance test on community vocabulary. So we closed those texts full of smiling, affluent White people and began to talk.

At first, my class could not quite believe that I wanted to hear from them. Despite their young age, so many had been silenced by classroom practices that rewarded their obedience and punished their curiosity that they were justifiably afraid to question the public transcript known as their curriculum. They kept their own oppositional knowledge hidden, relegating it to discussions on the playgrounds, on the streets, and in the privacy of their apartments. But because they were still young, they were able to come to voice much easier than those of us who have endured years of such silencing. With minimal prompting, they shared their feelings about the horror of their friend's death, especially their sense of vulnerability that something similar might happen to them. In some cases, they exploded, sharing deep-seated anger. Through dialogue, these children began to develop the voice so typical of any relatively powerless outsider group that begins to frame its own self-defined standpoint in hierarchical power relations of race, class, gender, and, in their case, age. Some blamed the victim, claiming that "he had no business being near that elevator anyhow." Others condemned his mother for being at work while it happened. "Why couldn't she stay home like she was supposed to?" one little girl queried. Still others wanted to "tell somebody" that something was wrong with the way that the people in their community were treated. One little girl summed it up—"It's just not fair, Miss Hill," she stated. "It's just not fair."

For me, this incident marked an important milestone in my growing recognition of the culpability of ideas in hierarchical power relations. Described by sociologist Dorothy Smith as a "complex of organized practices, including government, law, business and financial management, professional organizations, and educational institutions as well as the discourses in texts that interpenetrate the multiple sites of power" (1987, 3), power relations, or relations of ruling, permeate all aspects of everyday life. However, where Dorothy Smith's relations of ruling emphasize gender dichotomies that work with and through the economic class relations characterizing advanced capitalism, relations of ruling also encompass race, age, sexuality, and nationality.

Within these hierarchical power relations, the ideas produced by elite groups about community, difference, voice, justice, and many other topics matter. As Teun Van Dijk observes, "Elites have the means to manufacture consent. . . . This does not mean that all opinions of elites are always adopted by the public at large, but only that their opinions are well known, that they have the most effective means of public persuasion and the best resources for suppressing or marginalizing alternative opinions" (1993, 45).

Since those days of teaching second graders, I have come to see the importance of preschool through postgraduate education, collectively known as the Curriculum, to hierarchical power relations. Consisting of a body of knowledge accompanied by a specific constellation of classroom practices and administrative structures, the Curriculum operates as a contested location for knowledges of all sorts. On the one hand, the legitimated Curriculum includes the knowledge that most interests elite groups. Unfortunately, this public transcript far too often presents one version of the truth as being the only, ideal, and superior version. Moreover, such truth is often developed through racial segregation, gender homogeneity, and other exclusionary practices. Hierarchy occupies a central role in this Curriculum, where the goal for teachers and students alike lies in learning one's place in the pecking order. Despite the seeming hegemony of this Curriculum, it also sparks all sorts of rebellion. Thus, on the other hand, the Curriculum can and does generate critical thinking that leads to many unintended consequences. Although far too many classrooms present the Curriculum as universal truth, they simultaneously provide potential spaces of participatory democracy. The dialogue that I invited among my second-grade students, the ideas in their textbook, and I constituted just such a reworking of classroom space. Examining their ideas about community in the context of the concrete experiences of their everyday lives allowed those children to return to their text on "the community" with fresh eyes. The lesson that they needed had really begun.

My years in higher education have revealed another facet of the centrality of education to power relations in the United States—the Curriculum operates very much like "theory" does in the academy. Like the Curriculum, theory also cuts both ways. Social theory in particular can serve either to reproduce existing power relations or to foster social and economic justice. Far from being neutral, the very meaning and use of the term *social theory* represents a contested terrain. Narrow interpretations of social theory seem primarily concerned with studying the ideas of selected theorists from elite groups. It goes without saying that many of these theorists are "dead White males." But even if they were "living Latina lesbians" this approach would be shortsighted, because it treats theory as the individual commodity of selected luminaries. In my view, doing social theory involves analyzing the changing aspects of social organization that affect people's everyday lives. Social theory is a body of knowledge and a set of institutional practices that actively grapple with the central questions facing a group of people in a specific political, social, and historic context. Instead of circulating exclusively as a body of decontextualized ideas among privileged intellectuals, social theory emerges from, is legitimated by, and reflects the concerns of actual groups of people in particular institutional settings. This definition creates space for all types of groups to participate in theorizing about social issues. Moreover, it suggests that differences in perspective about social issues will reflect differences in the power of those who theorize.

Elite groups routinely minimize the workings of their own power in determining what counts as social theory, claiming that they merely want to protect universalistic standards of excellence. As a result, prevailing definitions of theory portray it as an ahistorical, static system of abstract logic, reason, or science that, when applied to social phenomena, suggests universal relationships between theory and practice. Separating questions of what counts as knowledge from questions of who decides what knowledge is—in effect, severing epistemology from power—privileges elites. As a result, much social theory produced either by members of elite groups or by individuals using standards legitimated by elite groups examines issues especially germane to elites. For example, most universities offer courses on managing some designated group. Beginning teachers learn how to discipline students, fledgling administrators study management techniques designed to get their staffs to work harder, and criminal justice students master skills of controlling deviant populations. Far fewer courses teach how to recognize and combat these strategies of control. Within this managerial climate, courses on union movements, Black political activism, global women's movements, and everyday subversive activities are few and far between.[1]

I've learned to think more broadly about social theory, beyond what I've found in the American academy. Although oppositional knowledge often takes diverse forms, in my view historically oppressed groups also produce social theories. Not only do the forms assumed by these theories—poetry, music, essays, and the like—diverge from academic theory, but the *purpose* of such theory also seems distinctly different. Social theories emerging from and/or on behalf of historically oppressed groups investigate ways to escape from, survive in, and/or oppose prevailing social and economic injustice. In the United States, for example, integrationist and Black nationalist political theories share the goal of analyzing and resisting the institutionalized racism confronting African-Americans. The challenging of economic class relations under U.S. capitalist development has a long, albeit muted, history in dissident social science. Feminism advocates women's emancipation and empowerment, and queer theory opposes heterosexism. Beyond U.S. borders, these and other issues occupy oppressed groups. Grappling with postcolonialism, groups from the Caribbean, Africa, and Asia struggle with new meanings attached to ethnicity, citizenship status, and religion in the increasingly diverse European nation-states. Social theories from these groups typically do not arise from the rarefied atmosphere of the imagination; instead, they often emerge in conjunction with freedom struggles. Although these social theories are far from perfect, they share a common feature of opposing oppression.[2]

It is not that elites produce theory while everyone else produces mere thought. Rather, elites possess the power to legitimate the knowledge that they define as theory as being universal, normative, and ideal. Legitimated theory typically delivers tangible social rewards to those who possess it. Elites simultaneously derogate the social theory of less powerful groups who may express contrary standpoints on the same social issues by labeling subordinate groups' social theory as being folk wisdom, raw experience, or common sense. Describing this process in the United Kingdom, writer Michelle Cliff observes that "one of the effects of assimilation, indoctrination, passing into the anglocentrism of British West Indian culture is that you believe absolutely in the hegemony of the King's English and in the form in which it is meant to be expressed. Or else your writing is not literature; it is folklore, and folklore can never be art" (1988, 59). In this sense, analyzing social theories in isolation from their embeddedness in race, class, and gender produces the objectified knowledge that characterizes hierarchical power relations (Smith 1990a).

In my view, critical social theory constitutes theorizing about the social in defense of economic and social justice. Stated differently, critical social theory encompasses bodies of knowledge and sets of institutional practices that actively grapple with the central questions facing groups of people differently placed in specific political, social, and historic contexts characterized by injustice. What makes critical social theory "critical" is its commitment to justice, for one's own group and/or for other groups. According to philosopher Iris Marion Young (1990), political thought of the modern period greatly narrowed the scope of justice present in ancient and medieval thought. Formerly, justice had been conceptualized as the virtue of society as a whole evidenced by orderly social institutions. If a society fostered individual virtue and promoted happiness and harmony among its citizens, it was just. Seeking to free individuals to define their own ends, liberal bourgeois societies abandoned these earlier ideas. Notions of justice under modern democracies became restricted to questions of distributing rights to individuals and regulating actions among self-defining individuals. My use of justice in *Fighting Words* differs from both of these uses. Neither of these approaches relies on relationships among *groups* in a society as an important indicator of social justice. Where group differences exist such that some groups are privileged while others are oppressed, achieving economic and social justice requires explicitly attending to these relationships. Thus, although individuals matter, I emphasize justice as a group-based phenomenon.

Although questions of justice and fairness typically fall outside the scope of traditional definitions of social theory, they emerge as central to critical social theory. Moreover, critical social theory neither remains completely absent from elite group histories nor emanates exclusively from oppressed groups. Members of elite groups who use their privilege to challenge unjust power relations often produce important critical social theory. Conversely, social theorists from oppressed groups do not generate uniformly emancipatory social theory. However, given the vested interest of members of elite groups in preserving their privilege and that of oppressed groups in challenging that same privilege, it stands to reason that critical social theory is closely aligned with the more generalized oppositional knowledge created by oppressed groups (Scott 1990).

All groups need to see how their views of truth remain limited by the workings of unjust power relations. In this sense, all groups potentially benefit from participating in a more broadly defined critical social theory. Just as the writers of my second graders' textbook on community failed to take my students' lives into account and thereby produced an impoverished text, the limited horizons of my second graders, imposed by the harsh conditions of their lives, restricted them to a similarly diminished understanding of community. The difference in these truths lay, in part, in the ability of one group to mandate that its view of community prevail over competing interpretations.

We are still quite far from a more democratic critical social theory that encourages textbook writers to take the lives of children like my second graders into account. Although it is theoretically possible for members of elite groups to relinquish privilege and to participate in a collaborative effort to develop critical social theory of the sort I envision, few actually do. Thus, the task of being critical continues to fall most heavily on those who are closest to the bottom.

My second graders from the 1970s are no longer children. If they survived until adulthood, they probably have second graders of their own who have encountered similarly narrow interpretations of community. However, the issues of "fairness" raised by those earlier second graders remain. This project is motivated and sustained by a deep desire to explore how social theory can be used to foster economic and social justice. As African-American intellectuals bell hooks and Cornel West observe, "Theory is inescapable because it is an indispensable weapon in struggle, and it is an indispensable weapon in struggle because it provides certain kinds of understanding, certain kinds of illumination, certain kinds of insights that are requisite if we are to act effectively" (1991, 34–35). Unfortunately, much important theoretical knowledge designed to provide understanding, illumination, and insights for effective action remains buried in the obscure, exclusionary language of academia. Over the years, I have encountered many individuals who want to grapple with theoretical ideas but who have been taught that social theory is too hard for the average person to understand. Undergraduates, some graduate students, and members of the college-educated public all express some distaste, if not distress, when confronted with what appears to be a theoretical (read boring) book.

What astonishes me is how many faculty members also express and frequently encourage these same reactions.

Fighting Words: Black Women and the Search for Justice explores two interrelated questions: What epistemological criteria best evaluate critical social theories that aim to oppose oppression? Furthermore, what standards might be used to determine how effectively a critical social theory confronts injustice? In cutting into these large questions, I confine my analysis to one critical social theory produced by one oppressed group in a specific historical situation. Although substantial attention has been paid to the epistemological dimensions of social theory produced by elite groups, the oppositional knowledge generally and the social theory in particular that emerge from oppressed groups typically has attracted considerably less attention. Despite long-standing claims by elites that Blacks, women, Latinos, and other similarly derogated groups in the United States remain incapable of producing the type of interpretive, analytical thought that is labeled theory in the West, powerful knowledges of resistance that toppled former structures of social inequality repudiate this view. Members of these groups do in fact theorize, and our critical social theory has been central to our political empowerment and search for justice. Social theory can be used to support hierarchical power relations. However, more importantly, critical social theory can also challenge unjust ideas and practices.

For me, one fundamental difficulty in writing this volume lay in exploring this question of epistemological criteria for oppressed groups' critical social theory while simultaneously invoking these same criteria in producing the volume. Such theory not only typically criticizes existing social arrangements, it often also seeks to change things. For elites, much social theory operates to obscure the workings of unjust power relations, especially those organizing the social relations in academia, where much social theory is currently produced. In contrast, critical social theory by those in an oppressed group and in defense of that group's interest in justice must attend to such power relations. The thematic content of the theory, daily practices that it generates, and evaluations of its effectiveness in challenging injustice all rely on its perceptions of power.

Anchoring my arguments in the experiences and ideas of African-American women was immensely helpful both in identifying core questions for the volume and in addressing this fundamental epistemological difficulty. This may seem simple, but at this historical moment, the relationship between groups and ideas is far from settled. *Black Feminist Thought,* my earlier work, published in 1990, set the stage for this volume. In that work, I aimed to demonstrate that African-American women had produced an oppositional knowledge that both emerged from a situation of oppression and was central to Black women's survival. Working in the late 1980s, I wrote against prevailing positivist truths that assumed that Black women in the United States were a collectivity but one that, for whatever reasons, had not produced any social theory of substance. In the political context of that historical moment, I chose not to explore heterogeneity among African-American women, because my goal lay in legitimating the existence of a Black women's standpoint. I aimed to validate a space for African-American women, in particular, where dialogue and disagreement could occur. Although *Fighting Words* builds on *Black Feminist Thought,* this volume reflects the political realities of a very different historical moment. Writing in the late 1990s against prevailing postmodern ideas of decentering and difference generates a new set of issues. Here the challenge to Black women's critical social theory lies not in a direct refutation of a Black women's intellectual tradition but rather in questioning the terms by which Black women exist as a collectivity. Without a collectivity or group, there can be no critical social theory that aims to struggle with the realities confronting that group. In other words, if African-American women's experiences are more different than similar, then Black feminist thought does not exist.

In response to these controversies, in this volume I both use and problematize Black feminist thought as a critical social theory to explore several significant questions. Each of the three parts of *Fighting Words: Black Women and the Search for Justice* explores a particular question. First, what issues does Black feminist thought confront *as* critical social theory? Just as my second graders faced formidable obstacles in getting their ideas and interpretations legitimated as knowledge, current power relations of race, gender, class, sexuality, and nation present similar challenges for oppressed groups. Second, what issues does Black feminist thought raise *for* critical social theory? My second graders' views of community contradicted those of their textbook, and probably those of other textbooks that disagreed with their textbook. Just as my second graders' perspectives constituted one important yet missing dimension of a complex analysis of community, so does Black feminist thought as critical social theory need to examine its relationship to a series of discourses that all appear to be constructing truths about similar things. Finally, what contributions can Black feminist thought make *to* critical social theory? Just as the textbook's portrayal of community was impoverished because its truth had been arrived at via exclusionary practices, so are existing knowledges similarly compromised when developed in undemocratic contexts. This suggests that new standards for evaluating knowledge are needed. Collectively, all three parts of *Fighting Words* explore Black feminist thought's potential contributions to developing adequate epistemological criteria for critical social theory.

These three questions shape the overall organization of the book in several ways. First, *Fighting Words* reflects a degree of eclecticism that results from dialogues with many intellectual communities. Because I read, listen, and travel widely, I encounter the content of many academic disciplines as well as the theoretical perspectives that permeate contemporary intellectual production. I try to take the best from positivist science, Marxist social theory, postmodernism, Afrocentrism, North American feminism, British cultural studies, and other intellectual traditions, and to leave the rest behind. Keeping multiple intellectual traditions such as these in mind, I invoke theoretical and methodological tools from different disciplines when they seem relevant to the goal of fostering economic and social justice. The strengths of this approach, I hope, emerge in innovative connections made among diverse ideas and phenomena. Its limitations, however, lie in risking insufficient depth in one knowledge. All around me, I hear colleagues paying lip service to interdisciplinary research. Many advocate collapsing artificial boundaries that distinguish theory from practice or academia from the so-called real world. Although this approach is ultimately rewarding, I want to remind readers that actually doing this type of work on a daily basis over a period of years remains extremely difficult.[3]

A second element of *Fighting Words* concerns my decision not to restrict my analysis only to ideas. I make an explicit effort to situate all theories that I examine in the social, political, and economic contexts from which they emerge and in which they operate. In this regard, my work participates in the traditions of the sociology of knowledge. Many of my students think that questions concerning knowledge and power relations originated with French philosopher Michel Foucault. However, in 1945, sociologist Robert Merton described this sociological subfield: "The sociology of knowledge came into being with the signal hypothesis that even truths were to be held socially accountable, were to be related to the historical society in which they emerged" (Merton 1973, 11). A seemingly eclectic combination of thinkers, including Karl Marx, Karl Mannheim, Antonio Gramsci, Robert Merton, Peter Berger, and Thomas Luckmann, has contributed to this area of inquiry. Although scholarship within the tradition of the sociology of knowledge in the United States historically has minimized the political dimensions of social organization, I explicitly attend to the power relations that frame knowledge, especially those of oppression. These, to me, relate most closely to group-based struggles for social justice.

This explicit contextualization also allows me to broaden my epistemological analysis beyond questions of truth. Western academics, especially theorists in the academy, seem especially preoccupied with the epistemological foundations of truth. For example, current debates emphasize how new social movements of race, gender, economic class, ethnicity, and sexuality have eroded former ways of validating truth. Such debates seemingly offer two choices. On the one hand, the notion of "universal" criteria for ascertaining truth that may be applied to all situations without regard to particulars—the legacy of science—persists. On the other hand, as philosopher Kwame Anthony Appiah suggests, "theory in the grand sense is surely yielding increasingly to a more particularized historical method" (1992, 65). From this perspective, universal truth is not possible. Instead, multiple truths exist. In the absence of standards for determining which truths have greater merit, a seemingly normless relativity sets in whereby all truths are equal. Because neither approach examines how hierarchical power relations influence the standards used in its epistemology, neither adequately confronts how power shapes what counts as truth. Moreover, both approaches avoid the question of justice as part of epistemological criteria applied to their own and other social theories. If oppressed groups controlled theoretical agendas, would this emphasis on truth be raised to this degree?

Third, *Fighting Words* spends little time analyzing the ideas of historical or contemporary social theorists, even those known as "critical theorists."[4] Some readers may be surprised that I do not evaluate well-known social theorists' ideas about a given phenomenon, for example, the worth of Jürgen Habermas's ideas about the public sphere for Black intellectual production or the implication of Jacques Derrida's notion of difference for racial hypersegregation in Philadelphia, or even what Habermas and Derrida have to say to each other. Works exist that engage in these types of analyses, and indeed this volume depends on this body of scholarship. Astute readers may notice that I rely on what are considered secondary works that examine primary works of social theory.[5] I remind these readers that the ability to rank scholarship into categories of primary, secondary, and tertiary importance reflects the power of those who classify. Since assessments of social theory reflect the agenda of the critic, I make my choices clear. I cite ideas and works when they seem to shed light on the three major questions shaping this volume, and I omit works that do not. Thus, the ideas in this volume are necessarily selective. Feminist philosopher Iris Marion Young's view of her own work parallels mine: "I claim to speak neither for everyone, to everyone, nor about everything" (1990, 13).

My treatment of my own subject position constitutes a fourth element of *Fighting Words*. Despite the risks associated with this stance, I place myself in selected chapters and thus model the process of working from a situated subject position. I realize that locating myself in my narrative runs certain risks. People from historically disempowered groups are typically not seen as theorists, and our work is not deemed theoretical unless we produce theory in ways comparable to highly educated White men. This presents a real dilemma for Black women intellectual workers. If we criticize elite discourse using its terms, we gain legitimation for our work by traditional standards. But by doing so, we may simultaneously delegitimate our work in the eyes of Black women who use different standards.

Fighting Words reflects one temporary resolution for these tensions. I write from a subject position and use it to illuminate how power relations affect individual and group readings of knowledges generated by elites and oppressed groups. In selected parts of the volume, I share examples from my own experiences. I am an African-American woman, and I certainly think that this reality shapes my arguments. However, I am also an academic, and my use of the impersonal language of academic discourse that erases me reflects my training as a social scientist. Academic discourses have distinctive strengths and limitations and, in some cases, express ideas not easily translatable into everyday speech or even into other specialized languages. Despite Black feminist theorist Patricia Williams's question "What is 'impersonal' writing but denial of self?" (1991, 92), in much of this volume, I invoke the authority of such writing to support my main ideas. The tensions of writing from a subject position within impersonal writing constitutes a contradiction, but it is one that I think mirrors theorizing from contradictory locations.

Finally, my choice of language in *Fighting Words* typifies my efforts to theorize differently. Unfortunately, we have so few models of legitimated social theory that foster dialogue among diverse groups that writing social theory typically means writing in a language of exclusion. A choice of language transcends mere selection of words— it is inherently a political choice. I see a great difference in trying to speak *to* someone, *with* someone, or *for* someone. Each suggests a different power relationship between the speaker-author and the intended or accidental audience and/or constituency. Moving among purposes of speaking to, with, and for someone generates difficult contradictions. With hindsight, I can see how my face-to-face contact with a wide range of potential readers for *Fighting Words* limited my ability to finish this book. Writing *Black Feminist Thought* involved imagining potential readers; in contrast, the people I met after 1990 at speaking engagements, in classes, and in informal conversations at more than one hundred schools, universities, professional gatherings, and other places left little room for fantasy. I realized the full range of the potential readership of *Fighting Words,* as well as the multiple languages that they used. I could not find a way to write outside the particular constellation of knowledge and power relations in which I am situated and which are reflected via multiple languages.

Rather than allowing my decisions about language to masquerade as seeming objectivity and apolitical authority, I am making my choices explicit. My choice of language for *Fighting Words* is both an intellectual and a political decision. Writing *Fighting Words* in a language that appears too "simple" might give grounds for criticism to those individuals who think that the complex ideas of social theory must be abstract, difficult, and inaccessible. The temptation for many in this group will be to possess and consume *Fighting Words* as if it were a commodity, a new theoretical candy bar with which to fight the boredom of the recycled academic theories currently clogging far too many scholarly publications. To this group, the scarcity of ideas becomes a measure of their worth. Populist ideas become devalued exactly because they are popular. This position reflects a growing disdain for anything deemed "public" and for the general public itself, a position that sadly seems to have infected many academic disciplines. At the same time, writing *Fighting Words* in language that demonstrates my grasp of the specialized languages of much contemporary academic discourse—or as former college president Johnetta Cole puts it, in "academic tribal language" (1993, 57–62)—needlessly excludes large numbers of people. The content of my ideas might be profoundly compromised by the process I use in sharing them.

The political implications of word selection further complicate this question of language. Robert Chrisman points out how choice of words creates frameworks that remove African-American protest and criticism from their specific historical and political contexts: "The general practice has been to de-racialize the African-American protest, eschewing terms such as 'black,' 'racism,' 'exploitation,' and 'oppression' in favor of 'minority,' 'ethnicity,' 'underprivileged,' 'disadvantaged,' or 'diversity'" (1992, xxxiii). Some audiences welcome language that mutes the effects of oppression, whereas others, like Chrisman, view such language as part of the problem. Because *Fighting Words* contextualizes critical social theory, this question of choosing words carefully is one I struggled with throughout the volume. I have aimed for consistency, but in places, readers will have to live with seeming contradictions.[6]

How could I possibly write for so many possible audiences in language that they would understand and find credible? In responding to this dilemma, I decided to write in the multiple languages used by the different audiences that I encounter on a daily basis. Moreover, I chose to place everything in this one volume to encourage different readerships to read outside what is comfortable for them. I have included a glossary of terms defining some of the more specialized language of academia that typically does not appear in popular dictionaries. Instead of bemoaning the fact that my migrations among multiple communities have left me with the speech of those communities, I decided to speak as many languages as I could, rather than feeling that I had to pick one in order to establish a "tone" for the volume. Although ideas generated in one language and one context typically lose something in translation, when the ideas are especially significant I think it is important to make the effort. As philosopher Elizabeth

Kamarck Minnich notes, "If we give up on the effort to speak across fields, theories, systems, 'isms,' and to people in many different countries, we also give up our responsibility as thinkers who care about as we depend upon democracy, especially in today's highly specialized, technologized, fragmented world" (1990, 10).

If you have been able to read this introduction, you are privileged. You do not belong to that shamefully large group of individuals who, because of substandard housing, inadequate nutrition, lack of recreational facilities, poor health care, chronic unemployment, and underfunded schools, have been denied literacy. I regret that the audiences that I would most like to reach may not be able to read this work. However, perhaps my efforts to make the ideas in this volume accessible will encourage many of you to use whatever positions you occupy as parents, students, scholars, lovers, neighbors, editors, siblings, journalists, teachers, and street intellectuals to make theoretical ideas in general, and perhaps those in this volume in particular, more comprehensible and therefore more important to more people than just a select few. Unfortunately, many of us who possess the specialized language of academia often do not even try to translate what are excellent ideas into a form that makes them understood by others. I remind these readers that to read on a high level of abstraction is itself a luxury. Privatizing and hoarding ideas upholds inequality. Sharing ideas through translation and teaching supports democracy. Black feminist theorist June Jordan provides a clear statement of the rationale that drives this project: "We do not sweat and summon our best in order to rescue the killers; it is to comfort and to empower the possible victims of evil that we do tinker and daydream and revise and memorize and then impart all that we can of our inspired, our inherited humanity" (1992, 29).

Part I

Black Women's Knowledge and Changing Power Relations

Learning from the
Outsider Within Revisited

Belonging yet not belonging presents peculiar challenges. As a high school student, I traveled across a largely invisible yet highly significant barrier. When I left my home in an African-American, working-class Philadelphia neighborhood to attend an academically elite public school for girls, passing through the high school doors signaled a unique demarcation between two types of communities. No lengthy bus ride cushioned the shift between my neighborhood and my school community, because, ironically, the high school was located in my own neighborhood. Sitting in class listening to official accounts that erased Black people from the public transcript, I could literally look through the windows and view the familiar terrain of a community and a people who, according to my teachers and the Curriculum, technically didn't exist or, if they did, certainly didn't matter very much.

The daily journey was difficult. I remained a stranger to most of the middle-class White girls who constituted the majority of my classmates. We were certainly friendly, but it was clear that I was not one of them. My teachers often did not see me—I was not an individual, I was an ambassador from my racial and economic group. Because I knew that my college aspirations and economic future largely depended on my teachers' and classmates' perceptions of me, I moved through my high school territory tentatively, trying to see myself as they saw me, living William E. B. Du Bois's notion of double consciousness (1961). Like others who find themselves in situations of being tolerated but not fully accepted, I became quiet and strategically conformist.

Although my classmates also journeyed to school, their power afforded them a degree of entitlement that I could only imagine. Even though they traveled through my neighborhood, the combination of being White, middle-class, and female guaranteed them protection and safe passage. Because they were assured that they would attend college, they relaxed into high school routines and focused on choosing their colleges with a casualness and a confidence that astounded me. They showed little interest in the community in which they were physically located, over which they clearly held dominion but to which they neither belonged nor felt accountable. A few used their privilege to become assertive and questioning. Some even stopped to look around. Most, however, simply occupied the territory.

Despite the pain and anger of experiences such as these, or perhaps because of them, my travels eventually disclosed some fundamental questions. I now see that I was searching for a location where I "belonged," a safe intellectual and political space that I could call "home." But how could I presume to find a home in a system that, at best, was predicated upon my alleged inferiority and, at worst, was dedicated to my removal? More important, why would I even want to?

I have since learned that neither my migration experience nor the changed consciousness that it engendered is unusual. In the United States, many individuals currently express feelings of being outsiders because they are Jews or Muslims in a fundamentally Christian country; or because they are Sansei, Chicanos, Chinese-Americans, Puerto Ricans, or Korean-Americans confronting notions of American nationality that insist on viewing them as foreigners (Takaki 1993, 1); or because they are physically challenged and face curbs that are too high and rest-room stalls that are too small; or because they are working-class White women whose subjective experiences with upward economic class mobility have been all but erased from dominant discourse (Higginbotham and Weber 1992); or because they are gays, lesbians, and bisexuals struggling to get insurance coverage for their partners; or because they are antiracist, feminist White men whose families often don't understand them—and the list goes on. Despite their divergent histories, their similar positions within unjust power relations seems to generate remarkably similar and recurring patterns of reactions to social injustice. Although contemporary writers from different race, gender, sexual, national, and economic class positions use varying terms to describe similar phenomena—*migration* (Cliff 1988), *displacement* (Said 1990; Martínez 1992), *border crossing* (Anzaldúa 1987), *curdling* (Lugones 1994), *marginality* (hooks 1990, 145–54), and *diaspora* (Chow 1993)—grappling with new social relations resulting from desegregation, postcolonialism, and civil war preoccupies a range of thinkers both in the United States and globally (Said 1978; 1993; Madrid 1988; Minh-ha 1989; Spivak 1993; Gilroy 1993). For members of historically oppressed groups, understanding arrangements of this magnitude requires rejecting the paralyzing constraints of putative "marginality" that alternately views outsiders as grateful ambassadors or unwelcome intruders. Replacing prevailing interpretations of how we are supposed to view ourselves with oppositional perspectives that not only redefine notions of marginality but reclaim marginal locations as places of potential intellectual, political, and ethical strength seems necessary.

For my own survival, I chose the term *outsider within* to describe the location of people who no longer belong to any one group. Initially, I used the term to describe individuals who found themselves in marginal locations between groups of varying power. This usage, however, reduces the construct to an identity category that resembles the "marginal man" of classical sociology.[1] More recently, I have deployed the term *outsider-within* to describe social locations or border spaces occupied by groups of unequal power. Individuals gain or lose identities as "outsiders within" by their placement in these social locations. Outsider-within spaces are riddled with contradictions. From the perspective of members of dominant groups such as the White girls in my high school, individuals like me who occupy outsider-within locations appear to belong, because we possess both the credentials for admittance and the rights of formal membership. However, as the case of African-Americans in the United States illustrates, formal citizenship rights do not automatically translate into substantive citizenship rights. Forty years after the landmark 1954 *Brown v. Board of Education* Supreme Court decision outlawing school segregation, large numbers of African-American children remained warehoused in crumbling, inferior, racially homogeneous schools. Black children's formal belonging as American citizens did not ensure first-class treatment. In the case of my high school, Whiteness conferred power, and I could never become White. Under conditions of social injustice, the outsider-within location describes a particular knowledge/power relationship, one of gaining knowledge about or of a dominant group without gaining the full power accorded to members of that group.

What began initially as a personal search to come to terms with my own *individual* experiences in diverse outsider-within positions led me to wonder whether African-American women as a *group* occupied a comparable location. At that point, I wrote an article entitled "Learning from the Outsider Within: The Sociological Significance of Black Feminist Thought" (1986) where I suggested that African-American women occupied just such a positionality. In particular, Black women's long-standing employment as domestic workers in private households comprised one archetypal migration story. This one occupational category has long dominated the work history of Black women in the United States. Given this shared social location, it seemed reasonable to explore how Black women domestic workers' daily journeys into White middle-class homes placed them in outsider-within locations in their places of employment. I also wondered about the effects that this migration experience might have on Black women's ideas. Experiencing two different types of intimate settings, namely, the households of both Black and White families, allowed Black women an angle of vision on both settings unavailable to members who exclusively occupied either. Such women gained insider knowledge about White middle-class family life yet biologically could never become full-fledged members of the White middle-class "family."

In both "Learning from the Outsider Within" and *Black Feminist Thought: Knowledge, Consciousness, and the Politics of Empowerment* (1990), I argued that Black women's migration experiences between two different communities and as workers within those communities generated a distinctive collective perspective on race, class, and gender relations that formed the basis for a Black feminist standpoint. African-American women in private domestic work encountered two types of knowledge. As full insiders within African-American communities, they acquired knowledge largely hidden to White people and other non-Blacks. Such women were often quite powerful within African-American communities, especially in Black churches and other social institutions of Black civil society (Berry and Blassingame 1982; Giddings 1984; Dill 1988b; Higginbotham 1993). Because they were members of a subordinated group that had to remain vigilant about resisting racial oppression, Black women actively participated in African-American resistance traditions, whether in small-scale and hidden positions (Rollins 1985; Dill 1988a), through traditional Black women's "community work" (Gilkes 1988; 1994), or as participants and leaders in large-scale Black social movements (Morris 1984; Adler 1992; Barnett 1993). At the same time, African-American women who worked this triple shift of unpaid family employment, low-paid domestic work, and Black community service often did so at substantial cost to their own well-being.

African-American women who came into contact with White communities via their forays into seemingly private spaces of White households also were exposed to another type of insider knowledge. Because they attended to the most intimate details of their employers' lives, African-American women in domestic service often possessed remarkable insights about White people and their everyday lives. Such women knew that White supremacist ideology was just that—knowledge produced by members of an elite group and circulated by that group to justify and obscure unjust power relations. Such women routinely returned to their Black families with stories of how unsuperior White people actually were (Rollins 1985). Even though their White employers may have treated them well, at times even imagining their domestic workers to be "like one of the family," Black women knew that they could never be full family members. Despite their grasp of insider knowledge, African-American women could never gain full insider power accorded to White family members unless the very terms of family membership changed.[2]

African-American women in domestic work thus possessed access to what James Scott (1990) calls the "hidden transcripts" of *both* Black and White communities. In this case, Black women had access to the private knowledges that groups unequal in power wanted to conceal from one another. However, Black women could exercise power only from positions of authority in Black civil society and not in private and public spheres controlled by Whites, namely, within White families or the social institutions of government, corporations, and the media. The knowledge generated while sitting around the kitchen table, waiting at the bus stop, planning church dinners, or acting in other safe spaces within African-American civil society was important for Black women's survival. Its characteristic themes reflected a fusion of ideas gained from working for "their" White families, as well as the distinctive worldview they crafted within African-American civil society.

Theorizing from outsider-within locations reflects the multiplicity of being on the margins within intersecting systems of race, class, gender, sexual, and national oppression, even as such theory remains grounded in and attentive to real differences in power. This, to me, is what distinguishes oppositional knowledges developed in outsider-within locations *both* from elite knowledges (social theory developed from within centers of power such as Whiteness, maleness, heterosexuality, class privilege, or citizenship) *and* from knowledges developed in oppositional locations where groups resist only *one* form of oppression (e.g., a patriarchal Black cultural nationalism, a racist feminism, or a raceless, genderless class analysis). In other words, theorizing from outsider-within locations can produce distinctive oppositional knowledges that embrace multiplicity yet remain cognizant of power.

In *Black Feminist Thought,* I provided a preliminary analysis arguing that African-American women had developed a self-defined intellectual tradition that encompassed this multiplicity. By demonstrating that Black women had crafted a self-defined intellectual tradition, that this tradition had its own standpoint growing from African-American women's outsider-within positionality in power relations, and that this standpoint in turn generated attention to certain themes and epistemological orientations, I analyzed Black feminist thought as oppositional knowledge. *Black Feminist Thought* recorded and legitimated Black feminist thought as one type of oppositional knowledge influenced by a particular outsider-within location. By positioning itself as documenting a tradition or canon, *Black Feminist Thought* aimed to legitimate Black women's intellectual production as critical social theory.[3]

The fact that so many African-American women have grown to womanhood able to resist the damaging effects of stereotyping demonstrates the significance of Black feminist thought for African-American women. After all, African-American women have been depicted as being stupid; having an "essential" animal-like sexuality, a "natural" willingness to serve, and an "innate" ability to cook; demonstrating a seemingly endless "strength" in the face of racism and sexism, cheerfulness in situations of profound poverty, and a willingness to put anyone and everyone always before ourselves; and being generally "bitchy" and disagreeable (Morton 1991; Jewell 1993). These attacks on Black women seem to be everywhere. They slap listeners in the face in the hard-hitting misogynistic lyrics of some contemporary rappers (Rose 1994; Crenshaw 1993). Through deeply entrenched beliefs such as the centrality of Black mothers in keeping Black people poor, they masquerade as scientific truths (Brewer 1988; Collins 1989). They permeate Black neonationalist dogma proclaiming a return to an Africa that never was and that certainly never will be again under conditions of a racialized global capitalism (White 1990). Surviving intellectual assaults of this magnitude requires oppositional knowledges that tell Black women, if only in the simplest terms, "Don't let anybody tell you who you are." The fact that Black women in the United States have survived at all is proof enough for me that Black feminist thought exists.

However, helping people survive and cope with harsh conditions is a far cry from trying to change those conditions. As filmmaker Trinh Minh-ha observes, "Theory is no longer theoretical when it loses sight of its own conditional nature, takes no risk in speculation, and circulates as a form of administrative inquisition. Theory oppresses when it . . . perpetuates existing power relations, when it presents itself as a means to exert authority—the Voice of Knowledge" (1989, 42). Black women domestic workers' placement in outsider-within locations certainly provides a useful starting point in investigating how subordination can stimulate "risk in speculation" needed for critical social theory. However, viewing Black women's ideas that emerge from one social context as a canon to be celebrated or criticized runs the risk of reducing Black feminist thought to an academic commodity. A better approach treats Black feminist thought as a dynamic system of ideas reactive to actual social conditions.

What works in one time or place may not work in others. The social conditions that generated a particular expression of Black feminist thought—U.S. Black women restricted to domestic work, living in racially segregated neighborhoods relatively untouched by drugs and crime—no longer exist. Documenting the former contributions of Black feminist thought to African-American women's resistance does not mean that contemporary Black feminist thought retains past oppositional meanings. Moreover, tactics for legitimating knowledge also change. Past strategies that helped Black feminist thought become accepted as critical social theory can lose effectiveness. As

African-American theorist Manning Marable cautions, "To be truly liberating, any social theory must reflect the actual problems of an historical conjuncture with a commitment to rigor and scholastic truth" (1993, 127). Although reclaiming and celebrating the past remains useful, current challenges lie in developing critical social theory responsive to current social conditions.

Black feminist thought *as* critical social theory confronts this fundamental issue of remaining dynamic and oppositional under changing social conditions. The two chapters in part I, "Black Women's Knowledge and Changing Power Relations," explore challenges confronting a Black feminist thought that aims to remain oppositional. Chapter 1, "The More Things Change, the More They Stay the Same: African-American Women and the New Politics of Containment," examines the significance of late-twentieth-century social conditions confronting Black women in the United States. Here the focus is on new strategies that lead to African-American women's subordination in the context of considerable social change. Chapter 2, "Coming to Voice, Coming to Power: Black Feminist Thought as Critical Social Theory," examines specific challenges facing a Black feminist thought that functions in this new social context.

One

The More Things Change, the More They Stay the Same: African-American Women and the New Politics of Containment

In 1994, senior financial analyst Bari-Ellen Roberts and a coworker filed a racial discrimination lawsuit against the Texaco Corporation. For Roberts, the decision was not easy. Even though she had been routinely passed over for promotion, she remained the highest ranking African-American woman in an executive position at corporate headquarters. The catalyst for the lawsuit concerned a promotion that Roberts and her coworkers all expected her to get. When her boss took a different job within the company, the vacated position was given to a White male executive with less experience. Questions about the promoted executive's lack of expertise garnered a predictable response—Roberts would simply have to train her new boss. "I was never really taken for my full potential," she reported. "They thought I should just be happy to be there."[1]

On one level, this story represents a fairly routine case of how middle-class African-Americans in the United States are aggressively recruited to join prestigious corporations, elite institutions of higher education, and other sites of institutional power, only to find themselves, upon arrival, confined to a new designated "place." In these situations, according to sociologists Joe Feagin and Melvin Sikes (1994), middle-class African-Americans learn to "live with racism," and they experience a disenchantment described by journalist Ellis

Cose (1993) as the "rage of the privileged class." As Roberts recalled, "The face they showed me as a customer and the face when I got in as an employee were totally different."

On another level, because Roberts and the other African-American employees who eventually joined the class-action suit engaged in group-based action, this situation remains noteworthy. In the 1980s and 1990s, legislative and judicial support for affirmative action and other group-based remedies for racial discrimination eroded.[2] African-Americans, in particular, came to recognize not only that rights of formal citizenship often failed to translate into substantive citizenship but also that the federal government could no longer be counted on to enforce legal remedies. In Roberts's case, rights of formal citizenship promising equal treatment in employment situations not only high-lighted its absence at corporate headquarters but simultaneously provided a legal foundation for a class-action lawsuit. Via this lawsuit, Roberts and her African-American coworkers hoped to gain substantive citizenship of equal treatment in the workplace.

Before we dismiss this lawsuit as racial business as usual in the United States, we should note that one feature distinguishes Roberts's story from other similar cases. While Roberts's class-action suit was in progress, someone delivered an audiotape to the press containing a transcript of a formal meeting among upper-level Texaco executives. The transcript of that meeting, in which the executives discussed the lawsuit, proved to be a smoking gun. Released in part because of the lawsuit, the transcript buttressed African-American employees' claims that routinized racially discriminatory practices characterized their work environment. On the tape, Roberts's superiors refer to her as a "smart-mouthed little colored girl," an allusion to her refusal to accept her second-class corporate citizenship. In a widely circulated segment of the transcript, several executives discuss the African-American employees who brought suit: "They are perpetuating an us-them atmosphere," one states. "I agree," responds another. "This diversity thing. You know how black jelly beans agree." And finally, the infamous line that resonated throughout the American media: "That's funny. All the black jelly beans seem to be glued to the bottom of the bag" ("Excerpts from Tapes," 1996).[3] Like the widely broadcast videotaped beating of African-American motorist Rodney King by members of the Los Angeles Police Department, for most African-Americans, the Texaco transcript revealed little that was new. Rather, what distinguished both the Rodney King video and the Texaco transcript was the documented public eye cast on practices that sociologist Philomena Essed (1991) labels "everyday racism" and that Himani Bannerji (1995) calls the "commonsense racism" permeating police activity, employment situations, and other dimensions of social structure in the United States.

In one sense, the organization of power confronting African-American women as a result of the civil rights and feminist gains of the 1960s and 1970s appears to be quite different from that characterizing earlier patterns of slavery and de jure segregation in the South. Bari-Ellen Roberts's arrival at Texaco certainly symbolizes the tangible gains that many Black women have attained, in part because of the long-standing, protracted struggles of African-Americans generally and Black women in particular. The fact that a sizable minority of African-American women have experienced social mobility into the middle class by gaining formal entry into historically segregated residential, educational, and employment spaces represents bona fide change. At the same time, however, other Black women remain disproportionately "glued to the bottom of the bag." According to various social indicators, African-American women and their children remain disproportionately poor, homeless, sick, undereducated, unemployed, and discouraged, leading some social scientists to posit that Black women in the United States are part of a growing, seemingly permanent urban "underclass" (Wilson 1987). The intractable poverty of Black people globally—in segregated inner-city neighborhoods in the United States; in urban areas in Britain and other advanced industrial nations; and in urban and rural areas of so-called undeveloped Third World regions in the Caribbean, in South America, and on the African continent—signals an entrenched fixity that gives the term *black bottom* an entirely new meaning. Although metaphors of travel, migration, and social mobility increasingly characterize local, national, and global population movement, this same movement seemingly replicates long-standing hierarchical power relations of race, economic class, and gender. When it comes to African-American women, it seems that the more things change, the more they stay the same.

Thinking through how this connection between change and fixity, traveling and standing still, migration and containment generates a new outsider-within location for African-American women represents one fundamental challenge confronting contemporary Black feminist thought. Black women in the United States seem to be facing a new politics of containment honed at this intersection of fixity and change. While continuing to be organized around the exclusionary practices attached to racial segregation, the new politics simultaneously uses increasingly sophisticated strategies of surveillance. Relying on the *visibility* of African-American women to generate the *invisibility* of exclusionary practices of racial segregation, this new politics produces remarkably consistent Black female disadvantage while claiming to do the opposite. Just how does this new politics of containment fit in with long-standing mechanisms of control?

Knowing Your Place: Public Spheres and Private Realities

Since its inception as a nation-state, the United States has wrestled with the contradictory nature of its promise of equality under the law and its actual social practices concerning African-Americans as a group or class.[4] Basic tenets included in the 1776 Declaration of Independence—all people were created equal; all people are endowed with certain unalienable or "natural" rights; and a government derives its power from the consent of the governed—constitute admirable ideals. However, during the transition from White settler society to new nation-state, vested interests regarding the status of enslaved Africans overrode these provisions. As a result, the almost 20 percent of the American population bound in slavery was relegated to the status of chattel or property. African-Americans received neither formal nor substantive citizenship rights. Delivering the Supreme Court's opinion in the 1857 *Dred Scott v. Sandford* case, Chief Justice Roger Taney summarized the Court's interpretation of the attitudes of the framers of the Constitution toward enslaved women and men of African descent: "They are not included, and were not intended to be included, under the word 'citizens' in the constitution, and can therefore claim none of the rights and privileges which that instrument provides and secures. . . . On the contrary, they were at that time considered as a subordinate and inferior class of beings" (qtd. in Estell 1994, 130). Within this constitutionally sanctioned form of institutionalized racism, Blacks as a group or class received differential treatment within American social institutions.

Race not only shaped African-American participation in institutionalized racism organized via slavery but also influenced the new nation-state's distinctly American notions of its public and private spheres. Typically, federal, state, and local governmental units constitute the state segment of the public sphere, with the franchise marking formal citizenship rights. Corporations, the media, civic associations, and all social institutions not attached to the state constitute civil society, the other segment of the public sphere. This bipartite public sphere is typically juxtaposed to a private sphere of home and family.[5] Race was deeply implicated in all of these meanings. In constructing the American public and private spheres, the 1790 census categories summed it up. The first U.S. census, administered in that year, relied on race, gender, citizenship status, and age in defining the American population. Six questions were asked of each household: the name of the family head, the number of free White males over age sixteen, the number of free White males under age sixteen, the number of free White females, the number of other free persons, and the number of slaves (U.S. Bureau of the Census 1979; Anderson 1988, 14).

These questions established a series of foundational categories that shaped American notions of public and private as well as American national identity. For free White men and women, gender emerged as one important feature that framed their status in the new nation-state. Free White men over age sixteen were deemed heads of households that contained free White women as their helpmates. Using age in reference to free White men only simultaneously gave individuals in this group the most individuality and valorized Whiteness and maleness as the most significant categories of belonging for the new nation-state. Moreover, placement in property relations influence citizenship rights. Since the status of free White women was so closely tied to their husbands and fathers, family households emerged as fundamental to economic class relations. The status of free White women was linked to that of men of their economic class.

In this construction of American national identity as White, free, and grounded in individualism and property relations, Black people as a class occupied a peculiar place. Whereas age was used to categorize free White males, and gender was used to classify free Whites, Blacks lacked age and gender specificity. Distributed among the remaining categories of other free persons and slaves, the majority of Blacks remained slaves. On the one hand, Black people remained *outside* the public sphere—they were Black, enslaved, and judged by their group membership, and they possessed no property, not even themselves. Enslaved African-Americans in the South had no rights of citizenship—

either first-class or second-class. Instead, they *were* the private property on which citizenship rights of White men and women rested. Because enslaved Africans stood outside citizenship, they participated in neither the government nor the civil sectors of the American public sphere. On the other hand, Black people as a group were curiously *inside* this same public sphere in a specific place of belonging reserved exclusively for them. Because they were Black, enslaved, and judged by their group membership, and because they lacked property, they lacked privacy rights accorded to individuals holding American citizenship. Just as animals are considered private property whose non-human status grants them no rights of privacy, African-Americans were categorized in a similar fashion.

As feminist scholarship quite rightly points out, the very categories of public and private, work and family, outside and inside rely heavily on specific gender configurations. For example, the notion of the public sphere as a White male domain of work, politics, and leadership gains meaning primarily when juxtaposed to its private-sphere alternative—the White female domain of family, domesticity, and intimacy that houses White women and children (Coontz 1992). During the slave era, free White females possessing formal citizenship rights simultaneously were denied many benefits of substantive citizenship because of their gender. The absence of the vote limited White women's ability to occupy positions of power both in the government sector and in many institutions of civil society. In practice, this meant that White women gained derivative citizenship rights from their association with men, primarily by being married to men with citizenship rights or by being the daughters of men with such rights. Since property relations worked so closely with race, marriage remained important not only in maintaining gender hierarchies but also in replicating racialized hierarchies of economic class structured through inter-generational property transmission (Collins 1997). Within this logic predicated on African-American exclusion from citizenship, family constituted the ultimate private sphere for Whites only. It regulated multiple dimensions of social organization, including sexuality, gender relations, citizenship rights, racial classification, and property relations (Collins forthcoming 1998b).[6]

The experiences of Black women, as members of an African-American collectivity, were profoundly shaped by these intersecting national, economic class, racial, and gender politics. Legally, Black women's gender remained unrecognized—the overarching category "slave" made no allowance for gender prior to the 1820 census (U.S. Bureau of the Census 1968, 147). In actual practice, however, gender mattered greatly. Black women's reproductive capacities led to a unique place in this racialized system of property relations. Just as any offspring of an animal's owner became his property, Black women's children became the property of their mothers' owners. Under slavery, Black women's bodies produced property and labor. After emancipation in 1865, Black women's children owned themselves and became units of labor. Black women's reproduction both produced actual populations central to economic class relations and served as an important site of boundary maintenance for the racialization of this process. Thus, in the United States, racialized slavery meshed with an intergenerational economic class disadvantage that was organized through and passed on via Black women's bodies.

Emancipation ushered in another form of institutionalized racism. Although emancipation granted African-American men formal citizenship, substantive citizenship for African-Americans as a class remained elusive. Two strategies of control—racial segregation and surveillance—emerged to limit and in most cases to reverse newly gained citizenship rights. Designed to exclude Blacks from owning property and exercising political power, racial segregation became increasingly significant in controlling African-Americans as a class. Targeted toward African-Americans as a group, racial segregation erased individuality and treated Blacks in the United States whose history lay in slavery as the 1857 Supreme Court's "subordinate and inferior class of beings." For example, rules prohibiting Black and White intermarriage, which lasted in some states into the 1960s, aimed in part to regulate the intergenerational transfer of property, that is, to maintain White wealth and its accompanying Black poverty. By excluding African-Americans from first-class citizenship, such control was also designed to keep Blacks as a group or class *outside* centers of power that might alter these racialized economic class relationships.

Some dimensions of racial segregation affected Black men and women in the United States fairly equally, whereas others had pronounced gender-specific effects. Residential housing segregation illustrates how exclusionary practices associated with racial segregation did not rely on gender. Depending on the unit of analysis measuring racial concentration effects, African-Americans have been and remain more highly geographically concentrated than any other racial group in the United States. Prior to 1900, because Blacks lived predominantly in the rural South, they experienced state-level racial segregation. Stated differently, Blacks were confined to a few southern states where they remained politically powerless. Moreover, in practical terms, although Blacks and Whites may have lived in close proximity in some urban areas, they less often interacted as equals. Black migration to urban areas in the first decades of the twentieth century shifted the geographic unit of housing segregation from the state to the neighborhood within a city. The creation of all-Black enclaves of ghettos continued housing segregation and its accompanying costs to Blacks. As statistical units, states and cities became more desegregated, whereas neighborhoods within cities did not. These patterns persisted until after World War II, when the federal government subsidized suburban development via low-interest mortgage loans and massive highway construction (Oliver and Shapiro 1995). During this period, cities themselves became primary units of racial isolation (Orfield and Ashkinaze 1991), with poverty among African-Americans being concentrated in cities (Wilson 1987; Goldsmith and Blakely 1992). Cities became Blacker while their surrounding suburbs developed as all-White enclaves. Thus, despite shifting patterns of racial segregation from states to neighborhoods within cities, to cities and suburbs themselves as the primary unit of organization, housing segregation remains fundamental in structuring African-American racial segregation (Massey and Denton 1993). Although gender was a factor *within* racially homogeneous spaces created by shifting patterns of residential housing, gender did not constitute a primary factor used to create and maintain racially segregated spaces.

At the same time, forms of racial segregation designed to exclude Blacks from political power and full citizenship rights had gender-specific dimensions. Rights attached to formal citizenship came slowly for African-American women. African-American men got the legal franchise in 1868 but saw it virtually eliminated by the establishment of a Jim Crow apartheid regime in the South by the turn of the twentieth century. Women as a group gained the vote through constitutional amendment in 1920. Legally, this meant that Black women gained formal citizenship commensurate with both White women and Black men. However, since the majority of Black women lived in the South, like Black men, they could not exercise this fundamental right of formal citizenship. After a protracted civil rights struggle in the South, the passage of the 1965 Voting Rights Act provided enforcement mechanisms designed to protect African-American efforts to exercise formal citizenship through voting. Thus, many African-American women have gained access to formal citizenship rights only since the 1960s.

Racial segregation has long been enforced through patterns of violence against African-American populations (Berry 1994). Historically, beatings inflicted by patrols on the lookout for runaway slaves or those traveling without passes, and the state-sanctioned mob violence against Blacks meted out by the Ku Klux Klan and other White supremacist organizations typified techniques used against Blacks. More recently, racial differentials in capital punishment in American penal institutions; cross burnings, arson, and other forms of harassment toward Blacks who desegregate White neighborhoods; and the ongoing issue of police brutality in urban Black areas have maintained the use of violence.

Racial segregation also generated some contradictions. Relegating African-Americans to homogeneous geographic space and political conditions, however inferior, simultaneously created the conditions for a Black public sphere, Black civil society, or Black community to emerge. Although this Black civil society was policed by outsiders, it could never be totally regulated or watched to the extent of erasing all privacy. In that space of Black public-sphere privacy, resistance to the injustices created by racial segregation emerged. From its inception, this Black civil society that was created within and in response to White controlled public and private spheres reflected contradictions of race, class, and gender that marked its origins and its purpose. Although it was a culture of resistance responding to institutionalized racism, its creation was far from voluntary. Unlike White ethnics and contemporary immigrants of color to the United States whose migration as individuals and family units is voluntary, Black civil society was honed in involuntary migration, conquest, and intergenerational slavery. By occupying a common collective position, African individuals became a group or class. Although the Black public sphere drew on African-derived traditions, over time Black civil society incorporated diverse cultural traditions to craft a distinctly African-American culture. In this ongoing process of cultural creation, Black civil society, like other American cultures, also incorporated the contradictions of its larger social context regarding race, class, gender, and sexuality into its very core. Designed to ensure African-American survival under extremely inhumane conditions, from its inception during slavery, Black civil society operated in secrecy. Rules of racial solidarity essential to its survival regulated Black behavior. Overall, racial segregation allowed the creation of a culture of resistance that was effective yet riddled with contradictions.

The limited privacy provided by Black civil society remained important in responding to surveillance, a second strategy of control that accompanied racial segregation.[7] Unlike racial segregation targeted toward African-Americans as a group, surveillance is aimed at African-American individuals. Racial segregation erases individuality—Blacks are treated as interchangeable members of a derogated group. In contrast, surveillance highlights individuality by making the individual hypervisible and on display. Whereas racial segregation is designed to keep Blacks as a group or class *outside* centers of power, surveillance aims to control Black individuals who are *inside* centers of power. In other words, surveillance becomes the strategy of choice in controlling African-Americans outside Black civil society when they enter the White spaces of the public and private spheres.

Surveillance was central to the larger context of racial etiquette described by sociologist Robert E. Park (1950) as the rules that govern interpersonal contact between racial groups. Park developed this term to describe the patterned race relations of Blacks and Whites in the segregated South. The rules of racial etiquette were designed to maintain social distance in situations where Blacks and Whites were in close proximity. Historically, the North needed far fewer of these rules of racial etiquette, because residential, educational, and employment segregation maintained a physical distance matching social distance between Blacks and Whites. In the South, where contact was frequent, racial etiquette required intense surveillance to ensure that Blacks would stay in their designated, subordinate places in White-controlled public and private spheres.

African-American women's experiences in the labor market illustrate these crosscutting relationships of racial segregation and surveillance. Black women's placement in domestic work resulted from race- and gender-specific labor market practices that relegated Black women to a narrow range of occupations (Amott and Matthaei 1991). Once in these occupations, Black women were managed by surveillance

tactics. Even though Black women's paid domestic labor was performed in private White homes, race, class, and gender relations within the public sphere determined its value. Serving as the testing ground
for surveillance as a form of control, domestic work held myriad contradictions. Unlike the labor of middle-class White women, Black
women's labor as domestic workers took them through the White,
male-controlled public sphere and inside the private sphere of the
White female-managed family. However, what was public for White
men and private for White women was highly public for African-
American women—inside was truly outside. Moreover, Black women's
participation in the public sphere via exploitive work in private homes
relied heavily on techniques of surveillance. Being constantly watched
ensured not only that African-American women were included in the
public sphere on the terms of the employer—low wages, poor working conditions, and no job security—but also that these same conditions weakened Black women's ability to resist racial segregation. Low
wages and job insecurity meant that Black people lacked economic
resources to purchase quality housing, schools, health care, and other
services, let alone to engage in political activism to challenge these
exclusionary practices.

Techniques of surveillance work especially well in situations of
proximity characterized by a power imbalance. Although Black domestic workers and White female employers shared the same gender,
race and class created significant power differences. White women
seemed to need the illusion that the Black women workers whom they
invited into their private homes felt like "one of the family," even
though they actually had second-class citizenship in the family (Rollins
1985; Dill 1988a). If Black domestic workers were truly like one of
the family, there would have been no need to watch them closely to
ensure that they didn't steal anything or spit in the soup. Surveillance
emerged to signal and control this power differential—White women
watched Black women because their race and class privilege allowed
them to do so.[8]

As with racial segregation, surveillance was enforced through violence. In this sense, Black women experienced physical violence and/or
the threat of such violence in public spaces. Their employment meant
that Black women lacked the protection afforded to "good" women
who remained at home. As workers, Black women faced threats of
sexual harassment and violence in their place of employment, the

White-controlled private sphere. At the same time, because they had to travel through racially segregated public space to get to their jobs, African-American women also faced threats of violence in White- and Black-male-controlled public space in the public sphere. For many, family households offered little protection. The domestic violence affecting many Black women was accompanied by surveillance tactics used to maintain gender oppression. Overall, Black women moved from their private households, through the space of Black civil society, through White-male-controlled public space, into White-female-managed family space, and back again. Each new location contained its distinctive form of surveillance, with Black women being watched every step of the way.

For African-American women, racial segregation and surveillance produced a powerful nexus of containment. On the one hand, racial segregation denied Black women formal citizenship rights and substantive citizenship rights. This reinforced Black women's exclusion from good jobs, education, housing, and health care that in turn inhibited their efforts to gain citizenship rights. Racial segregation fostered Black women's collective invisibility—an "out of sight, out of mind" consequence of exclusionary practices. On the other hand, placing individual Black women under surveillance, whether through domestic work performed in private homes or through the threat of violence that accompanied their lack of safety in public space, reflected the need to find ways to control subordinate populations who were inside centers of power.

African-American Women and Black Civil Society

Prior to the educational, housing, and occupational desegregation that characterized the 1970s, African-American women's political participation was rarely a matter of simply resisting institutionalized racism. Rather, positioned at intersections of class, race, nation, and gender, Black women in the United States tested the very definitions of citizenship by challenging notions of public and private, and the racial segregation and surveillance tactics necessary for the construction of such notions. Despite the theoretical significance of intersections of class, race, nation, and gender in shaping Black women's everyday experiences, deeply entrenched housing and occupational segregation mandated that Black women's activism would be expressed primarily through social institutions of Black civil society (Collins 1993).

In a Black public sphere organized in the context of deep-seated racial segregation, African-American women's struggle for rights of formal and substantive citizenship occurred largely via developing Black civil society. Traditionally, African-American women participated in political struggle not primarily as individuals lacking consciousness about their shared group position but as members of a historically constituted racial group identified as such in law, science, and custom (Sacks 1988). Historical legacies of group-based oppression such as slavery, colonialism, and racial segregation stimulated group-based resistance traditions organized primarily around race and institutionalized via the Black public sphere (Franklin 1992). Taking diverse forms and pursuing multiple political agendas, Black resistance focused on freedom (King 1992). Given Blacks' history of enslavement, freedom had palpable meaning. Gaining political rights and protections as first-class citizens involved acquiring formal citizenship and exercising it in the public sphere. Black women participated in shaping and running this Black public sphere from its inception.

Defined as a set of institutions, communication networks, and practices that facilitated responses to economic and political challenges confronting Black people (Dawson 1994), the Black public sphere, Black civil society, or Black community[9] became increasingly visible after emancipation. This sphere served as a fundamental arena that challenged both racial segregation and surveillance as strategies of control. Families, churches, fraternal organizations, and other institutions of the Black public sphere offered African-Americans protection from White surveillance. Also, the absence of surveillance meant that Black civil society fostered the planning of strategic responses to racial segregation in education, housing, employment, and public accommodations.

Within Black civil society, African-American women demonstrated a long history of maintaining Black-female-run organizations that allowed them to exert a distinctive form of leadership as "race women" (Reagon 1987; Higginbotham 1993). In contrast to the use of *race* in science as a term grounded in notions of biological inferiority and superiority, African-Americans infused the term *race* with a deeper meaning signifying cultural identity and heritage. Historian Evelyn Brooks Higginbotham refers to this as "the power of race to mean nation—specifically, race as the sign of perceived kinship ties between blacks in Africa and throughout the diaspora" (1992, 268). In this context, working for the "race" via community work constituted important personal and political achievements. Sociologist Cheryl Townsend Gilkes labels as "community work" Black women's political activism as "race women" within Black civil society. Within relatively self-contained African-American neighborhoods that accompanied housing segregation, community work consisted of activities to combat racism and to empower the communities to survive, grow, and advance in a hostile society (Gilkes 1994). The motto that described early-twentieth-century community work captures its essence—"lifting as we climb."

Three interrelated themes characterized African-American women's community work. The first stressed racial solidarity as fundamental to Black survival (Dyson 1993). Family, race, community, and nation all drew meaning from this notion of solidarity. In social conditions where racial violence targeted toward Black women and men was quite routine and was interwoven in the very fabric of the system, racial solidarity was not a luxury, it was essential (Berry 1994). More than three hundred years of legalized racial subordination in the United States convinced most African-Americans that sticking together and remaining unified could mean the difference between survival and death. In this context, fostering Black unity emerged as both a fundamental goal of Black political activism and a directive shaping the multiple strategies deployed by African-American women for achieving specific objectives (Franklin 1992). Racial solidarity framed both ends of the Black political spectrum. Political activism influenced by Black nationalism typically emphasized community self-reliance and development activities. Some organizations, such as fraternities and sororities, the Black independent schools movement, and Black churches, focused inward and targeted Black community development efforts in education, cultural activities, and community-based social services. In contrast, integrationist political activism targeted institutional policies. For example, organizations such as the National Association for the Advancement of Colored People (NAACP) and the Urban League challenged educational, occupational, and housing discrimination against Black people. Black women's political activism reflected similar diversity.

Racial solidarity also protected a Black identity continually bombarded with White supremacist images and ideologies. In a climate that routinely portrayed African-American women as sexually available servants, African-American men as violent rapists, and African-American children as miniature versions of their parents, institutions of Black civil society worked to shield their members from these and other ideological assaults. Families, churches, and other institutions provided buffers against attempts by news coverage, school curricula, movies, books, television, popular print media, and public transcripts of government and industry to dehumanize Black people. As a way of preserving their individual human dignity, Black children of both genders were encouraged not to take racism "personally." At the same time, a value system influenced by African origins fostered a collective "I," a sense of racial solidarity needed to both preserve traditions and offer a united front in response to white supremacist treatment (Hord and Lee 1995). Those who turned their backs on racial solidarity were censured, with names such as Uncle Tom and Aunt Tomasina reserved for the traitors. Everyone was involved in keeping everyone else under surveillance. Too much was deemed to be at stake to abandon this mutual policing.[10]

This deep-seated belief in the importance of racial solidarity fostered an emphasis on structural analyses of Black economic disadvantage, the second theme characterizing Black women's community work. Accompanying this focus on structural causes of Black suffering was a belief in the primacy of collective response to the problems Blacks confronted as a class. In her study of African-American political life in the transition from slavery to freedom, historian Elsa Barkley Brown examines the distinctive dynamics of this orientation toward the collective in the emerging Black public sphere of Richmond, Virginia:

> An understanding of collective autonomy was the basis on which African Americans reconstructed families, developed communal institutions, constructed schools and engaged in formal politics after emancipation. The participation of women and children in the external and internal political arenas was part of a larger political worldview of ex-slaves and free men and women, a worldview fundamentally shaped by an understanding that freedom, in reality, would accrue to each of them individually only when it was acquired by all of them collectively. (1994, 125)

In responding to racial segregation and surveillance, racial solidarity represented a reasonable and effective response to discrimination in housing, education, employment, health, and public access. Such racism was targeted not toward Black individuals but toward Black people as a racial collectivity. Without changes in rules, laws, practices, and customs that routinely discriminated against African-Americans as a class, little space for Black individualism existed. This attention both to structural sources of Black disadvantage and to group responses to oppression allowed Black women to interpret their individual activities in terms of the implications for development of African-Americans as a class. Whether an individual African-American woman accepted or rejected the belief that freedom would accrue to her only when it was acquired by African-Americans collectively remained less relevant than the consistency of family, church, and other institutions of Black civil society that continually advanced this idea.

Through this emphasis on systemic causes of and collective responses to Black disadvantage, African-American women community workers routinely advanced more complex political agendas within the assumptions of racial solidarity than is commonly realized. In particular, Black political organizations espousing Black nationalist philosophies are not perceived as hospitable environments for gendered analyses of Black women's oppression. For example, to this day the Universal Negro Improvement Association (UNIA), the political arm of the 1920s Garvey movement, remains the largest Black organization ever developed in the United States. Amy Jacques Garvey, wife of Marcus Garvey, not only participated in shaping the organization through her influential newspaper column but actually ran the organization in Marcus Garvey's absence. Especially striking in Amy Jacques Garvey's ideas are the connections she made between nationalism and women's liberation movements. Despite her claim that her primary dedication was to Black liberation, she believed that Black women represented the backbone of Black nationalist struggle (Adler 1992). Similarly, civil rights activist Ella Baker's vision of participatory democracy was cast in holistic terms. Baker thought that no feminist politics could be separated from an antiracist and economic justice agenda (Mueller 1990). As work on African-American women political activists indicates, Black women's feminist activities often occurred within all types of organizations (see, e.g., Naples 1991). In all, the work of Amy Jacques Garvey, Ella Baker, and other African-American women activists suggests that Black women in the United States historically approached politics primarily through a preexisting network of Black community organizations already positioned to work for economic and social justice for African-Americans as a class.

A third distinguishing theme of Black women's community work involved the centrality of moral, ethical principles to Black political struggle. Within organizational settings such as Black churches, African-American women expressed a commitment to ideas more broadly based than explicitly antiracist or feminist (Collins 1990). Traditionally, a belief in social justice worked closely with the theology of Black Christian churches (Cannon 1988). Joining this theological tradition to an organizational base that itself relied on collective effort, as was the case with the institutional base provided by Black churches, meant that African-American women were able both to find institutional support for and to tap an ethical tradition grounded in a broad view of social justice (Higginbotham 1993). Black churches, the fundamental organizations of Black civil society, provided an important arena for Black women's political activism for social justice. This moral, ethical tradition, especially as expressed within Black Christian churches, encouraged Black women to relinquish their special interests as women for the greater good of the overarching community. Rejecting individualist strategies that they perceived as selfish, Black women came to couch their issues as Black women within the egalitarian, collectivist ideological framework of Black women's community work, an approach that works well with womanist approaches to Black women's politics (Matthews 1989; Poster 1995). Within this interpretive framework, fighting on behalf of freedom and social justice for the entire Black community was, in effect, fighting for one's own personal freedom. The two could not be easily separated.

Within Black civil society, Black women's community work had several gender-specific outcomes that, although they may have benefited African-Americans as a collectivity, came at special cost for African-American women. One outcome of the emphasis on racial solidarity and collective approaches to social issues characterizing Black civil society concerned the pressure routinely placed on African-American women to eschew lobbying on their own behalf. Black women were taught to see their own needs as secondary to those of a collectivity of some sort, whether it be the family, church, neighborhood, race, or Black nation. In contrast to the model of organizing first around personal advocacy for one's own interests, many Black women initially entered community work through concern for specific loved ones in their lives, most often their children (Gilkes 1994). Working for social justice for particular loved ones often stimulated a heightened consciousness about the effects of institutionalized racism on African-Americans as a group. Black women saw their fathers and sons lynched, lost their children to guns and drugs, cared for their adolescent daughters' children, and visited their brothers in jail. As a result of this powerful catalyst for action, African-American women typically engaged in feminist political activism by broadening pre-existing analyses concerning racism and economic class exploitation to include the additional oppression of gender. Often their political work within Black organizations sensitized them to gender issues in the first place. Thus, Black women often encountered consciousness-raising experiences concerning gender not in the context of groups organized for this purpose but via daily interactions within organizations that formed the public sphere of African-American communities (see, e.g., Higginbotham 1993).

Efforts to separate the special issues confronting Black women from those of Black men were discouraged, as was personal advocacy by African-American women. Consider the following passage from a speech given at a 1971 NAACP Legal Defense Fund gathering, where civil rights activist Fannie Lou Hamer refused to separate Black women's issues from those of Black men:

> I used to think that if I could go North and tell people about the plight of the black folk in the state of Mississippi, everything would be all right. But traveling around, I found one thing for sure: it's up-South and down-South, and it's no different. . . . We have a problem, folks. . . . I'm not hung up on this liberating myself from the black man, I'm not going to try that thing. I got a black husband, six feet three, two hundred and forty pounds, with a 14 shoe, that I don't *want* to be liberated from. But we are here to work side by side with this black man in trying to bring liberation to all people. (Qtd. in Lerner 1972, 611–12)

Mrs. Hamer chooses to examine African-American oppression via the dual themes of racism and economic class exploitation in the "down-South" and "up-South." From the perspective of the widespread feminist political activism of the 1970s and 1980s, Mrs. Hamer's statement "I'm not hung up on this liberating myself from the black man, I'm not going to try that thing" can be read as a politically naive rejection of feminism. However, Fannie Lou Hamer's biography (Crawford 1990) reveals that she was anything but naive about oppression. As the twentieth child of a sharecropper family, like other Black Mississippians prior to the 1960s, Mrs. Hamer was denied an education and went to work as a timekeeper on a plantation. After eighteen years on this job, she attended a mass meeting on voting and was so inspired by the speeches that she agreed to be one of seventeen Black people who would try to register to vote. Mrs. Hamer's political activism began with this act and led to activities such as heading up a delegation at the 1964 Democratic National Convention that challenged its exclusion of Black representatives and organizing a food cooperative that was open to poor Blacks and poor Whites. This passage thus demonstrates a fusion of the norms of racial solidarity and an ethical tradition that defends all people, and an eschewing of a stance of personal advocacy.

Although Black women's community work certainly made significant contributions to Black political struggle, there were and are costs. The overarching emphasis placed on racial solidarity often promotes a paradigm of individual sacrifice that can border on exploitation. Many Black women encounter punishment if they are seen as too individualistic, especially those Black women who put themselves first. As mothers, wives, and churchwomen, Black women acquire responsibility for helping others cope with and resist racial segregation and surveillance, yet often they lack adequate resources and support in doing so. Pauline Terrelonge contends that a common view within African-American communities maintains that African-American women have withstood a long line of abuses mainly because of Black women's "fortitude, inner wisdom, and sheer ability to survive" (1984, 557). Connected to this emphasis on Black women's strength is the related argument that African-American women play critical roles in keeping Black families together and in supporting Black men. These activities have been important in offsetting the potential annihilation of African-Americans. As a result, "many blacks regard the role of uniting all blacks to be the primary duty of the black woman, one that should supersede all other roles that she might want to perform, and certainly one that is essentially incompatible with her own individual liberation" (Terrelonge 1984, 557).

Beth Richie's study of battered Black women (1996) reveals some startling findings regarding this paradigm of sacrifice. One significant factor in her study distinguished battered Black women from those

who were not—almost all of the battered women held privileged positions in their families of origin. As young girls, the African-American
women who were battered had seen themselves as important family
members, and other family members depended on them. But although
they held high self-esteem and felt powerful, their identities were also
wrapped up in pleasing and accommodating the needs of others. As
adults, this childhood strength, encouraged in so many Black girls,
translated into love relationships in which the "conditional nature of
the love, affection, respect, and the need to constantly work to maintain their status in relationships" (Richie 1996, 35) left them vulnerable to abuse. Richie thus explains the curious paradox of why strong
Black women adhering to the norms of racial solidarity would simultaneously be most susceptible to exploitation, in this case physical
violence:

> This sense of racial solidarity served to limit the women's self-
> determination, independence, and autonomy, leaving them vulner-
> able to gender entrapment that resulted in violence from their male
> partners. . . . The African American battered women excused the
> negative actions of men in their lives . . . while they held the women,
> including themselves, to a higher standard. . . . Historically based
> loyalty to family, therefore, got constructed as contemporary loyalty
> to men. (62)

African-American women's reluctance to challenge norms of racial solidarity can have some unfortunate consequences. By refusing
to engage in personal advocacy when appropriate, failing to claim existing personal advocacy as political, and adhering to a paradigm of
sacrifice, African-American women foster their own subordination.
For example, the resistance by some Black women to advocating
overtly "feminist" issues such as gender equality in education and employment, reproductive rights, and antiviolence initiatives stems in
part from the association of feminism with Whiteness. It also reflects a
widespread belief that Black women's particular concerns as women
are secondary both to those of Black men and to the needs of Black
civil society overall.

The Black civil society that generated these outcomes has under-
gone dramatic changes in the decades since 1970. Changing patterns
of the global economy, the wholesale denial of deeply entrenched
racial practices in the United States, and the emergence of a rhetoric of
color blindness arguing that institutionalized racism has disappeared

have all fostered several major shifts in Black civil society. One trend reflects the convergence of economic class mobility and geographic change. Since 1970, African-Americans living in poverty have become increasingly concentrated in poor, racially segregated inner-city neighborhoods (Wilson 1987; Squires 1994). With this concentration came a startling change in community organization—crumbling family structures, unemployment, gangs, drugs, and other social problems associated with blocked opportunity structures emerged with a vengeance in many Black inner-city neighborhoods. In this sense, both the structures and experience of Black poverty have radically changed.[11] A related trend concerns the expansion of a Black middle class created via upward social mobility. The existence of this group allegedly challenges long-standing notions that racial barriers cause Black disadvantage (Wilson 1978). A related factor concerns the changing patterns of residential segregation confronting African-Americans. The geographic dispersal of some African-Americans into desegregated neighborhoods has masked continued high levels of residential racial segregation overall, leaving many with the impression that more Black people live in integrated neighborhoods than actually do (Massey and Denton 1993). The changing images of Black people and Blackness itself in the mass media consistently mask the effects of continued racial segregation. Influenced by television and other media, many Whites believe, for example, that racism is no longer a problem for Blacks (Jhally and Lewis 1992).

These and other factors have affected Black civil society. Some argue that families, churches, and political organizations in Black civil society have become so ineffective in confronting racial oppression that a "Black public sphere does not exist in contemporary America" (Dawson 1994, 197). Media portrayals of race certainly challenge the importance of racial solidarity as the bedrock of both Black identity and Black political struggle. Grassroots organizations emerging from Black social movements face challenges in which political activism is less often resisted than weakened through co-optation (Gregory 1994). Moreover, the erosion of long-standing organizational bases for Black women's community work has led to decreasing numbers of African-American women who are able to engage in community work within segregated, self-contained Black neighborhoods.

Within a framework of Black women's community work stressing racial solidarity as a response to racial segregation and the centrality

of moral, ethical principles such as justice and freedom to Black political struggle, African-American women learned the importance of
working on behalf of Black families and communities and of seeing
their own needs as secondary to this larger, more significant political
struggle. However, the reorganization of power relations in the larger
public sphere raises entirely new questions concerning the actual and
potential relation of Black feminist thought to Black women's political
activism. Collectively, the continuation of racial segregation, the
emergence of new surveillance strategies, and changes in the organization of the Black public sphere have generated new patterns of containment that build on past practices yet differ from them. Where do
African-American women fit in this new politics of containment?

In a Public Place: African-American Women and the New Politics of Containment

Prior to the 1970s when racial segregation enjoyed the force of law
and custom, its visibility as the cause of Black disadvantage was clear.
When coupled with strategies of surveillance designed to regulate
Black women's exploitation in the labor market and use of public
space, the resulting combination of segregation and surveillance produced a distinctive nexus of containment. Although the processes that
fostered Black women's subordination were highly visible and socially
sanctioned, Black women's suffering remained hidden because Whites
had scant access to Black civil society. Nevertheless, despite the costs
attached to Black women's community work within a self-contained
Black civil society, African-American women found ways to resist
racial segregation and surveillance.

Institutionalized racism now demonstrates some curious contradictions—although neighborhoods, schools, and jobs are still highly
segregated by race in the United States, growing numbers of Whites
no longer see racial segregation and its accompanying discrimination
as producing these results (Blauner 1989; Hacker 1992). In an era of
formal desegregation, African-American women confront a new politics of containment. This politics operates not by excluding Black
women from formal American citizenship via the threat of a return to
legalized housing, educational, or employment discrimination. Rather,
it functions through more sophisticated strategies of control that
work *within* the boundaries of formal American citizenship. Although

social arrangements appear to be quite different—higher education is desegregated, Black images appear in the media, and Blacks have even served on the Supreme Court—social indicators of African-American women's disadvantage remain remarkably entrenched. Even though African-American women have rights of formal citizenship, they remain on the bottom of the social hierarchy.

Changing meanings attached to the terms *public* and *private* are deeply implicated in this new politics of containment. Historically, one effect of racial segregation lay in excluding African-American women from positions of authority in the state sector of the public sphere. Prior to the 1950s and 1960s, social welfare policies routinely denied legal protection, benefits, and services to African-American women. When, however, in the 1970s Black women, among others, laid effective claim to the vote and other public entitlements as well as to the public-sector jobs created in conjunction with the growth of the social welfare state, then the government itself came increasingly under attack.[12] Specifically, the dual path of Black women's gaining access to state services—for example, Black women's welfare rights activism in the 1960s gained them access to Aid to Families with Dependent Children (AFDC) benefits to which they were entitled (Amott 1990)—and Black professional women's increasing reliance on government-sector employment (Higginbotham 1994) contributed to perceptions that the state had been captured by African-American women and other "special interest" groups. As the government sector of the public sphere actually became more "public" and democratic, that is, more accessible to groups such as African-American women, government-sanctioned and/or -administered racial segregation became less effective as a strategy of control. Since affluent and middle-class Whites were apparently unwilling to share power in democratically run social institutions, the value of the social welfare state itself came under attack.[13]

Changing racial politics in the 1980s and 1990s dramatically reconfigured the valuation of the meaning of public generally and of the social welfare state as the quintessential public institution. When African-American women, among others, gained power within the government sector of the public sphere, this sector was increasingly abandoned by individuals and groups with power. Privatization now seems ubiquitous in the United States. Current efforts to privatize hospitals, sanitation services, schools, and other public services, and attempts to develop a more private-sector, entrepreneurial spirit in other services by underfunding them—evident in public radio and public television, and in the subcontracting of specific services via competitive bidding—illustrate this abandonment and derogation of anything public. Deteriorating schools, health care services, roads, bridges, and public transportation, resulting from public failure to fund public institutions, speaks to an erosion and an accompanying devaluation of anything deemed public. In this context, public becomes reconfigured as anything of poor quality, marked by a lack of control and of privacy—characteristics associated with poverty. "The living space of poverty is best described in terms of confinement: cramped bedrooms sleeping several people. . . . Not only is private space restricted . . . by the constraints of poverty, so too is public, institutional space, and purposely so. . . . [It is restricted by] overcrowded classrooms, emergency rooms, and prison facilities," observes philosopher David Goldberg (1993, 196). This slippage linking lack of privacy, poor quality, and poverty affects the changing meaning of public.

In the United States, much of this push toward privatization has covert yet powerful racial undertones. Post-World War II urban development, described in 1975 by African-American rhythm and blues artists George Clinton and the Funkadelics of Parliament as "chocolate cities surrounded by vanilla suburbs," has been joined by even more racially homogeneous exurbs. Many overwhelmingly White suburbs and exurbs support local governments that operate like private corporations. Within this "chocolate" and "vanilla" segregation, gated neighborhoods have sprung up, where residents tax themselves to support private police forces trained to protect residents from any obvious strangers. So-called neutral public space open to all has not been immune from this growing racial polarization. As the public spaces of shops and malls become increasingly hostile to African-Americans from all economic classes, possessing the formal right of citizenship to *be* in public space may not translate into substantive rights of equal treatment in public places. For example, African-American law professor Patricia Williams recounts how, when she aimed to enter a fashionable boutique in New York City during its business hours, she confronted a locked door while White patrons shopped inside (1991, 44–51). In 1995, a Black youth shopping in an Eddie Bauer warehouse outlet outside Washington, D.C., was accused of stealing his own shirt. Store security evicted him from the store shirtless, forcing him to return the next day with a receipt to prove that the shirt on his back was in fact his (Holmes 1995).

This new politics of containment signals a distinct reversal—the public sphere becomes a curiously confined yet visible location that increases the value of private services and privacy itself. Public places become devalued spaces containing poor people, African-Americans, and anyone else who cannot afford to escape. In the minds of many, the public sphere seems overpopulated by dangerous Black male criminals who have made the public streets unsafe, by "public children" from the so-called Black underclass who consume educational and social welfare services far exceeding their value to society, and by Black women whose refusal to work leaves them "married" to the state and living as "welfare queens" in public housing. Long-standing constructions of Blackness as inferior become intertwined with and central to constructing these changing meanings of public. Overlaying this new politics of containment is a rhetoric of tolerance, claiming that race and other such categories no longer matter. Rather than discrimination, market forces now produce social inequalities. In this context, privacy signals safety, control over one's home, family, and community space, and racial homogeneity—qualities that can be purchased if one can afford it.

African-American women's visibility as mothers and workers is deeply implicated in this changing valuation attached to the meaning of public and reconfigured patterns of institutionalized racism. Black women's social location signals a new politics of containment, but not in the historical sense of being hidden away in racially segregated neighborhoods with their inferior public services. Although racial segregation continues to exclude African-American women from quality education, housing, jobs, and health care, this new politics of containment relies much more heavily on surveillance tactics that fix Black women in the public eye. What we now seem to have is a curious reversal: practices of racial segregation that foster Black women's subordination seem increasingly hidden and invisible, whereas poverty and other effects of racial segregation on Black women become increasingly subject to public scrutiny. In this context, freedom represents not the move *into* the public sphere but the move *out* of it.

In this context of a reconfigured public, surveillance strategies become increasingly important. Unlike working-class Black women who virtually vanish, Black women on both ends of the Black economic class spectrum become especially visible in the media. Poor African-American women, especially those in female-headed households, end up disproportionately in the public eye. Despite poor African-American women's rights of formal citizenship, they remain watched in every-day life. Social welfare bureaucracies are instructed to monitor their Black female clients closely, ever vigilant to weed out the "welfare queens" enjoying public assistance. Assuming that African-American women are incapable of rational decision making and adult behavior, surveillance tactics associated with social welfare bureaucracies effec-tively infantilize poor Black women and serve as mechanisms of social control (Gilkes 1983a). Urbanization also highlights the visibility that poor Black women can encounter if unprotected in public space of all sorts. Black women remain watched in the White-male-controlled spaces of downtown areas and suburban neighborhoods, in their workplaces, and in the contested public spaces of Black civil society where White police and Black men struggle for control of the streets. In these spaces, Black women working odd hours and relying on pub-lic transportation still face the threat of violence as a major theme per-meating the surveillance they encounter as a result of being seen in the public sphere. Collectively, these tactics of surveillance in everyday life make it difficult for poor African-American women to exercise sub-stantive citizenship rights.

At the same time, *images* of poor Black women are watched by a public entranced by increasingly powerful media. Being fixed in the public eye via newspaper editorials, popular press, news coverage, doc-umentaries, and talk show appearances means that poor Black women become intensely "raced." Whereas the women as individuals become less visible, poor Black women become icons for Black women as a col-lectivity. Because working-class and poor Black women are members of an intensely raced group, the domestic violence, sexual promiscuity, strained family relations, and other personal difficulties that they en-counter in large part because of their race and economic class position become highly visible. Reinterpreted through an ideological apparatus that initially blames these women for their own poverty and for that of African-Americans as a class (Collins 1989), even more amazingly, Black women's poverty becomes associated with American national in-terests (Lubiano 1992). Wahneema Lubiano describes the power of the image of the "welfare queen" in linking Black women with a putative decline in the American quality of life:

> "Welfare queen" is a phrase that describes economic dependency—the lack of a job and/or income (which equal degeneracy in the Calvinist United States); the presence of a child or children with no father and/or husband (moral deviance); and, finally, a charge on the collective U.S. treasury—a human debit. The cumulative totality, circulation, and effect of these meanings in a time of scarce resources among the working class and the lower middle class is devastatingly intense. The welfare queen represents moral aberration and an economic drain, but the figure's problematic status becomes all the more threatening once responsibility for the destruction of the "American way of life" is attributed to it. (1992, 337–38)

Identified with and blamed for the deterioration of the American public sphere, poor Black women simultaneously become symbols of what's wrong with America, and targets of social policies designed to shrink the government sector (Lubiano 1992). Keeping icons such as the "welfare queen," the "Black matriarch," and "the bad Black mother" fixed in the public eye erases the workings of racial segregation that produce Black women's poverty and powerlessness, the personal difficulties attached to such poverty and powerlessness, and the icons themselves. In a context in which racial segregation, uneven development, and other structural explanations for Black women's devalued social status are erased by an avalanche of editorials, talk show trivia, and movies of the week, Black women's suffering itself becomes the spectacle that increasingly desensitizes its viewers.

Poor Black women's visibility in public discourse serves the important ideological function of erasing the workings of power relations; surveillance tactics targeted toward middle-class African-American women serve a similar function. Middle-class Black women also encounter racially discriminatory practices associated with the legacy of racial segregation (see, e.g., Orfield and Ashkinaze 1991; and Feagin and Sikes 1994). However, as a result of antidiscrimination legislation and affirmative action policies, many African-American women have achieved middle-class status. They are no longer excluded from good schools, good jobs, and quality public facilities and are typically in contact with Whites, often as equals and occasionally as superiors. Unlike working-class and poor Black women, who rarely supervise Whites or interact as equals with middle-class Whites, middle-class

Black women represent a threat. Where segregation used to keep Black women out of the classroom and boardroom, surveillance now becomes an important mechanism of control. As is the case for poor Black women, surveillance of middle-class Black women has a dual emphasis. Surveillance operates via strategies of everyday racism whereby individual women feel that they are being "watched" in their desegregated work environments. Surveillance also functions via media representations that depict the success of selected high-achieving Black women. Surveillance seems designed to produce a particular effect— Black women remain visible yet silenced; their bodies become written by other texts, yet they remain powerless to speak for themselves.

The surveillance that middle-class African-American women experience on a daily basis, especially when entering formerly race-and/or gender-homogeneous spaces, reflects a more sophisticated version of surveillance tactics initially developed for Black women domestic workers. For example, I had a conversation recently with a Black woman doctoral student in a program in management in a large midwestern university. As the first African-American woman likely to complete the program, she felt very watched. The chair of her department called her at the beginning of her office hours every week, claiming that he just wanted to see how she was doing. "He doesn't call anyone else," she observed, "just me." The use of space can also signal a new form of surveillance for middle-class Black women. On my visit to a different university, a Black woman graduate student shared a story of the conditions under which she had taken her preliminary examination. Unlike the seven other doctoral students who took the exam on that day, she alone was assigned to a room with a glass wall. All day long while she took her exam, people walked by, observing her. Ironically, the office she occupied that day was assigned to the lone Black woman member of the department's secretarial staff. Although these stories are anecdotal, they mirror accounts shared by other middle-class African-Americans (Cose 1993; Feagin and Sikes 1994). One can only guess at the effect that being constantly under surveillance has on other Black students and professionals who routinely try to achieve under similar conditions.

Within this situation of surveillance, middle-class Black women are watched to ensure that they remain "unraced" and assimilated. In contrast to the status of intensely raced poor Black women, middle-class status is achieved by constructing oneself according to this standard. Thus, keeping race at bay in the desegregated settings of work and neighborhood has clear economic and political consequences. Moreover, representations of middle-class and affluent Black women that are used to construct new standards against which the White public can assess middle-class Black women become especially important in an era of mass communication. In her incisive analysis of narrative structures of the 1991 Clarence Thomas confirmation hearings, Wahneema Lubiano (1992) identifies the "Black Lady Overachiever" as a new controlling image applied to middle-class professional Black women. The image of Claire Huxtable from the hugely successful *Cosby Show* of the 1980s provides a fictional representation of this new image.

Claire Huxtable certainly was a high achiever—she managed to complete four years of undergraduate training and three years of law school and to become partner in a New York law firm while having five children along the way. No matter that few Black women are law partners and that middle-class Black women have one of the lowest fertility rates of any group of American women—Claire's achievements were not due to any special favors; her hard work and college attendance were enough. Claire certainly modeled a view of Blackness that White America found highly comforting (Jhally and Lewis 1992). Never speaking in Black English, free of dreadlocks, braids, and other indicators of nappy hair, Claire demonstrated her Blackness largely through a love of jazz and Black art depicting an idealized southern Black experience. Claire made little mention of the three elements of Black women's community work. She exhibited minimal racial solidarity, preferring instead to associate with a rainbow of friends. Although she was comfortable expressing an identity as a woman, she rarely identified herself as part of a Black collectivity, especially a political one. Since she showed little evidence of attending church on a regular basis, her expression of a moral, ethical position, although present, was not tied to any recognizable traditions of Black political struggle. Ironically, though, Claire was "Blacker" than met the naked eye. By having five children, she reinforced images of hypersexed Black women with high fertility, and through the ease with which she juggled family, job, and household responsibilities, she reinforced long-standing notions that Black women possess a greater predilection for hard work without damaging consequences. Claire was so good at being a Black woman that we rarely even saw her working. And

Claire certainly was a lady—never appearing with a hair out of place, she remained calm and poised and always had time for her husband and children. Since her children miraculously escaped so many of the social problems that touch the lives of New York City's children of all economic classes (fortunately none of the Huxtable children had any serious problems with drugs, alcohol, pregnancy, school violence, police harassment, or rape) Claire was free to enjoy her beautiful, spacious home. No toilet scrubbing for Claire—as poet Nikki Giovanni once pointed out, "Real ladies don't know how to clean" (Giovanni 1970, 79).

In the absence of substantial racial integration in the United States that provides widespread contact with heterogeneous middle-class and affluent Black women, fictional characters like Claire Huxtable become highly salient in constructing mechanisms of surveillance applied to Black women professionals. Two high-profile media events where middle-class Black women aimed to use their visibility to challenge sexual and racial practices illustrate the significance of new forms of surveillance. The first, the treatment of Anita Hill during the confirmation hearings for Supreme Court justice Clarence Thomas, illustrates how a Black woman who chose to break silence was not believed and was even vilified. Anita Hill was highly visible during the confirmation hearings, yet the combination of her race and gender rendered her virtually invisible to much of the viewing public. In describing the use of stereotypes to achieve this outcome, Nell Painter suggests that Thomas "erected a tableau of white-black racism that allowed him to occupy the position of 'the race.' By reintroducing concepts of white power, Thomas made himself into 'the black person' in his story. . . . He cast Anita Hill into the role of 'black-woman-as-traitor-to-the-race'" (1992, 204). Playing on long-standing notions of racial solidarity whereby defending Black men was typically synonymous with defending the "race," members of Black civil society recognized Hill as a traitor. Although this strategy was incomprehensible to most White Americans, few images of Black women existed that *could* make Anita Hill comprehensible to the majority public. Even the Black Lady Overachiever image symbolized by Claire Huxtable did not fit—where were Hill's husband and five children? As Nellie McKay points out, because Anita Hill was Black and a woman but fit none of the stereotypes of Black women to which most White people were accustomed, the men running the hearings "could find no reference point for her, and therefore she had no believability for them" (1992, 285). The outcome of the hearings is well known—Thomas was confirmed. Although Anita Hill managed to gain a public hearing for her claims of sexual harassment, her treatment and the dismissal of the claims showed how Black women who break silence can be treated.

The case of Lani Guinier is also instructive in this regard. In 1993, President Bill Clinton nominated and subsequently rejected law professor Lani Guinier to head the Justice Department's Civil Rights Division. Guinier's nomination was bitterly opposed by conservative forces, who combed her law review writings and quoted her liberally out of context. The vilification of Guinier did not end with her ideas—her very persona was assailed. The more "raced" Guinier became, the less credible her ideas became. The *U.S. News and World Report* began an article on Guinier with the statement "Strange name, strange hair, strange writing—she's history," reports Patricia Williams (1995, 141). Labeled a "quota queen," Guinier was not allowed a public hearing to respond to her critics or even to summarize the views for which she was taken to task in the media. Forbidden for weeks to speak on her own behalf, Guinier pleaded on nationwide television for the opportunity to explain and defend her ideas in the open forum of a confirmation hearing. Guinier never got her public hearing. Unlike that of Hill, Guinier's treatment demonstrated that Black women in the public eye could be destroyed at will, with no opportunity for redress.[14]

Serving up a visible, unraced, yet powerless Black Lady Overachiever as a Horatio Alger with a Black female face dovetails with conservative analyses of African-American women's economic and political disadvantage. Under a new geography of class-stratified Black neighborhoods, poor Black women allegedly fail to get ahead because they lack images of what is possible. Conversely, middle-class Black women who refuse to serve as "role models" for their less fortunate sisters also garner blame. The emergence of racially homogeneous yet class-stratified Black neighborhoods creates new tensions among Black women across economic class. Since African-American women increasingly do not reside in areas conducive to a common Black civil society, Black women of varying economic classes do not encounter one another in their neighborhoods. Instead, they are much more likely to see one another in formal work settings where one group supervises the other (Omolade 1994, 62). In such settings, an overreliance on "role modeling" as a path for Black female empowerment seems shortsighted, because images of both groups obscure institutionalized power relations. Moreover, the success of selected unraced individual middle-class Black women becomes highly visible in blaming intensely raced poor Black women for their own poverty. If individual middle-class Black women can achieve success, the thinking goes, then individual poor Black women possessing the same content of character can achieve similar results. Taken together, the visibility of poor African-American women and the visibility of newly arrived Black professional women *both* obscure the workings of institutional power. Both sets of highly visible images also obscure the experiences of the majority of actual African-American women, namely, working-class Black women who fall into neither category.

Collectively, high-profile cases such as those of Anita Hill, Lani Guinier, and Bari-Ellen Roberts suggest that the public needs to see a few middle-class Black women in visible positions of authority. Juxtaposing in the public eye highly visible, seemingly unraced individual Black Lady Overachievers such as Roberts, Hill, and Claire Huxtable with the nameless, intensely "raced" Welfare Queens creates a new ethos of equality designed to obscure the workings of institutional power that discriminate against African-American women across numerous markers of difference. However, as the examples of Hill, Guinier, and Roberts suggest, when visible Black women find themselves routinely fixed in newly assigned and highly visible places such as these, long-standing civil rights discourses whose sole target is racial segregation can fall short. Hill, Guinier, and Roberts have not been excluded—they are now included in what appear to be positions of considerable power and influence. Despite their actual achievements, many think that these Black Lady Overachievers now want to use their positions to gain special favors: for Hill, any benefits that might accrue to her as an individual for filing a false claim of sexual harassment; for Guinier, quotas to serve Blacks as a special interest group; and for Roberts, the special favor of an unearned promotion. Not only does the visibility of Hill, Guinier, and Roberts suggest that the rhetoric of racial and gender equality really works, but their visibility simultaneously undercuts the claims of other African-American women that racial and sexual discrimination persists. At the same time, the treatment of these women that rendered them highly visible yet apparently powerless suggests that only apolitical middle-class Black women garner rewards. Claire Huxtable's lack of political race consciousness gained her the big house, solid marriage, good job, and well-behaved children, signaling a sepia-toned American dream. In contrast, Lani Guinier's politics got her silenced. Her experiences more closely resembled a nightmare.

Black Women's Activism Revisited

Traditional models of Black women's political activism that developed within Black civil society to address a historical politics of containment are clearly inadequate in addressing realities of the magnitude described in this chapter. The sophisticated mechanisms of surveillance that operate within current patterns of racial segregation generate a host of important questions for Black feminist thought. How can Black feminist thought craft resistance strategies for these new forms of control that seem to be hidden in plain sight? What are the effects of the changing contours of Black civil society on relations among African-American women? How effectively can Black women's community work be carried out under these new power relations among Black women? Which elements of Black women's community work should be saved, which should be transformed to meet new conditions, and which should be discarded? Is community work even relevant as a model for Black feminist praxis under these conditions?

As critical social theory, Black feminist thought must consider these and other questions and must do so from its own increasingly visible placement in the new politics of containment. Even though, in the words of the Godfather of Soul, James Brown, "Papa's got a brand new bag," the Texaco case illustrates that the black jelly beans continue to be glued together on the bottom of that new bag. The challenge for the African-American women who are distributed throughout this new bag lies in crafting a critical social theory dedicated to ungluing, if you will, all of the jelly beans of whatever color, gender, or economic status who remain stuck on the bottom. In the face of this difficult challenge, not only African-American women but all those committed to justice would do well to remember Fannie Lou Hamer's view of the "bag" that contains us all. As Mrs. Hamer once observed, "Whether you have a Ph.D., D.D. or no D., we're in this bag together" (qtd. in Lerner 1972, 613).

Two

Coming to Voice, Coming to Power: Black Feminist Thought as Critical Social Theory

Although many experiences have shaped my own understanding of the relationship between knowledge and power, one event stands out as pivotal. In 1970, I taught an experimental course called "The Black Woman" at the Martin Luther King Jr. Middle School in Dorchester, Massachusetts. The school itself resembled a prison—iron grates encased all of its windows, external doors lacking handles barred entry from the outside, and a stick-carrying assistant principal patrolled its interior hallways, routinely demanding hall passes from everyone, including unknown teachers like me. Despite this setting, my class of energetic eighth-grade Black girls remained full of questions. Since I had so few answers, I searched one of Harvard University's libraries for material on African-American women. I was stunned to find virtually nothing. Could it be, I wondered, that the absence of materials by and/or about Black women meant that our lives really were of little value? Or was something perhaps wrong with the library?

As Black feminist critic Mae Henderson points out, "It is not that black women . . . have had nothing to say, but rather that they have had no say" (1989, 24). Henderson's statement speaks to the importance that social theories produced by elites can have in maintaining social inequality (Van Dijk 1993). Designed to represent the interests of those privileged by hierarchical power relations of race, economic class, gender, sexuality, and nationality, elite discourses present a view of social reality that elevates the ideas and actions of highly educated White men as normative and superior. Thus, elite discourses measure everyone else's accomplishments in light of how much they deviate from this ideal. For example, social theories portraying Black people as intellectually inferior, criminally inclined, and sexually deviant emerged in conjunction with systems of political and economic exploitation such as slavery, de facto and de jure segregation, colonialism, and apartheid (Jones 1973; Said 1978; Richards 1980; Gould 1981; Delgado 1984; Gilman 1985; Asante 1987; McKee 1993). Similarly, theories of women's seemingly more emotional and less rational nature have long buttressed social arrangements designed to keep women ill educated and relegated to so-called helping professions (Keller 1985; Harding 1986, 1991; Fraser 1989; Smith 1990a, 1990b). These two traditions combine in shaping Black women's images and the discriminatory treatment condoned by those images (Collins 1990; Morton 1991; Jewell 1993; Mullings 1994). Racist and sexist assumptions that permeate much Western knowledge fail to wither away when the political arrangements that created them change. Instead they live on, having a life of their own (Minnich 1990; Torgovnick 1990). In this interpretive context, Black girls such as my eighth graders at Martin Luther King Jr. Middle School, the many African-American women whom I have known, taught, and learned from over the years, and many other groups labeled as Others have long had "no say" in determining the knowledge included in the American national "library" and, in turn, in holding the power that the "library's" knowledge defends.

Given the significance of elite discourses in maintaining power relations, knowledge produced by, for, and/or in behalf of African-American women becomes vitally important in resisting oppression (Fanon 1963; Cabral 1973). Such oppositional knowledge typically aims to foster Black women's opposition to oppression and their search for justice. Since oppression applies to group relationships under unjust power relations, justice, as a construct, requires group-based or structural changes. For Black women as a collectivity, emancipation, liberation, or empowerment as a group rests on two interrelated goals. One is the goal of self-definition, or the power to name one's own reality. Self-determination, or aiming for the power to decide one's own destiny, is the second fundamental goal. Ideally, oppositional knowledge developed by, for, and/or in defense of African-American women should foster the group's self-definition and self-determination.[1]

Historically, Black women's community work was organized in specific ways to foster these dual objectives. Based on the metaphor "lifting as we climb," the diverse patterns that such work took matched the contours of Black civil society. "Lifting as we climb" provided a certain analysis and prescription of Black civil society. Just as the shifting patterns of Black social organization require changes in Black feminist thought, the appearance of new slogans and metaphors applied to Black feminist thought highlights potential changes to this critical social theory. Metaphors provide interpretive frameworks that guide social meaning and serve as mental maps for understanding the world (Stepan 1990). Reflecting theoretical moves from more familiar to relatively unknown terrains, metaphors work by showing how a set of relations that seems evident in one sphere might illuminate thinking and action in other spheres. As Mary E. John observes, metaphors, "like other rhetorical devices, are tropical rather than logical instruments, which means that, depending upon their contexts and effective histories, they work *strategically*" (1996, 89; emphasis in original).

Given their significance, metaphors can provide suggestive road maps for thinking through new directions in Black feminist thought. In the 1970s, Black women encountered the feminist slogan "the personal is political," which, in part, operated as a metaphor in organizing feminist ideas and actions paralleling that of "lifting as we climb." As originally used, the phrase "the personal is political" pointed out how politics permeated everyday life. It also prescribed how actions in everyday life were important in challenging structural power relations. Consciousness-raising emerged as central to "the personal is political," because through it, individual women learned to see their individual lives in political terms (Sarachild 1978). Even though the slogan valorized individual experience or "voice," it linked such experiences to larger systems of structural power.

Since the 1970s, the phrase "coming to voice" has increasingly replaced the earlier feminist slogan "the personal is political." On the surface, this shift of replacing both "lifting as we climb" and "the personal is political" with a new metaphor seems to continue long-standing themes in Black feminist thought. If "voice" references the collective quest for self-definition and self-determination, Black women's searching for a "voice" in the United States is certainly not new. Anna

Julia Cooper's 1892 volume of essays, which provided the first book-length treatment of race, class, and gender in Black women's thought, is entitled *A Voice from the South*. As a leader in the Black women's club movement, Cooper certainly knew that breathing life into "lifting as we climb" required that Black women gain a collective voice. However, since the phrase "coming to voice" emerged in a different political context, it shares with and diverges from the earlier "lifting as we climb" and "the personal is political" in some significant ways.

In the context of the new politics of containment, "coming to voice" provides a potentially useful, albeit limited, metaphor for African-American women's political activism. As Black feminist theorist bell hooks (1990) points out, its three interrelated components—breaking silence about oppression, developing self-reflexive speech, and confronting or "talking back" to elite discourses—remain essential for Black women's journey from objectification to full human subjectivity. Hooks's term *self-reflexive speech* refers to dialogues among individual women who share their individual angles of vision. In a sense, it emphasizes the process of crafting a group-based point of view. In contrast, I prefer the term *self-defined standpoint,* because it ties Black women's speech communities much more closely to institutionalized power relations. Under current social conditions of racial segregation and sophisticated surveillance whereby Black women's "voices" are routinely stripped of their oppositional power, "voice" is not enough. Given the challenges facing contemporary Black feminist thought as critical social theory, what are the contributions and limitations of "coming to voice" as a metaphor for Black women's political activism?

Breaking Silence

Breaking silence enables individual African-American women to reclaim humanity in a system that gains part of its strength by objectifying Black women. Works by Black women writers such as Toni Morrison's *The Bluest Eye* (1970), Ntozake Shange's *for colored girls who have considered suicide / when the rainbow is enuf* (1975), and Alice Walker's *The Color Purple* (1982) broke silence about a series of painful issues confronting African-American women. For example, *The Bluest Eye* examines how images of Black women prove disastrous to Black girls. The latter two works explore how Black women claim subjectivity by refusing to be silenced—in Shange's choreopoem, by talking to one another; and in Walker's prizewinning volume, through the words of one Black girl who writes to God. But breaking silence is not just a literary tactic designed to heal Black women's victimization. For the most part, breaking silence can be a triumphant process in lived experience. Shirley Chisholm's autobiography, *Unbought and Unbossed* (1970), constitutes a lone voice within U.S. electoral politics of one woman who broke silence. Individuals like Chisholm who break silence lay the foundation for a collective group voice.

The benefits gained by individuals from oppressed groups who finally break silence explain, in part, why people do it. In *Crossing the Boundary: Black Women Survive Incest*, Melba Wilson discusses the importance that breaking silence can have for Black women survivors of childhood sexual assault. Wilson's advice remains instructive for oppressed groups in general: "There is no more righteous use of our anger than in directing it against those who have abused us; those who would abuse us and our children; or those who expect us to remain silent about our abuse" (1993, 200). By speaking out, formerly victimized individuals not only reclaim their humanity, they simultaneously empower themselves by giving new meaning to their own particular experiences. Racism, poverty, sexism, and heterosexism all harm their victims. For individuals, healing from this harm by making one's experiences and point of view public remains one of the most fundamental contributions of breaking silence.

Also important is the type of speech that individual Black women invoke in breaking silence. Like Black women's giving testimonials that often disrupt public truths about them, when Black women valorize their own concrete experiences, they claim the authority of experience. Even though Black women's autobiographical writings historically have remained largely unpublished and private, Black women wrote them anyway, because such writings challenged prevailing interpretations of Black women's experience (Braxton 1989; Franklin 1995). By invoking the authority of lived experience, African-American women confronted seemingly universal scientific truths by citing examples from their own experiences. The purpose was not simply to insert the missing experiences into prevailing wisdom. Instead, when effectively done, claiming the authority of concrete experiences used wisdom to challenge legitimated knowledge. Thus, breaking silence by claiming the authority of individual lived Black female experience offered an effective challenge to elite discourses claiming the authority of science.

Understanding the significance of breaking silence by invoking the authority of experience requires examining how knowledge is constructed within unjust power relations. Domination, whether of race, class, gender, sexuality, or nationality, produces public and private knowledges on both sides of power relations (Scott 1990). The public discourses of academia, government bureaucracies, the press, the courts, and popular culture constitute one type of knowledge (Van Dijk 1993). Controlled by elite groups, these public discourses typically count as legitimated knowledge—the knowledge included in the library—and these are the discourses that silence Black women. For example, consider the significance of the "mammy" image in shaping public discourse about Black women workers (Morton 1991; Jewell 1993). Mammy remains so fundamental to perceptions of Black women in serving or helping professions that, to keep their jobs, many Black women must give command performances rivaling that of Hattie McDaniel in *Gone with the Wind* (Rollins 1985; Dill 1988a). Even Black women professionals find ourselves doing "mammy work" in our jobs, work in which we care for everyone else, often at the expense of our own careers or personal well-being (Omolade 1994).

A second type of knowledge exists, the collective secret knowledge generated by groups on either side of power that are shared in private when the other side's surveillance seems absent.[2] For oppressed groups, such knowledge typically remains "hidden" because revealing it weakens its purpose of assisting those groups in dealing with oppression. African-American women's everyday theorizing constitutes such knowledge. In contrast to the public transcript about mammy, very different discussions about domestic work, secretarial work, and corporate mammy work can be heard when Black women talk to one another outside the surveillance of the public sphere. In these private spaces, domestic workers, clerical workers, and "mammified" Black women professionals can transform into nonsubservient, decidedly unmammylike mothers, aunts, sisters, and grandmothers (Rollins 1985; Dill 1988a). Drawing on traditional African-American cultures of resistance, conversations around the kitchen table become classrooms of learning about how to deal with oppression. Ironically, in fulfilling the emotional labor of caring for Whites, males, and/or the affluent, these same mammy workers gain access to their private, usually hidden knowledge. Thus, access to both public and hidden knowledge on both sides of power positions African-American women and other similarly situated groups to develop distinctive standpoints on hierarchical power relations.

Silencing occurs when Black women are restrained from confronting racism, sexism, and elitism in public transcripts because doing so remains dangerous. When individual Black women do break silence in situations of profoundly unequal power—from that of the secretary who finally tells off her boss, to that of Anita Hill's public accusations of sexual harassment against Clarence Thomas—breaking silence represents less a *discovery* of these unequal power relations than a *breaking through* into the public arena of what oppressed groups have long expressed in private. Publicly articulating rage typically constitutes less a revelation about oppression than a discovery of voice.

For African-American women as individuals, breaking silence thus represents a moment of insubordination in relations of power, of saying *in public* what had been said many times before to each other around the kitchen table, in church, at the hairdresser, or at those all-Black women's tables in student dining halls. Breaking silence in hierarchical power relations also generates retaliation from elite groups. As James Scott notes, "A direct, blatant insult delivered before an audience is, in effect, a dare. If it is not beaten back, it will fundamentally alter those relations. Even if it is beaten back and driven underground, something irrevocable has nonetheless occurred. It is now public knowledge that relations of subordination, however immovable in practice, are not entirely legitimate" (1990, 215).

Much of the public voice that Black women gained in the 1980s represents such a dare. Because individual African-American women broke silence in multiple arenas, Black women's collective voice is now public and known. Such voice challenges the legitimacy of public transcripts claiming Black female inferiority.[3] Because it represents profound public insubordination, this newly public voice was bound to generate new forms of suppression dedicated to resilencing African-American women.

African-American women as a collectivity are no longer silenced in the same way, in that Black women's public voice has gained much legitimacy. The 1980s and 1990s witnessed an explosion of works by and about Black women, designed to reclaim and highlight Black women's humanity.[4] If I went to the library today in search of materials, I would find substantially more work by and about Black women in the United States. Events such as Toni Morrison's winning the 1993 Nobel Prize for Literature (the first time a Black woman and a Black American was afforded such an honor), and the 1995 release of the movie *Waiting to Exhale,* based on Terry McMillan's enormously popular novel, speak to the increased visibility granted African-American women's ideas. Moreover, White women and Black men, among others, routinely acknowledge the contributions of Black women's ideas to their own work (Caraway 1991; Awkward 1995). These trends suggest that Black women's intellectual production has achieved some legitimacy. As theorist Ann DuCille points out, Black women academics "stand in the midst of the 'dramatically *charged* field'—the traffic jam—that black feminist studies has become" (1994, 593). This heightened visibility bears little resemblance to the past. Then, Black women were virtually invisible, whereas now, Black women's visibility constitutes a "traffic jam." The question is not whether opposition to Black women's breaking silence will emerge, but rather what form it will take.

In the context of a new politics of containment in which visibility can bring increased surveillance, breaking silence by claiming the authority of experience has less oppositional impact than in the past. During the heady days of the 1970s and 1980s, a critical mass of Black women acquired access to outlets for expressing their ideas. Then, breaking silence meant criticizing, in public, scientific and other academic "truths" that presented the experiences of White men as representative of all human experience. Such knowledge was characterized by a false universalism unused to open dissent. Closely linked to power relations, false universal perspectives reflected the efforts of a small group of people to exclude the majority of humankind from both education and the making of what we call knowledge. These few defined themselves not only as the inclusive kind of human but also as the norm for humanity and as the ideal human. "It is very strange to maintain that one small group of people is simultaneously the essence, the inclusive term, the norm, *and* the ideal for all," philosopher Elizabeth Minnich wryly observes (1990, 39), but that is exactly what paradigms positing the universality of elite White male experiences do. Moreover, the logic of color blindness and tolerance instituted in the 1980s aggravated this situation. In a context in which to talk of race at all meant that one was racist, it became even more difficult to tackle false universalism concerning race (Frankenberg 1993).

False universal perspectives could persist only in situations that either excluded Black women as agents of knowledge in their own behalf, or controlled via tactics of surveillance those Black women who were included. When confronted with an intellectual context grounded in false universalism, breaking silence by using Black women's concrete experiences constituted one effective strategy of resistance. For example, social-science claims that Black women were bad mothers could be countered with "That's not my experience or that of most Black women I know." When strategically deployed, using concrete experiences revealed that what science often presented as universal and true was not so at all. Concrete experience effectively destabilized seemingly scientific categories when such categories appeared unable to explain Black women's experiences and when Black women refused to accept the authority of those categories to explain their lives.

In situations when simply presenting Black female experiences decenters the false universalism accorded to elite White male experience, public acts of insubordination such as breaking silence can remain highly effective. Still, in hegemonic conditions in which dissent is more often absorbed than responded to, and in which Black women can become "fixed" in the public eye, the strategy of breaking silence may be rendered less effective (Winant 1994). In particular, whereas breaking silence within an identity politics grounded in concrete experiences has merit for *individuals,* as a *group* politic it contains the seeds of its own limitations. One such seed concerns the propensity of identity politics to be harnessed to the needs of the state. In describing the development of multiculturalism in Great Britain, Floya Anthias and Nira Yuval-Davis observe that "multiculturalism constructs society as composed of a hegemonic, homogeneous majority, and small unmeltable minorities with their own essentially different communities and cultures which have to be understood, accepted, and basically left alone" (1992, 38). Such approaches construct minority collectivities as basically homogeneous within themselves, speaking with a unified voice, and essentially different from one another. Over time, historically situated differences between oppressed groups become collapsed into and trivialized within an identity politics of unmeltable minorities characterized by essential differences. The power of the seemingly homogeneous majority remains intact, whereas the groups on the bottom compete with one another to receive increasingly small-er portions of the fixed segment of societal resources reserved for them. What begins as legitimate political protest by Black people and other similarly situated groups can degenerate into notions of "differ-ence" that don't make any difference at all (Hall 1992).

Not only does this state recasting of difference weaken group-based identity politics, it also dovetails with a distributive paradigm of justice that ignores structural oppression. Iris Marion Young (1990) notes that the distributive paradigm of social justice tends to focus on the allocation of material goods, such as resources, income, wealth, or the distribution of social positions, especially jobs. This emphasis ig-nores structural and institutional factors that determine distributive outcomes. Within this logic, social justice becomes reconfigured as "rights" that are distributed to "authentic" minority groups. Stated differently, justice becomes conceptualized as a bundle of static things, often in scarce supply, that are distributed to the most worthy. When coupled with state absorption and co-optation of identity politics, ad-hering to this model of justice leads to some unfortunate consequences.

One such consequence concerns competition among many groups to break silence in order to compete for social rewards distributed by the state. In the United States, African-American women have not been the only ones to "break silence." Many groups now do the same. Thus, current power relations are much more complex than the popu-lar conception that White men operate as a homogeneous elite using sophisticated strategies of control against a conglomeration of disad-vantaged groups allied in uncomplicated solidarity. Notions of an un-problematic unity among African-Americans, Asian-Americans, im-migrant groups, White women, and sexual minorities, among others, seem obsolete. When power is diffused throughout a social system, groups police one another to maintain their place in the pecking order (Foucault 1979; 1980a; 1980b). Just as African-American women in-teract with many groups that do not uniformly share Black women's efforts to foster justice, Black women's knowledge or collective voice interconnects with many others. Some remain dominant to Black femi-nist thought in some sense, whereas others are subordinate to it. In this situation in which multiple groups deploy strategies of control against one another, the process becomes one not just of breaking silence in response to one dominant group but of breaking silence with many different groups simultaneously. This climate of multiple "voices" greatly shifts the terms of the debate. Dialogues among the formerly silenced and their silencers seem simplistic. Instead, adversarial debates among multiple voices, all shouting to be heard, seem more common. Everyone wants to talk—few wish to listen.

An overemphasis on authenticity constitutes another unfortunate consequence of relying too heavily on brokering collective voice in an assumed marketplace of ideas with an eye toward achieving justice. Within a cacophony of group voices that break silence, different groups vie for center stage, often striving to be the most oppressed or the most different. Since experiences in a sense speak for themselves, individual qualifications to represent a group voice rest on being deemed an "authentic" representative of the essentially different minority group. Specifically, claiming that only African-American women can invoke the authority of experience to adequately depict "the Black woman's experience" creates a new form of silencing that, in effect, restricts Black women merely to breaking silence in a narrow box of authenticity. When combined with a parallel strategy of locating a person who looks the part, whose external appearance symbolizes essential difference, the limitations of breaking silence within this reformulated identity politics become magnified. In this setting, the actual ideas of the individual matter less than the person's seemingly authentic performance as a member of the affected, "different" group. This notion of authenticity became clear to me at a public lecture that I delivered on Black feminism at a large state university in the Northeast. One student was disappointed in my talk. When I asked why, the student revealed that he had expected me to look more like his image of a Black feminist. Where were my dreadlocks and African attire? Why wasn't I visibly angry, chastising White people for centuries of oppression? In brief, to him, because I had not "walked the walk and talked the talk," I was less authentic and thereby less credible.

Within assumptions of an essentialized identity politics recast within a distributive paradigm of social justice, examples such as these illustrate how the *person* is distilled to his or her *image* and becomes a commodity exchanged in the marketplace of ideas. African-American gay filmmaker and cultural critic Marlon Riggs's observations on the reception he received for his work on Black gay subjectivity satirize this form of appropriation: "Can we talk? But of course we can, queer diva darling, if you abide by the rules of the dominant discourse, which means, in short, you must ultimately sing somebody else's tune to be heard. That somebody is, of course, most often in part responsible for the historic gag in your communal mouth. . . . My mouth moves, but you hear your own words. What nature of ventriloquism is this?" (1992, 101–3). Ironically, performances of authentic difference—in Riggs's example, that of an authentic gay Black man—can be just as exclusionary as false universalism.

Adhering to these ideas regarding identity politics within a distributive paradigm of justice results in another unfortunate consequence. Ironically, because individual African-American women so often explore Black women's collective voice via narrative forms, their work can be appropriated and commodified by all sorts of people who build careers and profit from Black women's pain. As Ann DuCille observes, the current explosion of interest in Black women as literary and historical subjects "increasingly marginalizes both the black women critics and scholars in question and their black feminist 'daughters' who would further develop those fields" (1994, 596). As a result, the works of Black women writers are appropriated, analyzed, and returned in a form virtually unrecognizable to their creators (Christian 1988). Moreover, since appropriation and co-optation can take many forms, it is often difficult to distinguish between the treatment of Black feminist thought by thinkers such as Manning Marable (1983), Elizabeth Spelman (1988), Charles Lemert (1993), and Michael Awkward (1995), among others, from that of other scholars who merely insert individual Black women's narratives into long-standing reactionary frameworks. Fostered by the increasing significance of mass media, images, and culture in shaping our view of the political, Black women's texts can be used to give the illusion of actual political, economic, and social change. Describing how the works of Black women writers are used by dominant groups, Black feminist literary critic Hazel Carby contends, "For White suburbia, as well as for White middle-class students in universities, these texts are becoming a way of gaining knowledge of the 'other,' a knowledge that appears to satisfy and replace the desire to challenge existing frameworks of segregation" (1992, 197). In this sense, in a society that has retained many of its historical practices of apartheid in housing and education, Black cultural texts have become fictional substitutes for the lack of any sustained social or political relationships with Black people.[5]

This treatment of Black women's texts enables members of privileged groups who cannot deal with *actual people* who are constructed as different under hierarchical power relations to substitute the *idea* of difference for conflict-ridden interpersonal contact. This constitutes a new form of White privilege, one whereby White students may know more about Black women's commodified texts than actual Black women who are barred from the classroom. Unwittingly, the reliance of Black feminist thought on individual Black women's "voices" reinforces this tendency. Because many of the texts are "fictional" and "narrative," or because the visual images present a simultaneous closeness and distance, consumers of books and visual media can engage Black women's experiences with racism, sexism, and class exploitation without making any tangible changes in their own lives. Moreover, when individual Black women aim to break silence about the concrete experiences of their lives, often for reasons of self-empowerment, their narratives remain vulnerable to appropriation for other ends. When dissent becomes incorporated within the terms of elite discourse in this fashion, Black feminist thought is robbed of its oppositional potential.

Within this slippery terrain of a false universalism that coexists with an increasingly co-opted identity politics, breaking silence in some settings may be oppositional yet in others it may not. The efficacy of breaking silence thus greatly depends on its strategic use as one form of resistance suitable in certain social contexts. As the examples of Anita Hill and Lani Guinier suggest, under a new politics of containment wherein Black women can be highly visible yet rendered powerless, breaking silence may not work. Healing the internalized oppression of individual victims is not necessarily the same thing as challenging the conditions that created their victimization. In conditions of hegemony, even the righteous anger of the oppressed can be incorporated into a toothless identity politics in which difference becomes a hot commodity. In this new terrain, breaking silence may appear to confront power relations when in actuality it participates in their manufacture.

Developing a Black Women's Standpoint

Black women in the United States are at a decision point that in many ways mirrors that of other groups who recently "broke silence" and gained a collective group "voice." Building on pathbreaking works by Toni Cade Bambara, Ntozake Shange, Angela Davis, Toni Morrison,

June Jordan, Alice Walker, and Audre Lorde, among others, African-American women scholar-activists in the 1980s and 1990s developed a public "voice" (Collins 1990). However, although this collective voice has achieved a visibility unthinkable in the past, it operates in a greatly changed political and intellectual context. Reflecting the encroaching influence of the marketplace on all aspects of life, capitalist market relations have transformed Black women's writing into a hot commodity.

Beginning with the growth of capitalism in Europe in the 1600s and its export in conjunction with colonialism, slavery, and imperialism to people of color in Africa, Asia, and the Americas, notions of the commodification and ownership of property, ideas, and even people have been deeply woven into the very fabric of American society (Cox 1948; Baran and Sweezy 1966; Greenberg 1980; Marable 1983). In the United States, racial segregation and capitalist market relations go hand in hand. For example, by condoning slavery, the Constitution of the United States granted priority to property rights above human rights and thus laid the foundation for the subordinated status of African-Americans, Native Americans, women, and other American citizens (Bell 1987, 34–35). As critical legal theorist Patricia Williams observes, "Money . . . signals a certain type of relationship. So perhaps it is not just money that is the problem, but the relationship it signals" (1991, 31). Human relationships are profoundly affected by the increasing commodification of all aspects of our lives. Observes African-American philosopher Cornel West, "Respect goes to the person with the gun; that's what market forces lead to" (hooks and West 1991, 52).

In a capitalist political economy such as the United States, the exchange of commodities increasingly dominates all areas of life. This process fosters an intellectual climate in which everything—from bottled water to sexuality to actual people—becomes transformed into exchange values quantified for circulation in the marketplace (Jameson 1984; San Juan 1992, 73). As intellectual property, ideas, including Black feminist ones, have not been immune from this encroaching commodification. The synergistic relationship between commodified knowledge and commodified people is illustrated in Derrick Bell's analysis of how the racial composition of a law school's student population affects its perceived prestige (1987). If a school seems to have too many Blacks, it is perceived as not being as good as one that seems more White. In this case, knowledge becomes insepa-rable from the container in which it is packaged, namely, Black and White bodies, and the value of the knowledge is judged in relationship to its package.

In this context of commodification, knowledge validated by upper-middle- and upper-class White men becomes transformed into cultural capital that is systematically used to place people into niches within hierarchical power relations. Within these relations, Black feminist thought faces the danger of becoming just another commodified knowledge stripped of its critical edge. Initially, because it allowed African-American women access to one another's ideas, entering pub-lic space via books, movies, and print media proved invigorating. Thus, market relations initially facilitated Black feminist thought. Publishers put *The Bluest Eye* in the hands of many African-American women who had heard neither of Toni Morrison nor of Black women writers. However, in increasingly competitive global markets, any-thing that sells will be sold, regardless of the consequences. Black women's "voices" of all sorts now flood the market. And as with other commodities exchanged in capitalist markets, surplus cheapens value. Moreover, the fad of today can become the nostalgic memory of tomorrow.

Despite a host of important social issues that face African-American women as a collectivity, Black women's collective voice seems to be turning away from the types of concerns that traditionally preoccu-pied Black women who engaged in community work. This may reflect the recent success of Black feminist thought as a commodity in the academic marketplace. When the audience for Black feminist thought no longer is dominated by African-American women, market forces certainly will influence the content of Black women's "voice."

Given the high rates of poverty (Brewer 1988), poor health (Nsiah-Jefferson 1989; Avery 1994), restricted educational opportu-nities (Sands 1993), employment discrimination (Glenn 1985; Jones 1985; Amott and Matthaei 1991), violence (Arnold 1993; Wilson 1993), and other social problems confronting Black women in the United States as a group, this trend is unfortunate. Historically, in-fluenced by the importance of Black women's community work to Black civil society, Black women scholar-activists' intellectual produc-tion reflected a group standpoint that fused theory and activism.[6] Moreover, because African-American women confronted more than institutionalized racism, this Black women's standpoint addressed multiple forms of oppression. As Pauli Murray points out in her 1970 essay "The Liberation of Black Women," "Traditionally, racism and sexism in the United States have shared some common origins, displayed similar manifestations, reinforced one another, and are so deeply intertwined in the country's institutions that the successful outcome of the struggle against racism will depend in large part on the simultaneous elimination of all discrimination based on sex" (Murray 1995, 186). Building on the work of Murray, Toni Cade Bambara (1970), Shirley Chisholm (1970), and others, African-American women scholar-activists in the 1980s called for a new approach to analyzing Black womanhood. Claiming that African-American women's experiences are shaped not just by race but also by gender, social class, and sexuality, groundbreaking works by Angela Davis (1981), the Combahee River Collective (1982), and Audre Lorde (1984), among others, explored interconnections among systems of oppression. Subsequent works such as Deborah King's important essay "Multiple Jeopardy, Multiple Consciousness: The Context of Black Feminist Ideology" (1988) further explored this interconnected relationship, applying terms such as *matrix of domination* (Collins 1990) and *intersectionality* (Crenshaw 1991) to the connections among systems of oppression.[7]

Redefining Black women's resistance also preoccupied African-American women scholar-activists in the 1970s and 1980s. If Black women's oppression in the United States was multiply defined, then Black women's legacy of struggle against multiple oppressions merited an equally complex analysis. Written while she was in jail awaiting trial on charges for which she was ultimately acquitted, Angela Davis's groundbreaking essay "Reflections on the Black Woman's Role in the Community of Slaves" (1971) suggested that the theme of Black women's resistance to American slavery be reconsidered:

> Even as she [the female slave] was suffering under her unique oppression as female, she was thrust by the force of circumstances into the center of the slave community. She was, therefore, essential to the *survival* of the community. Not all people have survived enslavement; hence her survival-oriented activities were themselves a form of resistance. Survival, moreover, was the prerequisite of all higher levels of struggle. (Davis 1995, 205)

Following Davis's leadership, Black women intellectuals in the 1980s explored the multifaceted contours of Black women's resistance. Cheryl Townsend Gilkes's article "'Holding Back the Ocean with a Broom': Black Women and Community Work," published in La Frances Rodgers-Rose's highly influential edited volume *The Black Woman* (1980), signaled interest in seeing Black women not as objects of history but as historical agents. Much of the excellent scholarship produced by Darlene Clark Hine, Paula Giddings, Elsa Barkley Brown, and other African-American women historians in the 1980s and 1990s, as well as work by Doris Wilkinson, Jacqueline Johnson Jackson, Leith Mullings, Bonnie Thornton Dill, and many other social scientists, explored this legacy of struggle—its successes, obstacles, and defeats (see, e.g., Crawford et al. 1990; Barnett 1993; Higginbotham 1993; and Guy-Sheftall 1995). All aimed to generate a historical and contemporary "voice" for Black women as agents of knowledge. Through their scholarship, African-American women theorists of the 1970s and 1980s identified core themes concerning work, family, controlling images, motherhood, and sexual politics that formed the foundation for Black feminist thought that ensued in the 1980s and 1990s (Collins 1990).

Despite this legacy of a Black women's intellectual tradition nurtured by Black women's community work, recent Black feminist thought neglects many of the social issues affecting Black civil society. Instead, increasingly preoccupied with issues of individual and group identity, its gaze has turned increasingly inward. On one level, current interest in whether Black women's intellectual production should be named "womanism" or "Black feminism" mirrors the current preoccupation with questions of individual identity within academia. In this light, questions of what to name a Black women's standpoint constitute yet another minor academic debate. On another level, however, naming practices reflect a concern with crafting a Black women's standpoint that is sensitive to differences among Black women yet grounded in solidarity. In this sense, the question whether to call a Black women's standpoint womanism or Black feminism forces a rethinking of long-standing notions of racial solidarity that have been so central to Black women's community work. Thus, trying to name a Black women's standpoint not only demonstrates the heterogeneity among Black women but also highlights the ongoing and contested functions of self-definition in developing adequate political analyses of current social conditions.

In her acclaimed volume of essays *In Search of Our Mothers' Gardens,* Alice Walker introduced four meanings of the term *womanist.* According to Walker's first definition, a womanist is "a black feminist or feminist of color" (1983, xi). Thus, on some basic level, Walker uses the two terms virtually interchangeably. Like Walker, many African-American women see little difference between the two, since both support a common agenda of Black women's self-definition and self-determination. As Barbara Omolade points out, "Black feminism is sometimes referred to as womanism because both are concerned with struggles against sexism and racism by Black women who are themselves part of the Black community's efforts to achieve equity and liberty" (1994, xx). Despite similar beliefs expressed by African-American women who define themselves as Black feminists, as womanists, as both, or in some cases as neither, increasing attention seems devoted to delineating the differences, if any, between groups naming themselves womanists or Black feminists. The name given to Black women's collective standpoint seems to matter, but why?

Womanism

Alice Walker's multiple definitions of the term *womanist* shed light on the issue of why many African-American women prefer the term *womanism* to *Black feminism.* Walker offers two seemingly contradictory meanings of *womanist.* On the one hand, Walker clearly sees womanism as rooted in Black women's particular history of racial and gender oppression in the United States. Taking the term from "You acting womanish," the southern Black folk expression of mothers to female children, Walker suggests that Black women's concrete history fosters a womanist worldview accessible primarily and perhaps exclusively to African-American women. Womanish girls acted in outrageous, courageous, and willful ways, using attributes that freed them from the conventions long limiting White women. Womanish girls wanted to know more and in greater depth than what was considered good for them. They were responsible, in charge, and serious (1983, xi).

On the other hand, Walker aspires to a universal meaning of *womanist* that transcends particular histories, including that of

African-American women. Walker sees womanists as being "traditionally universalist," a philosophy invoked by her metaphor of the garden, where room exists for all flowers to bloom equally and differently. Despite this disclaimer, Walker implies that African-American women are somehow superior to White women because of their Black folk tradition. Defining *womanish* as the opposite of the "frivolous, irresponsible, not serious" *girlish* (1983, xi), Walker constructs Black women's experiences in opposition to those of White women. This meaning presents womanism as different from and superior to feminism, a difference allegedly stemming from Black and White women's different histories within American racism. Walker's much cited phrase. "Womanist is to feminist as purple to lavender" (xii) clearly seems designed to set up this type of comparison—Black women are womanist, whereas White women remain merely feminist.

This usage sits squarely in Black nationalist traditions premised on the belief that Blacks and Whites cannot function as equals while inhabiting the same territory or participating in the same social institutions (Van Deburg 1992). Since Black nationalist philosophies posit that Whites as a group have a vested interest in continuing a system of institutionalized racism, they typically see little use for African-American integration or assimilation into a system predicated on Black subjugation. Black nationalist approaches also support a Black moral superiority over Whites because of Black suffering (Pinkney 1976; Moses 1978).

Walker's use of the term *womanist* promises to African-American women who operate within these Black nationalist assumptions yet see the need to address women's issues within African-American communities a partial reconciliation of two seemingly incompatible philosophies. Although womanism raises the issue of gender, it simultaneously offers a distance from the "enemy," in this case, Whites generally and White women in particular. Because of its seeming endorsement of racial separatism, this interpretation of womanism offers a vocabulary for addressing gender issues within African-American communities without violating norms of racial solidarity of Black civil society. Geneva Smitherman's understanding of womanism taps this meaning. For Smitherman, a womanist refers to an "African-American woman who is rooted in the Black community and committed to the development of herself and the entire community" (1996, 104). This usage provides Smitherman and others continuity with earlier generations of "race women" who worked on behalf of Black civil society.

This use of womanism sidesteps an issue central to many White feminists, namely, finding ways to foster interracial cooperation among women. African-American women who embrace Black nationalist philosophies typically express little interest in working with White women—in fact, White women are defined as part of the problem (see, e.g., Welsing 1991). Moreover, womanism appears to provide an avenue for fostering stronger relationships between Black women and Black men in the United States, another very important issue for African-American women regardless of their political perspective. Again, Walker's definition provides guidance when she notes that womanists are "committed to survival and wholeness of entire people, male *and* female" (1983, xi). Many Black women in the United States view feminism as a movement that, at best, is exclusively for women and, at worst, is dedicated to attacking or eliminating men. Shirley Williams takes this view when she notes that in contrast to feminism, "womanist inquiry . . . assumes that it can talk both effectively and productively about men" (1990, 70). Womanism seemingly supplies a way for Black women to address gender oppression without attacking Black men.

Walker also presents a visionary meaning for womanism that dovetails with Black civil society's norms concerning the centrality of moral, ethical principles to Black political struggle. As part of her second definition of *womanist,* Walker has a Black girl pose the question "Mama, why are we brown, pink, and yellow, and our cousins are white, beige, and black?" (1983, xi). The response, "The colored race is just like a flower garden, with every color flower represented" (xi), both criticizes colorism within African-American communities and broadens the notion of humanity to make all people "people of color." Reading this passage as a metaphor, womanism thus furnishes a vision wherein women and men of different colors coexist like flowers in a garden yet retain their cultural distinctiveness and integrity.

This meaning of womanism also invokes another major political tradition within African-American politics, namely, a pluralist version of Black empowerment (Van Deburg 1992). Pluralism views society as being composed of various ethnic and interest groups, all of whom compete for goods and services. Equity lies in providing equal opportunities, rights, and respect to all groups. By retaining Black cultural distinctiveness and integrity, pluralism offers a modified version of racial integration premised not on individual assimilation but on group integration. Clearly rejecting what they perceive as the limited vision of feminism projected by North American White women, many Black women theorists have been attracted to the joining of pluralism and racial integration in this interpretation of Walker's womanism. Black women theologians, in particular, illustrate this use (Cannon 1988; Townes 1993; Sanders 1995). As an ethical system, womanism is always in the making—it is not a closed, fixed system of ideas but one that continually evolves through its rejection of all forms of oppression and its commitment to social justice.

Walker's definition thus manages to invoke three important yet seemingly contradictory philosophies that frame Black social and political thought in the United States. By claiming a moral and epistemological superiority for Black women because of their suffering under racial and gender oppression, Walker invokes Black nationalism. Through the metaphor of the garden, she embraces pluralism, and her claims that Black women are "traditionally universalist" call up integration and assimilation (Van Deburg 1992). Just as Black nationalism and racial integration coexist in uneasy partnership, with pluralism occupying the contested terrain between the two, Walker's definition of womanism demonstrates comparable tensions. By both grounding womanism in the concrete experiences of African-American women and generalizing about the potential for realizing a humanist vision of community via the experiences of African-American women, Walker depicts the potential for oppressed people to possess a moral vision and a standpoint on society that grows from their situation of oppression. This standpoint also emerges as an incipient foundation for a more humanistic, just society. Overall, these uses of Walker's term *womanist* create conceptual space to explore philosophical differences that exist among African-American women.

One particularly significant feature of African-American women's use of *womanist* concerns the part of Walker's definition that remains neglected. A troublesome line for many Black women who self-define as womanists precedes the often cited passage "committed to survival and wholeness of entire people, male *and* female." Just before Walker offers this admonition that womanists, by definition, are committed to wholeness, she states that a womanist is also "a woman who loves other women, sexually and/or nonsexually" (1983, xi). The relative silence of womanists on this dimension of womanism speaks to many African-American women's continued ambivalence in dealing with the links between race, gender, and sexuality, in this case, the "taboo" sexuality of lesbianism. In her essay "The Truth That Never Hurts: Black Lesbians in Fiction in the 1980s" (1990), Black feminist critic Barbara Smith points out that African-American women have yet to come to terms with homophobia in African-American communities. Smith applauds the growth of Black women's fiction in the 1980s but also observes that within Black feminist intellectual production, Black lesbians continue to be ignored. Despite the fact that some of the most prominent and powerful Black women thinkers claimed by both womanists and Black feminists were and are lesbians, this precept often remains unacknowledged in the work of African-American writers. In the same way that many people read the Bible, carefully selecting the parts that agree with their worldview and rejecting the rest, many people engage in selective readings of Walker's womanism.

Another significant feature of African-American women's multiple uses of womanism concerns the potential for a slippage between the real and the ideal. To me, there is a distinction between describing Black women's responses to racial and gender oppression in the United States as womanist, and using *womanism* as a visionary term delineating an ethical or ideal vision of humanity for all people. Identifying the liberatory *potential* within Black women's communities that emerges from concrete, historical experiences differs from claiming that these same communities have already *arrived* at this ideal, "womanist" end point. Refusing to distinguish carefully between these two meanings of womanism thus collapses the historically real and the future ideal into one privileged position for African-American women in the present. Taking this position is reminiscent of the response of some Black women to the admittedly narrow feminist agenda forwarded by White women in the early 1970s. Those Black women proclaimed that they were already "liberated," although this was far from the truth.

Black Feminism

African-American women who use the term *Black feminism* also attach varying interpretations to this term. According to Black feminist theorist and activist Pearl Cleage, feminism is "the belief that women are full human beings capable of participation and leadership in the full range of human activities—intellectual, political, social, sexual, spiritual and economic" (1993, 28). In its broadest sense, feminism constitutes both an ideology and a global political movement that confronts sexism, a social relationship in which men as a collectivity have authority over women as a collectivity.

Globally, a feminist agenda encompasses several major areas. First and foremost, the economic status of women and issues associated with women's poverty, such as educational opportunities for girls, industrial development, employment policies, prostitution, and inheritance laws concerning property, constitute important women's issues globally. Political rights for women, such as the right to vote, to assemble, to travel in public, and to hold office, as well as the rights of political prisoners, and basic human rights violations against women, such as rape and torture, constitute a second area of concern. A third area of global attention consists of marital and family issues, such as marriage and divorce laws, child custody policies, and domestic labor. Women's health and survival issues, such as reproductive rights, pregnancy, sexuality, and AIDS constitute another area of global feminist concern. This broad global feminist agenda finds varying expressions in different regions of the world and among diverse populations.

Using the term *Black feminism* positions African-American women to examine how the particular constellation of issues affecting Black women in the United States are part of issues of women's emancipation struggles globally (Davis 1989; James and Busia 1994). In the context of feminism as a global political movement for women's rights and emancipation, the feminism that African-American women encounter in the United States represents a narrow segment refracted through the binary thinking of American racial politics. Because the media in the United States portray feminism as a for-Whites-only movement and because many White women have accepted racially segregated institutions of all types, including feminist organizations, feminism is often viewed by American Blacks and Whites as the cultural property of White women (Caraway 1991). Despite considerable ideological heterogeneity that operates within the term *feminism,* unfortunately racial segregation in the United States and the hegemonic ideologies that accompany it typically obscure this plurality.

Despite their erasure in the media, many African-American women have long struggled against this exclusionary American feminism and have participated in what appear to be for-Whites-only feminist activities. In some cases, Black women have directly challenged the assumptions guiding feminist organizations controlled by White women in order to generate more inclusive feminist agendas (see, e.g., Matthews 1989 and Poster 1995). At other times, even though Black women's past and present participation in feminist organizations remains largely invisible—for example, Pauli Murray made many contributions as a founding member of the National Organization for Women—African-American women have participated in women's organizations. In still other cases, Black women have combined allegedly divergent political agendas. For example, Pearl Cleage observes that Black feminist politics and Black nationalist politics need not be contradictory: "I don't think you can be a true Black Nationalist, dedicated to the freedom of Black people *without* being a feminist, Black *people* being made up of both men and *women*, after all, and feminism being nothing more or less than a belief in the political, social and legal equality of women" (1993, 180).

In the United States, the term *Black feminism* also disrupts the racism inherent in presenting feminism as a for-Whites-only ideology and political movement. Inserting the adjective *Black* challenges the assumed Whiteness of feminism and disrupts the false universal of this term for both White and Black American women. Since many White women think that Black women lack feminist consciousness, the term *Black feminist* both highlights the contradictions underlying the assumed Whiteness of feminism and reminds White women that they are neither the only nor the normative "feminists." Because it challenges Black women to confront their own views on sexism and women's oppression, the term *Black feminism* also makes many African-American women uncomfortable. Even though they may support global feminist ideas, large numbers of African-American women reject the term *feminism* because of its perceived association with Whiteness. They are not alone in this rejection, since women of color globally have questioned the association of the term *feminism* with Western domination. Within this context, many Black women in the United States see feminism as operating exclusively within the term *White American* and perceive its opposite as being *Black American*. When given these two narrow and false choices, Black women routinely choose "race" and let the lesser question of "gender" go. In this situation, those Black women who identify with feminism must be recoded as either non-Black or less authentically Black.[8]

The term *Black feminist* also disrupts a long-standing and largely unquestioned reliance on racial solidarity in Black civil society (Dyson 1993). Using family rhetoric that views Black family, community, race, and nation as a series of nested boxes, each gaining meaning from the other, certain rules apply to all levels of this "family" organization (Gilroy 1992). Just as families have internal, naturalized hierarchies that give, for example, older siblings authority over younger ones or males over females, groups defining themselves as racial families invoke similar rules (Collins forthcoming 1998b). Within African-American communities, one such rule is that Black women will support Black men no matter what, an unwritten family rule that was manipulated quite successfully during the Clarence Thomas confirmation hearings. Even if Anita Hill was harassed by Clarence Thomas, many proclaimed in barbershops and beauty parlors, she should have kept her mouth shut and not "aired dirty laundry." Even though Thomas recast the life of his own sister through the framework of an unworthy welfare queen, Black women should have kept their collective mouths shut in deference to rules of racial solidarity (McKay 1992). By counseling Black women not to remain silent in the face of abuse no matter who does it, Black feminism comes into conflict with codes of silence such as these.

Several difficulties accompany the use of the term *Black feminism*. One involves balancing the genuine concerns of African-American women against continual pressures to absorb and recast such interests within White feminist frameworks. For example, gaining quality educations, jobs, and health care remains a strong focal point in the feminism of African-American women. Yet within some academic feminist circles, the emphasis on individualism, individual subjectivity, and personal advocacy implied in the politics of postmodernism (see chapter 4) saps Black feminism of its critical edge as a group-based, critical social theory. Contemporary Black women thinkers' efforts to explicate a long-standing African-American women's intellectual tradition bearing the label "Black feminism" can attract the attention of White women advancing different feminist agendas. Issues raised by Black women that are not seen as explicitly "feminist" ones (i.e., issues that do not affect only women) receive much less sanction. Even well-meaning White feminists can inadvertently consume the limited resources of African-American women who claim Black feminism. The

constant drumbeat of supporting White women in their efforts to foster an antiracist feminism diverts Black women's energy away from
addressing social issues facing African-American communities. Because Black feminism appears to be so well received by White women,
in the context of the segregated racial politics of the United States,
some African-American women quite rightly suspect its motives.

Another difficulty with Black feminism concerns the direct conflict between Black feminism and selected elements of Black religious
traditions in the United States. Given the significance of Christianity for
African-American women (see, e.g., Gilkes 1985 and Higginbotham
1993), any social movement that criticizes such a fundamental element of Black civil society will remain suspect. Moreover, the visibility
of White lesbians within North American feminism overall directly
conflicts with many Black women's article of faith that homosexuality
is a sin. Although individual African-American women may be accepting of gays, lesbians, and bisexuals as individuals, especially if such
individuals are African-American, Black women as a collectivity have
distanced themselves from social movements perceived as requiring
acceptance of homosexuality. Feminism in the United States appears to
be one such movement. As one African-American female student queried, "Why do I have to accept lesbianism in order to support Black
feminism?" The association of feminism with lesbianism remains a
problematic one for many Black women. Reducing Black lesbians to
their sexuality, one that chooses women over men, reconfigures Black
lesbians as enemies of Black men. This reduction not only constitutes
a serious misreading of Black lesbianism—African-American lesbians
have fathers, brothers, and sons of their own and are often embedded
in a series of relationships as complex as those of their Black heterosexual counterparts—it simultaneously diverts attention away from
more important issues (Lorde 1984). One might ask, who ultimately
benefits when the presence of Black lesbians in any Black social movement leads to its rejection by African-Americans?

The theme of lesbianism and its association with feminism in the
minds of many African-Americans also overlaps with another concern
of many African-American women, namely, their commitment to
African-American men. Sensitive to the specific issues confronting
Black men generally (see, e.g., Madhubuti 1990a and Dyson 1993)
and, as mothers, Black sons in particular (see, e.g., Golden 1995),
Black women in the United States routinely reject philosophies and
social movements that portray Black men as adversaries or enemies.

Thus, another difficulty confronting Black feminism concerns its perceived separatism—many African-Americans define Black feminism as being exclusively for Black women and as rejecting Black men. In explaining her preference for *womanism,* Shirley Williams notes, "One of the most disturbing aspects of current black feminist criticism [is] its separatism—its tendency to see not only a *distinct* black female culture but to see that culture as a separate cultural form having more in common with white female experience than with the facticity of Afro-American life" (1990, 70). Geneva Smitherman offers a similar criticism. In response to a press conference of Black women intellectuals who denounced the alleged sexism of the 1995 Million Man March in Washington, D.C., Smitherman notes, "Black women must be wary of the seductive feminist trap. White males hold the power in this society, not Black ones. . . . To launch an attack against the first mass-based, sorely needed, long overdue, positive effort by Black men on the grounds of sexism is to engage in a misguided, retrogressive brand of feminism" (1996, 105). Smitherman's criticism cannot be dismissed as the ideas of a woman who lacks feminist consciousness. Involved for years as a community activist and scholar in Detroit, Smitherman knows firsthand what is happening to Black youth in inner cities. Until White and Black feminists show some concern for those issues, they are likely to have little support from Smitherman and other self-defined womanists.

Williams and Smitherman offer a valid criticism of Black feminism in the United States, one that, in my mind, must be addressed if Black feminism is to avoid the danger of becoming increasingly separated from African-American women's experiences and interests. It also speaks to the larger issue of the continuing difficulty of positioning Black feminism between Black nationalism and North American White feminism. In effect, Black feminism must come to terms with a White feminist agenda incapable of seeing its own racism, as well as a Black nationalist one resistant to grappling with its own sexism (White 1990). Finding a place that accommodates these seemingly contradictory agendas remains elusive (Christian 1989b).

Talking Back

Whatever African-American women choose to name a Black women's standpoint, womanism and Black feminism encounter the issues confronted by any knowledge that aims to "talk back" to knowledges with more power. The chapters in part II investigate these issues in greater detail, but here I want to highlight one significant issue raised by the womanism/Black feminism analysis that is germane to this process of talking back. Articulating a Black women's standpoint under the new politics of containment confronts one fundamentally new challenge: how can Black feminist thought foster group unity while recognizing Black women's heterogeneous experiences? Ironically, the new public space provided by the successes of Black women scholar-activists in the 1980s and 1990s revealed differences among African-American women as individuals. Differences of sexuality, economic class, nationality, religion, region of country, and citizenship status all generate a substantial heterogeneity among Black women in the United States that is increasingly played out in public arenas. At this point, whether African-American women can fashion a singular "voice" about the Black *woman's* position remains less an issue than how Black women's knowledges collectively construct, affirm, and maintain a dynamic Black *women's* self-defined standpoint.

In essence, the discussion of whether to name Black women's intellectual production womanism or Black feminism participates in a larger discussion about the significance of difference for group self-definition. An identity politics that valorizes differences certainly helped create the conditions that allowed Black women to challenge the limitations imposed by racial solidarity. In particular, questioning notions of Black solidarity built on Black women's sacrifices has been beneficial. However, it is one thing to revitalize a politics organized around "lifting as we climb" by attending to difference among African-American women. It is quite another to replace that politics with one emphasizing different "voices," if not difference itself, as the theoretical anchor applied to Black women's experiences.

To me, overemphasizing differences among Black women while rarely, if ever, situating analyses in a context of Black women's distinctive group-based oppression in the United States is, at best, politically naive. If such neglect of social structure is also intentional, at worst, it is also dangerous.[9] Regardless of current academic fashions, I suspect that African-American women benefit much less from critical social theories organized around difference than do other groups. Take, for example, feminist theories and political movements controlled by middle-class and affluent White feminists in the United States. Within contemporary U.S. feminism, a well-intentioned effort to explore differences among women in order to build a multiracial, multicultural feminist movement has been under way for some time. Exploding the category "woman" aims to create space for new alliances among individual women across historical markers of difference. Such efforts at coalition building remain worthwhile, and I can see how White women who have had limited contact with Black women benefit from struggling with their own privilege, let alone how benefits might accrue to a women's movement that appears to tolerate difference. However, I am left wondering whether a similar politics organized around differences *among* African-American women would deliver comparable results and newfound freedoms for Black women as a group.

Although a politics organized around difference may expand the freedom of individuals already positioned to benefit from such emphases, African-American women as a group operate in a different political context. White women as a group can claim a legal history that respects their individuality and privacy, however regulated by domestic relations. This expectation of privacy is still denied large numbers of African-American women. Eliminating Black feminist thought as an expression of group-based knowledge and replacing it with a politics organized around difference may inadvertently foster a weakening of Black women's ability to resist injustice as a collectivity. The true irony here is that, like Black women's suffering that occurs in plain sight while the structural racial segregation that causes such suffering remains hidden, Black women's intellectual production that becomes overly preoccupied with differences among Black women may experience a similar fate. It may slowly disappear, all the while remaining in plain sight, with Black women as a collectivity left wondering what happened.

I suspect that the time has come to balance this issue of dialogues *between* African-American women and members of other groups with one of thinking through what types of themes beyond those of naming should permeate dialogues *among* Black women. In one sense, contemporary Black feminism, womanism, or whatever we or others in the academy name it in the future is a mature discourse. Since it has "come to voice," it now faces new issues. Because Black women's intellectual production now finds its way to Black women of all sorts, as well as to many other women and men who benefit from its ideas, its legitimation has been beneficial. However, under commodity relations, Black women are encouraged to sell their voices, and the more different they are from one another, the better. Novelty, rather than a continuation of long-standing concerns, becomes the selling point.

To recognize this process, one need only contrast Heidi Safia Mirza's edited volume *Black British Feminism* (1997) with the increasing specialization that characterizes Black feminist thought in the United States. Though its themes differ, the volume reminds me of works such as Toni Cade Bambara's *The Black Woman* (1970), Gloria Hull et al.'s edited volume *All the Women Are White, All the Blacks Are Men, But Some of Us Are Brave* (1982), Barbara Smith's *Home Girls: A Black Feminist Anthology* (1983), and other comparable anthologies reflecting dialogues among Black women in the United States in earlier periods. *Black British Feminism* manages to weave together diverse perspectives of Black British women to talk back to a public largely unaware that Black British women have a voice. As a foundational document, the volume contains an enthusiasm and excitement about coming to voice in a British context that has silenced this visible yet invisible minority. Within this volume of Black British women who self-define as "Black" (no small feat in that context), one sees a rich dialogue among established intellectuals such as Hazel Carby, Kum-Kum Bhavnani, and Ann Phoenix, as well as emerging thinkers such as Debbie Weekes, Tracey Reynolds, and Jayne Ifekwunigwe that presents a collective yet far from uniform voice. In part, this freedom to explore multiple dimensions of Black women's experiences from diverse perspectives reflects the significance of distinctive migration patterns to the United Kingdom and the distinctive meaning of *Black* in Britain. In the United States, racial segregation established more stringent and more limiting boundaries on lived Black experience, with corresponding effects on Black critical discourse (Wallace 1990).

Trying to name a Black women's standpoint certainly constitutes an important activity. However, whatever a Black women's intellectual tradition is called remains less important than, first, maintaining dialogues among Black women that are attentive to *both* heterogeneity among African-American women *and* shared concerns arising from a common social location in U.S. market and power relations; and, second, using this continually evolving knowledge to engage other critical social theories. So much of Black women's intellectual production is now filtered through an array of different speech communities, many of which serve important gatekeeping functions, that doing intellectual work in this climate necessarily changes the thought itself. The cost of visibility lies in the very real threat of having one's voice annexed in support of other agendas. I am reminded of a conversation I had with a Black female graduate student at a prestigious university who shared with me her interest in studying questions of Black women's knowledge and power relations. Although her decision to attend graduate school resulted from her deep interest in Black women's critical social theory, she quickly was told by potential committee members that since they had little interest in her topic, she would have to work on something more "marketable." The very interest that got her to school now had to be abandoned to gain the legitimacy to one day revisit this topic.

This woman's situation is far from unique. Many aspiring and established Black women intellectuals now create ideas for dissertation committees, tenure committees, journals, and the popular press—outlets that are all targeted to a liberal White public segmented into constituencies most receptive to the given intellectual. Writing to mainstream audiences to gain access to the public that one truly wants to reach is important and, far too often, necessary. However, as Zora Neale Hurston's continual struggles with her White patrons illustrates, visibility can exact high costs. Moreover, with the erosion of institutions of African-American civil society, much of this newer work remains unmediated. Many Black women doing intellectual work no longer encounter the heterogeneity of Black women's experiences in the everyday social interactions of Black civil society. As a result, although they are held accountable for what they say by a larger White public, even if their work deals with Black women, many see little reason to be accountable to Black civil society. Take, for example, the top four platform issues listed on the Web page of the organizers of the 1997 Million Woman March. The women who assembled in Philadelphia wanted the following: a probe into the Central Intelligence Agency's relationship to the influx of drugs in African-American communities; the development of Black independent schools; new mechanisms that would help Black women when they leave the penal system; and better health care services, with greater emphasis on preventive and therapeutic treatment. Other platform issues included support for Black women who want to become professionals, taking steps to curb homelessness and gentrification of urban neighborhoods, and increased support for all Black elderly. Many African-American women doing intellectual work certainly examine these issues, as do Black women activists. Yet none of these platform issues occupies a prominent place in contemporary Black feminist thought. Where is the book presenting a Black feminist analysis of African-American women and the drug industry? Where can we find a womanist treatment of Black independent schools? Without diligently attending to how the demands of the so-called universal audience and marketplace forces affect oppositional scholarship, Black women intellectuals, especially those deemed "public intellectuals," may lose their critical edge.

Although fostering dialogues among Black women in the here and now is important, of greater significance is reconceptualizing Black women's intellectual work as engaging in dialogues across time. The significance of writing books, making films, recording music, and producing other forms of cultural production lies in their power to foster dialogues among a diverse array of current and future readers, viewers, and listeners. I for one am immensely grateful that early-twentieth-century Black club women such as Anna Julia Cooper, Ida Wells Barnett, and others took the time to record their ideas. Their written record allows me to talk with them about patterns of injustice characterizing Black women's collective group history. Some of the most important ideas in Black women's intellectual history come from this sense of writing across time, of having dialogues with women who grapple with questions of injustice in unfamiliar social settings. Without listening to those who have come before, how can Black women prepare an intellectual and political space for Black women who will confront future, reconfigured injustices? Keeping a tradition alive differs from the popular conception of performing certain rites and rituals repeatedly and letting those rituals serve as tradition. Keeping a tradition alive lies in recognizing that African-American women will continue to confront a series of ongoing challenges stemming from systemic injustice. Although these challenges may be organized differently across time and place—the experiences of early-twentieth-century Black club women, Black women in the early 1970s, and contemporary Black British feminists cannot be collapsed into one another without doing serious damage—they share a commonality. When it comes to Black women in the United States and Black women globally, unfortunately, this commonality constitutes searching for justice.

Currently, no infrastructure exists for the type of rich dialogue that I envision. Instead, like all African-Americans in the United

States, Black women intellectuals remain under surveillance in racially segregated marketplace relations. Fostering dialogues among Black women across these complexities requires building new institutional locations that will continue to raise these questions across time. It also means legitimating one another's work despite bona fide differences emerging from the richly textured heterogeneity among Black women. Black women intellectuals would do well to remember that having the space to engage in dialogues of self-definition illustrated by the luxury of struggling over a name remains the privilege of only a select few. Twenty years from now, terms such as *womanism* and *Black feminism* may have little meaning, especially in the absence of actual social institutions dedicated to investigating Black women's critical social theory.

Overall, coming to voice in the public sphere without simultaneously coming to power in the social institutions that constitute it does little to challenge the injustices confronting African-American women as a collectivity. In this sense, those Black women teachers and administrators who publish little but who hold positions of power and authority in higher education, school districts, publishing avenues, and the media may have far greater impact on Black women's intellectual production than do a handful of handpicked academics. Without this type of structural power, Black women's position of having "no say" in determining the knowledge included in the American national "library" and, in turn, the power that the "library's" knowledge defends will persist. Including a few more books on Black women in the library or a few safe Black women's "voices" in the curriculum represents a step in the right direction. Those fortunate individual African-American women like me who find our work published and read certainly gain individual benefit from this politics. Although I like to think that our work makes a difference to more than just us, our loved ones, and a few empathetic colleagues, I also recognize how our work can be used toward quite different ends. Changing both the books in the library and the overall organization of the library requires far more than my or any other individual's coming to voice. After so many years of being silenced, individual voices like mine can provide comfort, if not inspiration, to individuals from many groups who, like African-American women, have been similarly silenced. I also know that, lacking a collective voice, individual voices like mine will become fainter until, one day, many may forget that we ever spoke at all.

Part II

*Black Feminist Thought
and Critical Social Theory*

On Fighting Words
with "Fighting Words"

When I worked as a college administrator in a small liberal arts college in the late 1970s, I shared the optimism of my colleagues that higher education in the United States had a bright future. Despite the contentious battles that led to the creation of Black studies, women's studies, and similar units, these programs asked new questions and, in doing so, revitalized college campuses. The changing contours of the college population itself certainly demanded a revised curriculum and a more diverse faculty. Students long separated by racial segregation, economic class differences, and gender-specific rules regulating appropriate activities for boys and girls now found themselves in the same classrooms, sharing the same academic space. Given this climate, I, among others, hoped that academia's professed commitment to free speech, exercised in conjunction with this new multicultural, inclusive curriculum, would foster greater tolerance among students.

Visiting college campuses of all types in the United States in the early 1990s, ironically, while presenting much of the material in this book, was an eye-opener. I knew that my own campus had experienced an unfortunate "racial incident," but I didn't suspect that so many other American colleges and universities had similar problems. The vast majority of faculty, students, and staff with whom I came in contact were genuinely concerned about building inclusive environments at their schools. Some of the problems they shared were heart-breaking. At one Ivy League university, I had dinner with two young Black women who became the center of national controversy when they complained about ongoing verbal harassment by some White male students. On a small rural campus, I met a Black woman who, because of her visibility as head of the student council, had received several death threats. During a dinner with faculty members of a large midwestern university, I listened to their frustration and embarrassment about their administration's inaction in responding to a "racial incident." When members of one of their fraternities had burned a cross, officials claimed that they could do nothing. Because the event occurred off campus, it was an "expression of free speech." On several campuses, African-American students experienced name-calling, racist graffiti in their dormitories, and death threats, and on one campus they were chased and beaten by an unruly crowd disappointed at the results of a baseball game (Walker 1994). Over time, it became clear to me that these and other "racial incidents" were far from isolated and consititued part of a larger pattern.

These incidents of racial harassment and violence escalated seemingly in tandem with a growth in assaultive speech, in which words are "used as weapons to ambush, terrorize, wound, humiliate, and degrade" (Matsuda et al. 1993, 1). If the cross-burning incident is any indication, some actions were protected as speech. This increase in violent acts and hate speech left not only me but also students, faculty, and administrators puzzled. Why did intolerance targeted against Blacks in particular but also against Jews, Asians, Latinos, foreign nationals, gays, lesbians, and bisexuals emerge among the first generation of college students exposed to ideas and practices claiming that categories of race, gender, class, nationality, and sexuality were unimportant in measuring human worth?

Explaining this seeming contradiction requires revisiting recent American history. Prior to the civil rights movement of the 1950s and the Black Power movement and federal civil rights legislation of the 1960s, inequalities distinguishing African-Americans from Whites were taken for granted. Whites could largely do as they pleased and say what they wanted to without repercussions. Describing the rules that governed interpersonal contact between racial groups, sociologist Robert E. Park (1950) developed the term "racial etiquette" to describe patterns of race relations in the racially segregated South. Southern rules of racial etiquette allowed Whites to address Blacks as "boy" and "girl" and to use their first names instead of surnames, while insisting that they themselves be addressed as "Mr." and "Miss" or "Mrs." The rules of racial etiquette were designed to maintain social distance in a situation where Blacks and Whites were in close proximity. Historically, the North needed far fewer of these rules of racial etiquette, because residential, educational, and employment segregation maintained a physical distance matching the social distance. Within the South, however, these rules mattered greatly. When in 1955, fourteen-year-old, Northern-born Emmett Till allegedly violated one of Mississippi's rules of racial etiquette—Till purportedly looked at a White woman—he was lynched.

Rules like those of racial etiquette also regulate academic speech in the United States. Although few of my colleagues are willing to admit it, within academia some of today's hate speech operated as business as usual in the past. Theories of Black inferiority have long permeated a range of natural and social-science disciplines.[1] During a period when African-Americans were excluded from higher education, academic disciplines produced their own regime of racial and other forms of etiquette. Historically, some academics showed little hesitation in expressing beliefs about Black inferiority and White superiority that would make many blush today. In a situation where, as David Goldberg points out, "power is exercised epistemologically in the dual practices of naming and evaluating" (1993, 150), social theories of Black biological and cultural inferiority were given free rein.[2]

When racial segregation predominated prior to World War II, racial thinking conventionally signified sets of negative associations of both individual characteristics (e.g., sexuality and criminality) and collective attributes (e.g., family structures and pathological cultural values) attributed to assumed biological differences between races. Rules of racial etiquette viewed Black intellectual achievement as an anomaly. Because "exceptional Blacks" were not like ordinary, normative African-Americans, their very existence became something to be studied. Racial desegregation of schools and jobs changed all this. Schools and workplaces were desegregated, fair housing legislation went on the books, and the de jure segregation characterizing public accommodations was dismantled. During this period, wholesale denial of the existence of racial inequality and injustice flourished in a climate of not talking about racism (Winant 1993).

As Blacks and Whites came into closer proximity, theories of Black inferiority became increasingly attributed to cultural differences (Barker 1990). Keeping races in their places in power relations required surveillance tactics designed, in part, to detect cultural differences. In current contexts, because they are still seen as being scarce, "exceptional Blacks" become something to be collected and owned. Within this logic, Black Lady Overachievers constitute a gender-specific version of a long-standing racial logic wherein the accomplishments of the "exceptional" middle-class Black woman sets her apart from the normative inferiority of the rest. This is the same logic that says that "Collins is the *only* Black woman doing theoretical work," which far too often has expressed the false belief "that Collins is the only Black woman who *can* do this type of intellectual work." The presence of small numbers of Blacks, even "exceptional" ones, also changed the rules of racial etiquette attached to formerly all-White spaces. Whites now felt themselves to be the targets of surveillance. Whites who spoke openly of their belief in Black inferiority found themselves censured and evaluated as "racist" and backward. A rhetoric of color blindness was instituted, so that to talk of race at all meant that one *was* racist (Frankenberg 1993). Overall, although rules of racial etiquette regulated how beliefs were expressed during this shift from biological to cultural inferiority, the core idea of Black inferiority persisted.

Race remained salient in American politics in the 1970s and 1980s, but how it was managed in social institutions and expressed in the marketplace of ideas changed dramatically. During the period of color blindness that worked with changing market relations, deeply entrenched and largely unchallenged beliefs about Black inferiority reappeared in racially coded language—language without an explicit reference to race but embedded with racial meaning nonetheless. Such speech reinforced long-standing beliefs about Black sexuality, criminality, stupidity, and laziness via gender-specific images of "street crime," "drug dealers," "quota queens," and "welfare queens" (Keith and Cross 1993, 14–15). Winant (1993) describes how this changing political climate led to the expansion of three interdependent varieties of conservative racial projects, namely, those of the far right, the New Right, and the neoconservatives. At the same time, the range of seemingly progressive racial projects instituted in the 1960s and 1970s collapsed into one "Radical Democratic" racial project. Although all these projects seemed to occur in the absence of much emphasis on race, Winant suggests that they actually were deeply grounded in a historical yet unspoken racist discourse.

These and other changes that marked the emergence of a rhetoric of color blindness created space for the reemergence of hate speech. According to a color-blind racial etiquette, hate speech breaks the rules of civility that characterize this imaginary culture of tolerance. From the perspective of dominant groups, incidents of hate speech and the racial violence that they often provoke can be assessed as isolated events, unfortunate incidents representing the price of protecting free speech and civil liberties in a democratic, color-blind, tolerant society. From the perspective of African-Americans as a group, such speech is less an anomaly than a visible, tangible manifestation of deep-seated ideas and practices that permeate and define the social structure itself. Ideas about race have not changed that much—what has changed are the rules of racial etiquette regulating how those ideas can be expressed. Hate speech and violent racial acts make up the speech that breaks through contemporary racial etiquette, expressing things that many people think but that are too polite to say in public. Although hate speech appears to come from nowhere, it actually is everywhere (Daniels 1997).

This correlation between the changing political climate in the United States and the synergistic emergence of hate speech and violent acts in the 1980s is not new. One need only examine the political climate from 1877 through the early 1900s when African-Americans lost hard-earned civil rights. The courts were central in legitimating the framework for this denial. This period witnessed a marked increase in racial violence, exemplified by the growing practices of lynching individual Black men and women and engaging in mob violence against Blacks as a group (Berry 1994). Not coincidentally, this was the same period when a science grounded in theories of biological determinism of racial and gender differences emerged. As speech communities, biology (Gould 1981), anthropology (Haraway 1989), and sociology (McKee 1993) all participated in formulating and legitimating theories of scientific racism dedicated to explaining assumed racial differences.

Given the significance of ideas, higher education and other locations that generate and regulate ideas take on added importance. Hate speech requires not merely material conditions that foster its emergence but also interpretive communities (or speech communities) that create frameworks for making it comprehensible. Such communities set the standards for what is acceptable speech; they help shape racial etiquette. The hate speech that emerged within academia in the 1980s and 1990s reflected changing student, staff, and faculty populations who encountered intensely "raced" contexts with no place to talk about them. Certainly the false universalism that preceded this period offered scant guidance. Moreover, the multiple voices of an identity politics that increasingly found itself co-opted and absorbed in adversarial debates discouraged cross-group contact and dialogue. In this sense, higher education both reflected the larger societal forces emerging from a new politics of containment and contributed to their outcome.

The "Fighting Words" Doctrine

If hate speech is a symptom of much deeper social processes, how might focusing on efforts to combat hate speech on college campuses shed light on the role of critical social theory in confronting hierarchical power relations? In the late 1980s and early 1990s, some legal scholars, themselves situated in a provocative intersection between law as practiced and law as theorized, proposed campus speech codes as one innovative response for resisting hate speech. Realizing that the term *fighting words* has a specific legal connotation, these critical race theorists sought to redefine certain expressions of hate speech as "fighting words" and thus to bring American jurisprudence more in line with international law (Matsuda 1989; Lawrence 1993; Matsuda et al. 1993). "Fighting words" consist of insults of such dimension that they either urge people to violence or inflict harm. Although the First Amendment to the Constitution is designed to protect political speech of all types, bomb threats, incitements to riot, obscene phone calls, "fighting words," and all speech that infringes on public order can be prohibited in the interests of the common good. Reclassifying hate speech as "fighting words" would remove its constitutional protection and thus expose it to regulation.[3]

Striking parallels exist between how some African-American women and members of other subordinated groups experience the speech of academia, particularly theories explaining racial and gender differences, and how hate speech can operate as "fighting words" for the targets of such speech. In both cases, the targets of hate speech and ideas that operate like hate speech often react in similar ways—through anger, flight, and silence. The response of the targets shows the power of speech and, by implication, how ideas expressed in speech shape power relations. Those victimized by hate speech often choose not to fight back. Words such as *bitch, nigger, Jew-boy, cunt, beaner,* and *faggot* can produce physical symptoms that "temporarily disable the victim, and the perpetrators often use these words with the intention of producing this effect," observes legal scholar Charles Lawrence (1993, 68). Although fear, rage, and shock may characterize the victim's reaction, she or he may not think of an appropriate response until much later. Moreover, the effect of dehumanizing language is often flight rather than fight. Mari Matsuda observes, "Targets choose to avoid racist encounters whenever possible, internalizing the harm rather than escalating the conflict. Lack of a fight and admirable self-restraint then define the words as nonactionable" (1989, 2355). In brief, "one of the key survival skills of subordinate groups has been impression management in power-laden situations" (Scott 1990, 3).

When confronted with theories about their own inferiority, Black women and other groups that have been historically marginalized within academia often demonstrate similar reactions to those who encounter hate speech. In the face of subtle yet pervasive verbal insults of contemporary racially coded academic discourse, some targets may remain silent. By their silence, they appear to demonstrate tacit agreement with the dominant discourse. Others simply leave the academy by dropping out of classes, remaining A.B.D.'s (all requirements completed but dissertation) in perpetuity, or, in the case of a woman of color serving on my dissertation committee, one day simply tack a sign to the office door that says, "I can't work here anymore. I'm not coming back."

Everyday routines in academia can reinforce a comparable silencing of those who oppose elite discourses. Although academic speech may not intentionally set out to harm its victims (unlike hate speech), its actual effects may be similar. For example, in her study of African-American women professionals in the Netherlands and the United States, sociologist Philomena Essed (1991) discovered that most of the women experienced so many examples of racist treatment that they saw these experiences as routine. Rather than respond to each incident, the women chose to adapt to the acts of everyday racism and rarely talked back or complained. To me, the absence of protest means that the women in Essed's study were harmed. Of greater significance is how their silence is viewed. The everyday, routine nature of such silencing results in the belief that the absence of opposition means that none exists. Similarly, although many African-Americans forced to study theories of their own inferiority may experience contemporary versions of scientific racism as "fighting words," the routine circulation of these ideas within academic marketplaces makes these ideas difficult to root out. The strength of these ideas emerges from their routinized, everyday nature.

Critical race theorists' efforts to use legal remedies to censure unpopular speech are designed to confront the harm generated by hostile speech. Law, like social theory, lends itself to a variety of purposes. Recall that social theory is a body of knowledge and a set of institutional practices that actively grapple with the central questions facing a group of people in a specific political, social, and historic context. On the one hand, both law and social theory generally support existing hierarchical power arrangements. The law establishes rules of conduct for legal knowledge and the society overall, whereas social theory establishes interpretive frameworks for academic etiquette and disciplinary knowledges. On the other hand, both the law and social theory can be put to critical or emancipatory uses. Thus, both can operate as critical social theories that foster justice. The presence of the First Amendment protects not only the speech of powerful groups but also that of less powerful groups (as its use by the civil rights activists in the 1950s and 1960s demonstrates [Walker 1994]). Critical social theories advanced from within biology, anthropology, sociology, and psychology, for example, illustrate how intellectuals can use ideas to resist injustice (Stepan and Gilman 1993).

Despite the reasons why critical race theorists aimed to regulate hate speech by redefining it as "fighting words," several questions remain concerning the effectiveness of this strategy. On the surface, developing critical social theory that confronts knowledges defending unjust social conditions appears to be relatively straightforward. One merely identifies the most problematic elements of dominant discourses and tries to silence them. Speech codes that censure objectionable speech implicitly support an approach of fighting fire with fire, a stance that argues, "You've silenced us for so long that now it's our turn to silence you back." However, the decision to fight the words of dominant discourses by censuring selected elements as "fighting words" can have unintended effects. From the perspectives of elites, such discourses create upheaval where none was thought to exist previously. Ironically, elites comfortable with engaging in racist speech without repercussion may view oppositional knowledges generally, and critical social theories by Black women and others specifically, as "fighting words."

The conceptual limitations of a "fighting words" stance, however, may go much deeper. Responses to "fighting words" often duplicate binary oppositional thinking, that is, thinking that constructs everything in one of two mutually exclusive categories (White/Black, man/woman, public/private, center/margin, powerful/powerless, reason/emotion, good/bad, or in this case, elite and oppositional discourses). Presenting only two options fails to recognize how the two categories gain meaning only in relation to one another. As philosopher K. Anthony Appiah argues, "The terms of resistance are already given to us, and our contestation is entrapped within the Western cultural conjuncture we affect to dispute" (1992, 59).

When it comes to critical social theory, this model of binary opposites that produces a "fighting words" approach ignores both the interconnectedness of knowledges and the accompanying difficulty of remaining oppositional in a context of multiplicity. For example, European positivist science emerged in oppositional response to the earlier "Dark Ages," when disease and disaster were seen as God's will. The notion of an "enlightened" way of thinking about the world, one grounded in individual rights and human reason, opposed superstition. This same science staunchly supported European colonialism and imperialism and thus operated as an elite discourse that helped structure relations of ruling. Thus, the positivist science that emerged as so central to a European modernity was constructed in response to two "dark" others—an internal, European dark past and an external, colonial dark "primitive." Postmodernism reflects similar contradictions. Often portrayed as an oppositional discourse to positivist science and other discourses of modernity, postmodernism nevertheless accepts some of the premises of modernity (Hartsock 1987). As with most discourses, both remain simultaneously elite and oppositional.

These types of linkages among discourses suggest that critical social theories represent degrees of emphasis rather than fundamental differences from elite discourses. In other words, no social theory is *inherently* dominant or oppositional—these categorizations gain meaning only in relation to one another. The oppositional nature of any social theory lies not within the essence of its constructs, paradigms, or epistemology. Instead, the types of socially constructed relations it has with other social theories—themselves representing varying patterns of dominance and opposition to yet other discourses, all changing through time—frame its oppositional practice.

Remaining Oppositional

For Black feminist thought, remaining oppositional involves challenging the constructs, paradigms, and epistemologies of bodies of knowledge that have more power, authority, and/or legitimacy than Black feminist thought. Evaluating such discourses involves invoking their progressive dimensions while rejecting their regressive tendencies. Because Black feminist thought raises a particular set of questions for social theory, it provides an especially useful lens for investigating the question of remaining oppositional.

Some African-American women aim to remain oppositional by working exclusively within the assumptions of standard academic disciplines and make noteworthy contributions to reforming such knowledge. Other Black women try to jump outside dominant intellectual frameworks and do something different. Some of the most exciting ideas, for example, those of Wahneema Lubiano, Kimberle Crenshaw, Elsa Barkley Brown, Tricia Rose, Evelynn Hammonds, and Patricia Williams, emerge in the work of African-American women who move among diverse intellectual frameworks. Thinkers such as these situate their scholarship in issues that are important to Black women, remain sensitive to the political implications of their work, and infuse their intellectual production with moral dignity.

Black feminist thought is connected to a range of discourses beyond sociology as science, postmodernism, and Afrocentrism, the three discourses examined in this section of *Fighting Words*. Drawing enabling elements from all three areas, Black feminist thought simultaneously stands in oppositional relationship to them. Moreover, these discourses have similarly contested relations with one another. Afrocentrism and postmodernism both operate as critiques of sociological knowledge derived from positivist science. Postmodern emphases on difference challenge certain premises of Afrocentrism, and sociological findings contest the unverifiable tenets of both postmodernism and Afrocentrism. Moreover, these three discourses, as well as Black feminist thought, remain connected to global feminism, queer theory, subaltern studies, critical theory, and other discourses that are not explicitly examined here.

Black feminist thought also contains the tensions of being simultaneously a dominant and a critical social theory. For example, African-American women's unwillingness to examine heterosexism's impact on Black civil society means that Black feminist thought can operate as an elite discourse in the view of Black lesbians, gays, and bisexuals. Similarly, the current dependence of Black feminist thought on an individual rights model associated with Western liberalism can reinforce an imperialist ideology that privileges African-American women holding American citizenship. Black feminist thought remains emancipatory in some dimensions, namely, conceptualizing power relations through intersections of race, gender, and class, yet dominant in others, namely, its relative silence on issues of sexual politics and on nationalism. For Black feminist thought, oppositionality represents less an achieved state of being than a state of becoming.

Given the intricacies of associations such as these, examining the actual and potential affiliation of Black feminist thought with selected discourses provides insights about remaining oppositional in complex intellectual and political contexts. By examining the relationship of Black feminist thought to American sociology as representative of contested science, the major tenets of postmodernism, and Afrocentrism as the contemporary expression of Black cultural nationalism, the three chapters in part II investigate this theme of remaining oppositional.

The basic question framing this section is straightforward: what is the actual and potential utility of each discourse for Black feminist praxis? The struggle of Black feminist thought for self-definition and self-determination constitutes a Black feminist praxis, a search for ideas that inform practice and practice that simultaneously shapes ideas. Each chapter examines a distinctive critical social theory of significance for Black feminist praxis. Although the three chapters share this common purpose, several issues distinguish their approach to this basic question.

One issue concerns the question of determining the boundaries of each discourse. Although intellectual issues remain important, determining the boundaries of a discourse involves much more than identifying its main ideas. Social theories not only have certain intellectual assumptions that distinguish them from one another, but they also reflect the political and social contexts in which they are situated. For example, sociology in the United States is simultaneously a profession, a discourse, and an imagined community (Cohen 1985). As a discipline, sociology functions as an arena in which individuals and groups promote their interests, pursue a social agenda, or struggle for power, often via the types of research and scholarship they produce. Extracting sociological knowledge either from sociology as a profession or from the collectivity of people who identify as sociologists robs the discourse of meaning. Sociological discourse could not exist in the absence of social practices.

Sociology, postmodernism, and Afrocentrism all have distinctive intellectual and political boundaries that frame their ideas and practices. As a social science that itself marks one boundary distinguishing the "hard" sciences from the "soft" humanities, sociology provides a particular site for examining boundary construction and transgression. Having emerged in the late 1800s as part of the modernist project of positivist science, sociology constitutes a particular type of discourse operating according to clearly defined rules and regulations. As a discipline that has produced substantial objectified knowledge, sociology in the United States has been implicated in relations of rule associated with disciplinary power (Smith 1987; 1990b). Sociology functions simultaneously as part of the ruling apparatus and as a site for contesting relations of rule. Thus, the political and intellectual context of American sociology explains not only the resulting exclusion of Black women from the community of scientists but also patterns in the knowledge generated about Black women as objects of knowledge within sociological literature. Through its examination of African-American women's initial exclusion from and subsequent inclusion within sociology, chapter 3 provides one angle of vision on the question of how politics shape boundaries of discourses and the knowledge that ensues.

Afrocentrism in the academy is the most recent and most tightly bound discourse of the three. Afrocentrism can be dated from the early 1970s and is expressed through a relatively uniform set of texts that were produced in a twenty-five- to thirty-year period. Primarily located in Black studies programs and departments in American higher education, Afrocentrism has a much smaller community of practitioners and institutional locations than does sociology. Afrocentrism also has a fairly tight linear history emerging from African-American student demands in the 1960s for changes in the curriculum. Even with this compact and easily located discourse, conflicts characterize its practitioners' beliefs about its purpose, effectiveness, and boundaries. Despite Afrocentrism's relatively brief history, when placed in the context of a much older Black nationalist politics, Afrocentrism represents a contemporary version of a long-standing strand of Black political theory.

Although the boundaries that define sociology and Afrocentrism seem fairly straightforward, the definition of postmodernism is far from clear. Most theorists agree on several premises: postmodernism constitutes a cluster of ideas that emerged after World War II; postmodern influences are global; European thinkers were central in creating and disseminating postmodernism; and postmodernism remains important across a range of disciplines. The loose constellation of discourses best known as postmodernism are developed and promoted by a diffuse, diverse collection of academic practitioners who, true to postmodern ideas, would not consider themselves to belong to a "discipline" in any traditional sense. Thus, although postmodernism is not attached to any one academic area, it simultaneously operates as a profession, a discourse, and an imagined community.

Where does one draw the boundaries around postmodernism? Is it truly new, as some argue, or is it really a critique of modernity that has yet to abstract itself from the assumptions of modernity? Rather than jumping into, as K. Anthony Appiah describes it, "the shark-infested waters around the semantic island of the postmodern" (1992, 140), I aim to position myself in an outsider-within location vis-à-vis postmodernism. Appiah's discussion of the connection between the postcolonial and the postmodern was immensely helpful to me. Confronting the politics of definition head-on, he questions how we might understand the "family resemblance of the various postmodernisms as governed by a *loose* principle" (143). This approach of identifying orienting strategies or Appiah's "loose principle" permeating a range of postmodernisms parallels my own. I recognize that it is virtually impossible to position oneself completely outside a given discourse and still be comprehensible. However, from this destabilized outsider-within location, I explore some core assumptions of postmodernisms of all types, especially those concerning race and gender as I experience them from within higher education in the United States.

A second feature of part II concerns the type of discourse analysis applied to the three discourses explored. As does *Fighting Words* generally, the chapters in this section fuse three strands of discourse analysis (Van Dijk 1993). First, discourses can be studied internally, that is, according to their structure, organization, and thematic content. This is typically the way that social theory is evaluated, especially for male social theorists. External factors such as the biography of a given theorist, the social and political conditions under which he did his work, the political economy of ideological production, and the like are typically excluded from consideration. A second approach makes these external factors more central to analysis. Since critical social theories, their creators, and the intended recipients of such theories are all embedded in broader social, cultural, and political settings, the interactions among social structures and ideas become part of discourse analysis. A final component of discourse analysis examines the relationships among the ideas of the theorist and those of his or her interpretive community of readers.

Although all three approaches are used in analyzing the critical social theories examined in part II, the chapters place varying emphases on each approach. In chapter 3, the investigation of the work of African-American women occupying outsider-within locations in sociology embeds its analysis within broader social, cultural, and political settings. In chapter 4, the analysis of the ties of postmodernism to hierarchical power relations also attends to the social, cultural, and political contexts in which postmodernism operates, as well as to the social cognition of the authors and audiences of postmodernism. In chapter 5, the exploration of how the gendered subtext of a 1960s Black cultural nationalism framed the subsequent domain assumptions of Afrocentrism in the academy illustrates a more traditional approach to social theory stressing its internal structure, organization, and thematic content.

A third feature distinguishing the three discourses concerns how each participates in contemporary power relations. To a far greater extent than either postmodernism or Afrocentrism, sociology is engaged with a rich array of contemporary social institutions and their accompanying public policies. Sociology aims to influence public policy in schools, all levels of government, the military, the economy, and the arts. Sociologists work in all of these locations. Thus, although potential audiences for sociological work remain much broader than professional sociologists, sociology is constrained by its embeddedness in hierarchical power relations. In contrast, practitioners of postmodernism remain largely confined to higher education and, as a result, write primarily to academic audiences. Although postmodern ideas are just now being translated into forms that make them more accessible to more than a select few, postmodernism does not aim to influence social institutions. Rather, postmodernism's criticisms of social institutions and policies circulate largely among academics. Afrocentrism occupies a distinct niche. Unlike other intellectual production produced in Black studies and in the academy overall, Afrocentrism aims to influence African-Americans both inside and outside the academy. Because it centers its practice on constructing new knowledge about African-Americans, Afrocentrism differs both from sociological objectives of influencing public policy and from postmodern aspirations to criticize everything.

Finally, all three chapters in this section aim to shed light on the issue of remaining oppositional. Critical social theories are typically plagued by the problem of extracting themselves from the complexities of power relations. They may be "oppositional" in some dimensions yet support hierarchical power relations in others. Although dominant social theories such as positivist science and postmodernism both offer emancipatory possibilities for oppressed groups, each also has been used in defense of existing relations of ruling. Because of these inherent tensions, histories of oppressed groups can be read as inventive ways of recasting dominant social theories for their own ends.

One major concern for Black feminist thought involves accessing the enabling dimensions of discourses dominant to it while rejecting their troubling implications. As Gayatri Spivak points out, "I have long held that in the arena of decolonization proper, the call to a complete boycott of so-called Western male theories is class-interested and dangerous. For me, the agenda has been to stake out the theories' limits, constructively use them" (1993, x). Each chapter in part II examines this question from a distinctive angle of vision. Because much critical social theory in American higher education seems preoccupied with postmodernism, it is often easy to forget that science, the signature discourse of modernity, remains immensely powerful. Bureaucracies of the state grounded in notions of knowledge and power legitimated by positivist science remain surprisingly intractable and, in fact, typically drive the research interests and structure of much of academia. Chapter 3, "On Race, Gender, and Science: Black Women as Objects and Agents of Sociological Knowledge," investigates how African-American women who gained entry to sociology as a profession recast sociology as science for forwarding the goals of Black feminist thought as critical social theory. The chapter explores contested patterns of participation in a mature discipline and thus sheds light on strategies of resistance from outsider-within locations. In chapter 4, "What's Going On? Black Feminist Thought and the Politics of Postmodernism," the investigation of the utility of postmodernism for Black feminist thought problematizes the question of oppositionality from a slightly different vantage point. It suggests that although the ideas of postmodernism initially shared much with and, in fact, were probably stimulated by the actions of social movements originating outside higher education, the current use of postmodernism as commodified knowledge weakens its radical potential. Chapter 5, "When Fighting Words Are Not Enough: The Gendered Content of Afrocentrism," explores how the "fighting words" stance of Afrocentrism compromises its effectiveness as a critical social theory. Using the lens of gender, the chapter examines how critical social theory that seeks merely to shout louder than its opponents and to silence them may win in the short term yet ultimately fail to produce systemic change.

Collectively, the chapters in this section question whether a "fighting words" paradigm can ever constitute sufficient grounds for constructing critical social theory. The actual resolution of the campus speech codes argument remains instructive in this regard. Despite several attempts to regulate hate speech on campus via campus speech codes, these remedies were all struck down in courts (Walker 1994). With these rulings, both the law and social theory reiterated their commitment to protecting unpopular speech. Although fighting words with the "fighting words" doctrine aimed to provide relief from harassment, simple censure failed to attack the foundation of the problem. Just as laws can protect behavior that is technically legal yet politically inflammatory and ethically indefensible, social theories may continue to be "truthful" by the standards of academia yet be equally problematic. Silencing anyone won't make any of this go away.

Three

On Race, Gender, and Science: Black Women as Objects and Agents of Sociological Knowledge

Since the 1960s, African-American, Latino, and Native American women and men have entered social-scientific professions in the United States in small but unprecedented numbers. Individuals from these and other historically excluded groups confront a peculiar dilemma. On the one hand, acquiring both the status and salaries enjoyed by their colleagues often require unquestioned acceptance of the domain assumptions or guiding principles of psychology, political science, economics, and other social-scientific fields. On the other hand, these same domain assumptions have long been implicated in institutionalized racism, gender oppression, and other relations of ruling. Finding a way to temper their critical responses while considering how such responses might jeopardize their newfound insider status constitutes a major challenge facing these new arrivals.[1]

African-American women's entry into American sociology illustrates the difficulties associated with outsider-within locations in academia (Collins 1986; Moses 1989; Wyche and Graves 1992). Historically, American sociology barred all but a few African-American women from its ranks. As a result, Black women appeared within sociological discourse as objects of knowledge. The small numbers of Black women receiving doctorates in sociology before 1960—one in 1937, one in 1945, and six in the 1950s—constrained Black women from influencing what counted as sociological knowledge. However, the fourteen or so African-American women earning doctorates in the 1960s encountered a rapidly changing intellectual and political landscape. This decade produced the first Black women who were able to act as visible agents of sociological knowledge as professional sociologists.[2]

African-American women's arrival in American sociology occurred in tandem with an intellectual phenomenon with special significance for sociology, namely, a reconfiguration of the meaning of science under conditions of postmodernity.[3] Seemingly characterized by the erosion of traditional centers of all types, postmodernity presents particular challenges to scientific understandings of the world, especially the functionalist and empiricist traditions of American sociology. Unlike physics, engineering, chemistry, experimental psychology, biology, and other disciplines conducive to experimental design, the subject matter of the social world defies laboratory control. Because social worlds result from human agency, they remain inherently dynamic and changing. Thus, although dominant traditions within American sociology have long aimed to bolster the status of sociology as a positivist science, other sociological traditions have recognized the limitations of defining sociology exclusively in scientific terms. Recently, many sociologists doubt the current status of sociology (see, e.g., Huber 1995). Since the 1960s, American sociology has changed to the point where some sociologists invoke a rhetoric of crisis to describe the current state of their discipline (Lemert 1995; Levine 1995).[4]

What is the connection between these two trajectories, namely, the inclusion of historical outsiders such as African-American women within scientific disciplines such as sociology, and the contested terrain of sociology as a science under conditions of postmodernity? Black women's deployment of sociology as science certainly sheds light on characteristic responses of groups who move from being objects to being agents of knowledge. However, the irony of Black women's arrival in the social sciences concerns its timing—African-American women entered the social sciences during a historical moment when postmodernism began to discredit scientific authority (Bauman 1992). Is the arrival of Black women within sociology and the seeming crisis in sociology an accidental convergence? Or are these trends linked on a more fundamental level?

Race, Gender, and Sociology as Science:
Black Women as Objects of Knowledge

During the formative years of American sociology from 1895 to 1920 and for several decades thereafter, exclusionary practices of race and gender combined to ensure that no African-American women participated as fully legitimated insiders in shaping what would count as sociological knowledge. Racial discrimination effectively prohibited African-Americans from educational opportunities and from professional opportunities to be employed as sociologists in the then-developing discipline. Although African-American men experienced considerable difficulty, they did enter sociology in small numbers. William E. B. Du Bois stands alone as an example of a Black scholar who worked within academic settings during these formative years.[5] White women fared somewhat better. Predominantly middle-class White women entered the profession, often as wives of prominent sociologists, but they could not achieve positions of authority within sociology (Deegan 1991; Roby 1992). In general, the barriers against both African-Americans and women meant that Black women remained barred from sociology until the 1950s.[6]

This absence of African-American women occurred during an extremely critical period for American sociology, one characterized by the emergence of scientific authority in explaining social realities (Ross 1991; Levine 1995). Examining major issues of the times, the sociology of this period focused on social-structural dimensions of human experience. European sociology confronted the effects of colonialism, capitalist industrial development, and the political upheavals that accompanied an increasingly politicized economic class structure. In contrast, in the United States, territorial expansion via conquering Native American populations and annexing parts of the Southwest, the management of Eastern European immigration, and the question of the limits of Black citizenship following the Civil War constituted dominant themes.

The exclusion of African-American women, among others, had direct effects upon sociological scholarship generally and resulted in Black women's treatment as objects of knowledge. First and foremost, the absence of Black women as bona fide subjects of study characterized both flagship sociological journals, the *American Journal of Sociology* (*AJS*), founded in 1895, and the *American Sociological Review*

(*ASR*), founded in 1936. For example, a survey of articles published in the *AJS* during the first hundred years of its publication reveals only two articles with titles indicating that they explicitly examine Black women's experiences. The first, "The Race Problem as Discussed by Negro Women" (Blauvelt 1900–1901) was written by a White female reformer who dutifully recorded Black women's conversations about race at a Chicago meeting of Black club women. The next article that explicitly examines African-American women is Cynthia Fuchs Epstein's "Positive Effects of the Multiple Negative: Explaining the Success of Black Professional Women" (1973).[7]

During the formative years of American sociology, African-American women's experiences remained embedded in the literature on race and thus reflected its assumptions. As a legacy of the founding categories of American citizenship—free White men, free White women, and slaves—Black women were not seen as women but were classified primarily as Blacks. Early on within sociological treatments of race, Black women became associated with crime and fertility, the theme of a Black deviance constructed around a degenerate sexuality resulting in prolific fertility. For example, Black women surface as prostitutes in an article by Monroe Work entitled "Crime among the Negroes of Chicago: A Social Study" (1900–1901), where the author compares crime rates for African-American men and women. Several articles on eugenics preoccupied early sociologists, among them pieces by Francis Galton (1904–1905; 1905–1906). An article by Edward A. Ross, "Western Civilization and the Birth Rate" (1906–1907), engendered a lively discussion in the journal. These emphases contrast sharply with William E. B. Du Bois's sociological research. The most extended treatment of Black women's experiences occurred in Du Bois's Atlanta University studies, where he systematically set out to complete an ongoing sociological analysis of African-Americans. Despite Du Bois's massive study *The Philadelphia Negro* (1967), as well as his subsequent work on Black families (see, e.g., Du Bois 1969) and other topics that illustrated a different interpretation of the meaning of race, his exclusion from sociological practice meant that his and similar views remained in the minority.

Work on race within American sociology reflected more general beliefs of scientific racism dependent, in part, on whether Blacks who symbolized American "primitives" could be assimilated into American society (Bash 1979). As James McKee points out, "Because they

[Blacks] had lived in rural isolation in the South, they were regarded as the nation's most backward people, and that was how they appeared in the sociological literature" (1993, 8). Largely provided by European anthropological discourses emerging with imperialism, the notion of Blacks as primitive helped establish a logic for understanding Africa and peoples of African descent (Torgovnick 1990; Said 1993). Black people in so-called primitive societies were increasingly cast as more natural, sexual, and primitive than Whites or others touched by the civilizing influences of European culture (Haraway 1989; Stauder 1993). Moreover, the emergence of a racist biology that linked inferiority with immutable biological differences meant that the stigma of race was seen as intergenerational and permanent. Africans carried the primitive's mark of immutable difference with them wherever they went.

African-Americans and Native Americans represented American versions of the primitive. In the United States, the big question was that of assimilation, especially as African-Americans gained citizenship rights after the Civil War. Ideas about non-White "primitives" in popular culture affected scientific work on evolution, species, culture, race, and other seemingly benign categories still used today. The treatment of race in sociology was profoundly affected by this overarching primitivist discourse as it intersected with racist ideas in biology and the political needs of assimilation. Within academia, the primitives came in all types, from "noble savages" that revealed to the West their childlike nature, to "bloodthirsty" Indians and cannibals. People who were not White and male were reduced to two major types of others—the childlike or the violent, or, in the case of Africans, both. Biology offered allegedly natural justifications for this primitivist discourse, a feature that affected sociology primarily in the area of intelligence and its role in framing cultural differences. As it infused scientific discourse, the primitivist discourse became increasingly reworked as the scholarship of scientific racism in general and sociology in particular (Lyman 1972; Bash 1979). A similar process operated within psychology that in turn entered the area of social psychology. In this construct, primitives served as proxies for the "untamed selves, the id forces," of the West. As Marianna Torgovnick notes,

> Primitives are our own untamed selves, our id forces—libidinous, irrational, violent, dangerous. Primitives are mystics, in tune with nature, part of its harmonies. Primitives exist at the "lowest cultural

levels"; we occupy the "highest," in the metaphors of stratification and hierarchy. . . . The ensemble of these tropes—however miscellaneous and contradictory—forms the basic grammar and vocabulary of what I call the primitivist discourse, a discourse fundamental to the Western sense of self and Other. (1990, 8)

Sociological research on race simultaneously reflected and contested these beliefs (Tucker 1994).

Sociological work on gender demonstrated comparable biases. Although this literature contained themes of great importance to African-American women, the assumption that "women" meant White women obscured Black women's experiences. Here the focus was less on women as a distinctive political and social group, and more on women's biology (Hubbard 1990; Fausto-Sterling 1992). Popular notions of White women's place within modern societies framed the study of gender within academic disciplines. Female social scientists were especially interested in the meaning of work and family for women. For example, Jane Addams's article on women in domestic work (1895–1896), one of the earliest articles published by a woman in the *AJS*, provides a trenchant analysis of the effects of this occupation on young women. Articles such as Charlotte Perkins Gilman's "How Home Conditions React upon the Family" (1908–1909) and Lydia Kingmill Commander's "The Self-Supporting Woman and the Family" (1908–1909) reveal the emphasis on family and work in this early gender literature. The literature on gender seemed particularly concerned with the conditions of working women, especially of those without families in urban areas, those heading families, and those in sweatshops.

During this period, the emphasis of racial scholarship on Black assimilation and the preoccupation of gender scholarship with themes of female employment reinforced one another within both popular culture and scientific discourse (Stepan 1990). Analogies between Blacks and White women were routinely used to give race and gender meaning. Blacks and White women both were viewed as childlike, a factor used to explain their supposedly inferior intelligence. White women and Blacks were also seen as more embodied, "natural," and controlled by their physical, biological essences. Both were viewed as having an inherent "nature" of some sort—for Blacks, violence, for White women, passivity. Collectively, these comparisons generated a situation in which race and gender gained meaning from one another, situated within economic class hierarchies that drew upon these ideas. Segregation would solve the perceived deficiencies of both groups. Seen as limited by their biology, childlike White women needed White male guidance, protection, and/or control. Remaining in the private sphere of home and caring for the family would protect middle-class White women from the dangers of the public sphere that, with urbanization and industrialization, was increasingly populated by poor people, immigrants, Black people, and "fallen" women. Blacks encountered a similar yet distinctive pattern of segregation. All Whites were perceived as needing protection from Blacks, who were associated with degeneracy, lack of civilization, and, in some circles, disease itself. Both approaches mandated categorization and placement of groups in their proper place in social hierarchies. Groups so constructed could be studied within assumptions attached to their place—women could be studied in their special place of racially homogeneous family life, and Blacks in their placement at the bottom of economic class hierarchies. Thus, social processes that created these categories in the first place, namely, restricting women to the private sphere and racially segregating African-Americans, could largely be taken for granted.

African-American women were profoundly affected by these intersecting discourses on race and gender that together helped structure core constructs, interpretive paradigms, and epistemologies of American social science. Overall, assumptions about Black women's assumed sexual promiscuity, lower morals, lower intelligence, and heightened fertility that paralleled those in popular culture became guiding assumptions of much subsequent social-science research. Whether a given researcher set out to prove or disprove these assumptions, they became the received wisdom to be addressed.

Understanding the treatment of Black women as objects of knowledge within sociology remains important in itself. However, these patterns also shed light on how domain assumptions shape the very definitions of science in general and sociology in particular. Ideas prominent in popular culture establish the taken-for-granted assumptions that frame any discourse. Some argue that ideas about gender and race shaped the founding domain assumptions of Western science (Harding 1986; Tucker 1994). Depending on how widely held and deeply entrenched popular beliefs may be, scientific fields take them as given and investigate *within* these assumptions as opposed to investigating the assumptions themselves. The case of African-American women in American sociology illustrates this larger phenomenon.

Configuring Black women as absent Others highlights sociological domain assumptions that determine the boundaries of legitimated sociological research. Take, for example, the long-standing sociological fascination with the theme of difference (Lemert 1995). Current use of the term encapsulates a series of sedimented meanings from the foundational period of sociology. In nineteenth-century Europe and the United States, the term *difference* signaled relations of supremacy and inferiority, of domination and subordination accompanying colonialism, imperialism, and slavery. Under the rubric of examining racial differences, nineteenth-century anthropology, sociology, psychology, and biology spent considerable time developing a scientific racism (Gould 1981; Stepan 1982; Barkan 1992; Tucker 1994) that not only degenerated into eugenics and social engineering projects in the early twentieth century (Haller 1984; Proctor 1988) but also demonstrates a remarkable resilience today (Duster 1990). Similarly, under the rubric of examining assumed sexual differences, a parallel scientific literature on women's inferiority emerged that was situated primarily in biology (Keller 1985; Harding 1986, 1991; Hubbard 1990; Fausto-Sterling 1992). In both cases, clear ties existed between the allegedly neutral commitment to scientific objectivity that generated theories of difference and the utility of scientific knowledge for justifying the subordination of Black people and women. In other words, these discourses on race and gender were simultaneously embedded in specific social hierarchies and in turn helped shape them (Goldberg 1993). Moreover, since Black women appeared in both discourses, both marked Black women's bodies as ultimate examples of this essentialized, immutable difference (Gilman 1985).

Seen against this backdrop, current sociological concerns with the question of "difference" (e.g., see Candace West and Sarah Fenstermaker's "Doing Difference" [1995] and the subsequent forum in *Gender and Society,* or Charles Lemert's identification of difference as a central yet obscured feature of sociological theory [1995]) represent less a new direction for sociology than a continuation of a traditional sociological preoccupation with investigating racial and gender differences. For example, the long-standing assumption identifying assumed differences in intelligence between Blacks and Whites as one important marker of racial difference reemerges in social-science research with remarkable frequency. Psychology, sociology, and biology have all at various points in their histories set out to measure these assumed differences instead of asking why such differences remain so fascinating (Gould 1981). Moreover, these approaches assume that differences lie somewhere in groups themselves, not in power relations that construct them. Overall, the assumption of difference remains far less questioned than are the consistent efforts to uncover the meaning of differences that, a priori, are assumed to exist.

Although they are rarely expressed in race- or gender-specific terms, current sociological debates concerning methodology may also configure Black women as different and justifiably absent because of that difference. For example, definitions of objectivity rely on conceptions of difference (Halpin 1989). Elevating rationality above emotion creates an objectivity wherein abstract, universal principles are more highly valued than particularistic, special interests. Within this binary oppositional thinking, Whiteness becomes configured as objective, fair, and impartial—the very qualities that distinguish scientists from nonscientists, who exhibit qualities of particularism. True scientists are able to comprehend the world via quantitative methodology. This link between the definition of scientist and the ability to engage in quantitative analysis has corresponding ties to political and economic interests. An increasing belief in quantifying the world by dividing everything into categories that could then be mathematically manipulated and hierarchically arranged and to which causal models could be attached for purposes of control was essential to the increase of bureaucracy as a particularly modern form of social organization (Max Weber's "iron cage" [1968]); to the emergence of statistical methods necessary for maintaining these bureaucratic forms (Smith 1990a; 1990b); and to an infrastructure amenable to the type of disciplinary surveillance essential to bureaucratic control (Foucault 1979).[8]

Reviewing the participation of sociology in shaping modernity sheds light on why American sociology aimed to establish itself as a science by using quantitative methodology. "Modern," secular societies viewed themselves as different from more "primitive" societies rooted in superstition and religion by defining their own characteristic form of social organization as "scientific." Rather than viewing modernity as a passive backdrop for the development of sociology, sociology helped manufacture and legitimate notions of modernity via knowledge about the primitive and about women's biology. These cognitive structures of scientific discourse in turn remain central in shaping public policy directed against people of color and women. They also work well with capitalist development. Thus, notions of science, race, gender, and modernity shaped one another's development (Said 1978; Gilroy 1993). Science emerged in this context, with the so-called soft social-science disciplines of sociology and anthropology being in a contested relation to the so-called hard sciences of physics, chemistry, and biology (Ross 1991).[9]

Contemporary sociological debates concerning appropriate sociological methodology inherited this race- and gender-specific history of the struggle of American sociology to become a science. The often heated debates about quantitative versus qualitative methodology not only have generated a voluminous literature (see, e.g., Sprague and Zimmerman 1989) but simultaneously tap the much deeper issue of the contested self-definition of sociology as a science.[10] In effect, what we have is a quantitative, abstract, objective macrosociology symbolizing the "hard" sciences—the male, the White, the Subject, the Universal—juxtaposed and defining itself in opposition to a qualitative, contextualized, interpretive microsociology referencing the "soft" sciences—the female, the Black, the Other, the Different. Paralleling this cognitive structure is a bureaucratic structure that has long made similar assessments of the membership of the profession. In brief, this perspective long equated the absence of Black women with excellence in the discipline and the presence of Black women with the seeming deterioration of the field. Increased attention to quantitative rigor allegedly addresses both of these concerns by reinstituting a cognitive structure that aligns itself symbolically with Whiteness, maleness, and elitism while simultaneously reproducing an accompanying hierarchy of social relations within the profession. Thus, what appear to be merely methodological questions mask deep-seated questions of the contested terrain of sociology as a science and its position in race and gender hierarchies.

This use of Black women's absence to frame sociological presence illustrates a peculiar form of logic (Minnich 1990). Grounded in circular reasoning, this logic uses mystified concepts such as the "primitive" in constructing faulty generalizations about Black women as being less intelligent and less sexually inhibited, and therefore less able to become "qualified" scientists; employs these faulty generalizations both to exclude Black women from the community of scientists and to construct an objectified knowledge about Black women framed within these domain assumptions; points to Black women's exclusion from sociology as "proof" that Black women make less capable scientists and that objectified knowledge about Black women is correct; and configures a true scientific identity based, in part, on the absence of Black women, who symbolize particularity, special interests, and the "different" Other against which science defined itself in the first place. Backed up by the political power of the state, this logic has shaped sociological constructions of Black womanhood specifically, as well as sociological perspectives on race and gender within sociology. More generally, this logic also frames sociological content, such as the treatment of difference, and sociological epistemologies, such as the weight given to quantitative methodology above other equally viable methodologies.

Given this fascination with difference and with quantitative methodology as the best way to understand the world, what happens if African-American women begin to enter sociology? What challenges confront Black women in fields where the absence of Black women is central to the discipline's definition of itself as a science? Since symbolism remains central to boundary maintenance of communities (Cohen 1985), absence becomes configured as absence of difference (embodied in both Blacks and women and thus accentuated in Black women). Beyond the actual conditions that Black women encountered or the behavior of Black women, their entrance into the profession potentially contains profound symbolic impact. By their presence, Black women transgress and change the very boundaries of what constitutes the discipline. Thus, presence creates issues where absence has long been the norm.

In a New Place: Black Women as Agents of Knowledge

African-American women did not become legitimated agents of sociological knowledge in any significant numbers until the 1950s and 1960s. From 1970 through 1990, a period when the numbers of students receiving higher education increased dramatically, the numbers of Black women earning doctorates in sociology also grew. Thus, Black women receiving doctorates in sociology prior to 1970 encountered a markedly different environment than did those after 1970.[11] How did these women respond to the treatment of Black women as objects of socio-logical knowledge? Given Black women's long-standing exclusion from sociology prior to 1970, the sociological knowledge about race and gender produced during their absence, and the symbolic impor-tance of Black women's absence to self-definitions of sociology as a science, African-American women acting as agents of knowledge faced a complex situation. To refute the history of Black women's unsuitability for science, they had to invoke the tools of sociology as science. However, as scientists, they simultaneously needed to chal-lenge the same structure that granted them legitimacy.

In unpacking how African-American women responded to these contradictions, I identify three historical periods: a period of contest-ed participation (1895–1960) that saw African-American women enter sociology in such small numbers that locating Black women's sociological research from this period remains difficult; a period of heightened visibility (1960–1970) when a small but highly visible group of Black female sociologists raised questions from within the profession; and a period of achieving critical mass (1970–1990) marked by the increase of Black women with doctorates. These struc-tural changes allowed African-American women to function as a small yet organized minority for Black women's concerns while serv-ing as a catalyst for intellectual developments in the field.[12]

Each period provided African-American women distinctive pat-terns of opportunities and constraints concerning how to deal with Black women's historical exclusion from American sociology. I sug-gest four possible responses to historical exclusions. First, surrender occurs when an individual uncritically accepts or "surrenders" to pre-vailing wisdom, in this case, Black women's acceptance of sociological domain assumptions of Black female inferiority. Second, seeming ac-ceptance occurs when an individual appears to agree with sociological domain assumptions but covertly resists them. In this sense, Black women sociologists may have retained rich "hidden transcripts" of resistance that saw sociology as a system of domination. However, they also knew that resisting openly remained too dangerous. In cases such as these, covert forms of resistance flourish yet must remain hid-den. As James Scott points out, "We may consider the dominant dis-course as a plastic idiom or dialect that is capable of carrying an enor-mous variety of meanings, including those that are subversive of their use as intended by the dominant" (1990, 102–3). A third response, that of critique, represents a more visible continuation of the rejection of sociological domain assumptions, one wherein individuals may openly resist some dimensions of sociology while upholding others. Finally, constructing new knowledge represents, in turn, a continuation of critique and represents the response to critiques that have openly occurred. Although each period hypothetically contains all four responses, only the period of critical mass allowed all four to be fully actualized.

Contested Participation: Trying to Be Heard (1895–1960)

Those few African-American women earning doctorates in sociology prior to 1960 were constrained by restricted opportunities that accompanied racial segregation. Their participation was contested in many ways, and their characteristic responses to this contestation ranged from surrender, to seeming acceptance, to laying a foundation for subsequent scientific critiques. These responses occurred both inside and outside the boundaries distinguishing sociology from other professions. This period marked a war of positionality, one in which practicing sociology outside the legitimated boundaries of the discipline in essence revealed the political nature of the boundaries themselves; in which earning a doctorate constituted a critique of sociological knowledge positing Black female inferiority; and in which, by one's presence, remaining in the profession at all, regardless of the content of scholarly work, resisted Black women's historical treatment.

The little we know about African-American women who practiced sociology completely outside the discipline provides insight into one pattern of contested participation. Consider, for example, the sociology of Ida Wells Barnett. Even though she never received a degree in sociology and is known primarily as a journalist, social reformer, and community activist, Barnett's work simultaneously validates and challenges two fundamental areas of scientific knowledge (Harding 1993). There is first the context of justification, the part of science in which hypotheses are tested and evidence gathered. For science, the context of justification rests on shared assumptions concerning empiricism and rationality. In the 1890s, Ida Wells Barnett conducted a statistical analysis of lynching in the South; used her empirical research to theorize about the connections between racism, gender discrimination against men, and class exploitation; and then actively opposed lynching by publishing her findings and trying to influence public opinion. Although Barnett is well known for her staunch opposition to lynching, what is often forgotten is that she justified her opposition using scientific tools of empiricism and rationality. Barnett's choice of subject matter foreshadows a second fundamental area of scientific knowledge, namely, the context of discovery. As the area in which hypotheses are selected and refined, this area refers to the process used to select problems worth studying. Because Barnett was not entirely situated within the guiding principles of early-twentieth-century sociology, she "discovered" lynching as a social problem worthy of scientific study. Had Black women like Barnett not been excluded from sociology, we might have seen social-science research by Black women who discovered comparable neglected issues grounded in tools of empiricism and rationality. Unfortunately, Barnett lacked access to the major journals and faculty positions that would certify her as a professional sociologist. Thus, her contributions and those of other similarly situated individuals remain lost to us.[13]

Another pattern of contested participation concerns those Black women who entered disciplines closely aligned with sociology. American sociology defined itself as a discipline by distinguishing itself from fields that were seen as being less scientific and more practical (e.g., social work) or fields using qualitative and less scientific research methodology (e.g., anthropology). Black women who entered these fields during the lengthy period of Black women's exclusion from sociology illustrate the type of sensibility that they might have brought to sociology. The case of Zora Neale Hurston is interesting here, for although Hurston is typically remembered for her groundbreaking novel *Their Eyes Were Watching God* (1978), she is less often discussed as an anthropologist. Her anthropological work, especially her treatment of Black culture and African-American women as agents within Black culture, demonstrates a sensibility concerning Black women markedly different from that expressed in traditional sociology. Hurston's continual struggles to practice her craft, her strained relations with the then-philanthropic funding structure for American sociology, and her relative poverty all reveal the difficulties that Black women confronted in remaining practicing professionals within any of the social-science disciplines.

Given this context, those few Black women who earned doctorates in sociology but who, for a variety of reasons, did not pursue careers as researchers could tell us much. In this regard, the career of Anna Johnson Julian, reportedly the first African-American woman who earned a doctorate in sociology, illustrates another pattern of contested participation. Julian earned a doctorate in 1937 from the University of Pennsylvania, writing a dissertation entitled "Standards of Relief: An Analysis of One Hundred Family Case Records."[14] However, she did not remain in sociology; instead she joined her spouse in running a very successful business.

Given the context facing these early entrants, the career path of Adelaide Cromwell Hill, who received a doctorate from the University of Pittsburgh in 1952, is especially noteworthy. Remaining in sociology as a professional sociologist, she neither surrendered nor accepted but created a scientific critique. The title of her dissertation, "The Negro Upper Class in Boston—Its Development and Present Social Structure," refutes long-standing assumptions that routinely portrayed African-Americans as exclusively poor. Hill's choice of topic thus breaks new ground in that it builds on E. Franklin Frazier's investigation of the Black bourgeoisie but examines affluent Blacks in a major urban area.

Hill's career remains exemplary for this period. In the absence of adequate qualitative data regarding the career patterns of the early entrants, it is difficult to assess the meaning of their participation within the discipline. However, a common thread seems to join the seven remaining Black women who earned doctorates in sociology prior to 1960. All completed doctorates, but they left few publications beyond the doctorate. Although the actual number of women remains too small for any valid generalization, I suspect that some may have worked primarily as teachers or administrators in historically Black colleges, universities, and secondary schools, or, like Ida Wells Barnett or Anna Johnson Julian, they made comparable contributions to Black civil society. Like other African-American women professionals of this period who faced extremely limited occupational opportunities, these women most likely made creative use of their sociological training but were excluded from careers as professional sociologists. Although they participated in sociology, their involvement resulted in minimal impact on sociological knowledge published in the major journals of the field.

These women represented the first group of African-American women who encountered sociological knowledge not as outsiders but as sociological insiders. They were able to see the contrasts between what sociological knowledge had long believed to be true about Black women and the framework they brought with them by virtue of their struggles to gain entry into the profession. The constrained opportunities they faced limited their choices of how to act upon their insights. As is the case today, some may have simply surrendered, whereas others practiced seeming acceptance. For Black women who surrender, remaining in sociology incurs a high cost. Some surrender by leaving the discipline in part or altogether. Those Black women who earn doctorates but do not aspire to be sociological researchers have in this sense surrendered. Although they make extremely valuable contributions in other areas, most notably teaching and administration, their withdrawal from the terrain of sociological research in essence surrenders this territory to those who remain. Others surrender by remaining in sociological research yet completely accepting its terms.

The dissertation content of many Black women might be interpreted as surrender, but their choice of topics could also be interpreted as seeming acceptance. This stance of seeming acceptance is especially important to those individuals who initially desegregated sociology or who now desegregate statistics, demography, and other quantitative areas of sociology. Even though scientific knowledge may have a profound impact upon their lives, Black women lacking the credentials that certify them as statisticians or demographers remain limited. When they criticize scientific practices and findings, they are typically accused of being insufficiently trained in quantitative methodologies to launch an informed critique. Lacking the authority granted scientific insiders, as outsiders they remain restricted to examining the terms of the insider knowledge. For example, feminist critiques of science have been forwarded primarily by philosophers (Harding 1986; 1991). As a result of the positioning of philosophers outside science, feminist critiques of science are often accused of not being knowledgeable about how science really operates. Those first entering scientific professions encounter similar conditions. Within this context, for many Black women new to the sciences, maintaining a posture of seeming acceptance becomes an especially useful strategy for survival.

Heightened Visibility: Critiquing Sociological Domain Assumptions (1960–1970)

Even though their numbers remained small, the approximately fourteen Black women earning doctorates during the 1960s encountered a greatly changed intellectual and political context. In contrast to the relative quiescence characterizing prior decades, these women entered sociology during widespread racial desegregation. During this one decade, they accumulated twice the number of doctorates in sociology than had been earned by African-American women during the preceding seventy-five years. Because these women encountered expanded opportunities to work as professional sociologists, several found faculty positions in sociology departments that could provide institutional support for their research. Drawing strength from both the civil rights and Black Power movements, their scholarship demonstrated a new insider critique of sociological knowledge, especially sociological treatments of race. In the context of social movements that themselves were aggressively engaged in critiquing social institutions, seeming acceptance began to give way to a growing emphasis on critique.

Black women earning doctorates in sociology in the 1960s encountered a sociological discourse lacking sustained critical engagement with Black women as agents of knowledge. However, they also found increased institutional support to remain sociological insiders and to use the idioms of science to critique sociology on its own terms. These women recognized that, as Dorothy Smith observes, "to begin with the theoretical formulations of the discipline and to construe the actualities of people's activities as expressions of the already given is to generate ideology, not knowledge" (1990a, 48). By using the tools of social science to evaluate sociological knowledge itself—for example, by questioning explanations of existing facts, proving the facts wrong, or generating new facts—their critiques questioned prior approaches to justification and discovery.

Using the tools of science itself in constructing their critiques allowed Black women to accept the guiding principles mandated by their newly achieved sociological membership but to change the meanings or valuations attached to them (a process known as transvaluation). By doing so, they could also recontextualize sociological knowledge by establishing a new context for existing sociological knowledge (Stepan and Gilman 1993). Invoking these strategies of transvaluation and recontextualization allowed Black women to argue that their interest lay less in castigating sociology as a positivist science and more in reforming sociology to make it a better science.[15] Black women sociologists often sought to redefine constructs originally developed within a context of discovery that included only White men—for example, rationality, individuality, agency, and humanity—so that they applied to all groups, including Black women. This approach destabilized existing meanings of core constructs in sociology by demanding that Black women be included. Traditionally, many sociological studies excluded Black people or women in their samples yet generalized to entire populations results gathered from homogeneous samples of White men. In this context, Black women who replicated these same studies with samples that included Black women basically criticized scientific knowledge. Something as simple as changing the composition of their sample provided "small wins" (Myerson and Scully 1995) and protected them from accusations of particularism with its attendant charge of irrationality. African-American women sociologists could study topics far removed from Black women's specific concerns yet challenge long-standing sociological domain assumptions.

Tracing the careers and work of three Black women sociologists who received doctorates in the 1960s illustrates the significance of this decade in fostering increasingly sophisticated strategies of critique. Stimulated by a sensitivity to Black women's objectification, scientific critique operates via the perspective brought to bear on sociological contexts of justification and discovery. The absence of overtly racial or gendered content in the scholarship of Black women sociologists does not signal the absence of critique. Cora Bagley Marrett's sociological career is exemplary in this regard. Neither Marrett's dissertation from the University of Wisconsin at Madison,"Consensus and Organizational Effectiveness" (1968), nor a coauthored publication in the *ASR* (Hage, Aiken, and Marrett 1971) set out explicitly to study Black women. However, Marrett's subsequent career can be seen, in part, as recontextualizing sociological knowledge by establishing a new context for existing sociological knowledge. For example, with Cheryl Leggon, Marrett served as coeditor of the first five volumes (1979–1989) of the serial publication *Research in Race and Ethnic Relations* for the JAI Press. Through these and other activities, she has demonstrated a quiet yet effective critique of sociological assumptions concerning inequities of all sorts.

The work of Jacqueline Johnson Clarke Jackson represents yet another trajectory of critique from inside the domain assumptions of sociology. Jackson's work signals a transition from the race-based work of earlier Black women sociologists such as Adelaide Cromwell Hill to the race-and-gender-intersectional work that emerged by the end of the decade. Jackson's dissertation, entitled "Goals and Techniques in Three Negro Civil-Rights Organizations in Alabama" (1960), focused on the civil rights movement, then a neglected area of study among sociologists (McKee 1993). Building on this foundation, her subsequent work on Blacks and aging and her important publications on Black women in the 1970s—Jackson's article "Black Female Sociologists" (1974) was the first to identify and summarize material on Black women in sociology—demonstrate a career path that would have been extremely difficult to pursue two decades earlier.

In contrast to Marrett and Jackson, Joyce Ladner's 1968 groundbreaking dissertation on Black adolescent girls, entitled "On Becoming a Woman in the Ghetto: Modes of Adaptation," constitutes the first dissertation within sociology that explicitly set out to examine Black women's experiences from the perspective of race, economic class, and gender. Four years later, Joyce Ladner's *Tomorrow's Tomorrow* signaled the beginnings of a fundamental shift from the race-only scholarship that preceded it to work on race, gender, and class intersectionality that emerged over the next two decades. Three aspects of *Tomorrow's Tomorrow* exemplify Ladner's use of scientific critique. First, by centering her study on the lives of Black women, Ladner broke with long-standing traditions denying Black women agency. Based on the notion that African-American girls have a unique, valuable perspective on the meaning of their own lives, Ladner contextualized her study of girls' ideas in the specific context where girls lived. She did not treat those ideas as free-floating normative beliefs. Instead, Ladner placed the experiences of the girls she studied in their historical context (she began with a discussion of slavery) and in their current context (the economics, social structure, and politics of the public housing project in which the girls lived). Moreover, because Ladner interviewed the girls, their voices emerge as central in her study. Second, the interpretive framework that Ladner deployed drew from several social-science traditions—race, class, and gender analysis—as well as from diverse research areas within sociology. Ladner's volume invokes the Marxist contribution of standpoint theory, the tools of qualitative research grounded in positivist science, and interpretive sociological traditions of social constructionism. Finally, Ladner's explicit goal was not to assist bureaucracies in controlling, managing, or working with the girls. Instead, her goal was empowerment, one linked to her explicit statements about her own struggles to become empowered as a sociologist.[16]

Ladner's groundbreaking work and that of other Black women sociologists from this period illustrates a range of responses to the challenges they faced. Seeming acceptance and strategies of scientific critique expanded to include more overt forms of critique. Once seeming acceptance and early critique legitimated the space for dissent, a full-blown critique could emerge. Subsequent African-American women critics noted several features, among them the general absence of Black women from social-science consideration; a treatment of Black women via the social problems framework, especially Black female identity and the construction of Black women as matriarchs; the tendency to discuss Black men and to generalize the findings to Black women; a parallel tendency to conduct studies on White women and to generalize findings to Black women; the use of social-science methodologies generally biased against Black people, women, and working-class people; and a generally limited list of topics that shaped social-science research on Black women, for example, studying women only in relation to their family roles, especially their relationships with males (Scott 1982). This overt critique set the stage for new strategies to emerge.

Achieving Critical Mass and Constructing New Knowledge (1970–1990)

In contrast to Black women's contested participation in sociology prior to 1960 or the small numbers of women who entered during the 1960s, the approximately 175 Black women earning doctorates in the 1970s and 1980s benefited from the critiques advanced by Black women who preceded them within the discipline. With their greater numbers, they were able to achieve a critical mass within sociology that allowed them to deepen preexisting critiques of prior decades and to participate in a cross-disciplinary endeavor of constructing new knowledge.

Building on the work of Jacqueline Johnson Jackson, Joyce Ladner, La Frances Rodgers-Rose, Doris Wilkinson, Gloria Joseph, and other African-American women earning doctorates in the 1960s, Black women sociologists in subsequent decades deployed a variety of strategies designed to recontextualize existing interpretations of Black women's experiences. Because of their greatly increased numbers, the techniques of critique became increasingly sophisticated, as did topics selected for study. In particular, because Black women's experiences had never fit within sociological assumptions positing the separation of family and work, critique focused on these two areas. Black family organization underwent considerable scrutiny. Topics such as disputing the portrayal of Black women as aggressive matriarchs, challenging notions that Black-female-headed households were a fundamental cause of Black poverty, and investigating new approaches to the growing problem of adolescent pregnancy among unmarried Black women all became open to new interpretations (see, e.g., Jarrett 1994). The voluminous literature produced by Black women exploring patterns of race and gender discrimination in education, housing, employment, and social services also relied heavily on scientific reasoning to refute long-standing interpretations identifying Black women's disadvantage as stemming from biological or cultural deficiencies (see, e.g., Higginbotham 1994). Much attention was directed to documenting Black women's inequality in comparison to other segments of the population, through topics as diverse as Black professional women's stress, and racial and gender discrimination.[17] Critiques consisted of invoking scientific reasoning to question explanations of existing facts, using the tools of positivist science by proving the facts wrong, or using the tools of science to generate new facts. All of these strategies were employed to challenge long-standing assumptions concerning African-American women, work, and family.

As the limits of critique became more evident, Black women sociologists moved beyond critique to construction. Over time, by challenging existing thinking that family and work constituted separate spheres, they began to apply similar analyses to sociological subfields. Within American sociology, race, economic or social class, and gender had long operated as distinct, nonoverlapping areas of inquiry, each with its own standards for credible scholarship. Black women's placement at the *intersections* of race, economic class, and gender raised questions concerning the possible connections among these distinct subfields.

Although examining these sorts of connections did not gain widespread visibility in sociological literature until the 1990s and still has not achieved analytical prominence in the two flagship journals of the discipline, the notion of race, class, and gender as mutually constructing systems emerged quite early in the work of Black women sociologists.[18] In particular, the work of Bonnie Thornton Dill and Cheryl Townsend Gilkes, who both earned doctorates in 1979, and Elizabeth Higginbotham, who earned a doctorate in 1980, explored how intersections of race, class, and gender as major features of social organization shape Black women's experiences. Bonnie Thornton Dill's research on Black women domestic workers (1988a) and her subsequent scholarship on family relations of women of color (1988b) not only treat African-American women as agents of knowledge but also examine the work/family nexus using an intersectional paradigm. Building on her empirical work on Black women community leaders, Cheryl Townsend Gilkes's scholarship (1985; 1994) examines African-American women's participation in Black churches and other social institutions of Black civil society via intersections of race, class, and gender. Elizabeth Higginbotham's research on the employment patterns of Black women (1994) demonstrates how sociological understandings remain impoverished by neglecting the effects of racial discrimination and occupational segregation by gender on economic class outcomes. Collectively, the work of these and other African-American women sociologists suggests that not race nor gender nor economic class alone could adequately explain Black women's experiences.

During this period, Black women demonstrated an increasing interest in applying intersectional analyses to a host of topics, to the point where, as Rose Brewer observes, "the 'race, class, gender' frame is the major theoretical lens through which black feminist theory is constructed. Alone, race, class and gender are rather sterile categories for black feminist thinking" (1989, 68). Although African-American women exerted intellectual leadership, their work participated in a much larger effort by scholars and activists from diverse race, class, and gender groups. Some of the most interesting sociological studies of Black women's experiences reflect this increasing attention to race, class, and gender intersectionality. For example, Dutch sociologist Philomena Essed's study of everyday racism experienced by Black women in the Netherlands and the United States (1991) begins from the assumption of intersectionality. Linda Grant's study of Black girls in first-grade classrooms (1994) explores the ways that race and gender intersect to discriminate against girls this young. Regina Arnold's analysis of African-American women in prison (1993) offers a race-, class-, and gender-inclusive interpretation of how young Black women become labeled criminals that differs markedly from the treatment of Black women as deviants in traditional literature. Similarly, Elaine Bell Kaplan's study of Black teenage motherhood (1997) relies on a paradigm of intersectionality. These and other works not only return subjectivity to Black women by treating them as agents of knowledge, they simultaneously demonstrate that race, class, and gender intersectionality is not merely an approach one *should* adopt, but an approach having conceptual and methodological merit.

In tandem with this intellectual shift, some Black women sociologists, in partnership with individuals from diverse race, class, and gender groups, created organizational and institutional space for the emerging interest in race, class, and gender studies. In the 1980s, the Center for Research on Women at Memphis State University (now the University of Memphis) sponsored curriculum workshops and research institutes in race, class, and gender studies for scholars across a range of academic disciplines as well as independent scholars and community activists. These workshops and research institutes not only fostered increased understanding of race, class, and gender intersectionality, they simultaneously organized a national network of academic and community intellectuals. The leadership of the center modeled the type of collaboration needed for intersectional work. No one thinker had all the answers, but pooling resources generated new directions and insights. Dill and Higginbotham constituted two of the three founders of this center, with Lynn Weber, whose roots in southern White culture stimulated her subsequent expertise in social class (see Vanneman and Cannon 1987), filling the third slot. Thus, from its inception, the center included scholars and activists of diverse races, genders, and disciplinary backgrounds in all levels of its organization. The two focal points of the center, women of color and women of the South, were designed to highlight groups historically excluded from knowledges of all sorts, including sociology. The success of the center demonstrates how Black women sociologists neither depended on traditional professional and disciplinary structures for examining race, class, and gender intersectionality nor saw intersectionality as particular to African-American women's concerns. Instead, they remained connected to sociology yet simultaneously built alternative institutional locations more hospitable to new ideas than were traditional sociology departments (Weber et al. forthcoming).

It is important to remember that although African-American women have been leaders in pursuing the burgeoning interest in race, class, and gender studies within sociology, this approach is not the intellectual property of Black women. African-American women did not create this emphasis within sociology on their own, nor are they now the exclusive contributors to this area of inquiry. Much exciting work published in the 1990s using intersectional analyses has emerged from sociologists of diverse backgrounds and is applied to a range of topics. Barbara Ellen Smith's study of women's political mobilization in the South (1995), Jessie Daniels's content analysis of contemporary White supremacist discourse in the United States (1997), and Esther Madriz's research on women's fear of crime (1997) all rely on intersectional analyses. Structurally, the formation of a section entitled "Race, Class, and Gender" within the American Sociological Association, which first offered program listings in the 1996 annual meetings, speaks to the growing interest in race, class, and gender studies. This growth within sociology parallels increasing interest in intersectional analyses in general, expanded to encompass intersections of nation (Gilroy 1987; Miles 1987, 1989; Yuval-Davis 1997) and of ethnicity (Anthias and Yuval-Davis 1992; Calhoun 1993).

By contributing to race, class, and gender studies, African-American women participate in a much larger interdisciplinary and collaborative effort. In the 1980s and 1990s, interest in intersectionality has emerged within and across a variety of academic disciplines (see, e.g., James and Busia 1994). In critical legal studies, Black feminist scholars invoke intersectional paradigms in rethinking the law (see, e.g., Scales-Trent 1989; Caldwell 1991; Crenshaw 1991; and Williams 1991). Black feminist literary criticism, in particular, contains a fairly voluminous literature paralleling the sociological notion of intersections of race, class, and gender (see, e.g., Christian 1989a; Wall 1989; and Awkward 1995), as does African-American women's history (Giddings 1984; Brown 1989; Higginbotham 1993) and the emerging field of Black cultural studies (see, e.g., Dent 1992; Mercer 1994; and

Rose 1994). Within the United States, scholarship by Latinas, Asian-Americans, and other women of color also relies on and exerts intellectual leadership in fostering intersectional paradigms. Research by Maxine Baca Zinn, Denise Segura, Dana Takagi, Aida Hurtado, and Nazli Kibria, among many others, contributes greatly to retheorizing work, family, immigration, and other topics through intersectional paradigms (see, e.g., Zinn and Dill 1994; and Chow et al. 1996). And, as is illustrated by the emergence of Black British feminism (Mirza 1997), this intersectional paradigm is not confined to the United States. Black women across diverse academic disciplines created a critical mass of Black women who not only participated in their respective fields but developed a variety of associations to create links across disciplines. This organizational base provided an infrastructure to pursue a strategy of generating alternative paradigms *within* traditional disciplines that were simultaneously linked together *across* disciplines. By participating in these diverse intellectual communities, Black women in sociology experience the depth gained by placement within sociology and the breadth of contact with thinkers working on similar themes in different academic disciplines.

This cross-fertilization across disciplines generates a specific set of methodological concerns for Black women in the sciences. Because it has been stimulated in large part by Black feminist scholarship in two areas outside the sciences—literary criticism and cultural studies—methodologically, race, class, and gender studies seems more in tune with qualitative research methods. Work in Black feminist literary criticism, Black women's history, and Black cultural studies all remain centered on Black women's subjectivity or "voice." These areas of inquiry contain space for Black women intellectuals to draw upon their own experiences as touchstones for developing race, class, and gender intersectionality. Some of the more significant Black feminist theory from these fields models a weaving together of personal narrative, stories, and critical social theory (see, e.g., Williams 1991 and Davies 1994). In this sense, scholarship on race, class, and gender intersectionality that is situated outside sociology generally and positivist sociology in particular seemingly aligns itself with qualitative sociological methodologies.

Sociology as science, with its emphasis on quantitative research methods, raises questions for Black women sociologists. Black women sociologists confront the dilemma of theorizing from their own

experiential positions informed by race, class, and gender intersectionality yet finding ways of doing so without relying solely on qualitative
research methodologies. Within this context, the responses of Black
women sociologists to the dilemma of synthesizing these two diverse
traditions—of legitimating their authority via positivist science, then
using that same science to validate qualitative approaches—seems especially complex. Deborah King's article "Multiple Jeopardy, Multiple
Consciousness: The Context of Black Feminist Ideology" (1988) remains one of the few works that applies quantitative research methodologies to the task of theorizing the paradigm of intersectionality
itself. However, the majority of African-American women sociologists
use the paradigm of intersectionality as a heuristic device that guides
their empirical research. In this sense, they rely on intersectional paradigms to generate themes within a context of discovery while using
standard research methodologies (i.e., qualitative and quantitative research methods) in their context of justification. This leaves one important question unanswered: how can quantitative methods further
our understanding of intersectionality both as a heuristic device that
helps explain other phenomena and as an entity to be studied in its
own right?

African-American Women, American Sociology as Science, and Postmodernity

Black women's actions as agents of sociological knowledge raise two
issues concerning shifting patterns of social-science knowledge in the
United States under conditions of postmodernity. The first issue concerns how American sociology as science can be reorganized and re-
legitimated in an era when African-American women, among others,
challenge both the content and the process of scientific knowledge.
Comparing established disciplines such as sociology to nation-states,
Donald Levine observes that "as the latter emerged worldwide in the
last few centuries to provide security, identity, prestige, welfare, and
civic rights for populations somehow historically connected, so the
disciplines emerged to provide professional status, intellectual identity, academic benefits, and collegial support for those who came to
profess them" (1995, 293). Just as decolonization has meant that
England, France, and other nation-states no longer benefit from an
imperial mapping of physical and political space, sociology, psycholo-

gy, political science, and other disciplines no longer "own" and control knowledge as they have in the past. Black women's ability to enter these disciplines with the entitlements of citizenship suggests that the very definition of sociology and comparable disciplines must change. Both ideas and people transgress the borders of these formerly sealed disciplinary entities, raising new questions concerning the identity of disciplines themselves. If, like-nation states, disciplines can no longer be defined in insider/outsider terms attached to people and ideas, how will they define themselves?

The changing organization of sociology remains both an outcome of postmodernity and a defining feature of it. Narrow definitions of sociology as science, especially those that prevailed during African-American women's exclusion, are no longer adequate. If there is a "crisis" confronting American sociology, it concerns the inability of sociology to reassure its traditional membership that its place in the disciplinary pecking order remains intact (Levine 1995). As cultural critic Edward Said observes, "Westerners may have physically left their old colonies in Africa and Asia, but they retained them not only as markets but as locales on the ideological map over which they continued to rule morally and intellectually" (1993, 25). Since the nature of rule is at stake, Black women's participation in disciplines such as sociology lies not on the periphery of these concerns but at the heart of the decisions confronting sociology as discourse and practice. Including Black women within sociology speaks to the process of democratization, whether the entity undergoing change consists of an academic discipline or formal citizenship in the U.S. nation-state.

To exercise intellectual leadership in thinking through changes of this magnitude, sociology cannot simply look back and bemoan the loss of the good old days when sociologists seemingly garnered respect. This simply rewrites history to the advantage of contemporary sociology. The absence of opposition and the speed and seeming collegiality with which sociologists historically made decisions was not synonymous with agreement and support from those standing outside the discipline. Outsiders were silenced—they were not supporters. Instead, American sociology must be reflexive concerning its own practice and its own strategies for reforming itself, and through this self-reflexivity must see itself as a particular location expressing a more general process of change. Leadership lies less in gaining the seemingly objective view assumed when one stands outside and above social relations, and more in seeing contingent and strategic possibilities. By examining its own intellectual and political practices, sociology is also positioned to develop empathy for similar struggles.

The second issue raised by African-American women's actions as agents of sociological knowledge concerns differences in contestation processes that groups in outsider-within locations deploy in challenging scientific knowledge. Groups such as African-American women face the question of how to invoke the legitimation function of science generated via the seeming objectivity of its epistemology, in order to challenge long-standing exclusionary practices as well as the knowledges generated by these practices. Given the inordinate power wielded by science as a discourse of power, crafting resistance strategies that appear to "buy in" while still aiming to resist should not be a surprising strategy. As James Scott points out, "What is rare . . . is not the negation of domination in thought but rather the occasions on which subordinate groups have been able to act openly and fully on that thought" (1990, 102). In this sense, Black women "buy into" sociology to challenge it or, once inside, see formerly obscured ways for critique and construction.

If the work of African-American women within sociology is any indication of the types of contributions made by Black women in science overall, one significant feature of Black women's scholarship is that it advances fewer critiques of the epistemological foundations of positivist science than, for example, the work of White North American women does (see, e.g., Keller 1985; Haraway 1988; and Harding 1986, 1991). Instead, Black women's sociological scholarship often appropriates the legitimation function of positivist social science to refute racist and/or sexist knowledge about African-American women and to buttress Black feminist knowledge claims. It would be a mistake, though, to view the absence of a sustained, visible critique on the part of African-American women of the epistemological foundations of sociology as science, as evidence that they lack such a critique. Instead, Black women's work within sociology demonstrates a sophistication associated with negotiating complex hierarchical power relations with an eye toward generating social change. In essence, Black women have realized that to destroy systems of power and authority— in this case, authoritative knowledge legitimated via science—without constructing alternative mechanisms of legitimation creates a vacuum into which existing systems of power merely reformulate.

Collectively, the corpus of work contributed by Black women as agents of sociological knowledge reflects diverse strategies used by outsiders entering communities from which they have traditionally been excluded. The disparate strategies deployed by African-American women sociologists seem targeted toward the specific contexts in which they had to learn how to "buy into" sociology without "selling out." Although Black women entering during the period of contested participation necessarily exhibited a narrower range of responses than those available today, their actions of seeming acceptance and scientific critique laid the foundation for more transformative strategies to emerge. Thus, although all reflect strategic responses to the challenges raised by a particular historical period, none is inherently better than the other. Individually, they each create part of the intellectual and political terrain that allows other strategies to flourish.

Despite these accomplishments, the question of how far these strategies will take groups in outsider-within locations remains open to investigation. As Black feminist theorist Audre Lorde points out, "The master's tools will never dismantle the master's house. They may allow us temporarily to beat him at his own game, but they will never enable us to bring about genuine change" (1984, 112). Lorde's often-cited quotation tells only part of the story. Although the "master" may have meant for scientific words to be used one way, reclaiming scientific tools and recasting them for different purposes can benefit both science and subordinated groups. Black women's actions within sociology seem to signal such a creative recasting. When it comes to the contributions of sociology to the powerful position that science occupies in the global political economy, relinquishing the "master's tool" of positivist science may be premature and, given the new politics of containment, quite dangerous.

Four

What's Going On?
Black Feminist Thought and
the Politics of Postmodernism

Like other oppositional discourses, Black feminist thought can never remove itself totally from the ideas expressed by more powerful groups. Although it challenges social theories dominant to itself, in order to be both comprehensible and legitimated it must use the constructs, paradigms, and epistemologies of these discourses. These tensions become apparent in the relationship of Black feminist thought to a loose constellation of academic discourses in the United States best known as postmodernism.[1] On the one hand, postmodernism opposes some of the core tenets of positivist science, structuralist literary criticism, and other discourses of modernity. Thus, postmodernism can foster a powerful critique of existing knowledges and the hierarchical power relations they defend. For example, postmodernism questions the taken-for-granted nature of categories such as race, gender, and heterosexuality and suggests that these seeming "biological truths" constitute social constructions. By focusing on marginalized, excluded, and silenced dimensions of social life, postmodernism destabilizes what has been deemed natural, normal, normative, and true. Overall, postmodernism rejects notions of epistemological and methodological certainty provided by the natural sciences, social sciences, and other discourses of modernity that have been used to justify Black women's oppression (Best and Kellner 1991; McGowan 1991; Rosenau 1992).

On the other hand, postmodernism undercuts selected dimensions of African-American women's political activism. For example, postmodernism rejects ethical positions that emerge from absolutes such as faith. It also eschews social policy recommendations—to make such recommendations requires advancing truth claims and advocating specific political actions stemming from those claims (McGowan 1991; Rosenau 1992). This absence of responsibility grounded in some sort of ethical stance is at odds with African-American women's long-standing contributions to Black civil society. Thus, although postmodernism provides a plausible response to dominant discourses and the politics they promote, it fails to provide direction for constructing alternatives.

This chapter has two main purposes. First, for readers who typically remain excluded, it highlights the "loose principles" permeating discourses of postmodernism (Appiah 1992). Such a task necessarily flattens differences among postmodernists, leaving those who operate within postmodernism to ask, "Exactly which postmodernism does she mean?" Although these readers may be frustrated by the generalizations in this chapter, to me, the exclusionary language barring access to postmodernism is part of the problem. Second, the chapter provides a preliminary assessment of these ideas in light of their actual and potential utility for Black feminist thought. Toward this end, I emphasize postmodernism as a series of ideas and practices. I focus on the contradictory nature of postmodernism—the difference between what it says and what it does.

In approaching these goals, I build on Charles Lemert's thesis (1992) that postmodernism can be seen as a social theory of difference that follows from decentering the social world using a methodology of deconstruction. Recall that critical social theory encompasses bodies of knowledge and sets of institutional practices that actively grapple with the central questions facing groups of people differentially placed in unjust political, social, and historic contexts. One might ask to what degree postmodernism is a critical social theory. Rather than examining the main ideas of postmodernism as concepts that can be proven correct or incorrect, I share David Wagner's view that it is more useful to view postmodernism as providing a series of orienting strategies that make theorizing possible.[2] As Wagner points out, "Strategies are directive; they tell us how to approach the sociological world, not what is true about the world" (1992, 210). Thus, I treat the three

main rubrics of decentering, deconstruction, and difference as orienting strategies for postmodern ideas and practices. Moreover, given the
embeddedness of knowledges of all types in relations of ruling (Foucault 1980a), these orienting strategies are used differently by intellectuals differentially placed in hierarchical power relations. Social theories of difference deployed by intellectuals who are privileged within
hierarchical power relations of race, class, and gender may operate
quite differently than comparable theories forwarded either by intellectuals emerging from the centers of oppressed groups or by those in
outsider-within locations. My approach explores the political implications of the three rubrics of decentering, deconstruction, and difference for developing Black feminist thought as critical social theory.

The Rubric of Decentering: Claiming Marginality

One common popular assumption that permeates academic discussions of postmodernism identifies the origins of postmodernism exclusively with leftist intellectuals in Europe and the United States. Steven
Seidman's otherwise excellent summary of the origins of postmodernism illustrates this approach. According to Seidman, postmodernism
emerged from the break of the French left from both the Communist
Party and Marxism in the 1970s, with leftist intellectuals in the United
States, particularly feminists and gays, becoming leaders of the postmodern in the American academy. Seidman argues that by the mid-
1970s, the left in the United States and in Europe became socially and
ideologically less effective in challenging centers of power. Composed
of a plurality of movements that each focused on its own local or particular struggle to build autonomous communities, these politics fostered a theoretical shift away from positivist science, Marxism, or
other theories of this type in the academy. Seidman quite rightly points
out that "the shift of leftist politics in the 1970s from the politics of
labor to the new social movements and to a post-Marxist social criticism forms an important social matrix for the rise of a postmodern social discourse" (1992, 50).

   Noticeably missing from Seidman's analysis is any mention of
race or Black women. It is not that Seidman is wrong—rather, his
focus may be too narrow. Consider the difference between Seidman's
account and that of Black feminist theorist Carole Boyce Davies, who
notes, "My contention is that postmodernist positions . . . are always

already articulated by Black women because we experience, ahead of the general population, many of the multiple struggles that subsequently become popularly expressed" (1994, 55). Or, as British scholars Michael Keith and Malcolm Cross observe, "The recently discovered postmodern condition of marginality and fragmentation, positively signified, has been lived and worked through for the last forty years, and more by racialized minorities in post-war metropolitan economies" (1993, 22). From this perspective, Black women's experiences prefigured the themes of contemporary postmodernism.

One such theme is an emphasis on decentering, namely, unseating those who occupy centers of power as well as the knowledge that defends their power. Typically applied in relation to elite White male power, the concept of decentering can apply to any type of group-based power. A standard strategy of decentering is to claim the power of marginality. For example, when in the 1970s and 1980s Black women and other similarly situated groups broke long-standing silences about their oppression, they spoke from the margins of power. Moreover, by claiming historically marginalized experiences, they effectively challenged false universal knowledges that historically defended hierarchical power relations. Marginality operated as an important site of resistance for decentering unjust power relations. Thus, the center/margin metaphor has been an important precursor to decentering as one rubric of postmodernism.

Postmodern claims to decentering introduce one important question: who might be most likely to care about decentering—those in the centers of power or those on the margins? By legitimating marginality as a potential source of strength for oppressed groups, the postmodern rubric of decentering seemingly supports Black women's long-standing efforts to challenge false universal knowledge that privileged Whiteness, maleness, and wealth. However, as with the changing interpretations associated with Black women's "coming to voice," current meanings attached to decentering as a construct illustrate how terms can continue to be used yet can be stripped of their initial oppositional intent (Winant 1994).

Tracing the changing interpretations attached to the center/margin metaphor from its initial affiliation with global postcolonial struggles and social movements of the 1960s and 1970s in the United States reveals a dramatic shift in meaning. As a literary metaphor, the language of centers and margins emerged in tandem with similar social-science emphases on core and periphery power relations. Designed to describe a range of unequal, exploitive political and economic relationships, these include the classical colonialism that characterized modern European nations' dominion over their oriental and African colonies (Said 1978; 1993); neocolonial relationships that juxtaposed the wealth of core industrial, developed nations of Europe and North America to that of the poverty of the largely colored Third World on the periphery (Said 1990); the geographic reversal of internal colonial relationships that viewed the affluence of White suburban communities in the United States as intimately linked to the poverty of Black inner-city neighborhoods (Blauner 1972); and the core and periphery industrial sectors that separated workers by race, class, and gender into segmented labor markets (Edwards 1979; Gordon et al. 1982; Bonacich 1989). In all of these cases, the construct of core/periphery relationships and its closely affiliated center/margin literary metaphor signaled unjust, hierarchal power relationships.

When embedded in an understanding of core/periphery relationships, this center/margin metaphor became a useful way of viewing Black women's experiences within hierarchical power relations in the United States (see, e.g., Glenn 1985; Dill 1988b; and Amott and Matthaei 1991). Within power relations that constructed Whiteness, maleness, and wealth as centers of power, African-American women were relegated to positions of marginalized Others. One "decentered" hierarchical power relations by claiming the marginalized and devalued space of Black womanhood not as one of tragedy but as one of creativity and power. Marginality certainly proved to be a productive intellectual space for many African-American women thinkers. In her essay "Choosing the Margin as a Space of Radical Openness," Black feminist theorist bell hooks presents the potential danger and creativity of theorizing on the margins of power:

> Those of us who live, who "make it," passionately holding on to aspects of that "downhome" life we do not intend to lose while simultaneously seeking new knowledge and experience, invent spaces of radical openness. Without such spaces we would not survive. Our living depends on our ability to conceptualize alternatives, often improvised. . . . For me this space of radical openness is a margin—a profound edge. Locating oneself there is difficult yet necessary. It is not a "safe" place. One is always at risk. (In hooks 1990, 129)

For African-American women as a collectivity, redefining marginality as a potential source of strength fostered a powerful oppositional knowledge (Collins 1990). Moreover, the work of Black women and other similarly situated groups participated in a much larger project that used the margins as a source of intellectual freedom and strength (see, e.g., Anzaldúa 1987 and Awkward 1995).

Despite these contributions, the continued efficacy of marginality as a space of radical openness remains questionable. Over time, the connections between the center/margin metaphor as a heuristic device and actual core/periphery relations became less clear. While continuing to reference power relations, talk of centers and margins became increasingly distanced from its initial grounding in structural, group-based power relations. Old centers of Whiteness, maleness, and wealth attached to core/periphery relationships in industrial sectors, labor markets, and among the colonial powers and their former colonies persisted. The center/margin metaphor, however, increasingly became recast as yet another ahistorical, "universal" construct applied to all sorts of power relations. Conceptions of power shifted—talk of tops and bottoms, long associated with hierarchy, was recast as flattened geographies of centers and margins.

Once decontextualized in this fashion, because all groups now occupied a flattened theoretical space of shifting centers and margins, decentering as a strategy could be more easily appropriated by groups situated anywhere within real-world hierarchical power relations. Decentering as a resistance strategy was no longer reserved for those actually oppressed within hierarchial power relations of race, class, and gender. Instead, decentering could now serve as a loose cannon/canon that could be aimed in any direction on this newly flattened center/margin power landscape. As Pauline Rosenau points out, part of the "magic" of postmodernism "is that its open-endedness and lack of specific definition is at once attractive to the affluent, the desperate, and the disillusioned of this world" (1992, 11). Even though the language continued to refer to social relations of race, class, and gender, decentering lost its initial analytical precision and assumed disparate meanings for groups differentially positioned within hierarchical power arrangements. Decentering increasingly became recast as a literary term, a decontextualized, abstract construct immersed in representations, texts, and intertextuality.

By attracting diverse intellectuals to an important collective enterprise, on the surface, decentering the power exerted via representations and texts appears promising. However, since dissimilar groups construct different meanings out of the *same* system of signs, we might

question what the term *decentering* means to diverse groups of intellectuals. Focusing on one group of academics who are privileged within the larger community of intellectuals sheds light on how groups'
placement within hierarchical power relations might shape their intellectual production. As political theorist Nancy Hartsock (1990) as-
tutely points out, some academic intellectuals who espouse postmodernism bear a striking resemblance to Albert Memmi's portrayal of
"colonizers who refuse" under conditions of classic colonialism.[3]
Memmi's discussion of colonizers' reactions to the privileges that
colonialism provided them (1965) offers a provocative metaphor for
understanding why theorists occupying positions of privilege might
be attracted to postmodernism at this particular historical moment.[4]
Although Memmi is clearly referring to European male response to
classic colonial situations, principally of the French in decolonization
struggles in Algeria in the 1960s, his analysis clarifies why certain intellectuals might find postmodernism particularly attractive.[5]

Memmi notes that, whether they like it or not, all colonizers benefit from colonialism. But although privilege is built into social structures, not all colonizers are comfortable with the power and privilege
that their status in the colonial system confers upon them. Some refuse
either by withdrawing physically from the conditions that privilege
them or by remaining to fight and change those conditions. As the
outsiders within the dominant group of colonizers, colonizers who
refuse typically act as power brokers who represent the interests of the
colonized natives to the colonizers who accept. By representing the
interests of the colonized and claiming to understand their standpoint,
members of this go-between group simultaneously challenge the colonial status quo and reproduce it. Although they understand how definitions of the colonized as "different" or as "Other" remain central to
the way colonialism functions, they oppose colonialism in the abstract
while continuing to enjoy its material benefits.

Despite their good intentions, when colonizers who refuse come
into contact with *actual* colonized people who speak out, as compared
to either *ideas* about colonized people or natives who remain silenced,
colonizers realize that their interests and those of the colonized are
fundamentally opposed. If colonialism were abolished and colonized
people were to gain power, little privilege would remain within new
social relations for former colonizers, even those who refuse. A decolonized world would offer to colonizers who refuse no place compara-

ble in power to that available under colonialism. As Memmi notes, "The left-wing colonizer refuses to become a part of his group of fellow citizens. At the same time it is impossible for him to identify his future with that of the colonized. Politically, who is he?" (1965, 41). Although colonizers who refuse may reject relations of ruling that privilege them, removing those relations simultaneously eliminates their identity and purpose. Memmi continues: "One now understands a dangerously deceptive trait of the leftist colonizer, his political ineffectiveness. It results from the nature of his position in the colony" (41).[6]

Memmi wrote in 1965 of members of classical colonial elites who could avoid the stark contrasts of privilege and penalty characterizing African and Asian colonies by returning home to the insulated homogeneity of France. A decolonized world linked via telecommunications into a global market offers no such escape. Postcolonial migrations of people from Africa, the Caribbean, and Asia to Europe demonstrate that self-contained, homogeneous European nation-states are largely relics of the past. Memmi's version of colonial relations also bears a strong resemblance to racial segregation in the United States prior to the 1970s. During that time, African-Americans were objects of knowledge, spoken about and for by sympathetic leftist intellectuals. As African-American women's experiences within sociology illustrate, the absence of Black people from higher education in any significant numbers, especially their absence from positions of authority, made this relationship palatable. In this regard, European decolonization and racial desegregation in the United States share important similarities. In both cases, the movement of people of color into formerly all-White spaces shattered the illusion of insider security maintained by keeping a safe distance from derogated outsiders. As Memmi observes, "It is not easy to escape mentally from a concrete situation, to refuse its ideology while continuing to live with its actual relationships" (1965, 20). In a sense, since there is no place to hide, intellectuals privileged by systems of race, class, and gender oppression must find new ways to "refuse" in proximity to those whose interests they formerly championed and who now inconveniently aim to "come to voice" and speak for themselves.

Thus, the problem that confronted colonizers who refused foreshadowed that facing contemporary leftist academics. Under a system of colonialism in which the natives were safely tucked away at a distance, colonizers who refused could claim solidarity with the marginalized and be praised for their efforts. However, what happens when the natives gain entry to the center? Recently desegregated institutions of higher education where African-Americans claimed legitimation as agents of knowledge created just such a new reality. Where do former allies of African-Americans and other dispossessed groups now belong? Some identify the changing configuration of personnel within higher education since the early 1970s as a "crisis" and spend considerable time wondering what to do about it (see, e.g., Levine 1995). Ann DuCille identifies the discomfort of many academics with the changing political climate in higher education when she observes that "a kind of color line and intellectual passing [exists] within and around the academy: black culture is more easily intellectualized (and canonized) when transferred from the danger of lived black experience to the safety of white metaphor, when you can have that 'signifying black difference' without the difference of significant blackness" (1994, 600). How comfortable are colonizers who refuse when the formerly colonized refuse to be objectified as "texts" amenable to scholarly manipulation? How should they handle groups of natives who express self-defined standpoints?

Although this newly decolonized world creates new patterns of interaction for everyone, by themselves these patterns do not explain why postmodernism remains so appealing at this historical moment. British cultural critic Kobena Mercer alludes to the links between privileged intellectuals who have lost their former positions as representatives of the oppressed and the type of social theory that these intellectuals might find attractive. In his discussion of the disillusionment of many intellectuals with economic class analysis, Mercer observes that

> a whole generation of postwar intellectuals have experienced an identity crisis as philosophies of Marxism and modernism have begun to lose their oppositional or adversarial aura. . . . What results is a mood of mourning and melancholia, or else an attitude of cynical indifference that seeks a disavowal of the past, as the predominant voices in postmodern criticism have emphasized an accent of narcissistic pathos by which the loss of authority and identity on the part of a tiny minority of privileged intellectuals is generalized and universalized as something that everybody is supposedly worried about. (1994, 288)

Edward Said forwards a similar claim: "After years of support for anti-colonial struggles in Algeria, Cuba, Vietnam, Palestine, Iran, which came to represent for many Western intellectuals their deepest engagement in the politics and philosophy of anti-imperialist decolonization, a moment of exhaustion and disappointment was reached. One began to hear and read how futile it was to support revolutions" (1993, 27). In her analysis of scholars engaged in Asian studies, cultural critic Rey Chow follows a similar logic. Chow's argument provides a suggestive link between Maoists, postmodernists, and colonizers who refuse:

> Typically, the Maoist is a cultural critic who lives in a capitalist society but who is fed up with capitalism—a cultural critic . . . who wants a social order imposed to the one that is supporting her own undertaking. The Maoist is thus a supreme example of the way desire works: What she wants is always located in the other, resulting in an identification with and valorization of that which she is not/does not have. Since what is valorized is often the other's deprivation—"having" poverty or "having" nothing—the Maoist's strategy becomes in the main a *rhetorical* renunciation of the material power that enables her rhetoric. (1993, 10–11)

If Hartsock, Mercer, Said, and Chow are correct, postmodernism may be more grounded in the needs of contemporary colonizers who refuse than is typically realized. Antiracist Whites grappling with their position in institutionalized racism, antisexist males coming to terms with patriarchy, White women who treated their domestic workers like "one of the family," and highly educated, affluent individuals from diverse backgrounds who must justify their own privileges in the face of the stark realities of chronic global poverty—all experience a "crisis" of identity of the loss of authority vested in old centers. Consider, for example, how the following definition of postmodernism matches the concerns of intellectuals for whom the world no longer brings the certainty of authority and identity:

> Postmodernisms are responses across the disciplines to the contemporary crisis of representation, the profound uncertainty about what constitutes an adequate depiction of social "reality." . . . The essence of the postmodern argument is that the dualisms which continue to dominate Western thought are inadequate for understanding a world of multiple causes and effects interacting in complex and nonlinear ways, all of which are rooted in a limitless array of historical and cultural specialities. (Lather 1991, 21)

One might ask which groups might be most unnerved by a "crisis of representation" that criticized long-standing criteria for authority and identity and which might welcome such a crisis with open arms.

The changed meanings attached to the rubric of decentering emerge in this political and intellectual context. Despite the seemingly oppositional content of postmodernism—its often-stated commitment to decentering of White male authority, subjectivity, and tradition—its use within the academy does very little to decenter actual power relations. In part, this situation reflects the identity of postmodernism as an academic theory. The placement of intellectuals almost exclusively within academia raises a valid question concerning how effectively academics can decenter power relations. African-American philosopher Cornel West points to the problems inherent in academic theories such as postmodernism:

> Even the critiques of dominant paradigms in the Academy are *academic* ones; that is, they reposition viewpoints and figures within the context of professional politics inside the Academy rather than create linkages between struggles inside and outside of the Academy. In this way, the Academy feeds on critiques of its own paradigms. These critiques simultaneously legitimate the Academy . . . and empty out the more political and worldly substance of radical critiques. This is especially so for critiques that focus on the way in which paradigms generated in the Academy help authorize the academy. In this way, radical critiques, including those by black scholars, are usually disarmed. (1993, 41)

The current academic pecking order privileges medicine, engineering, law, and the physical and natural sciences, all areas closely aligned with bureaucracies of power organized and administered through scientific principles. In this context, academic theories such as postmodernism seem unable to decenter the practices of their own institutions, let alone institutions of society overall.

In this academic context, postmodern treatment of power relations suggested by the rubric of decentering may provide some relief to intellectuals who wish to resist oppression in the abstract without decentering their own material privileges. Current preoccupations with hegemony and microlevel, local politics—two emphases within postmodern treatments of power—are revealing in this regard. As the resurgence of interest in Italian Marxist Antonio Gramsci's work illustrates (Forgacs 1988), postmodern social theorists seem fascinated with the thesis of an all-powerful hegemony that swallows up all resistance except that which manages to survive within local interstices of power. The ways in which many postmodernist theorists use the heterogeneous work of French philosopher Michel Foucault illustrate these dual emphases. Foucault's sympathy for disempowered people can be seen in his sustained attention to themes of institutional power via historical treatment of social structural change in his earlier works (see., e.g., Foucault's analysis of domination in his work on prisons [1979] and his efforts to write a genealogy linking sexuality to institutional power [1980a]). Despite these emphases, some interpretations of his work present power as being everywhere, ultimately nowhere, and, strangely enough, growing. Historical context is minimized—the prison, the Church, France, and Rome all disappear—leaving in place a decontextualized Foucauldian "theory of power." All of social life comes to be portrayed as a network of power relations that become increasingly analyzed not at the level of large-scale social structures, but rather at the local level of the individual (Hartsock 1990). The increasing attention given to micropolitics as a response to this growing hegemony, namely, politics on the local level that are allegedly plural, multiple, and fragmented, stems in part from this reading of history that eschews grand narratives, including those of collective social movements. In part, this tendency to decontextualize social theory plagues academic social theories of all sorts, much as the richly textured nuances of Marx's historical work on class conflict (see, e.g., *The Eighteenth Brumaire of Louis Bonaparte* [1963]) become routinely recast into a mechanistic Marxist "theory of social class." This decontextualization also illustrates how academic theories "empty out the more political and worldly substance of radical critiques" (West 1993, 41) and thus participate in relations of ruling.

In this sense, postmodern views of power that overemphasize hegemony and local politics provide a seductive mix of appearing to challenge oppression while secretly believing that such efforts are doomed. Hegemonic power appears as ever expanding and invading. It may even attempt to "annex" the counterdiscourses that have developed, oppositional discourses such as Afrocentrism, postmodernism, feminism, and Black feminist thought. This is a very important insight. However, there is a difference between being aware of the power of one's enemy and arguing that such power is so pervasive that resistance will, at best, provide a brief respite and, at worst, prove ultimately futile. This emphasis on power as being hegemonic and seemingly absolute, coupled with a belief in local resistance as the best that people can do, flies in the face of actual, historical successes. African-Americans, women, poor people, and others have achieved results through social movements, revolts, revolutions, and other collective social action against government, corporate, and academic structures. As James Scott queries, "What remains to be explained . . . is why theories of hegemony . . . have . . . retained an enormous intellectual appeal to social scientists and historians" (1990, 86). Perhaps for colonizers who refuse, individualized, local resistance is the best that they can envision. Overemphasizing hegemony and stressing nihilism not only does not resist injustice but participates in its manufacture. Views of power grounded exclusively in notions of hegemony and nihilism are not only pessimistic, they can be dangerous for members of historically marginalized groups. Moreover, the emphasis on local versus structural institutions makes it difficult to examine major structures such as racism, sexism, and other structural forms of oppression.[7]

Social theories that reduce hierarchical power relations to the level of representation, performance, or constructed phenomena not only emphasize the likelihood that resistance will fail in the face of a pervasive hegemonic presence, they also reinforce perceptions that local, individualized micropolitics constitutes the most effective terrain of struggle. This emphasis on the local dovetails nicely with increasing emphasis on the "personal" as a source of power and with parallel attention to subjectivity. If politics becomes reduced to the "personal," decentering relations of ruling in academia and other bureaucratic structures seems increasingly unlikely. As Rey Chow opines, "What these intellectuals are doing is robbing the terms of oppression of their critical and oppositional import, and thus depriving the oppressed of even the vocabulary of protest and rightful demand" (1993, 13). Viewing decentering as a strategy situated within a larger process of resistance to oppression is dramatically different from perceiving decentering as an academic theory of how scholars should view all truth. When weapons of resistance are theorized away in this fashion, one might ask, who really benefits?

Versions of decentering as presented by postmodernism in the American academy may have limited utility for African-American women and other similarly situated groups. Decentering provides little legitimation for centers of power for Black women other than those of preexisting marginality in actual power relations. Thus, the way to be legitimate within postmodernism is to claim marginality, yet this same marginality renders Black women as a group powerless in the real world of academic politics. Because the logic of decentering opposes constructing new centers of any kind, in effect the stance of critique of decentering provides yet another piece of the new politics of containment. A depoliticized decentering disempowers Black women as a group while providing the illusion of empowerment. Although *individual* African-American women intellectuals may benefit from being able to broker the language and experiences of marginality in a commodified American academic marketplace, this in no way substitutes for sustained improvement of Black women as a *group* in these same settings. In contrast, groups already privileged under hierarchical power relations suffer little from embracing the language of decentering denuded of any actions to decenter actual hierarchical power relations in academia or elsewhere. Ironically, their privilege may actually increase.

Although many intellectuals live with this contradiction between the content of their theorizing and their actual material conditions, how they respond to this incongruity varies considerably. The version of decentering that I describe here represents but one option. There are others. As James Scott points out, "Those renegade members of the dominant elite who ignore the standard script . . . present a danger far greater than their minuscule numbers might imply. Their public . . . dissent breaks the naturalization of power made plausible by a united front" (1990, 67). Those colonizers whose refusal is genuine represent more of a threat than is commonly imagined.

The Rubric of Deconstruction:
Ironic Circles and Other Practices

In its most general sense, deconstruction encompasses a constellation of methodologies placed in the service of decentering. Although it has a specific meaning within literary criticism (see, e.g., Lather 1991), it has taken on a more general meaning of dismantling truths. Deconstructionist methodologies aim to generate skepticism about beliefs that are often taken for granted within sociology, economics, psychology, and other social-scientific discourses of modernity. Such beliefs include the following: philosophy grounded in reason provides an objective, reliable, and universal foundation for knowledge; "truth" resides in knowledge gained from the appropriate use of reason; knowledge grounded in universal reason, not in particular interests, can be both neutral and socially beneficial; and science, as the exemplar of the legitimate use of reason, constitutes the paradigm for all true knowledge (Flax 1990). From a postmodern perspective, grand theories, or metanarratives, such as theories of institutionalized racism, Marxist theories of class exploitation, feminist theories of gender subordination, or Black feminist theories of intersectionality are neither desirable nor possible. Any political action derived from such absolutes becomes similarly suspect. Since no theory of absolute truth is possible under postmodernism, postmodernist theorizing becomes reduced to producing a narrative that explores some socially constructed reality (Fraser and Nicholson 1990). For this reason, postmodernist theorizing seems especially taken with textual analysis, seeing different texts or discourses as repositories for social constructions. Anything can be a "text" and thus is a possible candidate for deconstruction. By critiquing the texts of modernity, deconstructive methodologies also challenge the function of knowledge in legitimating power relations. Thus, via deconstructive methodologies, postmodernism aims to reconfigure the relationship between scientific knowledge, power, and society. Any discourse or theory that claims to explain universals is rejected (Weedon 1987; Fraser and Nicholson 1990; Seidman and Wagner 1992).

Deconstructive methodologies refute not just the context of scientific knowledge but the very rules used to justify knowledge. In this regard, intellectuals from oppressed groups can put deconstructive tools to good use. For example, through a complex array of strategies, African-American women in sociology "deconstructed" scientific contexts of discovery and justification. Deconstructive efforts to dismantle notions of subjectivity, tradition, and authority offer clear benefits for Black feminist thought. For example, White male subjectivity has long stood as normative for "human." Deconstructing this narrow view by exposing its particularity creates space for Black women to be redefined as fully human and to accrue the "rights" associated with being human. Similarly, although the traditions taught in the academic canon masquerade as universal, they actually forward a narrow set of human experiences. Deconstructive methodologies applied to the canon have proved useful in allowing Black feminist traditions to be included in legitimated knowledge.

I have found such techniques especially useful in my own work. Specifically, my analysis of the emergence of Black women as agents of sociological knowledge relies on deconstructive techniques. In chapter 3, I identify how the absence of Black women from sociology participates in the self-definitions of sociology as a science. Using insights from deconstructive methodologies, I treat sociology as text and challenge a series of sociological binaries—White male/Black female, objective/subjective, rational/emotional, scientist/nonscientist—as well as the effects of binary thinking on sociological subfields (e.g., race, class, and gender as separate areas of inquiry). Unpacking these binaries allows me to examine actual nonbinary social relations within sociology (specifically, the outsider-within location and its contributions to Black women's knowledge), as well as to sketch out a new conceptual space of intersectionality to replace the oppositions of race, class, and gender within sociology.

Despite these contributions, when it comes to the issue of the political implications of deconstructive methodologies for Black feminist thought, three issues merit special concern. The first involves the inability of deconstructive methodologies by themselves to construct alternative explanations for social phenomena. Deconstructive methodologies use three steps to "keep things in process, to disrupt, to keep the system in play, to set up procedures to continually demystify the realities we create, [and] to fight the tendency for our categories to congeal" (Lather 1991, 13). The first step consists of identifying the binaries or oppositions that structure an argument—for example, the center and its double or Other. Reversing or displacing the dependent term from its negative position to a place that locates it as the very condition for the positive term constitutes the second step. The third step involves creating a more fluid and less coercive conceptual organization of terms. The goal is to transcend binary logic by simultaneously being both and neither of the binary terms (Lather 1991). Thus, deconstructive methodologies aim to critique in order to evoke new ways of being outside the binary logic associated with science.

How often does this actually happen? Deconstructive methodologies yield impressive results when applied to ideas whose meanings emerge from binary categories such as Whites/Blacks, men/women, and other well-known dualities. In contrast to other approaches that fail to extract themselves from binary logic (see, e.g., the discussion in chapter 5 of the treatment of gender in Afrocentrism), deconstructive methodologies refute the very foundations of knowledge. However, when unanchored in power relations, the logic of deconstruction mandates that it apply deconstructive methodologies to its own practice. This can lead to multiple meanings, an endless string of interpretations, and the inability to construct alternative bodies of knowledge or truths (Bauman 1992, 131). Deconstructive methodology makes it difficult to develop alternative knowledge claims because to do so violates the fundamental premise of a deconstructive approach. Postmodernist theorists refuse to have a list of the practices or principles of knowledge that are implied in their own methodology installed as new theoretical centers of process or content. As feminist theorist Linda Nicholson points out, "Postmodernism must reject a description of itself as embodying a set of timeless ideas contrary to those of modernism; it must insist on being recognized as a set of viewpoints of a time, justifiable only within its own time" (1990, 11).

As the postmodern equivalent of the modernist dialectic, at best, deconstruction provides a corrective moment, a safeguard against dogmatism, a continual displacement. Unlike dialectical models that yield new constructions that are then challenged, deconstructive methodologies yield few new "truths." Because deconstructive methodologies must continually deconstruct their own practices, they cannot take themselves seriously. For example, the goal of Jacques Derrida's intertextuality is to generate an endless conversation among texts with no prospect of ever arriving at an agreed point (Bauman 1992, 130). Philosopher Richard Rorty's term *ironist* describes postmoderns' deconstruction of their own practices. Ironists hold radical and continuing doubts about vocabulary, realizing that arguments phrased in any vocabulary, including their own, remain questionable. "Irony creates confusion in order to say something that exceeds any logic," observes social theorist Charles Lemert. In this sense, "irony is the discursive form of postmodernism" (1992, 23). Unfortunately, postmodern discourse that is overly dependent on this element of never taking itself too seriously lacks authority. As a result, deconstruction remains ineffective as a strategy either to produce new theories about oppression or to suggest new politics that might oppose it. For Black women grappling with a new politics of containment in the United States, deconstructive methodologies operate more effectively as a critique of power than as a theory of empowerment.[8]

Lacking an inherent authority to explain reality leads to a second important concern: how does deconstruction gain credibility, legitimation, and authority? If scientific standards of rationality, verifiability, empirical data, and objectivity are rejected, what will take their place to make postmodernism convincing? Since deconstructive methodologies eschew internal mechanisms for legitimating themselves and in fact are dedicated to eradicating such absolutes, why does deconstruction have any credibility at all? I suspect that the answer lies in old ways of legitimating knowledge, that is, not so much in the logic of what is said but in the power of an interpretive community to legitimate what counts as knowledge (Mannheim 1954). Although deconstruction appears to belong to no one, it actually constitutes the cultural capital or intellectual property of specific groups of intellectuals who claim deconstruction as their own (Bourdieu 1990). In other words, for intellectuals who are skilled in deconstructing texts, the content of what is said remains less important than the ability of any given thinker to manipulate deconstructive methodologies. People become judged by their ability to "create confusion in order to say something that exceeds any logic." In some situations, the more confusing, the more value attached to the knowledge.

Given this situation, the exclusionary language often associated with deconstruction specifically and postmodernism in general takes on added importance. On the surface, the tendency of some postmodern authors to write in nonlinear styles by presenting their work as a pastiche of many voices challenges long-standing practices of knowledge validation. Traditionally, less-established writers secure the validity of their own ideas by preparing a list of citations of important thinkers whom the author can use to legitimate his or her own work. Whether the less-established writer agrees or disagrees with the ideas of scholars with established reputations matters less than the placing of his or her arguments near theirs. Thus, under commodity relations, mixing a known commodity with a lesser-known one theoretically enhances the value of the lesser-known argument. Through its language practices, deconstruction claims to challenge this type of reputational hierarchy. In discussing her writing style, Patti Lather explains why she uses this method: "In my own writing, the accumulation of quotes, excerpts and repetitions is also an effort to be 'multivoiced,' to weave varied speaking voices together as opposed to putting forth a singular 'authoritative' voice" (1991, 9). Despite Lather's good intentions, who she actually cites matters greatly. Although presenting different voices as if they were equivalent appears to flatten existing power relations, in real-world academic politics, some voices garner much more credibility than others. Authors of all texts, even those claiming affiliation with postmodernism, must put forth "authoritative voices," or why would we read them? Unfortunately, in far too many texts, the author's "authority" hides behind an often confusing way of presenting material. As Lather points out, "Postmodernism is easily dismissed as the latest example of theoreticism, the divorce of theory and practice. This tendency is compounded by the desire of those who write in these areas to want to 'interrupt' academic norms by writing inside of another logic, a logic that displaces expectations of linearity, clear authorial voice, and closure" (8). Unfortunately, writing within another logic necessarily excludes those who lack access to that new logic. It also damages those aiming to *claim* authorial voice within the old logic.

Postmodern reliance on exclusionary language has tremendous implications for African-American women's struggle for self-definition. As a result of a continual critique carried out in exclusionary language, little room remains to construct an identity grounded in an authorial voice of Black women. Moreover, when coupled with the minimal decentering of actual power relations in higher education, commodifying and exchanging the new language of postmodernism has become a new form of cultural capital in the academic marketplace. By performing a powerful gatekeeping function for those who lack access to the exclusionary language of postmodernism, the rhetoric of deconstruction can be used to maintain the status quo. As is the case with any commodity, scarcity determines its value. Despite postmodern lip service to decentering, the intellectuals writing articles, giving papers, populating the editorial boards of journals, and occupying positions of authority within academic disciplines seem remarkably similar to those of the past. To me, this is the ultimate postmodern irony. The ability to manipulate exclusionary language becomes yet another standard used to exclude Black women from legitimated intellectual work.

For those intellectuals currently privileged within hierarchical power relations, the issue of language appears to be a minor theme. As many speakers of standard American English as a second language know, in the United States, language signifies access to or exclusion from communities of power. Not possessing the language, whether written or oral, remains a major device used to maintain boundaries between insiders and outsiders. Exclusionary language usually results in exclusionary outcomes. "I feel that the new emphasis on literary critical theory is as hegemonic as the world it attacks," argues Black feminist theorist Barbara Christian. "I see the language it creates as one that mystifies rather than clarifies our condition, making it possible for a few people who know that particular language to control the critical scene. That language surfaced, interestingly enough, just when the literature of peoples of color, black women, Latin Americans, and Africans began to move to 'the center'" (1988, 71). How ironic—a major Black feminist literary critic sees the texts of Black women appropriated by and submerged within an exclusionary language of literary criticism that silences the creators of texts targeted for deconstruction.

Deconstruction raises a third issue especially germane to Black feminist thought. By challenging the notion of a self-defined Black women's standpoint, deconstructive methodologies undermine African-American women's group authority. Deconstructing identity, tradition, and authority simultaneously restricts Black women's appropriation of these marks of power in order to legitimate a Black women's standpoint. Black feminist literary critic Mae Henderson eloquently assesses the contradictory nature of deconstructive methodologies for African-American women:

> What is of value in the post-structuralist/deconstructionist school is that it aims at decentering what is essentially a white and male tradition and, in the process creating a space for the presentation of voices hitherto muted or marginalized. What is questionable is that it is a project that dismantles notions of authority . . . notions of tradition . . . and notions of subjectivity . . . during a period when blacks, feminists and other marginalized groups are asserting authorship, tradition and subjectivity. (In McKay et al. 1991, 23)

In essence, Black women cannot decenter Whiteness, maleness, and wealth as markers of power and at the same time claim the authority and power that these systems deliver.

Contextualizing the rubric of deconstruction within hierarchical power relations sheds light on why the treatment of authority, subjectivity, and tradition within postmodernism presents special problems for Black women in the United States. Grounding their authority in their ability to speak in self-defined voices as knowledge creators, African-American women have carved out a modest authority emanating from a Black feminist standpoint (Collins 1990). However, by rejecting the notion that "truths" such as Black feminist thought exist, deconstructive methodologies seem to be advocating the impossibility of objectivity or rationality for anyone, including Black women. From the relativist perspective implicit in extreme versions of postmodernism, no group can claim to have a better interpretation of any "truth," including its own experiences with oppression, than another. As a result, legitimation becomes plural, local, and embedded in practice (Fraser and Nicholson 1990). Taken to its extreme, methodologically, there is no ownership over the intellectual product or thought produced. The shift becomes one of moving from conceptions of oppressed groups producing their own truths and politics to notions of the alienated subjects endlessly deconstructing all truths.

The postmodern critique of history and tradition is similarly troubling. If traditions are discredited as mere "stories" told by "different voices," oppression and other macro-social-structural variables not only recede into the background, they implode and are encapsulated with postmodern views of hyperreality. From this perspective, reality collapses and the hyperreal becomes a model of a "real without origin or reality" (Rosenau 1992, xii). History and tradition are told not as linear narratives in which individual stories or voices are inserted, but as themes within individual narratives. Depending on which narrative is selected, this approach can lead to complete avoidance of specific political and social contexts. Because everything is contained within the narrative itself, no external, privileged position exists from which a critique of the absence of power dynamics may be launched. This move away from historical specificity that is associated with deconstruction resembles the long-standing apolitical ways of reading that are commonly associated with traditional literary criticism. "When historical specificity is denied or remains implicit," argues Valerie Smith, "all the women are presumed white, all the blacks male" (1989, 44).

Replacing group authority grounded in some notion of a shared standpoint emerging from a shared history, with the notion of collectivities of alienated subjects linked by strings of discursive moments presents a fundamental difficulty for Black feminist thought. What good is a theory that aims to dismantle the authority that Black women in the United States have managed to gain via group solidarity and shared traditions? By removing altogether the notion of a "center," that is, a belief in some sort of verifiable, objective knowledge that one can deploy with authority, the rubric of deconstruction disempowers the very same historically marginalized groups who helped create the space for postmodernism to emerge. Moreover, one might ask who benefits from a methodology that appears unable to construct alternative explanations for social phenomena suitable for guiding political action; legitimates its own authority via exclusionary language; and dismantles notions of subjectivity, tradition, and authority just when Black women are gaining recognition for these attributes. It is one thing for African-American women and similarly situated groups to use deconstructive methodologies to dismantle hierarchical power relations. However, it is quite another for members of privileged elites to appropriate these same tools for different purposes. The true irony is that elites can now undercut the bases of authority of those long excluded from centers of power while invoking their own fluency in the exclusionary language of postmodernism as the criterion used to keep the masses at the door.

The Rubric of Difference

As I discussed in chapter 3, the period from the 1880s through 1945 marked the high point of scientific interest in "racial differences" and "sexual differences." Thus, current scholarly fascination with the notion of difference within postmodernism represents less a new direction than a current manifestation of long-standing concerns of Western science. As Black feminist theorist Audre Lorde contends, much of Western European history has conditioned us to see human differences in simplistic opposition to each other. "We have *all* been programmed to respond to the human differences between us with fear and loathing," argues Lorde, "and to handle that difference in one of three ways: ignore it, and if that is not possible, copy it if we think it is dominant, or destroy it if we think it is subordinate" (1984, 115). Binary thinking legitimated by scientific authority proved central in generating this version of difference. Grounded in binaries such as White/Black, man/woman, reason/emotion, heterosexual/homosexual,

Eurocentric/Afrocentric, and self/other, science manufactured views of a world compartmentalized into either/or oppositional categories. Defining one side of the binary by the absence of qualities characteristic of the other side afforded one side normality and relegated the other to a deviant, oppositional Other. When linked to oppressions of race, gender, and sexuality, these ideas concerning oppositional difference helped construct the so-called essential group differences defended by biology and/or culture (Fuss 1989).

Using deconstructive methods, oppressed groups have challenged these notions of oppositional difference. Rather than rejecting the lesser identities of being Black in White supremacist systems or of being women under patriarchal domination or of being gays, lesbians, and bisexuals confronting compulsory heterosexuality, these groups have claimed the identity of the Other in political organizing. Identity politics of this type usually reverse the negative connotation attached to oppositional difference by valorizing the formerly negative side of the term. For example, a "woman's way of knowing" associated with living in a female body characterized by cycles, flows, and change has been offered as part of the identity politics of feminism (Belenky et al. 1986). Similarly, Afrocentrism remains predicated upon notions of "soul" or the essence of "Blackness" (Gayle 1971). Despite the limitations associated with these approaches, this type of identity politics fostered a group solidarity culminating in political resistance. Initially, its celebration of difference legitimated group challenges to the false universalism constructed from oppositional difference. However, as I discussed in chapter 2, in a context in which oppositional voices were routinely co-opted over time, politics organized around single axes of race, gender, or other badges of identity seemed increasingly doomed to failure.

Given the decreasing effectiveness of identity politics, what alternatives might a postmodern rubric of difference offer? Because postmodernism itself is a discourse of critique and not of construction, it hesitates to propose any alternative theories of difference other than those that emerge from within a critique. This stance of critique creates the illusion that postmodernism lacks a social theory of difference. However, the significance of the treatment of difference within postmodernism in the American academy may lie less in its critique of oppositional difference, and more in insights about difference that are embedded and thereby constructed within its critique.

Two distinctive political implications of constructions of difference within postmodernism merit review. The first deals with the important insight that the idea of difference is being increasingly commodified within relations of advanced capitalism (Jameson 1984). In situations in which ideas and cultural capital are increasingly important in maintaining power relations, the idea of difference can be easily transformed into a commodity that can be sold in the global marketplace. Moreover, the difference to be commodified is authentic, essential difference long associated with group differences of race, ethnicity, gender, economic class, and sexuality. "The Third world representative the modern sophisticated ideally sees is the *unspoiled* African, Asian, or Native American, who remains more preoccupied with her/his image of the real native—the *truly different*—than with issues of hegemony, racism, feminism, and social change," observes Trinh Minh-ha (1989, 88; italics in original). Within this logic, essential differences become commodified, marketed, consumed, and eradicated. This commodification and marketing of difference not only strips it of political meaning but reformulates it as merely a matter of style. For example, consider the commodification of difference in practices such as using kente cloth as part of the uniforms of KFC employees in selected African-American neighborhoods. The emergence of *Wiggers*, a derogatory term applied to White youth who want to possess the trappings of Black hip-hop culture—rap music, baggy clothes, gang colors—but who shun the actual Black people who create that culture also illustrates this trend. The parallels abound, including a similarity between academics who invoke postmodernism to analyze the texts of Black women writers in academic departments that remain lily-White. As British cultural critic Stuart Hall points out, postmodernism has a "deep and ambivalent fascination with difference—sexual difference, cultural difference, racial difference, and above all, ethnic difference. . . . There's nothing that global postmodernism loves better than a certain kind of difference: a touch of ethnicity, a taste of the exotic, as we say in England, 'a bit of the other'" (1992, 23).

Whether the object is Black women's texts or the latest hairstyles, celebrating differences by commodifying and consuming them works to defuse the righteous anger of historically oppressed groups. After all, it's hard to remain angry if the "authentic" Afrocentric culture upholding one's Black identity politics becomes glorified in advertisements selling clothes, tanning products, lip collagen, and the like. Like the surveillance techniques applied to "welfare queens" and Black Lady Overachievers in the media, this focus on difference hides in plain sight new power relations constructed from long-standing essential differences. Postmodernism seems to take a stand against this commodification. After all, much of the analysis of commodified difference is done by thinkers influenced by postmodernism. However, in its everyday practice, the way in which postmodernism has been inserted into the academy—for example, the appropriation of Black women's texts as voices—replicates practices associated with commodified differences.

A second implication of postmodern treatments of difference concerns the connections between difference and structural power. Up to this point, I have lumped all postmodernisms together, have treated them as one homogeneous discourse, and, some would say, have unfairly addressed my comments to one type of postmodernism. In actuality, the loose principles of postmodernism have been expressed along a continuum from extreme postmodern theories to reconstructive postmodern theories (Best and Kellner 1991).[9] One end engages in endless deconstructive activities, whereas the other tries to use postmodern ideas to reconstruct (but not construct) society. Conceptions of difference within postmodernism demonstrate similar patterns. However, arranging notions of difference along a continuum reveals a problematic analysis of structural power at both ends of the difference spectrum.

Because one end of the continuum—that occupied by extreme postmodern theories—takes deconstructivist reasoning to its logical extreme, it creates space for apolitical, often trivial differences. On this end, extreme constructionists argue that everything is constructed, all is in constant play, nothing is certain, and all social life consists of representations. This end emphasizes individual differences as well as differences within individual identities. Group-based differences become devalued and erased within strict constructionist frameworks. Instead, virtually all experience is seen as being historically constructed. Thus far, I have framed much of my argument in opposition to this extreme constructionist posture, because I remain skeptical of any analysis that decouples difference from its moorings in hierarchical power relations. Doing so allows socially constructed differences emerging from historical patterns of oppression to be submerged within a host of more trivial "differences." Difference can then be discussed as a question of individual identity, leaving behind the troublesome politics associated with racism, sexism, and other oppressions. In describing this problematic use of difference, Black cultural critic Hazel Carby observes, "The theoretical paradigm of difference is obsessed with the construction of identities rather than relations of power and domination and, in practice, concentrates on the effect of this difference on a (white) norm" (1992, 193). Or, as literary critic Chandra Mohanty states, such "difference seen as benign variation (diversity) . . . rather than as conflict, struggle, or the threat of disruption, bypasses power as well as history to suggest a harmonious, empty pluralism" (1989–90, 181). Under distributive paradigms of justice in which everyone is entitled to the same bundle of rights, for oppressed groups, diluting differences to the point of meaninglessness comes with real political danger.

The seeming fascination with identities of difference emerges in this practice of comparing stories of difference uprooted from ethical or political contexts. Such approaches minimize the significance of differences that are imposed from without—those resulting from oppression—and tacitly preserve the Enlightenment assumption of a freely choosing, rational human who is now free to be different. This is the liberal rational choice model applied to the issue of identity—one can emphasize or construct the different facets of one's subjectivity differently as one chooses. Whereas views of individual identity that valorize difference can benefit those already positioned to enjoy them, such approaches remain less promising for oppressed groups with readily identifiable biological markers such as race, sex, and age. As cultural critic Coco Fusco points out,

> The complete transfer of identity from essence to action, from innate property to consumable or reproducible activity, without any ethical referent or political grounding, is a form of cultural politics few blacks would benefit from, given the political and economic inequalities that continue to divide American society along racial lines. . . . This particular group of black cultural critics does not think of culture and identity without asking about politics—that is, about relations of power—and about ethics—, that is, about responsibility. (1992, 281)

Despite the surface validity of constructionist approaches to identity that emphasize not only individual differences but also differences within individuals, this approach erases structural power. Within systems structured along race, sex, gender, and sexual orientation, the fusion of these multiple identities determines one's overall place in a hierarchy. The fear is that once identity dissolves in a sea of meaningless differences, nothing stable and secure will remain upon which a politics of resistance can be built (Fuss 1989).

This emphasis on apolitical, often trivial differences that constitute individual subjectivity constrains Black women's collective political activism. As Black feminist theorist June Jordan points out, "The flipside of this delusional disease, this infantile and apparently implacable trust in mass individuality, is equally absurd, and destructive. Because every American one of us is different and special, it follows that every problem or crisis is exclusively our own, or, conversely, your problem—not mine" (1992, 16). Jordan points out that difference taken to its deconstructed extreme meshes smoothly with notions of liberal bourgeois individualism so essential to contemporary forms of domination. We learn to think in terms of individual solutions to what are actually socially constituted problems. If everything becomes conceptualized as local, personalized, and constantly negotiated in relation to shifting constructions of difference, then it becomes difficult to conceive of collective action. As Hazel Carby notes, "Because the politics of difference work with concepts of individual identity, rather than structures of inequality and exploitation, processes of racialization are marginalized and given symbolic and political meaning only when the subjects are black" (1992, 193).

Groups that have the most to lose appear least likely to replace both group-based notions of identity and any resulting identity politics with extreme constructionist understandings of difference. "Some of the most impassioned ratifications of the idea of an identity politics come from women of color," observes Diana Fuss (1989, 99). Both the critique of oppositional difference associated with identity politics and extreme constructionist treatments of difference that erase structural power ultimately undercut Black women's empowerment via self-definition. The development of Black feminist thought itself represents a hard-fought struggle to name oneself, to claim an identity that more accurately reflects Black women's lives and subjectivity. Individuals from groups that exercise real power run few risks in embracing identities organized around multiple differences, because they know that their power will remain intact. Consider Diana Fuss's comparison of lesbian and gay use of identity politics: "In general, current lesbian theory is less willing to question or to part with the idea of a 'lesbian essence' and an identity politics based on this shared essence. Gay male theorists, on the other hand, . . . have been quick to endorse the social constructionist hypothesis and to develop more detailed analyses of the historical construction of sexualities" (1989, 98). Since we must assume that Fuss's gay males are Whites, this group need not engage in identity politics because social institutions as currently constructed protect their interests.

The other end of the continuum on difference, occupied by reconstructive postmodern theories, appears unwilling to relinquish the possibility of a politically effective postmodernism organized around difference. Recognizing the implicit politics in any social theory, this end of the continuum aims to find a way to make postmodernism politically potent without supporting notions of oppositional difference. This end avoids extreme relativism by acknowledging the socially constructed nature of human differences of race, gender, and sexuality that emerge from "metanarratives," while simultaneously retaining a notion of something that is "essentially" human. Claiming that human beings are all the same under the skin, this model of difference works well in a current color-blind and power-evasive era when to see racial differences is to be racist and to point out gender differences is to be sexist (Frankenberg 1993). In this sense, this end of the continuum overlaps with, yet tries to distinguish itself from, liberal approaches to human difference.

Despite its contributions in maintaining a common ground for a politics of resistance, this version of difference also has limitations. Although I sympathize with the spirit of this effort to balance universality (human essence) with specificity (human difference), the use of these terms may undercut the goals of this reconstructive project. Grounding theories of human difference on a bedrock of essential human qualities that typically remains unexamined raises the troubling questions, who will constitute the essential human and, conversely, how will we know whether the list of "human essences" is, in fact, universal? Will White men remain, by default, the essential humans against which all others are now deemed equivalent? Moreover, this view of difference can also suppress more radical political responses to domination of race, class, and gender. Attention to the racism, sexism, class exploitation, and heterosexism that constructed these differences can become diverted as an effort to tolerate the differences that accompany an essentially human experience. Although humans can share commonalities, biology and culture can still be used to explain human differences. When differences are seen as benign, cosmetic variations on a common essence, tolerance becomes the strategy for constructing community. However, tolerance can be problematic. Historian Tessie Liu describes her puzzlement at the common reaction that her White students have when studying racism. Although they are highly sympathetic to the concerns of people of color, their tolerance is often coupled with the belief that racism does not affect them. Liu observes that tolerance "often encourages an ethnocentric understanding of differences because this form of comparison does not break down the divisions between *us* and *them,* between *self/subject* and *other*" (1991, 266).

Unless they explicitly deal with structural power relations and wealth, expressions of the rubric of difference within postmodernism present a conflictual terrain for Black feminist thought. The belief that people are all the same under the skin and that difference is a matter of superficial commodified style meshes with long-standing beliefs that attribute differences of power and wealth among Blacks, women, and other historically oppressed groups as being their own fault. Hazel Carby queries, "At what point do theories of 'difference,' as they inform academic practices, become totally compatible with, rather than a threat to, the rigid frameworks of segregation and ghettoization at work throughout society?" (1992, 193). To the end of this question, I might add, "and within academia itself."

Moving beyond Difference

Moving beyond difference (with its assumed question, difference from what?) to the conceptual terrain of intersectionality creates new conceptual space. By jettisoning the implicit assumption of a normative center needed for both oppositional difference and reconstructive postmodern tolerance for difference, intersectionality provides a conceptual framework for studying the complexities within historically constructed groups as well as those characterizing relationships among such groups. Drawing from the strengths of decentering and constructionist approaches to difference, the historical realities that created and maintain African-American women's particular history can be acknowledged, all the while recognizing the complexity that operates within the term *Black women*. Moreover, moving beyond difference to intersectionality may shed light on the mutually constructing nature of systems of oppression, as well as social locations created by such mutual constructions. In this sense, the postmodern legitimation of ongoing projects of oppressed groups to decenter power, deconstruct Western metanarratives, and rethink differences legitimates efforts to understand race, class, and gender intersectionality.

Despite these potential contributions, some might question whether postmodernism itself is part of the new politics of containment dedicated to maintaining hierarchy in desegregated spaces. In his essay "The New Politics of Difference," African-American philosopher Cornel West examines the oppositional nature not only of difference but of postmodernism overall:

> The new cultural politics of difference are neither simply oppositional in contesting the mainstream . . . for inclusion, nor transgressive in the avant-guardist sense of shocking conventional bourgeois audiences. Rather, they are distinct articulations of talented (and usually privileged) contributors to culture who desire to align themselves with demoralized, demobilized, depoliticized and disorganized people in order to empower and enable social action and, if possible, to enlist collective insurgency for the expansion of freedom, democracy and individuality. . . . For these critics of culture, theirs is a gesture that is simultaneously progressive and co-opted. (1990, 19–20)

Thus, the essential irony of the postmodern rubrics of decentering, deconstruction, and difference stems from the type of politics they suggest. Political struggles by people of color against racism, by women against patriarchy, and by gays, lesbians, and bisexuals against heterosexism fostered the decentering of Western beliefs about modernity. Yet the main ideas that grow from these struggles have been appropriated by a class of intellectuals who keep the language of resistance yet denude the theory of actual political effectiveness. This theory is then given back to people in a form that, because of the language used, becomes unusable for political struggle and virtually unrecognizable. The result is a discourse critical of hierarchical power relations that simultaneously fosters a politics of impotence.

Postmodernism neither gave African-American women license to decenter the authority of privileged White males nor planted the idea to do so. Rather, postmodernism provides powerful analytical tools and a much-needed legitimation function for those Black women and similarly situated intellectuals whose struggles take place in academic arenas. Thus, postmodernism can be a potentially powerful means for all of us who wish to challenge not just the results of dominant discourses but the rules of the game itself.

Five

When Fighting Words
Are Not Enough:
The Gendered Content
of Afrocentrism

In American higher education, Afrocentrism generates some curious contradictions. On the one hand, many African-American intellectuals staunchly support Afrocentrism, contending that its commitment to centering scholarship on people of African descent, its treatment of Black people as subjects rather than objects of history, its valorization of Blackness, and its attempts to speak to and not simply about Black people throughout the Black Diaspora provide African-Americans with a much-needed corrective to existing scholarship on race (Karenga 1978, 1982, 1988, 1990; Turner 1984; Asante 1987, 1990; Welsing 1991). Other respected African-American academics disagree. Defining Afrocentrism as an ideology or dogma, they claim that it romanticizes the African and rural African-American past while ignoring social issues in the urban Black present; suppresses heterogeneity among Black people in search of an elusive racial solidarity; forwards a problematic definition of Blackness as an essential, innate quality of a general ancestral connection to Africa; and remains male-centered and heterosexist (West 1993; hooks 1990, 103–13; Gilroy 1992, 1993; White 1990; Marable 1993; Gates 1992a; Ransby and Matthews 1993).[1]

Beyond these academic disagreements, Afrocentrism has a broader history and meaning. As one of several Black nationalist projects in the United States in the late twentieth century (Van Deburg 1992), Afrocentrism simultaneously represents and shapes Black political aspirations for freedom and justice. Much social theory rarely considers Black audiences except as markers of difference. In contrast, Afrocentrism speaks primarily to Black people by "centering" on their experiences and concerns. In a climate of postmodern criticism in which rhetoric of decentering holds sway, any discourse that "centers" on anything may seem hopelessly flawed. However, Black frustration within a new politics of containment provides one explanation why African-Americans seem more willing to accept Afrocentrism and other Black nationalist philosophies during a period when academics increasingly view nationalisms of all sorts with disdain. The resurgence of African-American interest in Black nationalism in the 1980s and 1990s may be a direct result of an increasingly conservative political climate in the United States, the deteriorating economic base in African-American communities resulting from changes in global capitalism, and the persistence of an increasingly sophisticated racial segregation (Massey and Denton 1993; Squires 1994).

Because Afrocentrism aims to influence the thinking and behavior of Black people outside academia, it participates in controversies unlike those affecting other discourses. Unlike most other academic discourses, Afrocentrism received substantial media coverage in the 1990s, most of it negative and centered on two themes. One concerned the inroads of Afrocentrism into the curricular offerings of urban public schools. Schools populated by predominantly African-American poor children that had been written off by everyone found themselves the center of attention when they tried to institute "Afrocentric" curricula. Another area of controversy surrounded the claim by some Afrocentrists that ancient Egypt not only constituted an African civilization but that it shaped subsequent European classical civilizations. This media controversy, in part, helped narrow understandings of *Afrocentrism* from its broader meaning as "Black consciousness." *Afrocentrism* increasingly described the "authentic" Afrocentrists garbed in traditional African attire. Nevertheless, despite the negative treatment in the popular press of both Afrocentric curricula and claims of African origins of civilization, *Afrocentrism* as synonymous with "Black consciousness" remains meaningful to Black youth (see, e.g., the autobiography of hip-hop artist Sister Souljah [1994]), to many African-American academics, and to African-Americans of diverse economic classes and genders in ways that social theories deemed more respected and more prestigious within higher education have yet to accomplish. I have found African-American college students receptive to "Afrocentric" course offerings, symposia, and programs. As part of a larger contingent of Black youth who see the devastation affecting their communities, many see Afrocentrism as the only critical social theory interested in addressing social problems of this magnitude (Lusane 1993).

The institutional placement of many Black intellectuals in higher education may also contribute to the persistence of Black nationalism generally and Afrocentrism in particular as one guiding interpretive framework for Black studies scholarship.[2] Despite considerable media attention to selected Black public intellectuals, most African-Americans in higher education experience far less privilege. For this group, Black studies programs have been vital. As Black studies initiatives proliferated at historically White universities in the United States, less celebrated African-American academics gained a crucial institutional niche that allowed them to become Black studies professionals, many within Black studies programs and departments. Moreover, the placement of Black academics in historically White institutions meant that such thinkers routinely encountered the residual effects of scientific racism that viewed Blacks as objects of knowledge in sociology, psychology, history, and other academic disciplines (Gould 1981; McKee 1993; Tucker 1994). With limited power to change these institutions, many Black thinkers turned inward toward the task of creating cultural communities that might provide them and their students solace on what were often hostile White campuses. Afrocentrism flourishes in these spaces.[3]

Given Afrocentrism's distinctive political and intellectual ties to Black nationalism, a deep-seated belief in the promise of Afrocentrism by many everyday African-Americans cannot be analyzed away as "false consciousness." This would only aggravate existing divisions between Black academics and African-Americans outside the academy, as well as growing divisions among Black intellectuals within higher education. Much more is at stake than merely questions of the logical consistency or empirical merit of Afrocentrism. As with Black nationalist philosophies in general, the appeal of having a "Black consciousness" or being "Afrocentric" lies, in part, in the ability of Afrocentrism to mean different things to different African-Americans.

Rather than trying to define Afrocentrism precisely or, worse yet, elevating one form of Afrocentrism over another and proclaiming it "correct," a more intriguing and useful approach lies in identifying the diverse ways in which African-Americans employ Afrocentrism as a system of meaning.

In this chapter, I confine my analysis to Afrocentrism as critical social theory within higher education. As critical social theory, Afrocentrism aims to theorize about social issues confronting Black people with an eye toward fostering economic and social justice. Rather than establishing a taxonomic framework designed to classify Afrocentric scholars (see, e.g., Darlene Clark Hine's useful discussion of Afrocentrism as one of three paradigms operating within Black studies [1992]), I examine selected "orienting strategies" (Wagner 1992) that frame the practice of Afrocentrism as critical social theory. As the progeny of a Black cultural nationalism that has been institutionalized within higher education, Afrocentrism adamantly claims to "fight the words" of traditional racist discourse. It aims to construct an oppositional social theory grounded in a "fighting words" paradigm. How effectively is Afrocentrism as critical social theory fulfilling this objective?

Although a variety of themes lend themselves to analyzing the oppositional nature of Afrocentrism, among them economic class, heterosexism, and religion, gender offers a particularly useful lens. Gender operates as a central yet largely unexamined tenet of most nationalist projects, whether the nationalism is forwarded by dominant groups in defense of institutionalized racism, colonialism, or imperialism, or by groups such as African-Americans who use nationalist aspirations to challenge hierarchical power relations (Yuval-Davis 1997). Although mainstream media portray Afrocentrism as a monolithic, static doctrine, Afrocentric intellectual production remains decidedly heterogeneous and incorporates diverse perspectives on a range of topics, including gender (Adler et al. 1991; Petrie et al. 1991). Despite this heterogeneity among individual scholars, neither Afrocentric intellectual production overall nor Afrocentrism in the academy has shown a sustained interest in gender. Neither the specific experiences of African-American women caused by gender oppression nor gender as a major category of analysis framing the experiences of both Black women and Black men has received sustained attention. Thus, Afrocentric treatment of gender might shed light on the challenges confronting critical social theories that embrace "fighting words" paradigms.

From Black Cultural Nationalism to Afrocentrism

Evaluating the effectiveness of Afrocentrism as critical social theory involves examining the gender politics in the version of Black cultural nationalism that emerged during the Black Power movement in the 1960s and early 1970s. Although Black nationalist movements have a long history in the United States (see, e.g., Pinkney 1976; Moses 1978; and Franklin 1992, 1995), Black cultural nationalism was the political and intellectual predecessor of contemporary Afrocentrism in the academy. For African-Americans, the 1960s represented a period of rising expectations about Black equality coupled with a growing realization that change would not come easily. The hopes generated by successful decolonization movements in Africa and the dismantling of de jure segregation in the United States stood in stark contrast to the seeming permanence of poverty and powerlessness plaguing Black urban communities. Disenchantment with civil rights, seen as an outmoded solution, led many younger African-Americans to Black nationalism and the search for a heroic national identity or "Blackness" that could serve as the basis for a reenergized political activism. Black cultural nationalism emerged in these social conditions and found its expression in the Black Arts movement, guided by a Black Aesthetic (Gayle 1971; Van Deburg 1992).

In contrast to other Black nationalist projects, Black cultural nationalism concerns itself with both evaluating Western treatment of Black culture as deviant (see, e.g., Gossett 1963; Jordan 1968; Gould 1981; Goldberg 1993; and McKee 1993) and constructing new analyses of the Black experience. Social-science scholarship on race typically sees Black culture in the United States in one of two ways. On the one hand, African-American contributions to mainstream culture have been deracialized and considered simply "American" or "universal." On the other hand, dimensions of African-American culture that have resisted absorption and remain distinctive are either neglected or dismissed as deviant (Crenshaw 1993). Consider the differential treatment afforded to jazz and Black English in dominant discourse. Despite their shared roots in African-derived philosophical frameworks—their expressiveness, improvisation, rootedness in dialogue, and valuing of individual sound or "voice"—dominant scholarship identifies jazz as the only "classical" music produced in the United States and routinely derogates Black language. Ignoring and minimizing the African origins and African-American practitioners of jazz, this approach effectively deracializes a major dimension of American culture. In contrast, when assessing Black language, dominant scholarship interprets the same African-derived characteristics as pathologies that retard African-Americans' social advancement (Smitherman 1977). The "Blackness" that created jazz remains ignored, yet the same "Blackness" that generates Black English is maligned.

Based on the premise that Black people make up a cultural nation, Black cultural nationalism aims to reconstruct Black consciousness by replacing prevailing ideas about race with analyses that place the interests and needs of African people at the center of any discussion (Asante 1987; 1990). For African-Americans, reclaiming Black culture involves identifying dimensions of an "authentic" Black culture that distinguish it from European-derived worldviews. Reconstructing Black history by locating the mythic past and the origins of the nation or the people (see, e.g., Diop 1974) is intended to build pride and commitment to the nation. These elements allegedly can be used to organize the Black consciousness of people of African descent as a "chosen people." Identifying the unique and heroic elements of the national culture, in this case, Black culture, ideally enables members of the group to fight for the nation (Fanon 1963; Karenga 1978).[4]

Four guiding principles or domain assumptions framed the Black Aesthetic of Black cultural nationalism (Gayle 1971; Dubey 1994). First, in the absence of any substantive African-American participation in sociology and other academic disciplines, social-science approaches had long viewed Black culture as "primitive," inferior, and deviant. In response to this scientific racism, the Black Aesthetic aimed to reconstruct a positive, philosophically distinct Black culture. Central to this reconstructed culture lay the thesis of "soul," interpreted as a condensed expression of the unconscious energy of the Black experience. Soul could not be acquired—one was born with it or one wasn't. Soul or essential Blackness was naturalized, and true believers either believed it existed or discounted it altogether. Thus, the concept of soul aimed to name the essential, authentic, and positive quality of Blackness (Rainwater 1970).

A second guiding principle of the Black Aesthetic involved reclaiming Black identity via this reconstructed Black culture. For African-Americans, institutionalized racism had severed this link between authentic Black identity and an affirming Black culture to create a "psychology of oppression" (Baldwin 1980). Internalized oppression substituted this authentic identity expressed via solidarity with the Black community, with an identity constructed on premises of scientific racism that deemed Black people intellectually and morally inferior. As a step toward recovering their identity and subjectivity, Black people needed to undergo a conversion experience of "Nigrescence" from "Negro" to "Black" (Cross 1971). Completing a four-stage transformation—preencounter, encounter with Whites, immersion in Black culture, and internalization of a new Black identity—distinguished "Negroes" mesmerized by Whiteness from authentic Black people prepared to participate in liberation struggles (Fanon 1967; Cross 1971; Nobles 1972).

A third assumption concerned the significance of maintaining racial solidarity grounded in a distinctive notion of Black community. Race became family, racial family meant community, and Black community symbolized the "imagined community" of nation (Anderson 1983). Reconstructing Black culture and grounding it in a family model of community organization gave newly "Black" people a home, a family to which they were linked by ties of blood. This stance joined the bonds of consanguinity, or blood ties, characterizing the racial family with the sense of political obligation that accompanies blood ties. Family metaphors and their unspoken assumptions about gender permeated Black nationalist discourse of this period. For example, Yosef Ben-Jochannan's influential volume positing African influence on European civilization was entitled *Black Man of the Nile and His Family* (1972). Family ties of consanguinity demand absolute submission because they are built not on political or social issues but on simple belonging (Appiah 1992).

Finally, when nurtured by this unified Black community relating as family, this newfound Black identity would stimulate a new politics for African-Americans. African-Americans in touch with their essential Blackness would be more willing to serve the Black nation, defined as a large, imagined Black community. This ethic of service to Black families, Black communities, and the Black nation, one wherein Black people would function as "brothers" and "sisters," emerged from the conversion experience of immersion in Black culture, re-claiming Black identity via racial solidarity.[5]

In the 1980s, Molefi Asante, Maulana Ron Karenga, and other African-American intellectuals basically imported these four principles into Black studies programs and departments and recast them as premises of Afrocentrism in the academy. Yet as each core theme traveled into the academy, it received a distinctive treatment reflecting the new politics of containment characterizing the 1980s and 1990s. The bulk of contemporary Afrocentric intellectual production, particularly that housed in Black studies programs, emphasizes the first core theme of the Black Aesthetic. Such scholarship explores the distinguishing features of Black culture through identifying the distinctive elements of an Afrocentric worldview (Karenga 1982; Asante 1987, 1990; Myers 1988).[6] Even though the term *soul* disappeared and was replaced by the search for the "essence" of Blackness, Afrocentrism retained this focus on opposing social-scientific constructions of Black culture as deviant. Recasting Black culture through an essentially Black and often celebratory corrective lens, African history (Diop 1974), philosophies (Serequeberhan 1991), religions (Mbiti 1969; Zahan 1979), and social systems (Thompson 1983) all generated new interest. The assumption guiding much of this research was that Black culture had an essential core. Uncovering the philosophical foundations of a distinctive African-centered, Black, or Afrocentric worldview expressed differently throughout the Black Diaspora would provide a new Afrocentric context for examining Black community organization (Herskovits 1990; Holloway 1990).

Building on the search for "soul" in the Black Arts movement, Afrocentric scholarship posited several distinguishing features of "essential Blackness." These features were a distinctive relationship of the Black individual to the Black community that fosters a connected definition of self (Myers 1988); a concern for harmony as a fundamental principle of community organization whereby individuals find their worth in relationship to a community, to nature, and to some supreme idea or being (Asante 1987); a relationship between the spiritual and material aspects of being wherein material life is not privileged over spirituality (Richards 1990); and a cyclical rather than linear conception of time, change, and human agency whereby individuals see their connectedness to all life and whereby the appearance of phenomena always change while the underlying essence remains basically unchanged (Richards 1980).

Efforts to verify how these key elements of the African philosophical tradition shaped African-influenced cultures throughout the Diaspora also stimulated scholarship on "classical" African civilizations (Asante and Asante 1990; Holloway 1990). Investigations of the roots of Black culture parallel efforts to reclaim Black history by empirically verifying how the elements of an African philosophical tradition have shaped Black history and, in some versions, Western civilization itself (Diop 1974; Bernal 1987; Brodhead 1987). This component has led to an increased interest in African civilizations and cultures, especially the study of ancient Egypt. Because Egypt was perceived as the original "Black" civilization serving as the philosophical foundation for all subsequent societies formed by people of African descent, interest in ancient Egypt or Kemet increased (Asante 1990; Karenga 1990).

Identifying elements of a distinctive Afrocentric worldview created the conceptual space for scholars to begin the painstaking task of reinterpreting a range of social institutions in Black civil society. Black family studies represent one area in which Afrocentric interpretations have challenged social-science assumptions of Black family deviance, especially in female-headed households (Sudarkasa 1981; Dickerson 1995). Studies of Black religious expression and spirituality make up another important area of scholarship on Black culture (Sobel 1979; Mitchell and Lewter 1986; Hood 1994). Black cultural production, especially music, dance, the visual arts, and literature, constitutes yet another area of important reinterpretation (Cone 1972; Thompson 1983; Asante and Asante 1990). Finally, Black language has benefited greatly from establishing a new normative center that is derived from African societies (Smitherman 1977).

Despite these contributions of 30 years of Afrocentric scholarship aimed at addressing more than 150 years of scientific racism, the definition of culture currently shaping much Afrocentric intellectual production runs the risk of limiting its effectiveness. Black cultural nationalism in the 1950s and 1960s was inspired by the use of culture in *actual* and not *imagined* national liberation struggles. As a result, the definitions of culture forwarded by thinkers such as Amilcar Cabral (1973) and Frantz Fanon (1963) differ markedly from those of today. These and other Black nationalist thinkers saw culture as dynamic and changing, a complex network of social practices that determine positions of domination, equality, and subordination (San Juan 1992). The close links that ideas and actions had in political struggle fostered a particular view of praxis grounded in a constantly tested Black culture.

In contrast, contemporary Afrocentric constructions of Black culture replace this dynamic self-reflexivity with an a priori set of cultural norms culled from the belief systems of selected African societies. These norms are often used as yardsticks for assessing normative qualities of Black culture (Asante 1990). Afrocentric preoccupation with forwarding "positive" views of Black culture stems from efforts to extract it from the uniformly "negative" constructions long permeating Western scholarship and popular culture. However, as Michele Wallace observes, "focus on good and bad images may be more fundamentally connected to the western metaphysical dualism that is the philosophical underpinning of racist and sexist domination than with radical efforts to reconceptualize black cultural identities" (1990, 19). Ironically, this type of thinking reifies the notion of a fundamentally good, essential Blackness increasingly submerged under an encroaching and inherently bad Whiteness. From this perspective, essential Blackness has much to offer an intellectually and spiritually bankrupt White world that has little of value (see, e.g., Welsing 1991).

Reconstituting Black identity, the second core theme of the Black Aesthetic, remains a less focused goal, yet unstated assumptions about identity permeate Afrocentric intellectual production. Work in Black psychology demonstrates efforts to use the core elements of Black culture to assist African-Americans in dealing with racial oppression. As prominent Afrocentrist Na'im Akbar observes, "We now know that psychology is not only what the European behavioral scientists have taught. We have a new grasp on the concept that Africans view the world differently" (1991, 36). Substantial scholarship aims to redefine a new basis for viewing African-American identity and personality (Baldwin 1980; Myers 1988; Akbar 1989; White and Parham 1990).[7]

As is the situation with Black culture, reconstructing Black identity faces its own set of challenges. In some cases, constructing a normative Black identity easily slips into attempting to describe the ideal, normative, and "authentic" Black person. The search for the "authentic" Black person as evidenced in the glorification of "pure" African biological heritage; the displacement of an essential Blackness from sight to sound by viewing orality, rhythm, and "soul" as the source of Blackness; listing components of the "normative" Black personality that can be used to measure African-American mental health; the belief that a Black essence or "soul" exists that is distinctive to Black people and that only Blacks can access—all have been accused of being instances of Black essentialism (hooks 1990, 103–13; Dyson 1992). In essence, this approach construes Black culture as a package of insulated traits possessed in varying degrees by Black individuals and then uses these traits to assess Black mental health.

Although designed to oppose scientific racism, Afrocentric definitions of culture and identity inadvertently rely on assumptions resembling those of positivist science. For example, positivist science claims that its tools can accurately depict reality. Within scientific contexts of justification, empiricism and rationality constitute tools that uncover the "truth" of social phenomena. Afrocentric views of culture and identity share this belief in a truth that is waiting to be discovered by the science of Afrocentrism. This theme of the embeddedness of Afrocentrism in scientific assumptions concerning culture and identity has had a deep impact on Black cultural criticism. African-American writers whose work seems to challenge dimensions of essential Blackness depicted as "truth" often encounter censure. For example, criticisms of Alice Walker's novels *The Color Purple* (1982) and *Possessing the Secret of Joy* (1992) often challenged Walker's accuracy in portraying the Black experience. Even though Walker never claimed that she was trying to "represent" or "depict" the Black experience, holding her work to this standard allowed for its dismissal.

In contrast to the treatment of culture and identity, the two remaining themes of racial solidarity and the ethic of service are treated less as areas of scholarly investigation and more as unquestioned rules that regulate relationships among professionals in some Black studies programs. Much less attention has been paid to examining the actual and potential mechanisms by which African-Americans create racial solidarity and/or engage in community service in Black civil society. Instead, Black-on-Black surveillance seems designed to ensure that racial solidarity and an ethic of service as articles of faith are observed. On some college campuses, maintaining racial solidarity at all costs often degenerates into policing the borders of who is authentically "Black." At times, this posture has proved extremely costly. For example, during the confirmation hearings of now Supreme Court justice Clarence Thomas, conservative Republicans manipulated this automatic invocation of racial solidarity to their own advantage.

Many African-Americans made the misguided assumption that, once on the bench, Thomas would demonstrate his racial loyalty by expressing an ethic of service to the Black community.

The lack of attention within Afrocentrism to current political and economic issues may stem, in part, from academic norms. Such standards support apolitical scholarship on culture, especially when displaced to a distant and safe past, while eschewing the more contentious contemporary African-American political realities. Molefi Asante has been producing Afrocentric arguments for years. When his work was deemed politically ineffective, he was left alone. But Asante's work became the center of controversy when it began to be used in shaping school programs in Milwaukee, Detroit, and Portland, Oregon. Only then was it publicly censured. Afrocentric analyses that suggest that psychological freedom must precede concrete political action also uphold academic assumptions. Treatments of Black identity, when confined to analyses of poor Black self-esteem and the need for more role models, represent another safe topic. Unfree minds limit Black participation in both racial solidarity and an ethic of service. The solution: fix the mind. These approaches sever analyses of culture and identity internal to African-American civil society from political challenges such as racial segregation and surveillance that originate outside Black communities. In other words, not only are culture and politics severed—a shrinking of the notion of praxis—but also the meaning of each becomes changed as a result of this separation. Thus, restricting Black intellectual activity to the terrain of culture and psychology may signal yet another strategy of co-optation characterizing the new politics of containment (Winant 1994). As Barbara Ransby and Tracye Matthews point out, "The Afrocentric prescription for progress is predicated upon the notion that the main problems confronting the African-American community and diaspora at this historical juncture are internal to the Black community itself. The problems are defined as cultural, behavioral and psychological, not as political, economic or structural. In other words—our problem is us" (1993, 59).

Comparing the power relations confronting Black cultural nationalism in the 1960s to those facing Afrocentrism in the 1990s sheds light on the contrasting views of culture deployed by both. The Black Arts movement of the 1960s clearly reflects a stance of "strategic essentialism" (Spivak 1993, 1–25) whereby an essentialist Black culture played a pivotal role in Black nationalist struggles. However, intellectuals from that era recognized that national culture can become problematic for liberation struggles if the moment of "strategic essentialism" hardens into dogma. Cabral (1973), Fanon (1967), and others never meant Black essentialism to be the organizing principle of Black social organization. Instead, they saw culture as one tool essential for political liberation.

The question for African-Americans concerns whether we are still in such a historical moment. Will producing a national culture of Blackness yield political results similar to those characterizing earlier historical periods? More important, who benefits from Black essentialist positions that appear unable to generate theoretically compelling arguments for political practice? In a paper appropriately entitled "Afro-Kitsch," film critic Manthia Diawara scathingly alludes to the political limitations of some versions of Afrocentrism:

> Until Afrocentricity learns the language of black people in Detroit, Lingala in Zaire, and Bambara in Mali, and grounds itself in the material conditions of the people in question, it is nothing but a kitsch of blackness. It is nothing but an imitation of a discourse of liberation. Afrocentric academics fix blackness by reducing it to Egypt and *kente* cloth. Hence, like Judaism, Christianity, and Islam, Afrocentric social theory has become a religion, a camp movement, where one can find refuge from the material realities of being black in Washington, D.C., London, or Nairobi. (1992, 289)

As currently constructed, some dimensions of Afrocentrism seem designed to soothe their advocates comfortably ensconced in teaching and research positions in higher education. Their value as critical social theory seems much more questionable.

Gender and the Black Aesthetic

As the discussion in chapter 1 of African-American women and Black civil society suggests, Afrocentric domain assumptions of culture, identity, solidarity, and service have markedly different implications for African-American men and women. These differences stem in large part from the Afrocentric reliance on Black Aesthetic notions of community, which in turn rely on mainstream views of family. As in nationalist movements globally, women and gender have proscribed functions (Yuval-Davis 1997). Using the experiences of selected White middle-class families as normative, 1960s gender ideology posited that "normal" families maintained a dichotomous split between the public sphere of the political economy, reserved for men, and the private sphere of family, relegated to women. These nuclear families in which benevolent male authority ruled, with women assuming their proper, natural roles as wives and mothers, reproduced appropriate gender roles for men and women (Andersen 1991; Thorne 1992). Within this interpretive framework, strong African-American women in Black families and in Black civil society were labeled deviant (Zinn 1989; Coontz 1992). Moreover, the seemingly flawed gender roles in African-American families fostered a slew of problems, among them Black poverty, criminality, poor school performance, and adolescent childbearing. In other words, by not reflecting dominant gender ideology, Black families reproduced Black cultural deviance that in turn fostered Black economic class disadvantage (Collins 1989).

Despite writings of Black feminists disputing these views (see, e.g., essays in Toni Cade Bambara's *The Black Woman* [1970]), in the absence of a Black feminist political movement, these views were incorporated into Black cultural nationalist agendas. Autobiographies of Black women activists from the Black Power era describe the sexism in Black cultural nationalist organizations. For example, Elaine Brown (1992), a former leader of the Black Panther Party for Self-Defense, describes the sexism in this revolutionary Black nationalist organization. Brown also identifies similar practices in US, a Black cultural nationalist movement led by Maulana Ron Karenga, the creator of Kwanzaa and a figure closely associated with Black studies in higher education. Echoing Brown, Angela Davis (1974) also reports elements of sexism in Karenga's Black cultural nationalist organization. Brown, Davis, and other, less prominent Black women assumed a particular place in Black cultural nationalist efforts to reconstruct authentic Black culture, reconstitute Black identity, foster racial solidarity, and institute an ethic of service to the Black community. Although Black cultural nationalism staunchly opposed racial oppression, it ironically incorporated dominant ideologies about White and Black gender roles into its domain assumptions. Consider the following passage, quoted at length, from Imamu Amiri Baraka, in 1970 a prominent Black cultural nationalist in the United States. In his article entitled "Black Woman," Baraka offers an especially concise example of the gender ideology that permeated Black cultural nationalism:

We do not believe in "equality" of men and women. . . . We could never be equals. . . . Nature has not provided thus. . . . But this means that we will complement each other, that you, who I call my house, because there is no house without a man and his wife, are the single element in the universe that perfectly completes my essence. You are essential, to the development of any life in the house, because you are that house's completion. When we say complement, completes, we mean that we have certain functions which are more natural to us, and you have certain graces that are yours alone. We say that a Black woman must first be able to inspire her man, then she must be able to teach our children, and contribute to the social development of the nation. How do you inspire Black man? By being the conscious rising essence of Blackness. . . . By race, by identity, and by action. You inspire Black Man by being Black Woman. By being the nation, as the house, the smallest example of how the nation should be. So you are my "house," I live in you, and together we have a house, and that must be the microcosm, by example, of the entire Black nation. Our nation is our selves. (1970, 8)[8]

Although participants in Black nationalist projects certainly differed in their adherence to these beliefs, in its bold assertion of typically more diffuse assumptions, Baraka's rendition remains unusual and therefore useful. The significance of this passage lies in its particularly concise statement of the gender ideology permeating 1960s Black cultural nationalism. Moreover, it illuminates how key ideas about gender framed subsequent assumptions of Afrocentrism. Four areas are of special significance. They are the importance attached to controlling Black women's reproduction and sexuality; the significance of Black mothers in passing on Black culture; the notion of complementary gender roles as points of departure in constructing Black masculinity and Black femininity; and the symbolic association of Black women with the nation.

First, since women are the only group who can biologically reproduce the population of Black families, communities, or nations, regulating Black women's reproduction becomes central to nationalist aspirations. Controlling biological reproduction to produce more of one's own "people" or, depending on political and economic policy, more or fewer of an outsider group's "people" typifies nationalist philosophies generally and Black nationalist philosophies in particular (Yuval-Davis 1997). Responding in large part to eugenicist scientific and public policies long leveled against Black people and others deemed socially undesirable (Davis 1981, 202–21; Haller 1984; Kevles 1985;

Duster 1990), Black nationalist projects claim that without sufficient population there can be no Black individuals whose identities are in question. Without population, the Black nation ceases to exist. Within this intellectual and political context, Black nationalist projects of the 1960s often opposed contraceptive and reproductive services for African-American women. Viewing such services as genocide, they argued that because family planning services were largely White-run, such services represented a continuation of long-standing eugenics policies targeted toward Blacks. In a climate of medical experimentation on Blacks typified by the then-in-progress Tuskegee syphilis experiment (see, e.g., Jones 1993), claims of government-initiated efforts to eliminate the Black population appeared highly plausible. However, although the Black nationalist phrase "have a baby for the nation" made good political rhetoric, it failed to address the issue of who would care for the population born. Despite their analyses, Black nationalist groups often found themselves at odds with the African-American women who were left to raise the future warriors of the nation with few resources. These women often viewed the denial of reproductive services quite differently.

Controlling Black women's biological reproduction raises the accompanying issue of who would control Black women's sexuality. Assumptions about Black women's sexuality central to relations of ruling also influence Black nationalist projects (Collins 1990). For example, Baraka's passage mirrors dominant gender ideology that divides women into two opposed categories: the virginal, married, good girls, contrasted to the sexually promiscuous, immoral, unmarried, bad girls. Within this oppositional difference, good girls are sexually active only within the context of marriage and family. In contrast, bad girls represent the sexualized woman, who lacks the protection of marriage and whose sexuality renders her deviant. Within this context, African-American women who embody the "conscious rising essence of Blackness" are to be protected, revered, and seen as good women, whereas those who fall outside this union with a Black man garner less favor. This model legitimates Black women's sexuality only in relation to Black men, yet it offers no parallel legitimation of Black male sexuality in relation to attachment to Black women. Moreover, statements such as "a Black woman must first be able to inspire her man" suggest that the primary utility of Black women's sexuality lies in inspiring her Black man in the privacy of their home.

Controlling Black women's sexuality simultaneously addresses another issue of great concern within Black nationalist projects. By reversing the color hierarchy of White supremacist beliefs that derogate darkness, Black becomes beautiful. If "the blacker the berry, the sweeter the juice" typifies standards of Black beauty and moral authority, Black women remain far superior to White women and other women of color in their ability to produce the authentic Black bodies that this ideology requires. Moreover, keeping the race biologically "Black" directs attention to policing Black women's sexuality. Black women who sleep with "the enemy" place Black families, Black communities, and the Black nation at risk, for this choice perpetuates the bastardization of the Black race. As mothers of the race, Black women need to be good girls, and good girls do not sleep around. Within a sexual double standard, Black women become mothers of the nation while Black men serve as warriors in the revolution. As warriors, they maintain the right to sleep with, own, and in some cases rape the women of the alien nation, in this case, White women, while receiving praise for these actions (see, e.g., Eldridge Cleaver's *Soul on Ice* [1968]). This ideological framework constrains Black women and Black men differently, with patterns of choices made by actual African-American women and men reflecting their struggles with this unstated yet powerful gender subtext of reproduction and sexuality within Black cultural nationalism.

The significance of African-American women as mothers in passing on Black culture also constitutes a significant feature of Black nationalist projects. Within nationalist philosophies, the people of a nation not only exist as a measurable, quantifiable population but also represent a group occupying and/or dispersed from a homeland and possessing a national culture symbolic of the nation (Anthias and Yuval-Davis 1992). Since nationalism remains closely associated with notions of self-determination over territory and homeland, Black women, by virtue of their association with land, family, and homes, become keepers of the family, home, community, and nation (Collins 1998a and forthcoming 1998b). For example, Baraka notes that the collective self-determination of a people is expressed through building a "nation" composed of "houses." These houses form a microcosm for the nation as a whole. Thus, the family becomes the approved, natural site where Black culture and racial identity are reproduced. Viewing families as the building blocks of nations, in conjunction with identifying women's actions as more central to the family's well-being and functioning within the house and community than men's, elevates Black women's responsibilities as mothers in certain ways. Since women typically carry the burden of child care responsibilities within African-American households, conceptualizing family as intricately linked with both community and nation effectively joins women's activity in socializing the young in individual households to that of transmitting the symbols, meanings, and culture of the Black nation itself. Viewing African-American women as moral mothers or keepers of the "nation," Baraka argues that Black women must be able to "teach our children, and contribute to the social development of the nation." Maintaining elements of culture such as language, ways of living, and cultural values of a people is essential to the continuation of the national group. Through their activities as mothers, Black women reproduce authentic Black culture, in this case, the positive qualities that would ensure the loyalty of members of the national group. Thus, Black women's highest accomplishment becomes inspiring Black men and keeping "house," the building block of the nation.

With so much vested in glorifying the mother, Black women who fail to fulfill these functions can face only censure. A distinction can be made between those women who uphold the values of the nation but do not adhere to them and those women who, by refusing protection, challenge the premises of the system. Within this framework, Black gays, Black lesbians, and Black women who embrace feminism all become suspect, because each group in its own way challenges the centrality of motherhood for Black families, communities, and ultimately the Black nation. The homophobia in Black cultural nationalism seems linked to the belief that maintaining a conservative gender ideology is essential for Black families, communities, and the Black nation. As Henry Louis Gates Jr. points out, although the ideology of Black nationalism does not have any unique claim on homophobia, "it is an almost obsessive motif that runs through the major authors of the black aesthetic and the Black Power movements. In short, national identity became sexualized in the sixties in such a way as to engender a curious subterraneous connection between homophobia and nationalism" (1992b, 79). Overall, those Black women who fail to have children or who reject the gender politics of the heterosexist nuclear family face being labeled racial traitors or lesbians.

As Baraka points out, Black women's actions as mothers, although extremely important, remain secondary to the objective of "inspiring their men." Thus, Black women's partnership with Black men via gender-appropriate nation-building endeavors constitutes a third key idea about gender. The thesis of the complementarity of men and women working in partnership in building strong Black families and communities functions as a deep root in Black cultural nationalism. In this discourse, complementarity symbolizes equality, so that the revered Black mother role complements the benevolent yet warrior-like father. But although equality and complementarity are related, they are not the same. Baraka flatly states that African-American men and women can never be equal. By this, he endorses natural, separate identities for men and women that parallel the notion of natural, complementary identities for Blacks and Whites. This notion of gender complementarity dovetails with an ethic of service in which Black women and men exhibit racial solidarity by submerging their individual needs, goals, and concerns to those of the Black community as a collectivity. Theoretically, all sacrifice so that racial solidarity can be maintained. But in actual everyday life, African-American women typically sacrifice more.

Not only are Black women supposed to reproduce the population of the new nation and to pass on national culture but, within the confines of gender complementarity, they also are expected to serve as symbols of the national family or national culture to be protected and preserved. Symbols of American nationalism such as Mom, God, the flag, and apple pie are deeply gendered images. They revolve around a nexus of traditional nuclear family values with a nurturing mother at the center under the protection of a supportive husband/father/ good citizen and watched over by a powerful male God. Although Black cultural nationalism alters the symbols of the nation through the creation of a Black liberation flag, a Black value system, and Black holidays such as Kwanzaa, it simultaneously imports the notion of women as symbolic of the nation. Tactics such as referring to Africa as "Mother Africa" and identifying it as the mythical homeland of Black people scattered throughout the Black Diaspora promote gender-specific images. Within Black cultural nationalism, as its "conscious rising essence," only certain Black women symbolize the nation "by race, by identity, and by action." In this sense, Black women become defined as "keepers of the race" both literally and symbolically.

Black community, race, and nation understood through the rubric of family thus become constructed on certain notions of gender that, although not as explicit as Baraka's rendition, depend on African-American women's and men's adhering to a particular gender ideology. Black women's contributions remain both biological—as mother, she physically produces the children for the nation as well as provides sexual services for male warriors—and symbolic or cultural—as mother, she socializes Black children for the nation through exemplary role modeling of authentic Black femininity. In contrast, Black men claim masculinity by protecting their households, their communities, and their nation, as symbolized by their Black women.

The dangers here for African-American women become clear. If protecting Black women becomes conflated with the construction of Black manhood, any woman who is seen as unworthy of this protection becomes a threat to the entire community and is thus open to group censure. It's one thing to refuse to have a baby for the nation and yet to support the importance of that activity. It's quite another to reject the role itself as part of the heterosexual nuclear family under Black male leadership. The actions of an individual woman are far less threatening than what her rebellion symbolizes to the entire community.

Gender and Afrocentrism

The guiding principles of Afrocentrism reflect Black cultural nationalism's emphases on reconstructing Black culture, reconstituting Black identity, using racial solidarity to build Black community, and fostering an ethic of service to Black community development. More important, the unexamined yet powerful gender ideology of Black cultural nationalism concerning reproduction, motherhood, gender complementarity, and Black women's symbolic association with nationalist aspirations is also present in the fighting words stance of Afrocentrism.

Most commonly, discussions of Black culture operating within Afrocentric domain assumptions exclude gender altogether and discuss Black "people." In some versions, the phrase "the Black man" stands as proxy for Black people. However, in far too many cases, "the Black man" really refers to men, suggesting that the experiences of Black men adequately represent those of African-Americans overall. This approach both renders the distinctive experiences of African-American women invisible and reinforces the notion that if

Black women are not explicitly discussed, then the discourse itself lacks a gendered analysis. Thus, although it may appear that Black women in particular and a gendered analysis in general remain absent from efforts to reconstruct Black culture and Black identity, Black women's absence and invisibility structure the very terms of the argument advanced.

Another approach to Black culture consists of incorporating the work of a few clearly exceptional Black women, but only if these Black women worthies do not challenge preexisting Afrocentric assumptions. For example, Harriet Tubman is routinely portrayed as the "Moses of her people" because she meets a standard of greatness derived from male experience, namely, military leadership in warfare. Women whose accomplishments seem to advance the dual goals of furthering the development of a positive Black culture and fostering positive Black identities without challenging prescribed gender roles within Black communities also garner the status afforded to Black women worthies. In some cases, only part of the African-American woman can be claimed—her nationalist part is embraced, but any feminist, socialist, antiheterosexist ideas that challenge Afrocentric domain assumptions are conveniently omitted. For example, Mary McLeod Bethune's contributions to Black civil society by founding a college for Black youth, if they are mentioned at all, remain more prominent than her contributions as a skilled negotiator within Franklin Delano Roosevelt's "kitchen cabinet." Her community development activities reinforce norms of Black motherhood within Black civil society, whereas her participation in the public sphere challenges views that such activities are best left to African-American men. Even the most radical Black women worthies may have trouble recognizing themselves within the Afrocentric canon. Despite Angela Davis's socialist-feminist, antiracist political analysis, reconfiguring her image as the essence of a 1960s-style "authentic" Black woman—signified by presenting Davis as wearing a large "natural" hairstyle—effectively recasts her complex political activism in terms of a more simplistic cultural nationalist framework. As Davis herself notes, "It is both humiliating and humbling to discover that a single generation after the events that constructed me as a public personality, I am remembered as a hairdo. It is humiliating because it reduces a politics of liberation to a politics of fashion" (1994, 37).

In response to the obvious exclusion of Black women in analyses of Black culture, some Afrocentric scholarship tries to present African-American women's experiences as equal and complementary to those of African-American men. Responding to earlier patterns of the exclusion and marginalization of African-American women, Black women scholars in particular aim to correct the Afrocentric record by highlighting Black women's activities in shaping Black culture and history. Although volumes such as *Women in Africa and the African Diaspora* (Terborg-Penn et al. 1987) foster Black women's visibility within Afrocentrism and work within the assumptions of complementarity, they disrupt gender ideology relegating Black women exclusively to home and family, because they highlight Black women's activities in Black civil society. In this volume exploring Black women's resistance in African, Caribbean, and African-American societies, several authors suggest that Black women's activities have not been confined to the so-called private or domestic sphere. Works such as this create conceptual space to investigate how African-American men and women both have been central to the creation and continuation of Black culture in the areas of religion, music, language, and families. This focus on Black women's complementary contributions to Black culture challenges views of Black culture as male-created and male-defined. For example, by demonstrating Black women's contributions to the creation and continuation of Black culture, Bernice Johnson Reagon's work on Black women as cultural workers (1987) deepens Afrocentric analyses of Black culture. Similarly, Niara Sudarkasa's reconceptualization of African women's gender activities (1981) provides a much needed perspective for understanding African-American women.

The outpouring of works by contemporary Black women writers in the United States can be seen as an initial corrective to the male bias in African-American literature. On the one hand, by focusing on different yet equally important themes permeating Black civil society, such writers illustrate complementarity and demonstrate solidarity with Black men (Tate 1983). For example, anthropologist and novelist Zora Neale Hurston writes of Black life and culture—contact with Whites does not figure into her greatest work, *Their Eyes Were Watching God* (1978). In contrast, Richard Wright, Hurston's contemporary, writes of interracial interaction, primarily among men. Hers is affirmation, his is protest. Both offer valid approaches to African-American experience, for Black affirmation and protest against White domination can be seen as complementary parts of the same process (Jordan 1981). Yet one has traditionally been elevated above the other as superior. Reclaiming the ideas of Hurston and other Black women writers redresses these long-standing imbalances.

On the other hand, African-American women writers' treatment of reproduction, sexuality, and motherhood definitely breaks with the Black cultural nationalist idealized gender ideology of men as warriors and women as nurturers. Black women writers' works are revealing on this point primarily because, unlike social scientists or historians, fiction writers encounter fewer requirements to depict reality and instead can explore its contested nature. For example, Alice Walker's fiction has long been criticized because, although it invokes traditional Black culture, it simultaneously refuses to valorize that culture's construction of gender. Like Walker, other African-American women writers increasingly eschew uniformly positive treatment of Black culture and instead situate themselves within the space created by Black nationalist discourse to rework some of the themes of that discourse (Dubey 1994).

Despite its appeal in reinforcing long-standing norms of racial solidarity, the hypothesis of gender complementarity can be applied only to selected topics. Far more attention has been paid to positing areas of Black women's equality with Black men in an imagined ancient African past than to exploring gender complementarity within either contemporary Black civil society in the United States or contemporary African societies. For example, in her popular and controversial volume *The Isis Papers: The Keys to the Colors* (1991), Frances Cress Welsing claims that the Black classical civilization of Kemet fostered a gender complementarity whereby women and men were essentially equal. Her argument suggests that prior to European-installed institutionalized racism, Africans in Kemet lived an idyllic life. Ransby and Matthews disagree, claiming that "the great African past which we are told we need to recreate is also a patriarchal past in which men and women knew their respective place. These unequal gender roles are then redefined euphemistically as 'complementary' rather than relationships of subordination and domination" (1993, 59). Historical settings of African antiquity appear to be more amenable to this type of reinterpretation than contemporary African-American civil society. This is because historical analyses of this nature cannot be easily disproved, and because applying similar arguments to contemporary conditions would generate a storm of protest. Reactions such as those of historian E. Frances White, who notes, "The ideology of complementarity and collective family continues to work against the liberation of black women" (1990, 75), would surely arise. Given these caveats, locating complementarity in the distant past represents a wise decision.

In responding to sustained Black feminist criticisms from Toni Cade Bambara (1970) through E. Frances White (1990), more recent Afrocentric scholarship acknowledges the significance of gender but relegates it as secondary to the more pressing cause of fighting racism. Working within the assumptions of gender complementarity, scholars such as Molefi Asante (1987; 1990), Linda Jane Myers (1988), and Haki Madhubuti (1990a; 1990b) acknowledge differences in male and female experiences but minimize the effects of gender oppression in the lives of both Black women and Black men. Lip service is paid to Black women, but gender as a major category of analysis can be ignored. For example, in *Kemet, Afrocentricity, and Knowledge*, widely acknowledged as a central text in contemporary Afrocentrism, Asante advises his readers to incorporate gender as a principal cosmological issue in Afrocentric inquiry. Afrocentric researchers must be cognizant of "sexist language, terminology, and perspectives," counsels Asante, and should investigate the "historic impact and achievement of women within the African community" (1990, 9). Asante further advises his readers to "examine the roles women have played in liberating Africans and others from oppression, resisting the imposition of sexist repression and subjugation, and exercising economic and political authority" (10). Asante's advice is especially odd, given that he makes little mention of gender in this volume despite his advice that it be taken seriously. Eschewing intersectional analyses of race, class, and gender, this approach assumes that only Black women are affected by gender, that Black women's political activism should be analyzed solely within the Black nationalist race as family framework, and that sexism is something that exists *outside* this racial family. As a result, gender has little explanatory power.

Including Black women worthies, incorporating material on Black women, and investigating Black women's experiences within assumptions of gender complementarity all expand the knowledge base about Black women. Given the sorry history of social-science scholarship on African-Americans in general and Black women in particular, Afrocentric efforts, however flawed, can serve a purpose. Unfortunately, however, these correctives typically fail to challenge how gender influences the domain assumptions of Afrocentrism concerning culture, identity, solidarity, and service. They reinforce notions of Black women as people who curiously escaped the effects of sexism. Within these constraints and in the absence of any sustained interest in intersectional analyses of race, class, and gender, certain dimensions of Black women's experiences in the United States cannot be adequately addressed. Reconceptualizations of rape, violence, and the overarching structure of sexual politics (Davis 1981; Hall 1983; hooks 1990); of Black women's political activism and resistance outside traditional family models (Gilkes 1983b, 1988, 1994; Terborg-Penn 1986); of the relationships between work and family for both Black women and Black men (Higginbotham 1983, 1994; Dill 1988a, 1988b); of reproductive rights issues such as access to family planning services, and Black women's rights of choice (Davis 1981); of homophobia and its impact on Black identity, families, and communities (Smith 1983; Lorde 1984); and of the ways race, class, and gender interlock in framing Black women's poverty (Brewer 1988; Omolade 1994) are all topics currently explored in Black feminist thought that are routinely neglected by those working exclusively within Afrocentric domain assumptions.

Despite its contributions, Afrocentrism as critical social theory remains unable to address the inherently problematic stance toward gender that plagued the Black Arts movement. The Black Arts movement did contain the seeds for a quite different gender ideology. For example, the first groundbreaking book of contemporary Black feminist theory, Toni Cade Bambara's edited volume *The Black Woman*, published in 1970, contains several essays by Black women whose feminist ideology developed in large part within the context of Black nationalist struggle. Despite this resource, Afrocentric scholarship conveniently ignores these Black feminist analyses, choosing instead to incorporate a conservative gender analysis. Moreover, because the Black Arts movement catalyzed not only Afrocentrism but also a Black feminist movement in the 1970s and 1980s (Dubey 1994), the failure of Afrocentrism to examine its own gendered ideology represents a profound missed opportunity. Unfortunately, as a discourse following both the Black cultural nationalism of the 1960s and 1970s and Black feminist analyses of the 1970s and 1980s, contemporary Afrocentrism seems to have taken only one to heart.

How Oppositional Is Afrocentrism?

On the surface, developing Afrocentrism as critical social theory appears to be relatively straightforward. Afrocentric thinkers should simply identify the most problematic elements of established scholarship on race, criticize these components, and construct alternatives to them. However, this uncomplicated, reactive posture generates additional problems. As African-American writer James Baldwin once observed, "You cannot escape the pathology of a country in which you're born. You can resist it, you can react to it, you can do all kinds of things, but you're trapped in it" (Baldwin and Mead 1971, 24). In the case of Afrocentrism, merely reacting duplicates the binary thinking that divides social reality into White oppressors and Black oppressed. Presenting only two groups distorts both groups' experiences and fails to recognize how the two categories gain meaning from one another.

Notions of White oppressors and Black oppressed also rely on the same gender ideology. Feminist critiques remind us that Afrocentrism confronts a positivist science that is not just overtly racist but deeply sexist as well (Keller 1985; Hubbard 1990; Fausto-Sterling 1992; Harding 1986, 1991). Despite its trenchant critique of scientific racism, Afrocentrism turns a blind eye toward the sexist bias of that same science. Afrocentrism may "resist" and "react" to the premises of racial scholarship, yet it remains "trapped" in its premises concerning gender. Thus, although Afrocentrism assumes a "fighting words" posture in response to institutionalized racism, on a deeper level the nature of its critique inadvertently supports the intellectual frameworks that legitimate hierarchical power relations.

In the context of scientific racism, the very existence of Afrocentrism as an avowedly antiracist project speaks to its oppositional intent. Because the guiding principles of Afrocentrism have been formed largely within the domain assumptions of a science it opposes, it remains limited as critical social theory, as its treatment of gender illustrates. Since the predominantly male practitioners of Afrocentrism experience Western science as "fighting words," in response they generate "fighting words" of their own. Without grounding their analyses in more complex notions of culture and society that deconstruct all binary thinking, Afrocentric countermyths can reinforce the very categories they aim to oppose. For example, reclassifying Kemet as "Black" does little to challenge the cognitive frameworks that juxtapose civilization to primitivism (White 1987). Reversing the value attached to the color symbolism legitimated by scientific racism leaves the system itself intact—only the colors of the players have changed.

Unfortunately, for African-Americans in search of antiracist critical social theory grounded in lived Black experience, Black nationalist projects such as Afrocentrism often appear to be the only game in town. Afrocentrism seems increasingly effective in attracting those segments of Black civil society who, for a variety of reasons, see little hope that racial integration can solve economic and social injustices. Given the racial polarization in the United States, Afrocentric reliance on Black essentialism may not be as misplaced as a *political* strategy as some Black public intellectuals believe. Afrocentric discourse that treats Blackness as a free-floating, ahistorical essence expressed differently at different historical moments provides continuity with the past and gives members of communities so constructed an identity and purpose that provide guidance for the future. In this sense, criticisms that Afrocentrism remains riddled with troublesome essentialist thinking that harms both women and men, especially when advanced by Black intellectuals who have minimal current contact with racial segregation, typically fall on deaf ears. Despite the limitations of Afrocentrism as critical social theory, its strong pro-Black posture, combined with its masculinist thrust, contributes to its popularity among many African-Americans. The Nation of Islam, a competing Black nationalist project, has long recognized the effectiveness of us/them binary thinking as a strategy for mobilizing African-Americans. Few of the estimated eight hundred thousand Black men and their female supporters who attended the 1995 Million Man March in Washington, D.C., expressed concern about Black essentialism and its purported suppression of differences among Black people. They were there in a show of unity. If Black academics in the United States tried to organize a rally of that magnitude, how many African-Americans would attend? Moreover, in a climate in which hate speech escalates and racial violence targeted toward African-Americans gains strength from the resurgence of scientific racism resurrected by the far right, essentialist thinking continues to enjoy widespread success at mobilizing large numbers of Whites in defense of White privilege. In a situation in which, for example, thirty-two southern Black churches in the United States experienced arson fires in an eighteen-month period preceding the 1996 presidential campaign, Black essentialism may be the best defense against White essentialism. While intellectuals in academia deconstruct everything, including their own leftist politics, little remains on which to construct a new politics capable of responding to unemployment, police brutality, teen violence, adolescent childbearing, AIDS, and other social issues of pressing concern to African-Americans.

Black people in the United States need critical social theory that provides leadership and hope in the face of these troublesome conditions. In this sense, the distinctive and fundamental contribution of Afrocentrism may be one that, as of yet, other theories cannot match. Philosopher Cornel West suggests that nihilism, or the feeling that life has no meaning, constitutes a new, fundamental threat to African-American existence: "Nihilism is not overcome by arguments or analysis; it is tamed by love and care. Any disease of the soul must be conquered by a turning of one's soul. This turning is done by one's own affirmation of one's worth—an affirmation fueled by the concern of others. This is why a love ethic must be at the center of a politics of conversion" (1993, 19). West may have touched upon why, despite its problematic treatment of gender, economic class, and sexuality, Afrocentrism remains important to both Black men and Black women. In a climate of institutionalized racism that valorizes Whiteness, Afrocentrism offers an affirmation of Blackness, a love ethic directed toward Black people. In this sense, it reaches out to everyday African-American women and men in ways lost to even the best antiracist, feminist, Marxist, or postmodern academic social theories. Whereas sociology provides knowledge and postmodernism stresses tools of critique, Afrocentrism offers hope.

Despite this essential contribution, the fighting words of Afrocentrism appear increasingly ineffective in both changing the academy and guiding Black political activism. Exclusivity in the name of nation building eventually fails. Fear of dissent undermines the creativity that must lie at the heart of truthful, sustained, and meaningful struggle. An Afrocentrism that remains analytically self-critical of its own ideas, practices, and practitioners could seriously engage questions of gender, economic class, nation, and sexuality. By situating itself in dynamic versus essentialist definitions of Black culture, such a revitalized Afrocentrism might manage to craft an elusive racial solidarity simultaneously sensitive to Black heterogeneity and difference and prepared to engage in principled coalitions. Until that day, domination is domination, no matter who is doing it. Any critical social theory that counsels African-American women or any other group to be silent and step back in the name of an ill-defined unity hurts Black women, cheats African-American communities of the best talent and leadership, and ultimately impoverishes us all.

Part III

Toward Justice

Moving beyond Critique

As a child growing up in an African-American, working-class Philadelphia neighborhood, I wondered how my mother and all of the other women on our block kept going. Early each workday, they rode long distances on public transportation to jobs that left them unfulfilled, overworked, and underpaid. Periodically they complained, but more often they counseled practicality and persistence. Stressing the importance of a good education as the route to a better life, they recognized that even if Black girls married, big houses, maids, and blended family bliss as idealized on the popular television show *The Brady Bunch* were not guaranteed for us. Their solution: we, their daughters, were to become self-reliant and independent.

Despite their practicality, these same Black women also held out hope that things would be better for us. They vigorously advised that we'd better be ready *when* (not if) the door of racial segregation opened and opportunities became available to us. Despite troubles in their own love relationships, they encouraged us to hold out for a "good man." "Keep your eyes on the prize," they exhorted, whether the prize was a desegregated society or loving sexual relationships. They always encouraged us to dream.

Looking back, I am struck by how many of the prizes that the women on my block urged us to imagine were clearly visionary in the context of their lives. Ever pragmatic about their everyday struggles to pay the mortgage, pacify the boss, and keep children in line, these women simultaneously envisioned the unrealized possibilities for themselves and their loved ones. How did they manage to prepare us for lives that none of them had ever lived?

The Black women on my block possessed a "visionary pragmatism" that emphasized the necessity of linking caring, theoretical vision with informed, practical struggle (James and Busia 1994). A creative tension links visionary thinking and pragmatic action. Any social theory that becomes too out of touch with everyday people and their lives, especially oppressed people, is of little use to them. The functionality and not just the logical consistency of visionary thinking determines its worth. At the same time, being too practical, looking only to the here and now—especially if present conditions seemingly offer little hope—can be debilitating. As Black feminist anthropologist and former college president Johnetta Cole observes, "While it is true that without a vision the people perish, it is doubly true that without action the people and their vision perish as well" (1993, 75). Maintaining a balance between these seeming opposites is required.

Traditionally organized as "grand narratives," most critical social theories have been characterized by linear thinking—they have points of origin, straight-line conceptions of time, overt or covert prescriptions concerning how to better the world, and imagined, utopic end points. For example, positivist science rejects its twin predecessors medieval science and religion by arguing that the logic and empiricism of the scientific method will bring order to the perceived chaos of the world. Responding to the exploitation characterizing the global capitalism that housed such science, Marxist social theory identifies class struggle as the engine of social change and envisions a socialist utopia as the end point of capitalist exploitation. Identifying imperialism as the problem, Pan-Africanism promises a Black utopia to those who join in Black consciousness movements dedicated to liberating the African motherland and reestablishing a long lost Black homeland. Emerging primarily from the imaginations of the theorists themselves, theories such as these create predetermined definitions of freedom as the logical end points of natural evolution or human struggle. When these linear models fail to deliver, their visions of freedom seem increasingly unattainable and often irrelevant. Lacking tangible results, straight-line visionary thinking can be easily dismissed. Even as they move people to action, linear visions ironically disempower their followers when the utopic end of the line fails to materialize. Why try to work for something that one knows can never happen?

Critical social theories that completely reject visionary thinking can err in the other direction. Social engineering projects that tinker with poverty, homelessness, institutionalized racism, illiteracy, domestic violence, and other social problems through incremental reforms represent technical Band-Aids slapped on historically entrenched, systemic social problems. In the United States, American citizens clamor for recipes, rules, and quick-fix solutions that give the illusion, if not actual evidence, that things are getting better. When short-term solutions fail, apathy and cynicism flourish. Events such as the Los Angeles rebellion of 1992 and the significant differences in African-American and White American perceptions of the 1995 O. J. Simpson murder acquittal both signal an increasing and often frightening racial polarization in the United States. Decreasing support for public institutions of all sorts reflects a growing disillusionment that things will ever change. This climate of public apathy simultaneously fosters and reflects critical social theories that eschew visionary thinking and moral absolutes. Ironically, such theories may have unintended opposite effects. Postmodernism as practiced within some academic disciplines provides a compelling case of a discourse that counsels local, pragmatic action as a stimulus for change but whose actual politics undermines its own critical edge. Deconstruction often runs in circles, with all efforts leading back to where one started. Without some larger vision, continual deconstruction that looks at the specific, the concrete, the everyday can foster a nihilism as crippling as that accompanying the death of utopic visions. Moreover, because deconstruction often targets science, Afrocentrism, Marxism, and other linear narratives that provide utopic visions, it destroys hope without constructing any alternatives. As Edward Said observes, "There is nothing to look forward to: we are stuck within our circle. And now the line is enclosed by a circle" (1993, 27).

Black women's visionary pragmatism may offer one way to sidestep Said's gloomy impasse of the line of linear thinking enclosed by a deconstructive circle. The notion of visionary pragmatism more closely approximates a creative tension symbolized by an ongoing journey. Arriving at some predetermined destination remains less important than struggling for some ethical end. Thus, although Black women's visionary pragmatism points to a vision, it doesn't prescribe a fixed end point of a universal truth. One never arrives but constantly strives. At the same time, by stressing the pragmatic, it reveals how current actions are part of some larger, more meaningful struggle. Domination succeeds by cutting people off from one another. Actions bring people in touch with the humanity of other struggles by demonstrating that truthful and ethical visions for community cannot be separated from pragmatic struggles on their behalf.

Sadly, both my childhood neighborhood and the version of visionary pragmatism expressed by its African-American female residents no longer exist. The curious combination of fixity and change that characterizes neighborhoods such as mine gives meaning to the phrase "the more things change, the more they stay the same." Since 1970, the quality of life in Black working-class communities like the one I grew up in has changed dramatically in the United States. Four back-to-back recessions in the 1970s, coupled with a new politics of containment in the 1980s and 1990s, have effectively eroded or eliminated the quality public education, job opportunities, and social services that working-class and poor children need to become productive adults. Unlike my Boston second graders, or the eighth-grade girls in my first class on Black women, or even me as a child, today's working-class and poor African-American children grow to adulthood in communities increasingly plagued by drugs, violence, substandard housing, underfunded schools, AIDS, and a constellation of heartbreaking social problems. Not only do many of these children fail to dream, many don't expect to live to adulthood. They are not alone, for their experiences resemble those of far too many White children and other children of color in the United States, as well as poor children living in far less affluent nation-states. If I were attending my former Philadelphia high school today, the least of my worries would be fixing the curriculum to be more inclusive of African-American women's experiences. Some days, the ironies that I confront regularly seem overwhelming. While my academic colleagues and I wax on about the relative merits of sociology, postmodernism, and Afrocentrism, far too many children continue to suffer and die.

What contributions can critical social theory in general, and Black feminist thought in particular, make to addressing realities of this magnitude? As the new politics of containment indicate, social conditions confronting oppressed groups change, often in quite unexpected ways.

Who could have anticipated how deeply the combination of racial desegregation and drugs, violence, and hopelessness in poor African-American neighborhoods would tear the very fabric of Black civil society? Who could have predicted that the texts of Toni Morrison, Alice Walker, and other prominent African-American women thinkers would be commodified, circulated, and often celebrated in institutions of higher education while African-American enrollment drops in those same institutions? Who could have anticipated that the emerging self-defined voices of Black women acting as agents of knowledge would be dismissed as essentialist, thus fostering a double silencing? Now that Black women's community work seems increasingly ineffective, what will replace it?

Despite these challenges, the fundamental question raised by the Black women on my block remains: how can scholars and/or activists construct critical social theories that prepare future generations for lives that we ourselves have not lived? Black women's visionary pragmatism certainly did this for me and, I suspect, for many other African-American women. Given this tradition, what insights can Black feminist thought gain from its foundation in Black women's praxis?

Moving beyond Critique

The myriad responses to one simple question that my students have routinely asked over my years of teaching tell me much about them. "How will I know when I've sold out?" someone asks, or, in its more generic form, "Is buying in selling out?"

Some of my students are confused by the question itself. They simply don't understand it because they never think to question the terms of their own participation in hierarchical power relations. In order to learn, they must keep the intellectual, the personal, and the political sharply compartmentalized, even if it means living with heartbreaking contradictions. They are afraid to think, to feel, and to try. Holding fast to the belief that knowledge and power are two entirely separate things, these students refuse to relinquish views of themselves as blameless consumers of knowledge conceptualized as ahistorical, timeless truth. The irony is that in maintaining these distinctions, they deny part of themselves. Although most are privileged by one or more systems of race, gender, economic class, nationality, and sexuality, most are simultaneously disadvantaged in some fashion by these same systems.

Others claim that they'll never sell out. Exhibiting a striking absence of self-reflection, they're really quick to tell me what's wrong with everyone else. All sorts of variations of these types of thinkers exist. Doctrinaire Marxists who revel in recounting the last union struggle, old-guard academics who see themselves protecting "standards of excellence" from the likes of people like me, radical lesbian feminists who brand their sisters who sleep with men as politically backward, kente-cloth-garbed Afrocentrists who take the phrase "stuck in the sixties" to an entirely new level, even those few Black women intellectuals who see their feminism as superior to everyone else's—all qualify. Anointing themselves as the chosen ones who own the correct knowledge, these people simultaneously uphold and are blinded by the banner of their self-proclaimed perfection.

Still others understand the question but remain uncertain as to where they fit in. Many students who are privileged within hierarchical power relations come to see the harm done by institutionalized racism, sexism, class exploitation, and other forms of oppression. Dominant ideologies trumpeting the inherent superiority of maleness, Whiteness, heterosexuality, wealth, Christianity, and the "American way of life" no longer ring true for them, if they ever did. "Everyone can make it in America if they just work hard enough," "the system is basically fair," "anyone who is poor deserves it," "if they don't like America the way it is, they can just leave it," and other everyday platitudes sound hollow. Those who sense these contradictions between ideologies that explain injustices and the ways oppression operates do so from varying sites of privilege. Regarding race, for example, many African-American students face the constant reminder "don't forget your roots." The pull of group traditions grounded in racial solidarity tells them that although they as individuals may be doing well, far too many group members are not. Despite such traditions urging them not to "sell out" by becoming useless for Black political struggle, attending school as successful students is itself an endorsement of "buying in." White students confront a different dilemma. Unquestioned buying in is the cost of their success. Students who recognize their participation in multiple sites of privilege may risk being labeled "race traitors." In a context of institutionalized racism, selling out means rejecting White privilege. Students who are differentially privileged by hierarchies of gender, economic class, sexuality, and citizenship status face similar issues. They certainly don't want to collude with injustice, but they remain uncertain as to how to use their privilege, however tenuous, for different ends.

Essentially, "Is buying in selling out?" asks, what standards should be used to assess everyday behavior in a context of injustice? What rules should be followed, what criteria should be applied to determine whether the individual's actions constitute—to put it crudely—part of the problem or part of the solution? The answer is simple yet profoundly complex. Because each action must be evaluated in its own particular context, none is inherently a sellout. That's the simple part. The complexity lies in the question itself. To me, selling out is defined by *forgetting to ask the question at all*. Stated differently, losing self-reflexivity represents a sure sign that one is beginning to sell out.

A similar set of criteria can be applied to critical social theory. How will we determine whether a critical social theory increasingly supports social injustice rather than challenging it? In approaching this question, appearances can deceive. Some social theories concern themselves with seemingly progressive content—they study oppression and the like—while their own politics replicate hierarchy. Similarly, other social theories may make scant mention of anything deemed political yet make a difference in the everyday lived experiences of large numbers of people. Is the former progressive because its content is oppression? Is the latter reactionary because it makes no mention of Black women? Answering these questions certainly requires that critical social theory remain cognizant of the terms of its own participation in actual hierarchical power relations. This raises additional questions. Does critical social theory that is attentive to power require different epistemological standards? How do we assess critical social theories that concern themselves not only with hierarchical power relations as a subject of study but also with their own participation in those power relations? If we forget to ask about power relations, how can we know that a given critical social theory has not sold out?

The sociology of knowledge provides a useful conceptual framework for thinking through these questions (Merton 1973). In particular, standpoint theory offers especially rich insights for analyzing the intellectual and political terrain in which Black feminist thought operates. Standpoint theory posits a distinctive relationship among a group's position in hierarchical power relations, the experiences attached to differential group positionality, and the standpoint that a group constructs in interpreting these experiences (Hartsock 1983; Harding 1986). In part II, I analyzed selected bodies of knowledge by treating them as standpoints emerging from and expressing the worldviews of specific communities of practitioners for which Black women somehow decenter assumptions of the discourse. For example, the analysis of sociology in chapter 3 claims that privileged knowledges developed through exclusionary practices produce distorted sociological truths. The emphasis on how Black women approached sociology within and in opposition to this privileged standpoint speaks to the question of what happens when differences in standpoint collide within one interpretive community. To demonstrate how what appears to be progressive can operate as a privileged, commodified knowledge for its group of practitioners, the treatment of postmodernism in chapter 4 contextualizes knowledge within hierarchical power relations. It examines how intellectuals from dominant groups resemble "colonizers who refuse," experiencing an increasingly desegregated world. It explores how this group increasingly appropriates the language (of "centers," "margins," and "difference") associated with other groups' standpoints while rejecting the actual politics associated with those standpoints. In chapter 5, the treatment of the flawed gender analysis within contemporary Afrocentrism investigates what happens when standpoints of oppressed groups incorporate some of the guiding principles of discourses that they oppose. In all three cases, I treat the ideas of sociology, postmodernism, and Afrocentrism as standpoints advanced by specific groups of people, while using ideas and techniques gained from these same areas to conduct my analysis.

Thus far in *Fighting Words*, I have emphasized critique by keeping elements from these and other social theories in play. However, one can neither "play at" things nor keep them "in play" forever. At some point, we must each take a stand and be very clear about where we stand. Although I like to think that much of *Fighting Words* is innovative or, failing that, minimally interesting, remaining in a stance of critique leaves one perpetually responding to the terms of someone else's agenda. Although critique remains valuable, without moving to the next of step—taking a stand by constructing new knowledge—critique can become a predictable and decreasingly effective strategy. As the limitations of the Afrocentric fighting words stance suggests, constructing oppositional knowledge solely around an axis of critique is effective only up to a point. The next step lies in moving beyond critique and crafting something new.

Despite the risks associated with this step, in part III, "Toward Justice," I aim to move beyond critique in order to take a more proactive stance toward knowledge. By exploring how standpoint theory remains relevant for Black feminist thought, chapter 6, "Some Group Matters: Intersectionality, Situated Standpoints, and Black Feminist Thought," initiates this process of moving beyond critique. Since standpoint theory is closely aligned with group-based strategies long useful for resisting racial and/or economic class segregation, rethinking the question how social groups are actually constituted in the United States seems relevant for considering any group consciousness they might exhibit. In this chapter I explore a variety of themes germane to the oppositionality of standpoint theory, namely, the significance of distinctions between individual- and group-level phenomena for any analyses of standpoint theory; the possible contributions of intersectionality as a heuristic device for conceptualizing social groups and their ensuing knowledges; the ways in which Black women's lived experiences in the United States shed new light on groups organized through intersections of race, economic class, and gender; and the ways in which more complex notions of group composition emerging from intersectional analyses might generate equally complex group standpoints. Turning a lens of self-reflexivity on standpoint theory, chapter 6 provides a preliminary synthesis of ideas developed elsewhere in *Fighting Words*.

Although I rely heavily on standpoint theory in *Fighting Words*, this means neither that I consider myself a "standpoint theorist" (whatever that means to those who might characterize my work in this fashion) nor that I unilaterally dismiss other social theories as less valuable. To me, all social theories have something to offer. For example, sociology, postmodernism, and Afrocentrism all remain useful in assessing whether a critical social theory has sold out. Through its attention to social structures, sociology serves as an important corrective to the current emphasis on individualism. Sociology provides a language for talking about social structure. Similarly, postmodernism provides important intellectual tools for examining cultural products as texts. Because reading is always active and dynamic, the professed (albeit rarely achieved) commitment of postmodernism to decentering power and deconstructing narratives that support such power provides a series of tools that keep everything moving. The commitment of Afrocentrism to Black people introduces the question of what the potential and actual effects of ideas on people are and how central considerations of these types of connections should be to evaluating critical social theory.

I think that some theories work better for certain concerns than others and that the challenge lies in appropriately deploying multiple social theories for the task at hand. Social scientists routinely see the connections between the types of questions asked and the need to match appropriate research methodologies to those questions. A similar process might guide the use of social theory wherein different social theories lend themselves better to some questions than others. Within this logic, one criticizes a theory from within the boundaries of what it sets out to do. From these multiple critiques comes the potential for constructing something new from the strategic use of multiple social theories. Moreover, using social theories in this fashion requires a continual critique not only of the theories themselves but also of one's practice. Constructing new knowledge requires taking these types of risks. Critics who hide behind their critiques of others' work or, worse yet, build careers solely based on their ability to criticize others really should question their own practice. How safe it must feel to be able to criticize or "play at" critique without taking responsibility for outcomes. Knowledge for its own sake, without the accountability to have one's work make a difference to anyone, must be nice. However, as difficult as it is to do, I think it remains vital never to forget the value of self-reflexivity. In postmodern terms, deconstructing one's own practice remains essential.

The View from Here: Constructing Epistemology

Given my expressed objective to explore epistemological criteria for critical social theory produced by and in defense of oppressed groups, *Fighting Words* has thus far made little mention of epistemology. Current epistemological criteria for critical social theory seem especially preoccupied with questions of truth. Whether we're talking about the defenders of positivist science who claim that one truth can be determined if we all agree on responsible ways to go about it, or their postmodern critics who argue for multiple truths that take context into account, academic approaches to critical social theory typically stress the search for truth as fundamental. However, conceptualizing critical social theory as the search for truth(s) already posits a separation between knowledge and power that may be more imagined than real. Despite their commitment to truth, many of the truths produced by anthropology, biology, sociology, political science, history, and other academic disciplines manufactured consent for colonialism, imperialism, slavery, and apartheid. As the critiques of these truths demonstrate, entire populations were deemed objects of knowledge, with their experiences repackaged into forms useful for domination and rule.

Claims that exploring truth(s) should be the primary purpose of critical social theory also limit epistemological options. Emphasizing truth confines one either to a singular, modernist Truth or to multiple postmodern truths that far too often seem locked in combat with one another in yet another example of binary thinking. Certainly, investigating the criteria for the truth of a given critical social theory remains important. However, from the perspective of oppressed groups, this emphasis on truth is too limited, because it overshadows other potentially significant criteria for evaluating critical social theories of all types.

Take, for example, the significance of power relations in determining truth(s). In *Fighting Words,* I explicitly weave issues of context throughout the entire volume. In particular, my repeated contextualization of a range of theories within particular hierarchical power relations is designed to demonstrate that what constitutes truth changes markedly when context is taken into account. Like other critical social theories, Black feminist thought faces the question of remaining oppositional in changing power relations. I suggest that it do so by broadening the epistemological criteria it uses in evaluating its own practice. Because content changes, I am less concerned with the actual content of the thought—I remain awed at how quickly interpretations of "coming to voice" shifted in the 1980s and how media assaults narrowed the meaning of the term *Afrocentrism* in the 1990s. Instead, I read social theory in relation to the specific historical conditions in which it emerges. I think it is important to identify how critical social theory remains dynamic in changing conditions. Since an inherent danger exists in critical social theory "becoming institutionalized, marginality turning into separatism, and resistance hardening into dogma" (Said 1993, 54), self-reflexivity via self-criticism seems crucial.

Thus, a fundamental goal for critical social theory consists of broadening its epistemological criteria beyond truth to develop the self-reflexivity to keep its practice oppositional.

Toward this end, chapter 7, "Searching for Sojourner Truth: Toward an Epistemology of Empowerment," explores contributions that Black feminist thought can make to critical social theory. In particular, it examines how contemporary Black feminist thought might build upon the notion of visionary pragmatism as a conceptual framework for its own praxis. Three interdependent questions weave throughout the chapter that collectively suggest a greatly expanded definition of epistemological criteria for critical social theory.

First, does this social theory speak the truth to people about the reality of their lives? Patterns of whose knowledge counts, whose is discredited, and which standards are used to determine the difference encompass much more than logical consistency or empirical verification, the hallmarks of traditional epistemology. Because reason and truth have so long been coded as White and male, it is difficult to accept truths that come from new sources. As is illustrated by Black women's treatment as objects of knowledge, arguments about empirical verification and logical consistency often turn out to be about much more than truth. Even postmodern attacks upon reason as the linchpin of Western civilization rely on reason in constructing their arguments. This shift away from traditional epistemology raises a series of questions about what was formerly taken for granted. Who are the "experts"? Why do we believe what these experts say? Who decides what counts as knowledge? In this sense, critical social theory requires new mechanisms of validating truth that contextualizes truth(s) in power relations.

A second question for critical social theory concerns its stance toward freedom—its vision of emancipation as well as the pragmatic strategies it suggests. Does this social theory equip people to resist oppression? Is this social theory functional as a tool for social change? All social theories, whether critical or not, have an explicit or implicit theory of freedom and resistance embedded in them. Freedom constitutes, in one sense, the inverse of oppression. However, the content and approach to resistance differ markedly. For example, the fighting words stance of Afrocentrism, coupled with its emphases on reclaiming Black culture and constructing an authentic Black identity as prerequisites for Black political action, valorizes consciousness in theorizing political resistance. In this critical social theory, ideas precede actions to such a degree that action often never happens. At the same time, Afrocentrism owes much of its focus to standpoint theory and to the type of identity politics attached to raising consciousness in order to facilitate political action. Yet versions of identity politics that harden into essentialist dogma also frame a particular type of political action. Even social theories that seemingly eschew politics of all sorts implicitly contain a theory of emancipation. Positivist science preaches reformism through gathering data, thinking through logical options, testing new approaches, and then instituting large-scale changes when testing is complete. This incremental approach to social change differs markedly from other approaches grounded in conflict. Questioning how a social theory empowers people to resist oppression thus evaluates the adequacy of that theory of resistance.

Finally, does this critical social theory move people to struggle? For oppressed groups, this question concerns how effectively critical social theory provides moral authority to struggles for self-definition and self-determination. The necessity of an ethical foundation as the vision for a critical social theory such as Black feminist thought becomes increasingly important in an era when power relations are being so dramatically reformulated. As French theorist Michel Foucault notes, "The ideal point of penalty today would be an indefinite discipline: an interrogation without end, an investigation that would be extended without limit to a meticulous and ever more analytical observation, . . . a file that was never closed" (1979, 227). Turning Foucault's "interrogation without end" on its head generates freedom struggles "without end" *against* such disciplinary power. The search for justice as an ongoing, principled struggle resists disciplinary power relations and gives meaning to everyday life.

Because the search for justice has been central in African-American women's history, I emphasize an ethical framework grounded in notions of justice as specific cultural material for exploring this more general question of moral authority for struggle. This emphasis on how the search for justice grants moral authority to Black women's freedom struggles sheds light on the difference between doctrine and faith. In the same way that some view social theory as unchanging systems of rules to be applied uniformly to all social phenomena, doctrines constitute fixed and timeless systems of beliefs to be followed blindly. In contrast, faith constitutes a *process* whereby individuals and groups use an ethical framework grounded in deeply felt beliefs to construct meaningful everyday lives. In other words, the difference lies in distinguishing between theory as a dogma or closed system of ideas to be verified and tested, and theory as a story or narrative operating as an open system of ideas that can be retold and reformulated. How Bible stories are used illustrates this process: Everyone knows and shares the same story. However, the changing collectivity constructing such stories—new interpretations, listeners, tellers, and the context itself—changes the meaning of the story with each retelling. Moreover, congregations are moved to struggle by their moral, ethical principles. Deep caring characterizes this type of struggle. Whereas doctrines can become discredited, faith persists.

Writing *Fighting Words* has given me a better sense of not only how the women on my block kept going but why they were able to do so. Certainly their visionary pragmatism was shaped by a commitment to truth, a belief in freedom, a concern for justice, and other ethical ideals. They clearly had an arsenal of pragmatic skills that helped them deal with difficult situations. However, I think that their ability to persist was rooted in a deep love for us. Theirs was not the individualized, sexualized, private, romantic love currently commodified and marketed by American media, but rather a proclaimed, actively struggled-for, passionate love ethic. In a society in which little Black children are written off to this day, they loved us when no one else did and as no one else could. I want to be clear—I am not glorifying mother love as some sort of natural, instinctual female condition. Rather, I talk of the power of intense connectedness and of the way that caring deeply for someone can foster a revolutionary politics. When informed by truths, armed with tools of resistance, and moved by faith in justice, proclaimed love that struggles without end can make a profound difference.

Six

Some Group Matters: Intersectionality, Situated Standpoints, and Black Feminist Thought

In developing a Black feminist praxis, standpoint theory has provided one important source of analytical guidance and intellectual legitimation for African-American women.[1] Standpoint theory argues that group location in hierarchical power relations produces shared challenges for individuals in those groups. These common challenges can foster similar angles of vision leading to a group knowledge or standpoint that in turn can influence the group's political action. Stated differently, group standpoints are situated in unjust power relations, reflect those power relations, and help shape them.

I suspect that one reason that the ideas of standpoint theory (in contrast to the vocabulary deployed by standpoint theorists, including the term *standpoint theory* itself) resonate with African-American women's experiences lies in the resemblance of standpoint theory to the norm of racial solidarity. Created in response to institutionalized racism and associated with Black nationalist responses to such oppression (see, e.g., Franklin 1992; Van Deburg 1992), racial solidarity within Black civil society requires that African-Americans stick together at all costs. The civil rights and Black Power movements certainly demonstrated the effectiveness of Black politics grounded in racial solidarity. In the former, racial solidarity among African-Americans lay at the center of a multiracial civil rights effort. In the latter, racial solidarity was expressed primarily through all-Black organizations. Collectively, these movements delivered tangible political and economic gains for African-Americans as a group (but not for all members within the group). Differences could be expressed *within* the boundaries of Blackness but not *across* those same boundaries. In this sense, the notion of a Black women's standpoint gains meaning in the context of a shared Black consciousness dedicated to sustaining racial solidarity. Notions of racial solidarity and a shared Black women's standpoint both invoke explicitly political objectives. Just as adhering to racial solidarity was important for Black emancipation in the United States, so might a collective Black women's standpoint be seen as essential for Black feminist praxis. Since Black women, like African-Americans overall, are oppressed as a group, collective as compared to individualized strategies remain important.

Much has happened since the 1970s. Depending on their placement in hierarchies of age, gender, economic class, region of the country, and sexuality, African-American women encounter new challenges associated with the new politics of containment in the United States. These changes require fresh ideas that analyze the complexities of contemporary lived Black experience and suggest adequate political responses to them. The intellectual climate currently housing Black feminist thought has also changed. In academic contexts influenced by postmodern rubrics of decentering, deconstruction, and difference, the norm of racial solidarity itself has come under increasing attack. Within Black cultural studies in particular, critiques now stress how racial solidarity has far too often been constructed on the bedrock of racial authenticity and essentialism (see, e.g., Dyson 1993; West 1993; and chapter 5 of this book), leading some to emphasize the pitfalls of unquestioned racial solidarity for African-American women (Grant 1982; Terrelonge 1984; Richie 1996). Academic feminism in North America takes aim at similar targets. Whereas Black academics question the utility of racial solidarity in addressing social issues of lived Black experience, feminist theorists increasingly criticize standpoint theory on theoretical grounds (Hekman 1997). Collectively, many Black and/or feminist academics question the assumptions that underlie solidarities of all sorts. This has great implication for Black feminist praxis generally, and a Black women's standpoint situated in unjust power relations in particular.

Given these shifting patterns, the situated standpoints that Black women collectively construct, and even the question of whether African-American women self-define as a group, become vitally important. In historical contexts in which racial segregation more visibly organized geographic, symbolic, and political space assigned to African-Americans, the links between a group's common positionality in power relations, the shared experiences that accompanied this commonality, the mechanisms for constructing group standpoints, and the significance of group standpoints for political activism were fairly straightforward. Under the changed conditions that accompany the new politics of containment, however, these links are neither clear nor assumed. Despite the historical significance of the ideas of standpoint theory to African-American women, questions remain concerning the efficacy of group-based identities of this sort for contemporary political struggles. In situations in which increasingly sophisticated practices, such as controlling populations through constant surveillance (Foucault 1979), as well as strategies of everyday racism (Essed 1991) and symbolic racism (Jhally and Lewis 1992), obscure the continued effects of institutionalized injustices of all sorts, political theories that seem to advocate pulling together and storming the factory gates can seem simplistic. Moreover, the decreasing effectiveness of an identity politics currently associated with standpoint theory raises questions of its continued relevance (see chapter 2). Are group-based identities that emerge from standpoint theory and the politics they generate still empowering for African-American women? Do group-based identities such as those advocated by standpoint theory ultimately disempower African-American women because they unduly suppress differences and heterogeneity among Black women? Quite simply, in what ways, if any, does standpoint theory remain relevant for Black feminist thought?

Intersectionality and Social Groups

Since standpoint theory remains predicated on the notion of a group with shared experiences and interests, addressing these questions requires revisiting the connections between African-American women's identities as individuals and Black women's historically constituted group identity. Individuals can assemble associations by coming together as already formed persons. African-American women who join sororities come as individuals and participate as voluntary members.

In contrast, a historically constituted group identity is neither fleeting nor chosen. As Iris Marion Young points out, "One *finds oneself* as a member of a group, which one experiences as always already having been" (1990, 46; emphasis in original). For example, for the vast majority of the population in the United States, race creates immutable group identities. Individuals cannot simply opt in or out of racial groups, because race is constructed by assigning bodies meaningful racial classifications. Gender marks the body in a similar fashion.[2] Within the framework provided by their historically constituted group identity, individuals take up and perform their classification in diverse ways. African-American women, for example, all encounter some variation of what is expected of them as "Black women." How individual Black women construct their identities within these externally defined boundaries varies tremendously. However, it also occurs in response to the shared challenges that all Black women encounter.

Within unjust power relations, groups remain unequal in the powers of self-definition and self-determination. Race, class, gender, and other markers of power intersect to produce social institutions that, in turn, construct groups that become defined by these characteristics. Since some groups define and rule others, groups are hierarchically related to one another. Within this overarching hierarchical structure, the ways in which individuals find themselves to be members of groups in group-based power relations matters. In some cases, individuals may be aware that their classification in a particular group matters, but they have little contact with other group members or believe that group membership is not important in everyday lived experience. Other groups have clearly defined histories, traditions, and patterned forms of behavior dedicated to ensuring that individual members "find themselves" as members of groups quite early in life.[3]

I stress this difference between the individual and the group as units of analysis because using these two constructs as if they were interchangeable clouds understanding of a host of topics, in this case, assessing the contributions of group-based experiences in constructing standpoints.[4] The type of reductionist thinking that uses individual experience to theorize group processes falters, because the treatment of the group in standpoint theory is not synonymous with a "family resemblance" of individual choice expanded to the level of voluntary group association. The notion of standpoint refers to groups having shared histories based on their shared location in unjust power relations—standpoints arise neither from crowds of individuals nor from groups analytically created by scholars or bureaucrats. Common location within power relations, not the result of collective decision making of individuals, creates African-American women as a group. What collective decision making does produce is a determination of the *kind* of group African-American women will be in a given social context.

Under race-only or gender-only conceptual frameworks, it is fairly easy to see how unjust power relations create social groups. Within binary thinking, men rule women and Whites dominate Blacks in schools, the labor market, government organization, and other social institutions. However, the emerging paradigm of intersectionality problematizes this entire process of group construction. As a heuristic device, intersectionality references the ability of social phenomena such as race, class, and gender to mutually construct one another. One can use the framework of intersectionality to think through social institutions, organizational structures, patterns of social interactions, and other social practices on all levels of social organization. Groups are constructed within these social practices, with each group encountering a distinctive constellation of experiences based on its placement in hierarchical power relations. African-American women, for example, can be seen both as a group that occupies a distinctive social location within power relations of intersectionality and as one wherein intersectional processes characterize Black women's collective self-definitions and actions. Whereas race-only or gender-only perspectives classify African-American women as a subgroup of either African-Americans or women, intersections of race, class, and gender, among others, create more fluid and malleable boundaries around the category "African-American women." Within this logic, Black women as a historically constituted group in the United States are no less real—how the group is theoretically defined, however, changes markedly.

Intersectionality thus highlights how African-American women and other social groups are positioned within unjust power relations, but it does so in a way that introduces added complexity to formerly race-, class-, and gender-only approaches to social phenomena. The fluidity that accompanies intersectionality does not mean that groups themselves disappear, to be replaced by an accumulation of decontextualized, unique individuals whose personal complexity makes group-based identities and politics that emerge from group constructions impossible. Instead, the fluidity of boundaries operates as a new lens that potentially deepens understanding of how the actual mechanisms of institutional power can change dramatically even while they reproduce long-standing group inequalities of race, class, and gender. As Kimberle Crenshaw points out, "Intersectionality captures the way in which the particular location of black women in dominant American social relations is unique and in some senses unassimilable into the discursive paradigms of gender and race domination" (1992, 404). In this sense, African-American women's group history and location can be seen as points of convergence within structural, hierarchical, and changing power relations.

Given the tendency of state power to manipulate groups that rely too heavily on narrowly defined identity politics, it is especially important to keep intersectional analyses of group construction in mind. In their assessment of how the government policy of positive action (affirmative action) in Great Britain effectively weakened racial and ethnic identity politics, Floya Anthias and Nira Yuval-Davis (1992) identify an important pitfall confronting groups that allow themselves to be constructed around essentialist definitions. When state distribution of social rewards in relation to group membership fosters a situation of group competition for scarce resources, policing the boundaries of group membership becomes much more important. Anthias and Yuval-Davis illustrate how initial efforts to express self-defined group standpoints can easily be co-opted by state powers that recognize and use identity politics for their own interests.

Retaining this focus on groups constructed within and through intersectionalities remains important for another reason. Intersectionality works better as a substantive theory (one aimed at developing principles that can be proved true or false) when applied to individual-level behavior than when documenting group experiences. The construct of intersectionality works well with issues of individual agency and human subjectivity and thus has surface validity in explaining everyday life. Individuals can more readily see intersections of race, gender, class, and sexuality in how they construct their identities as individuals than in how social institutions rely on these same ideas in reproducing group identities. On the level of the individual, using race, class, gender, sexuality, and national belonging as mutually constructing categories of experience that take on shifting meanings in different contexts makes sense. It is perfectly reasonable to compare, for example, an individual African-American woman to an individual White American woman and to ask how each constructs an identity informed by intersections of race, class, and gender across varying social contexts. On the level of the individual, these kinds of comparisons work, because the unit of comparison—the individual—is deemed equivalent, constant, and not in need of analysis.

Unfortunately, the compatibility of intersectionality with individual-level analyses can foster the consequence of elevating individualism above group analyses. This valorization of individualism to the point where group and structural analyses remain relegated to the background has close ties to American liberalism. Despite the significance of racial, ethnic, economic, and other types of groups in U.S. society, individualism continues as a deep taproot in American law and social theory. David Goldberg describes the roots of liberalism:

> Liberalism is committed to *individualism* for it takes as basic the moral, political, and legal claims of the individual over and against those of the collective. It seeks *foundations* in *universal* principles applicable to all human beings or rational agents. . . . In this, liberalism seeks to transcend particular historical, social, and cultural differences: It is concerned with broad identities which it insists unite persons on moral grounds, rather than with those identities which divide. . . . Liberalism takes itself to be committed to equality. (1993, 5; emphasis in original)

Whether we are talking about the explicit individualism of bourgeois liberalism or the explicit individualism permeating postmodern renditions of difference, individualistic models define freedom as the absence of constraints, including those of mandatory group membership. Freedom occurs when individuals have rights of mobility into and out of groups—the right to join clubs and other voluntary associations or to construct their subjectivity as multiple and changing. Little mention is made of the collective struggles that preceded any group's gaining individual rights of this sort. Within this logic, race, class, gender, and the like become defined as personal attributes of individuals that they should be able to choose or reject. Thus, because it fails to challenge the assumptions of individualism, intersectionality when applied to the individual level can coexist quite nicely with both traditional liberalism and a seemingly apolitical postmodernism.

When discussing intersectionality and group organization, however, assumptions of individualism obscure hierarchical power relations of all sorts, from race- and gender-only perspectives through more complex frameworks such as intersectionality. Can one argue that African-American women and White American women as *groups* are so equivalent that one can take the reality of the social group itself as an assumption that does not need to be examined? Moreover, not only does intersectionality, when applied to the level of groups, become more difficult to conceptualize, but because groups do not operate as individuals do, intersectionality on the group level becomes difficult to study. When examining structural power relations, intersectionality functions better as a conceptual framework or heuristic device describing what kinds of things to consider than as one describing any actual patterns of social organization. The goal is not to prove intersectionality right or wrong, nor to gather empirical data to test the existence of intersectionality. Rather, intersectionality provides an interpretive framework for thinking through how intersections of race and class, or race and gender, or sexuality and class, for example, shape any group's experience across specific social contexts. The existence of multiple axes within intersectionality (race, class, gender, sexuality, nation, ethnicity, age) means neither that these factors are equally salient in all groups' experiences nor that they form uniform principles of social organization in defining groups. For example, institutionalized racism constitutes such a fundamental feature of lived Black experience that, in the minds of many African-American women, racism overshadows sexism and other forms of group-based oppression. In contrast, if the literature on the social construction of Whiteness is any indication (see, e.g., Frankenberg 1993), despite their comfort with identifying themselves as women, many White women in the United States have difficulty seeing themselves as already part of Whites as a group. Although African-American women and White American women participate in the same system of institutionalized racism and sexism, each group assigns a different salience to race and gender. Race and class and gender may *all* be present in *all* social settings in the United States, yet groups will experience and "see" them differently. Within this logic, examining historically constructed groups that exist not in theory but in everyday practice requires having an open mind about what types of groups will actually be uncovered.

Given the significance of both group membership and intersectionality, African-American women's group classification and its connection to intersectional analyses of Black women's common history become important. African-American women participate in two distinctive yet overlapping ways of organizing groups in the United States, one organized around a race-class axis and the other around the axis of gender. Because both operate as defining principles of American national identity—recall the race-gender categories of "free White men," "free White women," and "Slaves"—both constitute groups in which Black women find themselves members quite early in life. However, despite the significance of, on the one hand, race-class groupings and, on the other, gender groupings as core forms of social organization, race, class, and gender mutually construct one another in historically distinctive ways.

Although race, class, and gender may share equal billing under the paradigm of intersectionality as a heuristic device, most African-American women would identify race as a fundamental, if not the most important, feature shaping the experiences of Black women as a group. Race operates as such an overriding feature of African-American experience in the United States that it not only overshadows economic class relations for Blacks but obscures the significance of economic class within the United States in general. Even though race and economic class are intertwined, mutually constructing, and intersecting categories, race is often manipulated to divert attention from economic class concerns (Katz 1989; Quadagno 1994). At the same time, race and economic class are such tightly bundled constructs in shaping actual economic outcomes in the United States that one construct loses meaning without referencing the other. Recall that in interpreting the intent of the framers of the Constitution, Chief Justice Roger Taney referred to African slaves as "a subordinate and inferior class of beings" (qtd. in Estell 1994, 130). In this remark, Taney uses a language of class to describe a racialized population and thus illustrates how race and class often stand as proxy for one another. For the sake of argument, I'll refer to this relationship as one of articulation between race and class or, for the context of the United States, race-class intersectionality.[5]

As women and men, African-Americans also encounter gender as a fundamental organizing principle of social structure. Race and economic class not only articulate with one another but also intersect with gender. Although race and gender both mark the body in similar (but not identical) ways, in the United States they are organized in social relations quite differently. Race-class intersections operate primarily through distancing strategies associated with racial and economic seg-regation. Groups remain separated from one another and do not see themselves as sharing common interests. Blacks and Whites, labor and management are defined in oppositional terms. Although race-class groups may be in close proximity—slavery certainly represented full employment for Blacks coupled with close proximity to Whites—they do not see themselves as sharing common interests. For African-Americans in particular, segregated spaces of all sorts—in particular, housing segregation with its concomitant effects on educational op-portunities, employment prospects, and public facilities—accentuate these oppositional relationships. In contrast, gender is organized via inclusionary strategies where, via family, neighborhood, and religious groups, women live in close proximity to or belong to common social units with men. Women are encouraged to develop a commonality of interest with men, despite the gender hierarchy operating within this category of belonging.

Examining how race and class, on the one hand, and gender, on the other, have been historically organized in the United States sug-gests that they represent two divergent ways of constructing groups, each with different implications for the meaning of standpoint theory. African-American women's positionality within both race-class collec-tivities and gender collectivities as two overlapping yet distinct forms of group organization, provides a potentially important lens for evalu-ating standpoint theory overall. Specifically, standpoint theory seems useful in analyzing issues associated with a new politics of contain-ment that places Black women in segregated housing, schools, and jobs designed to keep them on the economic "bottom." But stand-point theory seems less applicable to gender relations in the United States. Because women are separated from one another by race and class, they face different challenges both in conceptualizing themselves as a group at all and in seeing themselves as a group similar to race-class groups. This suggests that standpoint theory might be better suit-ed for particular types of groups or, alternately, that groups formed via different mechanisms have varying relationships with standpoint theory.

I realize that in an intellectual climate in which viewing race, class, gender, sexuality, and nation as intersecting categories of analysis has now become more accepted, highlighting differences between race-class and gender as forms of organization may seem counterintuitive to some and intellectually conservative to others. However, despite my commitment to intersectionality as an important conceptual framework, continuing to leave intersectionality as an undertheorized construct contributes to old hierarchies (and some new ones) being reformed under what I see as a new myth of equivalent oppressions. In the United States, to be a Black woman is not the same as to be a White gay man or a working-class Latino. Similarly, Black women's collective experiences differ from those of White gay men and working-class Latinos. Although these experiences are all connected, they are not equivalent. Moreover, in a situation in which far too many privileged academics feel free to claim a bit of oppression for themselves—if all oppressions mutually construct one another, then we're all oppressed in some way by something—oppression talk obscures actual unjust power relations. Within these politics, some groups benefit more from an assumed equivalency of oppressions than others. Although this approach is valid as a heuristic device, treating race, class, and gender as if their intersection produces equivalent results for all oppressed groups obscures differences in how race, class, and gender are hierarchically organized, as well as the differential effects of intersecting systems of power on diverse groups of people.

Black women's social location in the United States provides one specific site for examining these cross-cutting relationships among race, class, and gender as categories of analysis. It's particularity may also shed light on how rethinking the connections between social group formation and intersectionality points to the potential relevance of standpoint theory for Black feminist praxis. In the next two sections of this chapter, I examine two groups in which African-American women "find themselves"—race-class groups in the United States, and gender-organized groups shaping women's experiences. My analysis is not meant to be exhaustive but instead sketches out some patterns for beginning to examine how intersectionality might relate to situated standpoints.

Race-Class Group Formation: Standpoint Theory Revisited

Reviewing the origins of standpoint theory in a more general theory of economic class relations associated with the critical social theory of Karl Marx sheds light on race-class intersectionality in the United States generally and standpoint theory in particular. Although current scholarly attention restricts its attention to standpoint theory, the idea of experiential bases of knowledge is much broader than Marxist social theory. Social theorists as diverse as American functionalist Robert Merton, German critical theorist Karl Mannheim, and French postmodernist Michel Foucault all explore the experiential base of knowledge to some degree. Marxist social thought, however, most clearly situates knowledge within unjust power relations.[6]

Although Marx may be better known for his analyses of capitalism and socialism, I find that revisiting Marx's historical work provides new directions for conceptualizing how race and economic class mutually construct one another in the United States.[7] Marx's 1852 essay *The Eighteenth Brumaire of Louis Bonaparte* provides a historical examination of how economic class relations both constrained and shaped human agency during a period of social uprising in France. The following passage from this work contains several interrelated ideas that collectively provide an interpretive context for understanding how economic class represents a specific type of group formation.

> In so far as millions of families live under economic conditions of existence that separate their mode of life, their interests and their culture from those of the other classes, and put them in hostile opposition to the latter, they form a class. In so far as there is merely a local interconnection among these small-holding peasants, and the identity of their interests begets no community, no national bond and no political organization among them, they do not form a class. They are consequently incapable of enforcing their class interest in their own name. (Marx 1963, 124)

Four features of economic class analysis are germane to conceptualizing how race-class intersectionality in the United States constitutes a particular type of group formation. First, although economic class remains rooted in economic analysis, dual meanings of economic class exist. On a specific level, economic class refers to the economic status of historically identifiable groups in capitalist political economies such as the United States. Concentrations of economic power (owning income-producing property), political power (running workplaces and the government), and ideological power (controlling the schools, media, and other forms of representation) distinguish economic classes from one another (Higginbotham and Weber 1992). Analyses that define the middle class as comprising managerial and professional workers, the working class as encompassing factory workers and clerical workers, and the underclass as populated by workers who move between secondary labor-market jobs, government transfer payments, and the informal economy represent one important dimension of economic class relationships. Relying on analyses of segmented labor markets, industrial sectors, or other indices of placement in political economy, these approaches attribute economic class outcomes to economic causes (Baran and Sweezy 1966; Edwards 1979; Wilson 1978, 1987).

Ways of conceptualizing class relations exist other than those accompanying the familiar labor market, industrial sector, and human capital variables. Understanding classes whose "economic conditions of existence" distinguish them from other groups requires situating those groups in the specific history of their society. This history might resemble the familiar bourgeoisie and proletariat of Marxist conflict theory constructed from studies of industrializing, racially homogeneous nineteenth-century European societies. However, in the postcolonial, desegregated contexts of advanced capitalism, Marxist class categories seemingly lose validity. The approach taken to constructing class, however, remains valuable. Rather than starting with a theory of how capitalist economies predetermine economic classes, analysis *begins* with how social groupings are actually organized within historically specific capitalist political economies. Class categories are constructed from the actual cultural material of historically specific societies. This is exactly the method that Marx used in constructing his class categories—the bourgeoisie and proletariat were not theoretically derived categories but emerged from historical analysis.[8]

Analyzing class relations via historically concrete, lived experience sheds light on race-class intersectionality in the United States. One might ask whether African-Americans "live under economic conditions of existence that separate their mode of life, their interests and their culture from those of other classes" or, alternately, whether African-Americans continue to bear the intergenerational costs associated with the denial of citizenship stemming from their being branded "a subordinate and inferior class of beings." For African-Americans, group positionality is determined less by theoretical categories constructed within assumptions of distinct discourses of class or race, and more by actual lived Black experience. Although economic outcomes remain fundamental to conceptualizing Black economic class relations, such relations may not be defined *solely* by labor markets, industrial sectors, and other economic criteria. A more complex analysis of class formation might encompass an intersectional analysis attentive to institutionalized racism, slavery as a mode of production, and other factors shaping the social location of African-Americans as a group. The forces constructing African-Americans as a group living under economic conditions that distinguish them from other groups in the United States are far more complex than simple economic determinism.

This leads to a second feature essential for exploring how race-class intersectionality in the United States might foster a specific type of group formation—the necessity of historic specificity in examining both economic class relations and any standpoints that might ensue. Nowhere is it written that only two or three classes exist. Yet this parsimonious number persists. It seems just as reasonable to argue that actual class relations are much more complex. Since Marxist class analysis is heavily influenced by its origins in racially homogeneous European societies as well as its construction of class categories from the individual's relationship to capital and labor, it underemphasizes the importance of race in conceptualizing class. However, given how institutionalized racism and capitalism have constructed one another in the United States (Marable 1983), restricting analysis to a few economic classes shorn of racial meaning oversimplifies a series of complex relationships. Rather than taking a class analysis developed for one specific historical context—for example, Marx's discussion of the bourgeoisie and proletariat developed for nineteenth-century France or industrializing England—and applying it uncritically to other social settings, one might assume that differently organized class differences will *always* characterize unjust power relations.

This shift in perspective that both views class relations in more than purely economic terms and generates class categories from actual lived experience creates space to examine how social hierarchies construct group or class relationships with visible economic dimensions. It also creates space to think about class in relation to race, nationality, and ethnicity (see, e.g., Anthias and Yuval-Davis 1992). Within the United States, race, ethnicity, and nationality have long been intertwined in historically complex ways in producing pronounced economic inequalities among groups (Takaki 1993). Moreover, the institutional mechanisms by which unjust power relations of class, race, nation, and ethnicity are organized are similar—namely, separation and exclusion. Issues of purity and separation, whether of geographical space or occupational and employment space, or in school curricula, the media, or other forms of symbolic space, appear central to maintaining unjust power relations of race, class, nation, and ethnicity in the United States. Despite a rhetoric of individualism associated with liberalism, Americans seem to be profoundly group-oriented. As sociologist Joseph Scott succinctly puts it, "Group rights are the American practice; individual rights are the American promise" (1984, 178).

If groups with historically identifiable histories and traditions have become the focus of class analysis (class cannot operate in the abstract—it always works through actual lived experience), African-Americans participate in class relations in particular ways. The complexity of class analysis is limited only by the degree of specificity used to delineate groups with shared "economic conditions of existence." Class relations can thus be drawn with broad brush strokes, as in the case of nineteenth-century industrializing England, or more finely crafted into intersectional categories such as race-class intersectionality in the late-twentieth-century United States. Within this logic, race-class groups are constructed less from theoretical models advanced by governmental officials and academics, and more from actual group histories.

A third feature of class analysis that is especially germane to both group formation and race-class intersectionality in the United States concerns the nature of class as a construct. Class does not describe a "thing" but rather a *relationship* among social groups unequal in power. Classes represent bounded categories of the population, groups set in a relation of opposition to one another. Within Marxist social theory, group relationships describe power relations such that one group's privilege is predicated upon another group's disadvantage. One group or class exploits the other, excludes the other from equitable social rewards, or somehow benefits from the other's disadvantage. The main insight here concerns the relationship between group structure, group membership, and unjust power relations. Groups become defined largely by their placement within historically specific power relations, not from choices exercised by individual group members concerning issues of identity and belonging.

From this perspective, it makes little sense to talk about the middle class as an entity or a thing unto itself, because such a class could not exist without other economic classes to which it is linked in relationships of, at best, mutuality and, at worst, exploitation. In a similar fashion, historically in the United States, the notion of Whiteness as a meaningful group category was formed in relation to Blackness as a separate and allegedly inferior way of constructing groups. Moreover, these group relationships within race-class intersectionality persist over time. Although patterns of race-class intersectionality may be distinctive for any given era, the basic oppositional relationships among groups constructed within and linked by these intersections remain constant. As long as the basic relationship of intergenerational disadvantage and privilege in which White and Black individuals "find themselves" persists, the relationship is one of class.

I stress the intergenerational nature of this process of mutually constructing privilege and disadvantage because, in the United States, such relationships remain organized through family units. With the important exception of feminist analyses of the family, the concept of family remains simultaneously underanalyzed and fundamental to how people conceptualize groups of all sorts. In his discussion of class, Marx identifies families as the unit of class analysis. Recall the passage quoted earlier: "In so far as millions of *families* live under economic conditions of existence that separate their mode of life, their interests and their culture from those of the other classes, and put them in hostile opposition to the latter, they form a class" (1963, 124; emphasis added). Consider how differently that passage would read if the term *individuals* were substituted for the term *families*. In this passage, classes are constructed not from the building blocks of *individuals* but from those of *families*, the same building blocks of nations, races, and ethnic groups. Thus, class, race, and nation all become linked in a common cognitive framework that relies on separation and exclusion to define family groups. This shift from the individual to the family as the basic unit of class analysis leads to very different notions of how hierarchical power relations become reproduced over time. As the long-standing debate on Black family deviance indicates, most Americans seem comfortable with the idea of the intergenerational transfer of property from one generation to the next, as long as the property under consideration is *cultural* capital. Any resulting inequalities can then be attributed to the workings of good or bad parenting. However, analyzing how the intergenerational transfer of *wealth*, or actual capital, participates in shaping these same outcomes leads to different conclusions (Collins 1997). Here one encounters inherited patterns of opportunity or disadvantage, based on the class position of one's family. Moreover, if family is used to conceptualize other types of groups—race as family, nation as a large extended family, ethnicity as a large kinship group—then relations within the family and the treatment of family members and outsiders become significant to social relations of all sorts (Collins forthcoming 1998b).

Rather than trying to determine the essential features that distinguish African-Americans from other social groups, a more fruitful approach might explore how African-Americans participate in race-class intersectionality in the United States at any given time, especially in oppositional relationships with other groups. This approach accommodates a dual emphasis on fixity and change. On the one hand, intergenerational patterns of family inequality in which Whites and Blacks largely replicate the economic status of their parents signal the fixed nature of race-class intersectionality in the United States. On the other hand, because history is seen as changing, race-class formations also change, as the new politics of containment suggests, often in quite dramatic ways. Within such changes, opportunities for struggle continually are being remade. Historicizing race-class relations as specific power relations in this way not only highlights how race-class relations change over time but also reintroduces the question of human agency in bringing about such changes.

Exercising agency in response to and/or in behalf of a group requires *recognizing* groups by seeing how past circumstances have profound effects on the present. Thus, a final dimension of class approaches to group formation specifically related to race-class intersectionality in the United States concerns the centrality of group culture and consciousness in developing self-defined group standpoints. Shared disadvantage and shared interests are not sufficient—*separate* modes of life that distinguish groups from one another remain important. Although structural features such as shared location in the economy can bring people into proximity who have common economic interests, they do not become classes without some sort of self-defined group knowledge. Individuals within the group must develop and proclaim a consciousness of their connections with one another, and the group itself must come to see its relationships with other groups within this same system of power relations:[9] "In so far as there is merely a local interconnection among these small-holding peasants, and the identity of their interests begets no *community,* no national bond and

no political organization among them, they do not form a class"
(Marx 1963, 124; emphasis added). In other words, a group consoli-
dates its class interests through community infrastructures that actively reproduce its particular group interests for its own membership.

Historically, African-Americans have recognized themselves as a
group in this way, with shared interests constructed in opposition to
those of more powerful Whites as a dominant group. The longevity of
Black nationalism in Black civil society stems in part from its repeated
denouncements of institutionalized racism, coupled with an insistence
that Blacks center political action on lived Black experience. Recall
that Black cultural nationalism encourages African-Americans to
claim an independent Black culture. Aiming to develop a radical Black
consciousness that recognizes how existing race-class relations are unjust, such a culture is designed to give voice to Black political struggle.
In exploring these relations, African-American legal scholar Derrick
Bell has the Curia, fictional Black women judges, point to the importance of situated standpoints for theories of Black liberation:

> Some of you . . . will leave here seeking theories of liberation from
> white legal philosophers, who are not oppressed, who do not per-
> ceive themselves as oppressors, and who thus must use their impres-
> sive intellectual talent to imagine what you experience daily. Black
> people, on the other hand, come to their task of liberation from the
> battleground of experience, not from the rarefied atmosphere of the
> imagination. (1987, 253)

Bell's fictional account in which the Curia chides Black people
who fail to trust their own experiences with racism, who deny the perspectives that often emerge from these experiences, and who look to
Whites for answers resonates with the type of independent thinking
advocated by Black nationalist leader Malcolm X, who once advised a
group of Black youth to think for themselves (Collins 1992a). Within
this framework, culture, consciousness, and political struggle become
inextricably intertwined.

Overall, the ideas of standpoint theory seem more suited to
groups structured via segregated spaces such as residential racial segregation, employment discrimination, and other exclusionary practices characterizing race-class intersectionality in the United States.
Despite its insights into the workings of power through segregated
spaces, this race-class approach to group construction routinely fails
to address hierarchy *within* groups that are differentially positioned

within unjust power relations. This failure to address internal hierarchy has great implications for constructing group standpoints. Even though a social group may occupy a distinctive structural location within hierarchical power relations, it can simultaneously remain quite uninformed about unjust power relations operating within its own boundaries. Thus, one fundamental challenge lies in ensuring that neither group practices nor any ensuing standpoints replicate other hierarchies, particularly those of gender and sexuality.

Gender and Group Formation

Because women in the United States are distributed *across* groups formed within race-class intersectionality, gender raises different issues. Long-standing exclusionary practices that separate women by race, economic condition, citizenship status, and ethnicity result in social groups that *include* women, organized via these categories. For example, Black women and White women do not live in class-stratified women's neighborhoods, separated from men and children by processes such as gender steering, bank redlining that results in refusal to lend money to women's neighborhoods, inferior schools in women's inner-city neighborhoods due to men moving to all-male suburban areas, and the like. Instead, for the most part, Black and White women live in racially segregated, economically stratified neighborhoods (Massey and Denton 1993). The experiences they garner in such communities, especially via the powerful social institution of family, reflect the politics of race-class intersectionality in the United States. Stated differently, although women in the United States may share much as women, residential patterns, schools, and employment opportunities that routinely sort women into clearly defined categories of race, economic class, ethnicity, and citizenship status mean that few opportunities exist for having the type of intimate, face-to-face contact that would reveal women's "shared economic conditions," if they exist at all, let alone for organizing around those conditions.

At the same time, as a collectivity, women experience distinctive gendered mechanisms of control that remain specific to women's patterns of inclusion within race-class groups. Specifically, regardless of actual family composition, all women encounter the significance of American society's preoccupation with family. As a familiar and seemingly natural form of group organization, the idea of family serves as a particular foundation on which many types of groups are built (Collins 1998a). Members of all sorts of collectivities are often encouraged to treat one another as "family," a perspective illustrated by family references to, for example, the "brothers" in gangs, the "sisterhood" of feminist struggle, the Black "mothers" of the church, and the founding "fathers" of America. Recall that Marx himself falls back on the image of the family as the smallest social unit having a shared interest. By definition, families stick together against outsiders. Within idealized notions of family, family units protect and balance the interests of all of their members—the strong care for the weak, and members contribute to and benefit from family membership in proportion to their capacities. Though there may be differentiation within the family, family members share a common origin through blood and a commonality of interests.

By providing compelling arguments that family functions as a primary site for conceptualizing and organizing women's oppression, feminist scholarship challenges these assumptions. Analyses of bourgeois family structure or the traditional family ideal, in particular, unpack the relationship between particular ideas of family and gender oppression. Defined as a natural or biological arrangement based on heterosexual attraction, a normative and ideal family consists of a heterosexual couple who produce their own biological children. Formed through a combination of marital and blood ties, the traditional family ideal views this nuclear unit as having a specific authority structure, arranged in this order: a father-head earning an adequate family wage, a stay-at-home wife and mother, and children. Assuming a relatively fixed sexual division of labor, wherein women's roles are defined as primarily in the home and men's in the public world of work, the traditional family ideal assumes the separation of work and family. Viewing the family as a private haven from a public world, family is seen as held together through primary emotional bonds of love and caring (Andersen 1991; Thorne 1992).

Feminist scholarship reveals that despite a rhetoric of equality in this ideal, a good part of women's subordination is organized via family ties. In contrast to idealized versions of family, actual families remain organized around varying patterns of hierarchy. As Anne McClintock observes, "The family image came to figure *hierarchy within unity* as an organic element of historical progress, and thus became indispensable for legitimating exclusion and hierarchy within nonfamilial social forms such as nationalism, liberal individualism and imperialism" (1995, 45). Thus, because the family is perceived as a private sphere that is naturally and not socially constructed, relying on the traditional family ideal as a model for group organization replicates a naturalized hierarchy. For women, domination and love remain intimately linked. Through their contribution of socializing family members into an appropriate set of "family values," women participate in naturalizing the hierarchy within the assumed unity of interests symbolized by the family while laying the foundation for systems of hierarchy outside family boundaries. As people often learn their place within hierarchies of race, gender, ethnicity, sexuality, nationality, and class from their experiences within family units, they simultaneously learn to view such hierarchies as natural social arrangements, as compared to socially constructed ones. As feminist analyses of family suggest, women's families remain central to their subordination. Moreover, because women's shared economic conditions as women remain organized within families across race-class groups, women remain disadvantaged in seeing their connections with other similarly situated women.

Developing group culture and consciousness for all women as a collectivity involves extracting them from historically constituted groups within which family serves as part of the conceptual glue giving meaning to race, class, ethnicity, and nation. It also involves creating a new group identity based on gender affiliation. For women as a collectivity, building this type of group constitutes an intellectual and political project distinctly different from that confronting groups organized via the segregated spaces of race, class, ethnicity, and nation. Moreover, differences in group construction and the challenges that face different types of groups have implications for any ensuing standpoints. Using standpoint theory both as a tool for analyzing gender relations in the United States and as a strategy for organizing women raises a different and complex set of issues. Because women are distributed across a range of race-class groups, all women confront the initial task of developing a shared understanding of their common interests as women. However, they must do so in close proximity to, and often in sexualized love relationships with, members of the group that allegedly oppresses them. Since women must first construct a self-definition as a member of a group, ideas may precede the building of actual group relations. Women certainly know other women within their own race, economic, ethnic, and/or citizenship groups, but most have difficulty seeing their shared interests across the vast differences that characterize women as a collectivity. The process of constructing a group standpoint for women differs dramatically from that confronting groups with histories of group-based segregated spaces. Women come to know themselves as members of a political collectivity through ideas that construct them as such.

By invoking the rhetoric of family in constructing women's groups and any hoped-for standpoints that might follow, a feminist politics may inadvertently undermine the logic of its own organization. The longed-for group solidarity promised under the rubric of "sisterhood" posited by contemporary feminists seems designed to build a community among women that is grounded in shared conditions of existence. However, imagining multicultural, multiethnic, multiracial, multiclass women's groups predicated on family-based notions of sisterhood is much easier than building such communities across lived, institutionalized segregation. The path from women conceptualized as a numerically superior "minority group," through feminist organizing designed to generate a shared consciousness of women's oppression or standpoint under the banner of sisterhood, to building actual women's groups organized around sisterhood encountered considerable resistance, much of it from African-American women and other similarly situated women (Dill 1983).

White American feminist critiques of standpoint theory may emerge in part from discouragement with the seeming failure of feminist struggles for sisterhood. In part, the increasing attraction of postmodernism for many White American feminists may lie in its deconstructive move. By arguing that multiracial, multicultural women's collectivities are neither desirable nor possible, postmodernism seems to offer a way out. Turning attention away from challenging women's oppression to deconstructing the modern subject provides conceptual space to sidestep the theoretical failures of Western feminism. If women cannot be organized as a group, then groups themselves must go, and everything associated with them, including standpoints. Although this theoretical move seems highly plausible when directed toward the fragile solidarity of women, applying similar deconstructive moves to groups organized through segregated spaces of race and economic class remains far less convincing. Despite well-intentioned gestures (e.g., placing "race" in quotation marks to signal the socially constructed notion of race as a category of analysis), declaring a moratorium on using the word *race* does not make housing segregation, underfunded inner-city schools, and employment discrimination any less real.

Because groups respond to the actual social conditions that they confront, it stands to reason that groups constructed by different social realities will develop equally different analyses and political strategies. For example, White American feminist thinkers who theorize that feminist standpoints are untenable may be inadvertently expressing the standpoint of a group that has no need of such thinking. Moreover, despite the support and leadership of many women's studies professionals for intersectional analyses, such support may evaporate quickly if any real sharing of power appears on the horizon. Ironically, within unexamined assumptions of individualism, intersectionality can be reconfigured so that it makes things worse. Just as academic talk of centers and margins flattened and in some cases erased hierarchical power relations, the construct of intersectionality used to analyze differences among women can be similarly depoliticized. When extracted from hierarchical power relations, recognizing differences among women can become so watered down that power simply vanishes.

In a fundamental way, African-American women are caught in the cross fire of two different ways of organizing groups. Race, class, nation, and ethnicity all rely heavily on segregation and other exclusionary practices to maintain hierarchy. In contrast, because women often find themselves in close proximity to men, gender relies more heavily on surveillance and other inclusionary strategies of control targeted toward the proximate other. Because it reproduces the naturalized hierarchy that also informs the self-definitions of race-class groups, the idea of family permeates both types of group organization. On the one hand, due to its overreliance on a gender-blind racial solidarity constructed via family metaphors, Black civil society fosters a problematic paradigm of sacrifice for African-American women. On the other hand, because structural power attached to race-class intersectionality in the United States can be recast within apolitical frameworks of differences among women, White American feminist theories in particular maintain the illusion of gender solidarity while allowing hierarchy to be reformulated via actual practices. For African-American women, hierarchy flourishes in *both* approaches to constructing groups.

Situated Standpoints and Black Feminist Thought

How might these complexities introduced by intersectionalities and group organization shed light on the relationship between standpoint theory and Black feminist thought? A more intricate view both of African-American women as a group and of any accompanying Black women's standpoint might emerge by first agreeing that African-American women have a shared (though not uniform) location in hierarchical power relations in the United States. The existence of group interests means neither that all individuals within the group have the same experiences nor that they interpret them in the same way. Acknowledging a shared location means neither that African-American women's experiences become collapsed into stereotypes of welfare queens or Black Lady Overachievers, nor that images of "natural," "African," or "real" Black women that are conjured up in Black nationalist discourse constitute what is shared. A paradigm of intersectionality stressing how race, class, and gender mutually construct one another suggests that unitary standpoints of the type associated with traditional racial solidarity are neither possible nor desirable. However, if groups themselves need not be organized via essentialist principles, neither do group-derived standpoints. Group-based experiences, especially those shared by African-American women as a collectivity, create the conditions for a shared standpoint that in turn can stimulate collective political action. But they guarantee neither that such standpoints will follow nor that efforts to develop standpoints constitute the most effective way of empowering a group in a given context.

Shared group location is better characterized by viewing Black women's social location as one of a heterogeneous commonality embedded in social relations of intersectionality. Despite heterogeneity among African-American women that accompanies such intersections, differences in Black women's experiences generated by differences of age, sexual orientation, region of the country, urban or rural residence, color, hair texture, and the like theoretically can all be accommodated within the concept of a shared standpoint. When it comes to oppression, there are essentials. A passage in *The Eighteenth Brumaire* speaks to this critical element of what might actually be shared: "Men make their own history, but they do not make it just as they please; they do not make it under circumstances chosen by themselves, but under circumstances directly encountered, given and transmitted from the past" (Marx 1963, 15). "Shared" refers to the "circumstances directly encountered, given and transmitted from the past," not to uniform, essentialist responses to those conditions. Stated differently, a shared standpoint need not rest on a list of essential rules or Black feminist articles of faith to which Black women must subscribe in order to be considered a true sister. Rather, it rests on the recognition that when it comes to being African-American women in the United States, as Fannie Lou Hamer points out, "we're in this bag together" (qtd. in Lerner 1972, 613).

By primarily emphasizing only one historically specific dimension of hierarchical power relations, namely, economic classes in industrializing political economies, Marx posited that, however unarticulated and inchoate, oppressed groups possessed a particular standpoint concerning the "bag" they were in, that is, their own oppression. Contemporary analyses of social structure that stress the complexity created by intersections of race, economic class, gender, ethnicity, sexuality, and nationality ask how to invoke a comparable complexity in defining and studying groups. What we now have is increasing sophistication about how to discuss group location not in singular "fighting words" paradigms of economic class, race, or gender, but with a growing recognition of the significance of intersectionality. This suggests that the complexity characterizing African-American women's group identity under a new politics of containment will generate a comparably sophisticated Black women's standpoint.

As the preceding discussion of race-class and gender groups suggests, actually thinking through this complexity represents a daunting task. However, at a minimum, it points to the need to develop a more sophisticated language for discussing social groups that takes power relations into account. Traditional discussions of standpoint theory leave this notion of group unexamined, if they make mention of it at all, allowing unexamined family metaphors to fill the void.

Because actual family relations are rarely fair and just, using family as metaphor for constructing an understanding of group processes can duplicate inequalities that are embedded in the very definition of what constitutes a well-functioning group. This has profound implications for any group that understands its internal dynamics through the lens of "family." Since the 1970s, increasing numbers of African-American women have recognized how this notion of naturalized hierarchy within a family constitutes a problematic organizing principle for the organization of actual Black families. However, challenging conceptions of Black civil society that naturalize hierarchy among African-American men and women has proved more difficult. This recognition requires questioning long-standing norms that simultaneously have used family language to define African-Americans as a race and have often conceptualized Black political struggle via the rhetoric of family.

Protesting gender hierarchies internal to Black civil society certainly framed the feminism of African-American women participating in the civil rights and Black Power movements of the 1960s and 1970s. As Frances Beale succinctly observed in "Double Jeopardy: To Be Black and Female," her groundbreaking 1970 essay,

> Unfortunately, there seems to be some confusion in the movement today as to who has been oppressing whom. Since the advent of black power, the black male has exerted a more prominent leadership role in our struggle for justice in this country. He sees the system for what it really is for the most part, but where he rejects its values and mores on many issues, when it comes to women, he seems to take his guidelines from the pages of the *Ladies' Home Journal*. (Beale 1995, 147–48)

Beale's comments reveal how African-American women's placement in political struggles organized by both race and gender reveal two overlapping and important uses of family in constructing groups. On the one hand, a Black civil society in which race-as-family metaphors are used to construct group identity misses potentially problematic internal hierarchies such as those of gender and sexuality. On the other hand, African-American women who see themselves as part of a women's collectivity organized around women's subordination within families confront the ongoing difficulties of organizing across deeply entrenched patterns of segregated space.

In thinking through these relationships, it may prove useful to revisit standard sociological categories of macro-, meso-, and micro-levels of social organization yet to view them as organized within and through power relations. Hierarchical power relations operate on all three levels—no one level "rules" the others. Collectively, these levels of social structure frame what Black women as a group are, what they do, and what they might think. On the macro level, schools, labor markets, the media, government, and other social institutions reproduce a social position or category of "Black woman" that is assigned to all individuals who fit criteria for membership. One does not choose to be a "Black woman." Rather, one "finds oneself" classified in this category, regardless of differences in how one got there. On the meso level, Black women as a group encounter accumulated wisdom learned from past interactions between what was expected of them as Black women and what they actually did. On this level, Black women develop strategies for how African-American women grapple with these socially assigned positions. On the micro level, specific contexts of everyday life provide each Black woman multiple opportunities to play the social role of "Black woman" as it has been scripted or to negotiate new patterns. In this sense, each Black woman constructs the type of Black woman she chooses to be in different situations. All of these levels work together recursively, shaping one another to create specific social outcomes.

In analyzing the question of situated group standpoints, the meso level provides considerable insight on how Black women's group organization mediates between categories that are socially assigned to Black women and options that individual African-American women perceive in constructing their unique ways of being Black women. Although all Black women remain defined by the social role of Black women, how individual African-American women act in specific situations depends on at least two factors. The distinctive patterns of their individual biographies constitute one important factor. In addition, their access to historically created and shared Black feminist wisdom, for want of a better term, matters. This is of immense importance for Black feminist thought, because it suggests that Black women's collective, lived experiences in negotiating the category "Black woman" can serve a purpose in grappling with the new politics of containment. Despite its importance, scholarship on this meso level that examines Black women's agency in accessing cultural knowledge to construct individual expressions of self within socially defined categories of "Black woman" remains modest. What does exist, however, is provocative. Signithia Fordham's study of "loud Black girls" in education (1993) reveals strategies deployed by Black women who routinely encounter institutional silencing. Jacqueline Bobo's study of Black women as cultural readers (1995) informs us that Black women do not sit passively by, watching movies and believing everything they see. Rather, they actively negotiate cultural meanings.

Developing Black feminist thought as critical social theory requires articulating a situated standpoint that emerges from rather than suppresses the complexity of African-American women's experiences as a group on this meso level. British sociologist Stuart Hall's notion of articulation works well here—the idea of "unity and difference," of "difference in complex unity, without becoming a hostage to the privileging of difference as such" (qtd. in Slack 1996, 122). Such a standpoint would identify the ways in which being situated in intersections of race, economic class, and gender, as well as those of age, sexuality, ethnicity, and region of the country, constructs relationships *among* African-American women as a group. At the same time, a situated standpoint would reflect how these intersections frame African-American women's distinctive history as a collectivity in the United States. This involves examining how intersectionality constructs relationships *between* African-American women and other groups. Thus, the challenge confronting African-American women lies in constructing notions of a Black female collectivity that remain sensitive to Black women's placement in distinctively American hierarchical power relations, while simultaneously resisting replication of these same relations within the group's own ranks.

The ability of Black feminist thought to make useful contributions to contemporary freedom struggles hinges on its ability to develop new forms of visionary pragmatism. Within the new politics of containment that confronts African-American women, visionary pragmatism in turn hinges on developing greater complexity within Black women's knowledge. In this regard, remaining situated is essential. Vision can be conjured up in the theoretical imagination, yet pragmatic actions require being responsive to the injustices of everyday life. Rather than abandoning situated standpoints, becoming situated in new understandings of social complexity is vital. Despite the importance of this project, changes in Black civil society, coupled with the growing importance of academia as a site where Black feminist thought is produced and circulated, raise real questions concerning the future of this type of functional knowledge. Whether Black feminist standpoints survive remains to be seen.

Seven

Searching for Sojourner Truth: Toward an Epistemology of Empowerment

> My name was Isabella; but when I left the house of bondage, I left everything behind. I wa'n't goin' to keep nothin' of Egypt on me, an' so I went to the Lord an' asked him to give me a new name. And the Lord gave me Sojourner, because I was to travel up an' down the land, showin' the people their sins, an' bein' a sign unto them. Afterward I told the Lord I wanted another name, 'cause everybody else had two names; and Lord gave me Truth, because I was to declare the truth to the people. (Qtd. in Sterling 1984, 151)

How did Isabella Baumfree, an illiterate, newly emancipated, poor Black woman, dare to name herself? Stepping outside the conventions of 1832, Truth created her own identity and invoked naming as a symbolic act imbued with meaning. Refusing to be silenced, Truth claimed the authority of her own experiences to challenge the racism, sexism, and class privilege of her time.

Often presented as important to Black feminism (Guy-Sheftall 1986; Joseph 1990), Sojourner Truth's ideas are important in and of themselves. Moreover, as a figure who has been appropriated by a range of groups in defense of disparate agendas (Painter 1993), Truth has taken on the status of an icon. The power of Truth as a Black feminist intellectual (an appropriation that suits my purposes) lies in her complexity, in the fact that she lends herself so well to multiple interpretations. What I find compelling about Sojourner Truth is that her biography suggests an epistemology of empowerment that has helped me think through critical social theory in general. Recall that critical social theory encompasses bodies of knowledge and sets of institutional practices that actively grapple with the central questions facing groups of people differentially placed in specific political, social, and historic contexts characterized by injustice. Sojourner Truth's life serves as a metaphor for all parts of this definition. Not only did she produce knowledge and engage in particular social practices, she also faced injustices that remain remarkably similar to our own.

Sojourner Truth's biography speaks to the significance of her movement among multiple communities, the impact that these diverse groups had on her worldview, and the potential significance of Truth's life for an epistemology of empowerment. Truth was born into slavery but experienced the distinctive form practiced in the North. Despite being sold several times as a child, Truth knew both of her biological parents. She spoke Dutch, and when she was sold to English-speaking owners, she experienced the language barrier of not being understood. Her older sisters and brothers were sold away, yet Truth was able to see her own children grow to adulthood. Emancipated in 1827 by New York state law, Truth possessed insider knowledge of slavery but also experienced mobility out of slavery into the status of freedperson. Since she lived both in upstate New York and in New York City after emancipation, Truth was well aware of both rural and urban life. She was one of the few African-Americans in the White Christian evangelical movement, as well as one of the few Black women who spoke out about women's rights (Painter 1993; Washington 1993). Thus, Sojourner Truth's travels through multiple outsider-within locations may explain in part her remarkable ability to see things differently than others of her time did. She was visionary in her ideals concerning equity and justice yet pragmatic about the political actions needed to make justice a reality. The richness of Truth's biography signals a significance that far exceeds her individual life.

Although Sojourner Truth's and African-American women's particular experiences stimulated my ideas for this chapter, my analysis has implications beyond these specific origins. Social theories emerging from and/or on behalf of historically oppressed groups investigate ways to escape from, survive in, and/or oppose prevailing social and economic injustice. Black women in the United States are but one such group engaged in developing this type of social theory. Just as Black women's group location within hierarchical power relations creates the conditions for a distinctive standpoint, this same positionality simultaneously limits what will be visible. Since a standpoint is not something that a group possesses but rather something that involves the ongoing process of negotiating heterogeneous commonalities, Black women do not "own" an epistemology of empowerment. Rather, by using Sojourner Truth's ideas and experiences as a touchstone or metaphor, I hope to sketch out some key considerations for moving toward an epistemology that opposes injustice.

Migration, Outsider-Within Locations, and Contextualized Truth

Sojourner Truth's mobility as a "sojourner" among multiple outsider-within locations highlights the importance of social contexts in determining truth. Because Truth lived in a Black woman's body, her position in the world certainly shaped her position on her world. A traveler, a migrant who transgressed borders of race, class, gender, literacy, geography, and religion largely impenetrable for African-American women of her time, Truth remained an outsider within multiple communities. Just as Sojourner Truth was situated in the context of hierarchical power relations, searching for truth requires similar contextualization. For her, resolving the tensions raised by her migratory status did not lie in staying in any one center of power and thereby accepting its rules and assumptions. Rather, Truth explicitly breached group boundaries. By selecting the name Sojourner, Truth proclaimed that specialization and movement were both required in legitimating truth claims. No truth was possible without a variety of perspectives on any given particularity.

Individuals like Truth who accept their placement in outsider-within locations can formulate remarkable critical social theory. Biographies of many African-American intellectuals demonstrate how movement through outsider-within locations can catalyze creativity (Braxton 1989; Franklin 1995).[1] In her autobiography, Angela Davis (1974) describes how migrating from the South to the North and from the United States to Europe stimulated insights largely unavailable to African-Americans who are denied such experiences. Her pathbreaking analyses of the intersections of race, gender, and class in framing

Black women's experiences under slavery (1981) reflect the insights she gained from her movement among multiple interpretive communities. Realizing that when it comes to injustice, all social locations provide opportunities for struggle, Davis embraced both social theory and political activism in her work. "The new places, the new experiences I had expected to discover through travel turned out to be the same old places, the same old experiences with a common message of struggle" (1974, 120), she observes. Each new location provided Davis a new vantage point for constructing critical social theory.

Truth's and Davis's travels stimulated new angles of vision. More important, their movement violates implicit assumptions concerning segregated spaces and Black women's appropriate place in them. Michel Foucault's analysis of disciplinary power points to the importance of segregated space as a guiding metaphor for thinking through African-American women's experiences in outsider-within locations. Arguing that disciplinary power operates by enclosing individuals in assigned spaces, Foucault observes, "This machinery works space in a . . . flexible and detailed way. It does this . . . on the principle of elementary location or *partitioning*. Each individual has his own place, and each place its individual" (1979, 143; emphasis in original). Since they are defined by the place they occupy in a series and by the gap that separates them from others, individuals categorized in this fashion become interchangeable. One Black woman is the same as any other, and all are different from everyone else. People are classified hierarchically and assigned metaphorical and actual places where they belong. Their location in those places (whether they are geographic neighborhoods or scientific categories of race) determines their rank (Foucault 1979, 145). The actual people remain less important than their placement in this overarching arrangement. Moreover, this logic of disciplinary power shapes the organization of bodies of knowledge. Ideas are assigned disciplinary places where they belong, and their location in their disciplines determines their value. In this sense, hierarchical power relations are mapped onto physical space that in turn reproduces symbolic space.[2]

Sojourner Truth's biography provides a metaphor for this type of journey, an ongoing search that views truth as a process negotiated in outsider-within places, as compared to a finished product that one finds in the center of either actual segregated places or symbolic disciplinary spaces. Since intellectuals are simultaneously located in and

moving through all sorts of positions within the metaphoric disciplinary space as well as within actual academic disciplines, their intellectual production and the positions they take will be similarly varied. As
Black British cultural critic Kobena Mercer points out, "In matters of
war, positioning is everything" (1994, 7). Some intellectuals seem to be
at home in the centers of what appear to be self-contained, interpretive
communities. They accept the premise that "each individual has his
own place, and each place its individual" (Foucault 1979, 143), even if
it disadvantages them. Theorizing from these old centers generates distinctive perspectives on the world: the former location generates elite
knowledge used to support oppression; the latter, the "hidden transcripts" of oppressed groups that can be either emancipatory or not
(Scott 1990). Other intellectual workers migrate through to the bor-
derlands, boundaries, or outsider-within locations linking communities
of differential power. As temporary sojourners, they pause and look
around before returning to former home communities or moving on to
new ones. Whether by choice or by design, still others find themselves
permanently exiled in these outsider-within locations, unable to return
home to old centers and never gaining entry into new ones. There, as
permanent sojourners, they continue to search for meaning. In these
outsider-within spaces, some sojourners approach truths.

On the one hand, journeying and migration benefit individuals in
some specific ways. Individual migration reveals and breaks down
segregated spaces of all sorts. Black women's migration experiences
into formerly White and/or male academic disciplines illuminate how
migration can stimulate individual creativity. The work of Black
women writers who embrace migration and movement certainly has
made important contributions to Black women's intellectual production. For example, making extensive use of migration as a metaphor
for Black women's experiences, Carole Boyce Davies (1994) provides
a useful overview of Black women's connections to migration literature. Decrying the fixity of the term *Black women* that she sees characterizing Black feminist discourse in the United States, Davies counsels embracing fluidity, movement, and flexibility as a frame for Black
feminist theorizing. Ironically, in her criticisms of what she perceives
as the fixity of American Black feminism, Davies draws on the legitimation of intellectual space created by African-American women to
forward her own agenda. If there were no womanism or Black feminist
thought, nothing would exist for her to criticize. Writing not from the

fixity of racial segregation in the United States but from her position as a Caribbean migrant, Davies still finds hope generated in migration. Embracing migration and movement can also spur some important coalitions among individuals of all sorts who move into and through outsider-within locations. Like African-American women as a group, other similarly situated groups develop oppositional knowledges influenced by their proximity to more powerful groups. The historical invisibility of Black feminist thought and the hidden transcripts (Scott 1990) of other subjugated knowledges make them no less real. Individuals who manage to migrate from these subordinated groups often find that they share common themes, interpretive paradigms, and epistemological orientations. Moreover, White "race traitors," feminist men, and other individuals critical of their own privilege can also move into outsider-within spaces (see, e.g., Pratt 1993). Outsider-within locations allow individuals from these diverse places to meet and compare notes.

On the other hand, neither the relationships among people in outsider-within locations nor the knowledges produced in these spaces are inherently progressive. Within American higher education, for example, the myth of equivalent oppressions creates a new kind of individualism in outsider-within spaces. Although individual intellectuals in higher education may appear to be similarly disadvantaged, actual power relations create neither uniform privileges nor uniform disadvantages. Although being marginalized in intersections of race, class, gender, sexuality, and/or citizenship places many well-meaning intellectuals in higher education in common border zones, these same systems of power reproduce hierarchies within outsider-within locations. For example, within academia, African-American and White women seemingly share outsider-within positionality. Yet although female academics theoretically occupy equivalent locations in relation to each other, they are far from equal in academia itself, and certainly not in the United States as a whole. As appealing as it may be, it is impossible to shed the meanings attached to the socially assigned groups of race, economic class, nationality, and sexuality in which one finds oneself. Constructing oneself anew in the liberatory space of a shared outsider-within identity is difficult.

Since individuals emerging from differently ranked social groups have similar yet conflicting interests, migration and journeying to outsider-within locations may not yield uniformly progressive social theories. As Michael Awkward observes, "I have attempted to suspend disbelief, to interrogate actively the consequences of border crossings, including my own, rather than assume a predictably transgressive outcome" (1995, 15). Individual intellectuals can subsist in outsider-within locations and produce social theory that not only is *not* critical but may actually support injustice. Philosopher K. Anthony Appiah's criticism of the ways in which postcolonial intellectuals broker the idea of postcoloniality in the marketplace of academic ideas describes this situation:

> Postcoloniality is the condition—a relatively small, Western-style, Western-trained, group of writers and thinkers who mediate the trade in cultural commodities of world capitalism at the periphery. In the West they are known through the Africa they offer; their compatriots know them both through the West they present to Africa and through an Africa they have invented for the world, for each other, and for Africa. (1992, 149)

Black female intellectuals who trade a Black feminism or womanism in defense of their careers, especially if they aim to install their version as more authentic than others, are equally suspect. Thus, it is important to resist the temptation to recast outsider-within locations, their residents, and their accompanying knowledges as a homogeneous space characterized by an inherently progressive identity and politics.

Despite these caveats, gaining greater clarity about the ways in which the social location of intellectuals shapes their intellectual production offers the possibility of creating both new ways of theorizing and new types of critical social theory. This becomes possible when, for example, African-American women intellectuals who find themselves in outsider-within locations between many groups of unequal power critically use selected ideas from the knowledges generated by these groups (e.g., science, postmodernism, Afrocentrism, standpoint theory, and feminism) to construct truth(s) while journeying toward truth. To gain a fresh angle of vision, theorizing in these outsider-within locations often involves pausing in the typically uncomfortable disjuncture between conflicting knowledges. One is never "at home" anywhere, but, unlike Alfred Schutz's "stranger" (1944) or Karl Mannheim's "marginal intellectual" (1954), one is always situated somewhere in actual power relations. Pausing at the disjuncture represents the thought of one moment in time, a place in the dynamic process of theorizing. Since the locations where outsiders may pause are multiple and changing, critical social theory honed in outsider-within spaces reflects these dynamics.

Situating Black feminist thought as discourse and practice in relation to other discourses and their practices highlights the importance of moving through multiple contexts. Ironically, to be situated and moving at the same time is not a contradiction. As contexts become multiple, critical social theory reflects comparable complexities. Chicana theorist and poet Gloria Anzaldúa's work provides a glimpse of this process of continually moving among discourses in contextualizing and generating truth. For Anzaldúa, contextualizing truth via movement fosters a critical social theory unavailable to those who ground their truth in the centers of any one interpretive context. Invoking the metaphor of the snake shedding its skin, Anzaldúa queries, "Why does she have to go and try to make 'sense' of it all? Every time she makes 'sense' of something, she has to 'cross over,' kicking a hole out of the old boundaries of the self and slipping under or over, dragging the old skin along, stumbling over it. It hampers her movement in the new territory, dragging the ghost of the past with her" (1987, 49). Anzaldúa describes the difficulty of always remembering one's past, the process of "dragging along" the "old skin" of science, Afrocentrism, standpoint theory, feminism, and the like. How nice it would be to move easily through these social theories, leaving them as dead and discarded skins of prior, "incorrect" periods of intellectual inquiry. Being a traveler, always attending to context ("old skin") yet always moving ("slipping under or over" the possibilities and limitations of social theories), is difficult. However, Anzaldúa also points to the utility of this approach for contextualized truth:

> It is only when she is on the other side and the shell cracks open and the lid from her eyes lifts that she sees things in a different perspective. It is only then that she makes the connections, formulates the insights. It is only then that her consciousness expands a tiny notch, another rattle appears on the rattlesnake tail and the added growth slightly alters the sounds she makes. (49)

On Naming and Proclaiming the Truth

Sojourner Truth's chosen name speaks to the power relations associated with truth, illustrating that the act of naming has special significance. Truth recognized that the power relations that framed the truth about her life were so unjust that she could not even name herself. In the context of her time, Truth was an object to be named at will by masters. Rejecting her slave name, "Isabella," Truth proclaimed, "I wa'n't goin' to keep nothin' of Egypt on me, an' so I went to the Lord an' asked him to give me a new name." By selecting Sojourner Truth as a name more in keeping with how she saw herself, Truth highlights the power of naming in creating new realities. In a similar fashion, academic masters have the power to define academic disciplines within segregated disciplinary space. Describing these connections between naming and power, Pierre Bourdieu notes, "Social agents struggle for . . . symbolic power, of which this power of constitutive *naming,* which by naming things brings them into being, is one of the most typical demonstrations" (1990, 55; emphasis in original). In this context, Truth's refusal to accept the names or interpretations routinely applied to social phenomena, including herself, constituted an act of profound defiance.

Naming oneself and defining ideas that count as truth are empowering acts. For those damaged by years of silencing, Truth's act speaks to the significance of self-definition in healing from oppression. However, Sojourner Truth's biography also points to the importance of actively proclaiming truth. Although important, private naming is not enough—truth must be publicly proclaimed. James Scott observes, "Although we have expressly avoided using the term *truth* to characterize the hidden transcript . . . the open declaration of the hidden transcript in the teeth of power is typically experienced, both by the speaker and by those who share his or her condition, as a moment in which truth is finally spoken in the place of equivocation and lies" (1990, 208). By claiming that she was to "declare the truth to the people," Sojourner Truth saw her intellectual and political task not as one of fitting into existing power relations but as one of confronting injustice—to speak the truth "in the place of equivocation and lies." Believing that speaking the truth in a context of domination constituted an act of empowerment, of all the possible names, Isabella Baumfree named herself Truth.

By proclaiming truth, Sojourner Truth's actions invoke a Black women's testimonial tradition long central to naming and proclaiming the truth. Although testimonials to God within organized church settings illustrate one important dimension of this tradition, the act of testifying is epistemologically significant as well. Within a narrow use of the testimonial, individuals testify within a community of believers such that each testimonial spurs others on to greater faith. However, a broader use of the testimonial involves testifying the truth to cynics and nonbelievers. Within a more generalized testimonial tradition, breaking silence, speaking out, and talking back in academic settings constitute public testimonials. Moreover, linking this tradition to a search for justice politicizes it. For Black women in the United States, testifying for or publicly speaking the truth, often about the unspeakable, not only recaptures human dignity but also constitutes a profound act of resistance.

Epistemologically, the act of proclaiming truth speaks to the significance of dialogue in constructing truth, especially dialogue across substantial differences in power. Although Sojourner Truth certainly could have named herself in isolation, proclaiming the truth required a community of listeners. It mattered neither that many of the listeners in her day cared little for what she had to say nor that they were more powerful. In a sense, her boldness foreshadows the civil rights, Black Power, and other social movements of the 1960s and 1970s that effectively used the media to proclaim new truths. Despite the discomfort and conflict that typically accompany this type of dialogue, singular and/or multiple truths can be accessed only by open proclamation from a variety of locations.

In approaching the question how truth might be dialogically determined by groups with competing interests, the works of African-American women writers offer some intriguing ideas. Searching for a deeper understanding of the complexity of Black women's "voice," Mae Henderson describes Black women's voice as both a "dialogic of difference and a dialectic of identity" (1989, 21). In the former, African-American women speak from a location that highlights differences from others, whereas in the latter, they negotiate aspects of Black womanhood that are shared with others.[3] Thus, the contours of Black women's "voice" are simultaneously confrontational (in response to different interests) and collaborative (in response to shared interests). The complexity of Black women's voice reflects this difference/identity, both/and quality, one that, to Henderson, can be seen in Black women writers' ability to "speak in tongues." In describing this practice, Henderson invokes the experience of Black women in the Pentecostal Holiness Church (the Sanctified Church) of speaking in unknown tongues as a sign of being chosen or of holiness.

Henderson suggests two connotations of speaking in tongues. The first involves the ability to speak in diverse, known languages, especially to speak the multiple languages of public discourse. The second consists of the private, particular, closed, and privileged communication between the congregation and the divinity. Inaccessible to the general congregation, this second meaning of speaking in tongues is outside the realm of public discourse. Henderson claims, "It is the first as well as the second meaning which we privilege in speaking of black women writers: the first connoting polyphony, multivocality, and plurality of voices, and the second signifying intimate, private, inspired utterances" (23).

Although Henderson confines her analysis to Black women's literature, her analysis of speaking in tongues suggests provocative new epistemological directions for critical social theory. Henderson's analysis of speaking in tongues provides a metaphor for the interaction of logic, creativity, and accessibility, a metaphor for producing contextualized truth that is actively named and proclaimed in multiple voices. She states, "Also interesting is the link between the gift of tongues, the gift of prophecy, and the gift of interpretation" (1989, 24.) This link suggests intriguing connections among three ideas: the gift of tongues, or the ability to produce social theory that is accessible to diverse groups of people who speak different "tongues"; the gift of prophecy, or what we might call creativity and inspiration; and the gift of interpretation, the more familiar notion of rationality or logic. Separating truth from the world in order to construct truths about the world may not be necessary. As Sojourner Truth's biography suggests, other options exist.

Freedom Struggles and Critical Masses

When it comes to resistance, Sojourner Truth's significance lies less in her being a role model to be emulated than in the symbolic meaning of her many freedom struggles. Although Truth is best known for her speeches against slavery and for women's rights, her patterns of resistance demonstrate a knack for resisting on multiple fronts. Using her voice to name and proclaim truth did not constitute her sole means of resistance. By going to court to sue a former owner who had illegally removed one of her children to the South, Truth recognized and used law as an instrument of social change. Moreover, Truth felt compelled to take direct action when such action seemed unavoidable. For example, she was evicted from a train for refusing to adhere to racially segregated practices. Truth's life thus seems to model a view of resistance that takes Malcolm X's words "by any means necessary" to heart.

Using her voice, pursuing legal remedies, and taking direct action all contribute to Truth's lushly textured notion of freedom. Freedom was not an intellectual project for Truth. Born a slave, freedom was real for her. Historian Darlene Clark Hine describes the centrality of freedom for Sojourner Truth and her contemporary Harriet Tubman:

> For both Truth and Tubman, freedom, and the unrelenting quest for freedom, was the mainstay of their identities. Their passionate embrace of freedom was born not of some abstract commitment to the Constitution or the noble sentiments embodied in the Declaration of Independence, but out of the reality of their enslavement and oppression. They knew firsthand what it meant to be owned by another, to be considered little more than a cow or a mule. Truth and Tubman also mastered the survival skills slavery and multiple oppression required. Slavery, and resistance to it, were the defining moment of the birth of black women's oppositional consciousness. (1993, 343)

Truth's fusion of visionary ideas about freedom (a vision informed by race, class, and gender intersectionality), as well as pragmatic actions taken in search of freedom (legal action, individual protest, speeches, etc.), shaped her resistance.[4]

In crafting freedom struggles that resist the new politics of containment, Black feminist thought might build on this tradition of visionary pragmatism. For African-American women, questions such as "In what ways does Black feminist thought equip Black women to resist oppression?" and "In what ways is Black feminist thought functional as a tool for social change?" are more than academic concerns. Answers to these questions have palpable implications not only for Black women in the United States but also for members of other similarly situated groups. Black feminist thought and other critical social theories either explicitly or implicitly include ideas about resistance. Any critical social theory that energizes African-American women to struggle in the context of everyday life will be more valuable than social theories that, no matter how logical, correct, contextually true, or eloquently proclaimed, foster hopelessness. Moving African-American women to political action requires providing a comprehensive array of pragmatic actions that can work in everyday life. Grounded in the belief that everybody can contribute something to a freedom struggle, such a theory recognizes that not everyone can make the same contribution, nor should they.[5]

Sojourner Truth's path of initially struggling for her own freedom and then expanding her actions and ideas to encompass broader freedom struggles is not unusual. Just as Truth grounded her struggles in concrete experience but refused to limit them to her particular experience, contemporary Black feminist thought might emulate a similar relationship between the particular and the general. Since Black feminist thought has now succeeded in its initial efforts to gain some visibility, Black women can move beyond their particular experiences without losing sight of the specificity of those experiences. In *Fighting Words,* for example, I stress the specificity of African-American women's involvement in a new politics of containment. I neither claim that all groups experience this emerging politics in the same way nor present African-American women's experiences as a new universal reality. Rather, just as being situated yet moving does not constitute a contradiction for knowledge developed in outsider-within locations, being simultaneously particular and universal is also possible. Black feminist thought must remain situated in African-American women's particular experiences yet must also generate theoretical connections to other knowledges with similar goals. It must preserve its particular but must learn to see its particular in universal terms. Stated differently, Black feminist thought can be conceptualized as a particular intellectual freedom struggle that must engage (both confrontationally and collaboratively) with other intellectual freedom struggles without losing sight of the specificity of its own situation.[6]

For the moment at least, Black women's intellectual production has visibility that provides new opportunities for thinking through Black women's pragmatic, everyday freedom struggles. Since much of African-American women's political activism in particular situations remains unrecognized as political activism, even by many Black women themselves, it remains unconnected to more universal freedom struggles (e.g., those for human rights). Moreover, most discussions of politics focus on male behavior in the public sphere and assume self-interest as a motivation for participation. In contrast, actions that derive from a concern for collective good—one major dimension of women's political activism—are rarely incorporated into contemporary political analyses. Nancy Naples's study of the political practice of women community workers in low-income neighborhoods reveals a reluctance on the part of Black and Puerto Rican women to identify their community activism as "political." As Naples points out, "Most of the workers did not define themselves a political people, feminists, radicals, or socialists. They simply believed that they were acting to protect their communities" (1991, 491). A similar study of a group of elderly Black women who successfully managed co-op buildings in Harlem found that the activities of women in co-ops linked domestic life and cooperative organization. Both leaders and tenants in success-ful co-ops likened their buildings to a family. Elderly Black women be-came leaders not only because of their special abilities but also be-cause of their membership in long-standing social networks, as well as their histories of reliance on such networks for survival (Saegert 1989). Yet because women's behavior in both of these cases could not be coded within dominant norms of political self-interest, their ac-tions were not defined as political activism.

In recasting the political to encompass Black women's everyday freedom struggles, the term *critical mass* seems especially useful. I like this term because it is already in everyday use and has a variety of interrelated meanings.[7] One meaning views a critical mass as a neces-sary catalyst for some other, larger action to occur. In the history of protest movements, the term refers to small subgroups of especially motivated individuals who form a critical mass that sets collective action in motion. For example, the four students who sat in at the Woolworth's lunch counter in Greensboro, North Carolina, in 1960 formed an organized critical mass that galvanized Black and White students across the American South to take similar action. Borrowing from business, the term is applied to a threshold of vendors needed to launch a successful product line. The turning point or threshold at which hype turns into reality constitutes the onset of critical mass. The term *critical mass* also refers to a group of people who take action in response to their criticisms of some policy or dimension of social organization. Although they may express a critical consciousness, they become a critical mass when they take action.

All of these meanings of *critical mass*—a catalyst for change, a threshold or necessary turning point at which action can occur, and an action taken by an organized minority—permeate African-American women's pragmatic, everyday freedom struggles. In this sense, Black feminist thought might aim to build critical masses of all sorts, certainly among African-American women, but also between Black women and other similarly situated groups. The term *critical mass* seems especially malleable in this regard. On the one hand, there exists a need to build a critical *mass* or threshold group of people who act as catalysts for change. *Mass* does not necessarily mean large numbers of people, as in "mass" culture and "mass" media. Instead, *mass* can mean some sort of political threshold associated with action. On the other hand, a need for a *critical* mass—a group, however defined, that is equipped to analyze its situation—also exists. Developing more complex understandings of critical mass might provide new directions for contemporary freedom struggles.

Moral Authority, Black Women's Spirituality, and Justice

Reading about Sojourner Truth's accomplishments, I remain awed at how she managed to persist under such extremely difficult circumstances. In my own work, I have access to telephones, computers, fax machines, steady employment, health benefits, decent housing, and multiple forms of literacy. All enable me to do this kind of work. Despite this level of Western privilege, however, some days I become discouraged. Sojourner Truth possessed none of these advantages. How did she manage to keep going?

Sojourner Truth's sustained commitment to social justice raises one important question for any critical social theory: does this social theory move people to struggle? I use the word *move* intentionally to refer to the power of deep feelings. This type of passionate rationality flies in the face of Western epistemology that sees emotions and rationality as different and competing concerns (Jaggar 1989). Described by Audre Lorde (1984) as the power of the erotic, deep feelings that arouse people to action constitute a critical source of power. Sadly, within capitalist marketplace relations, this erotic power is so often sexualized that not only is it routinely misunderstood but the strength of deeply felt love is even feared. Spirituality fully realized, for example, is a passionate, deeply felt affair. People are moved to do all kinds of things when they genuinely care. Ideas that engage this deep love, caring, and commitment can energize people and move them to struggle. Moreover, given the vulnerability of deep feelings to be annexed by systems of power, moral authority must lie at the heart of meaningful social theory, providing, as Cornel West suggests, "a chance for people to believe that there is hope for the future and a meaning to struggle" (1993, 18).

Like Sojourner Truth, Black women often approach this search for meaning by expressing a deep-seated concern with the issue of justice, not just because they either think justice is logical or see pragmatic reasons for pursuing it, but because they *believe* that achieving it is the right thing to do.[8] Moreover, as was true for Sojourner Truth, people often feel compelled to take action against injustice when they care deeply about something. The ability of a social theory to engage deep feelings in searching for justice suggests a complex redefinition of the personal. As opposed to interpretations of "the personal is political" that aim to micromanage individual actions in defense of misguided political "correctness," personal actions grounded in ethical frameworks (such as the search for justice) become infused with political meaning. When feelings are involved—when individuals *feel* as opposed to *think* they are committed—and when those feelings are infused with self-reflexive truths as well as some sort of moral authority, actions become fully politicized.

As they are for other groups with histories of oppression, ideas of freedom and justice are especially important for Black women in the United States. Even though Black women's concern for justice is shared with many others, African-American women have a particular group history in relation to justice. Spirituality, especially that organized though and sanctioned by Black Christian churches, provides one important way that many African-American women are moved to struggle for justice. Defined as a collective expression of deep feeling that occurs within an overarching moral framework, spirituality remains deeply intertwined with justice in Black women's intellectual history.[9] Spirituality moves many Black women and thus influences Black women's critical social theory in particular ways. My concern in this section lies less with the *content* of Black women's vision of what makes social theory meaningful to them (i.e., with particular expressions of spirituality) and more with the way Black feminist thought represents a culturally specific, distinctive expression of a more general *process* of being moved to struggle.

Sojourner Truth's biography suggests a process in which thinking and feeling do not work at cross-purposes but, rather, seem to energize one another. Her spirituality served as a vehicle that clearly moved her struggle for justice. It is almost as if Truth developed a deep love for justice and expressed her passionate commitment to it through her freedom struggles. As is the case for many African-American women, Truth's spirituality found expression through a Christian religious ethos whereby she talked directly to "the Lord" and where "the Lord" gave her the name Truth. When Sojourner Truth was asked by a preacher if the source of her preaching was from the Bible, she responded, "No honey, can't read a letter. When I preaches, I has jest one text to preach from, an' I always preaches from this one. My text is, 'when I found Jesus!'" (qtd. in Grant 1992, 41). Truth's understanding of Jesus appears consistent with an African-American women's moral tradition of seeing the world as infused with an importance that supersedes any one human being or group of human beings. In a carefully constructed and comprehensive assessment of African-American spirituality, Dona Richards offers a deeply textured analysis of its significance within African-American culture. Noting the difficulty of discussing spirituality using the language of Western intellectual discourse, Richards observes, "Spirit is, of course, not a rationalistic concept. It cannot be quantified, measured, explained by or reduced to neat, rational, conceptual categories as Western thought demands. . . . We experience our spirituality often, but the translation of that experience into an intellectual language can never be accurate. The attempt results in reductionism" (1990, 208). Thus, spirituality is not merely a system of religious beliefs similar to logical systems of ideas. Rather, spirituality comprises articles of faith that provide a conceptual framework for living everyday life. Sojourner Truth's biography reveals the profound influence that the evangelical movement had on her ethical standards, her notion of struggle, and her journey to proclaim the truth. Truth describes the importance of spirituality, expressed as a belief in God, in her everyday life: "No, God does not stop to rest, for he is a spirit, and cannot tire. . . . And if 'God is all in all,' and 'worketh all in all,' . . . then it is impossible he should rest at all; for if he did, every other thing would stop and rest too; the waters would not flow, and the fishes could not swim; and all motion must cease" (qtd. in Washington 1993, 86–87). For Truth, God was to be worshiped at all times, in all places, throughout time, and without rest.

For many Black women in the United States, Christianity provides symbols invoked in crafting and expressing this ethical tradition infused with spirituality.[10] Jesus constitutes one such symbol. According to Black feminist theologian Jacqueline Grant, Black women see Jesus as a nonconformist, a model of wholeness, and a person who affirms women as persons created equally with men. By interpreting Jesus as a cosufferer, an equalizer, and a liberator, Black women appropriate the symbols of Christianity and infuse them with a moral authority that guides everyday life:

> As the Resurrection signified that there is more to life than the cross for Jesus Christ, for Black women it signifies that their tri-dimensional oppressive existence is not the end, but it merely represents the context in which a particular people struggle to experience hope and liberation. Jesus Christ thus represents a three-fold significance: first he identifies with the "little people," Black women, where they are: secondly, he affirms the basic humanity of these, "the least"; and thirdly, he inspires active hope in the struggle for resurrected, liberated existence. (1989, 217)

In brief, Jesus is committed to social justice.

In her volume *Black Womanist Ethics*, Katie Cannon develops a model of Black women's ethics that is deeply tied to this ethos of spirituality. According to Cannon, Western ethical ideals are predicated on the existence of freedom, defined as having a wide range of choices. Dominant ethics make a virtue of qualities that lead to economic success—self-reliance, frugality, and industry. Dominant ethics also assume that a moral agent is basically free, possesses individual rights, and is self-directing. Each person retains self-determining power in a raceless, genderless, classless rational-man theory on which notions such as liberal individualism, moral worth, and distributive justice rest. For people experiencing oppression, these assumptions are inaccurate. In a context of racial segregation, the everyday texture of African-American life requires an alternative moral agency that challenges and replaces these beliefs. In investigating this moral agency, Cannon looks not to biblical sources but to the tradition of Black women's literature. Cannon claims that this literary tradition forms the best available written repository for understanding Black women's ethical values. For Cannon, this tradition "documents the 'living space' carved out of the intricate web of racism, sexism, and poverty" (1988, 7). It parallels African-American history and conveys the assumed values in the Black oral tradition.

Using this understanding of the connections between deep caring, moral authority, and freedom struggles for justice creates a dramatically different political and intellectual ethos for African-American women. Spirituality broadly defined continues to move countless African-American women like Sojourner Truth to struggle in everyday life. "In addition to the necessity for us to be political, we must be spiritual," contends poet Sonia Sanchez. "Our spirituality will keep us from becoming cynical, from becoming bitter, from becoming harsh. Our politics combined with our spirituality will keep us from becoming like the people that we are now trying to replace" (qtd. in Chandler 1990, 362). As Black feminist literary critic Barbara Omolade observes, "The reliance on the spiritual center for answers, explanations, and focus is the strongest opposition to Western social and natural science. All questions can't be answered through objectivity, and certainly Black woman's power and knowing can't be understood without a knowing of her spirit and spiritual life" (1994, 112). Historically, Black women invoked spirituality through family, church, and other institutions of Black civil society. This spirituality encompassed a distinctive ethical core, one that not only gave moral authority to African-American women's ideas and actions but also fostered survival. To Dona Richards, African-Americans survived the horrors of the Middle Passage, the slave experience, and subsequent institutionalized racism because of the "depth and strength of African spirituality and humanism" (1990, 207).

African-American women's active participation in the civil rights movement cannot be explained fully by either their commitment to truth or their skill in crafting critical masses. It took passion to confront fire hoses, dogs, and guns, a deep caring linked with a vision of how their individual efforts constituted part of some larger ethical struggle. Moreover, the freedom songs, many of which were secular versions of music sung in Black churches, were central to helping marchers and protesters sustain the struggle. For example, Fannie Lou Hamer's rendition of "This Little Light of Mine" spoke to the uniqueness of each individual in that collective struggle. Similarly, the Freedom Singers, in which Bernice Johnson Reagon was a young singer, produced music that gave heart to the struggle. The civil rights movement typifies a freedom struggle with close links among spirituality, moral authority, and social justice. Black women participated in the civil rights movement not because it was logically defensible to do so but because it was the *right* thing to do. In this context, "rightness" encompassed more than mere logic or rationality—"rightness" emerged from faith and had moral authority.

The moral authority that emerges from this type of spirituality becomes increasingly significant in a secular world grounded in the commodity relations associated with profound injustices. After all, how does a group of people persist when each day brings new ways of relegating them to the bottom of a social hierarchy? How do African-American women struggle in a place where the black jelly beans remain stuck to the bottom of the bag from one generation to the next? Critical social theory infused by a deeply felt, politicized spirituality operates in a special place—it steps *outside* the assumptions of social theories expressing either purely theoretical quests or narrow pragmatic concerns. Moreover, in the absence of being moved toward justice, the quest for contextualized truth, the naming and proclaiming of truth, and the building of critical masses constitute secular, pragmatic concerns. Even the most intellectually gifted and politically savvy students, faculty members, parents, managers, and book editors become discouraged. Although secular, pragmatic concerns clearly matter, in the absence of deep caring infused with ethical or moral authority, freedom struggles become increasingly difficult to sustain.

Rather than being seen as yet another content area within Black feminist discourse, a concern with justice fused with a deep spirituality appears to be highly significant to how African-American women conceptualize critical social theory. Justice constitutes an article of faith expressed through deep feelings that move people to action. For many Black feminist thinkers, justice transcends Western notions of equality grounded in sameness and uniformity. Elsa Barkley Brown's discussion of African-American women's quilting (1989) points us in the direction of conceptualizing an alternative notion of justice. In making their quilts, Black women weave together scraps of fabric from all sorts of places. Nothing is wasted, and every piece of fabric has a function and a place in a given quilt. Black women quilters often place in juxtaposition odd-sized scraps of fabric that appear to clash with one another. Uniform size is not a criterion for membership in the quilt, nor is blending in with all the other scraps. Brown reports that viewers of such quilts who evaluate aesthetic beauty in terms of sameness, repetitive patterns, and overall homogeneity are often disoriented. These quilts may appear chaotic, yet patterns that are initially difficult to see become apparent over time.

In a similar fashion, those who conceptualize community via notions of uniformity and sameness have difficulty imagining a social quilt that is simultaneously heterogeneous, driven toward excellence, and just. In this regard, neither the false universal perspectives on truth discussed in chapter 2 nor the postmodern treatment of difference explored in chapter 4 has been able to generate compelling alternatives for unjust practices. False universal perspectives claim that seemingly universal standards (whether of truth or beauty) should be held up for all members of the social fabric to replicate. Within this logic, just communities are accomplished by making individuals fit into some overall pattern. When each piece has an equal right to achieve its place in some preestablished setting, then justice has been adequately distributed. Postmodern notions of difference criticize these notions yet have difficulty generating compelling alternatives. The extreme constructionist views of difference offer little hope for achieving community. Within their logic, no social quilt is possible. All that remains is a pile of unrelated scraps of fabric. Reconstructive postmodern views that retain tolerance for difference may also inadvertently rely on notions of uniformity and sameness in constructing just communities. As long as patterns in the overall social quilt remain uniform, tolerating an occasional scrap of difference is allowed. One need not like a scrap that sticks out within the overall pattern of homogeneity—one need only tolerate its presence. Indeed, in an era of commodified difference, symbolic inclusion of scraps of difference that divert attention from overall social injustices can appear to promote social justice while upholding unjust power relations.

Brown's analysis of quilts points to a much more radical notion of justice. Although Brown's analysis makes little overt mention of justice, viewing quilts as a metaphor for community highlights different ways of conceptualizing justice within communities. Her notion of difference held in balance in one quilt suggests a notion of justice that balances the whole and its different parts. Brown presents a vision of a just community constructed in response to aesthetic and pragmatic concerns, one in which all people are represented and none left out, no matter how small or seemingly insignificant the individual scrap of fabric. A textbook containing this vision of community would forget neither those second graders I taught so long ago nor the children of today. Moreover, Brown's vision is not merely an academic concern. Black women activists such as Fannie Lou Hamer and Ella Baker brought similar sensibilities to their freedom struggles. In particular,

Baker's notion of participatory democracy suggests a pragmatic approach to achieving Brown's vision of community.

Black feminist poet and essayist June Jordan has long offered an uncompromising stance on the issue of justice. Jordan counsels us to move beyond, as she puts it, "the paralysis of identity politics," because, as she observes, "there is available to me a moral attachment to a concept beyond gender and race. I am referring to the concept of justice" (1992, 168). Angered by the increasing depoliticization of the language of struggle, Jordan points to the connections among moral authority, freedom struggles, and justice. In her essay entitled "Where Is the Rage?" she links deep feelings of rage with a passion for justice:

> The neglected legacy of the Sixties is just this: unabashed moral certitude, and the purity—the incredible outgoing energy—of righteous rage. I do not believe that we can restore and expand the freedoms that our lives require unless and until we embrace the justice of our rage. . . . If we do not change the language of current political discourse, if we do not reintroduce a Right and Wrong, a Good or Evil measurement of doers and deeds, then how shall we, finally, argue our cause? (178)

As for those who lack the commitment to struggle for justice, Jordan offers the following challenge: "No matter how desolate our condition, there is someone else depending on our humanity for his or her rescue" (114).

When I embarked upon the journey from my Philadelphia neighborhood to the unfamiliar terrain of my high school, then to my class of Boston second graders, and on to the often troubled campuses of higher education in the 1990s, I had no idea that my journey would take me so far. Much has changed since I started. Former concerns about my identity or difference seem less important these days, for too much is at stake. Because situations characterized by injustice are ubiquitous, I neither bemoan my discomfort nor worry whether I "belong" when I find myself in situations of privilege. When tempted to complain about some dimension of my life, I try to remember that my condition is far from desolate, and that holding fast to my humanity might matter to others. On a daily basis, I try to remember that even though I "buy in" to much of what is around me, I cannot forget to ask whether I've "sold out." In my current terrain of struggle—the often seductive yet vital world of higher education—these remain important lessons.

As Italian philosopher Antonio Gramsci observes, "For a mass of people to be led to think coherently and in the same coherent fashion about the real present world, is a 'philosophical' event far more important and 'original' than the discovery by some philosophical 'genius' of a truth which remains the property of a small group of intellectuals" (Forgacs 1988, 327). Although political struggle requires good ideas, it also needs much more. Without some sense of where we're going and why we want to go there, and some "righteous rage" to spur us on, we won't even know if we're headed in the right direction. As Barbara Ransby and Tracye Matthews remind us, "It is a complex journey from consciousness to the concrete politics of empowerment, and one which is, by definition, full of contradictions and detours. It is perhaps most important, individually and collectively, simply to stay on the right road" (1993, 68). In these endeavors, critical social theory matters, because it helps point the way. If critical social theory manages to move people toward justice, then it has made a very important difference.

Notes

Introduction

1. In the United States and across the globe, economically privileged, seemingly heterosexual, White men with citizenship in the United States or former European colonial powers occupy positions of power in government, corporations, universities, and the media. Despite the tremendous heterogeneity that exists among American and European White men, elite discourses typically depict this group's worldview as homogeneous and hegemonic. During the nineteenth and well into the twentieth century, when people of color, women, and working-class people were excluded from basic literacy, let alone positions of authority in schools, the media, and other sites of knowledge production, academic disciplines such as biology, anthropology, sociology, and psychology seemed preoccupied with proving the inferiority of these excluded groups (Jones 1973; Gould 1981; Stepan 1982, 1990; Harding 1986, 1991; Torgovnick 1990; Morton 1991; McKee 1993). Intellectual biases in the Curriculum reflect the legacy of this elite group's need to generate ideological justifications for its right to rule.

2. For classic general works on resistance, see, for example, Memmi (1965) and Freire (1970). Selected works on resistance emerging primarily from antiracist struggle include Fanon (1963), Breitman (1965), Marable (1983, 1991), and Walters (1993). Selected works dealing with resistance under capitalist development include Baran and Sweezy (1966), Forgacs (1988), and Bonacich (1989). For works aiming to theorize intersectionality and resistance traditions, see Davis (1981, 1989), Caraway (1991), and Anthias and Yuval-Davis (1992).

3. French theorist Pierre Bourdieu describes a similar process of intertextual readings. For a discussion of issues of working across interpretive communities, see Bourdieu (1990, 147–49). In a moment of uncharacteristic clarity, Bourdieu notes, "The method of analysis that I am proposing cannot really be put into operation other than at the cost of an enormous amount of work" (148).

4. Critical theory references a tradition of thinking loosely organized in two branches—the first centered on the Institute for Social Research, established in Frankfurt in 1923, and the second on the more recent work of Jürgen Habermas (Held 1980). Although the ideas of critical theorists influence this volume, I rely on a broader definition that approximates the approach taken by Craig Calhoun (1995), who examines postmodernism and standpoint theory as examples of critical social theory. Thus, critical theory as a school of thought is one example of the more general category of critical social theory.

5. The literature of secondary works that analyze primary works is quite vast. For example, three texts that examine sociological theory from widely different perspectives appeared in 1995 alone (Lemert, Levine, Mouzelis). Three secondary works that take similarly divergent views of postmodernism include volumes by Best and Kellner (1991), McGowan (1991), and Rosenau (1992). Works by Goldberg (1993) and Omi and Winant (1994) survey racial theory, and the important volume by Anthias and Yuval-Davis (1992) summarizes a range of theories of race, ethnicity, class, gender, and nation.

6. For example, astute readers may notice that I incorporate several meanings of class in *Fighting Words*. In its most general use, *class* refers to a general category or group of people who have some sort of shared condition. In its more restricted use, it refers to a group of people with a shared economic condition. When referring to this more restricted use, I use the term *economic class* whenever possible, or the more familiar *social class* when it clearly refers to economic class relations.

Learning from the Outsider Within Revisited

1. The discussions of marginality, especially marginal intellectuals, in classical sociological theory shed some light on social theory developed in outsider-within locations. Sociologist Georg Simmel's essay on the sociological significance of what he called the "stranger" (1921) provides one perspective on how living on the borders of a group may lead to different types of theorizing. Some of the potential benefits include (1) Simmel's definition of *objectivity* as "a peculiar composition of nearness and remoteness, concern and indifference"; (2) the tendency for people to confide in a "stranger" in ways they never would with each other; and (3) the ability of the "stranger" to see patterns that may be more difficult for those immersed in the situation to see. Mannheim (1954) labels the "strangers" in academia "marginal intellectuals" and argues that the critical posture that such individuals bring to academic endeavors may be essential to the creative development of academic disciplines. More recently, Young's analysis of the five dimensions of oppression (1990) identifies marginalization as one key component.

2. Barbara Neely's mystery series beginning with *Blanche on the Lam* (1992) provides an enjoyable fictional account of these relationships. In the opening novel, Blanche goes undercover as a domestic to hide from the law. Her view of her new White family is fascinating.

3. With hindsight, I now see that there are several issues involved in creating a tradition, especially a Black feminist one. First, attempts to specify a canon necessarily minimize differences among members of the group. I decided that highlighting sameness and thereby legitimating Black women's right to *have* an intellectual tradition would have more impact on Black women's being taken seriously than would writing my work as just another individual "voice" so easily appropriated by a range of other, more powerful discourses. Another issue concerns the very definition of canon. Critiques of *Black Feminist Thought* typically use a narrow definition of canon, treating it as a decontex-

tualized system of ideas unrelated to actual social conditions. It quickly became apparent to me that Black women's intellectual tradition could not be explained without sustained attention to the status of Black women as a group in power relations. As Michele Wallace points out, "I . . . realized that to define a 'tradition' that integrates black female critical voices is to be forced to confront the way in which such voices have been systematically excluded from previous notions of 'tradition.' It is, in other words, a 'tradition' of speaking out of turn. The reasons for this are not inherent in the nature of black women, but are, rather, structural: they derive from the 'outsider' position we tend to occupy in critical discourse" (1990, 215).

1. The More Things Change, the More They Stay the Same

1. All quotations of Bari-Ellen Roberts in this section can be found in an article based on an interview with Roberts that is reported in Boulton (1996). Roberts's failure to be promoted apparently was not related to her qualifications. She reported that she had endured a series of racially discriminatory acts at Texaco before filing the lawsuit—she was excluded from attending executive training seminars, going on foreign trips, receiving high-profile assignments, and making presentations before senior executives—the same responsibilities Roberts had routinely been given during her 9½ years at Chase Manhattan Corporation. In that previous position, Roberts had served as a vice president overseeing a staff of twenty, including five other vice presidents. Roberts's treatment by her later employer parallels the employment discrimination reported by African-Americans in general. For a discussion of racial differences in employment, see Hacker (1992). An overview of employment discrimination and current remedies can be found in Ezorsky (1991). See Feagin and Sikes (1994) and Cose (1993) for work on middle-class African-Americans and employment discrimination. Despite her successful lawsuit, Roberts has left Texaco and has published a book-length analysis of the case.

2. Building on the legal framework established by the 1954 *Brown v. Board of Education* school desegregation case, the Civil Rights Act of 1964, and other significant legislation, several landmark employment discrimination cases against corporations were argued in the 1970s. For a cursory review of landmark decisions, see Scott (1984). Ezorsky (1991) provides a more extensive treatment of the same topic.

3. The transcript was made of a meeting in August 1994 among senior officials of Texaco, a giant oil company that reported $36.8 billion in 1995 revenues (White 1996b). The meeting was secretly taped by a former personnel director who, after he was fired, turned the recording over to the plaintiffs in the racial discrimination suit. According to the transcript, the executives openly discussed shredding minutes of meetings and other documents that were sought by the Black employees to bolster their claim that Texaco discriminated against minorities in promotions and fostered a hostile work environment. The embarrassing transcript catalyzed a speedy resolution of the lawsuit. As one journalist queried, "Why did it take more than two years of legal action by six aggrieved black employees, the leak of an embarrassing tape recording and the threat of a boycott to get Texaco to live up to the fine-sounding promises in its glossy equal-opportunity brochures?" (White 1996a.)

4. The term *class* has several meanings that are used throughout this volume. In its most general sense, *class* means "group," as in a class of second graders, or Blacks as a class of people. Iris Marion Young provides a definition of *group* that parallels my use: "A social group is a collective of persons differentiated from at least one other group by cultural forms, practices, or way of life. Members of a group have a specific affinity with one another because of their similar experience or way of life. . . . Groups are an

expression of social relations" (1990, 43). According to Young, *oppression* refers to structural phenomena that suppress a group. Thus, relegating Blacks as a group to the bottom of power relations constitutes oppression. Within this logic, economic oppression becomes one type of group oppression that works with and through others. Thus far, I have used the term *economic class* to refer to a group of people who share a common placement in a political economy. In this sense, historically Blacks constituted an economic class because the vast majority of African-Americans lived in similar economic and political conditions. This meaning of *economic class* parallels the term *social class,* which has a vast literature attached to it. Since, like the term *outsider within, social class* is also often reduced to an identity category (e.g., working-class Black women, middle-class White men), I decided to use *economic class* to signal the structural relations that frame group formation. I take up these issues in greater detail in chapter 6.

5. This section relies on Jürgen Habermas's (1989) groundbreaking analysis of the emergence of the public sphere and its relation to European bourgeois society. Although Habermas makes little mention of gender and social class, and even less of race, his ideas have attracted considerable interest among academics in the United States. Habermas could generate his notion of the public only by ignoring the private spheres of home and family and therefore leaving them undertheorized. The omission of slavery and colonialism also limits the generalizability of Habermas's perspectives on the public sphere. In this section, I collapse into a few pages a diverse and lively discussion about issues of public and private that transcend law, political science, philosophy, women's studies, and other disciplines.

6. Whereas in this section I focus on the split between the public and private, philosopher David Goldberg points to an interesting parallelism between notions of private/public and inside/outside: "Citizens and strangers are controlled through the spatial confines of divided place. . . . For modernity, inside has tended to connote subjectivity, the realm of deep feelings, of Truth; outside suggests physicality, human difference, strangeness. The dichotomy between inside and outside also marks, as it is established by marking territory. . . . This dichotomy between inner and outer intersects with and is both magnified and transmuted by another one central to the condition of modernity: the dichotomy between public and private" (1993, 186).

7. The theme of surveillance is closely tied to French philosopher Michel Foucault's notion of disciplinary power. Foucault argues, "In a society in which the principal elements are no longer the community and public life, but, on the one hand, private individuals and, on the other, the state, relations can be regulated only in a form that is the exact reverse of the spectacle" (1979, 216). He continues: "Our society is one not of spectacle, but of surveillance . . . the hierarchical, permanent exercise of indefinite discipline" (217). In this sense, disciplinary power is exercised via surveillance.

8. This notion of power differences giving one group the right to watch another has some interesting parallels. One concerns the tradition of White women in anthropology and their involvement in recording "native" experiences of nonwhite peoples. Donna Haraway's discussion of White women, photography, and primatology (1989) provides a provocative view of the use of the camera as an important tool in situations of conquest.

9. Multiple meanings operate under the term *community* (Cohen 1985). Evelyn Brooks Higginbotham (1992) presents the connections between family, race, and nation as if they were unproblematic. In contrast, other authors explore how racism and nationalism as ideologies of power gain meaning from one another (see Miles [1987; 1989], and Balibar and Wallerstein [1991]). For views on the links between family,

kinship, and race, see Liu (1991) and Guillaumin (1995). Analyses of gender and nation can be found in Yuval-Davis (1997).

10. This notion of solidarity was not merely a response to racial oppression. Even in the absence of racial oppression, Black people expressed distinctive beliefs concerning the relationship between the individual and the community. Molefi Asante (1987; 1990) and other Black studies scholars suggest that the Black Aesthetic defined Eurocentric ontology as negatively individualistic, one in which the individual finds his or her fullest expression of existence in isolation from or in opposition to humankind, nature, or some supreme idea or being. In contrast, the Black Aesthetic viewed individuality and subjectivity as constructed via a communal Black self, a concept whereby individuals develop their individuality in the context of community. One of the best-known examples of this orientation occurs in the call-and-response pattern of Black church services and within Black popular music. The individual preacher's or singer's individuality is affirmed by community response; without such response, the call of individuality would be meaningless. Paradoxically, without community there can be no individuality. This was the foundational, normal, or authentic Black identity, one grounded in African-derived philosophies. For discussions of the Black Aesthetic associated with the Black cultural nationalism of the 1960s and its construction of individuality, see Gayle (1971), Dubey (1994), and my discussion in chapter 5 of Afrocentrism as a legacy of the Black Aesthetic.

11. William Julius Wilson's work has been challenged by scholars who refute his claim that the Black middle class has escaped unscathed from racial inequality. See, for example, Geschwender and Caroll-Seguin's analysis of the continued disadvantage of African-Americans (1990), Essed's investigation of new patterns of everyday racism for racially integrated situations (1991), Feagin and Sikes's study of the Black middle class (1994), and Oliver and Shapiro's research on differential patterns of Black and White wealth (1995).

12. These attitudes persist in the 1990s. In *White Lies* (1997), Jessie Daniels reports the results of her extensive examination of contemporary White supremacist publications. Daniels finds not only a discourse in these publications that is racist and sexist, but also one that is deeply distrustful of the government. Repeatedly, they comment on how the government has sold out to special interests. To Daniels's surprise, the arguments expressed in these extreme publications strangely mirror more mainstream public discourse.

13. Race and economic class differences shape varying attachments to this process of dismantling the social welfare state in the United States. The truly wealthy have never been subject to sustained scrutiny in the public sphere. Preferring the privacy afforded by private schooling and the like, they influence public policy primarily through campaign contributions, taxation policies, and similarly circumspect practices. In this context, the increasing attacks on the social welfare state by middle-class and working-class White men in particular may be far more beneficial for elite group interests than is popularly recognized. Reflecting a growing perception on the part of White men that the federal government in particular is overly conciliatory to Blacks, women, homosexuals, and other so-called special interests, efforts to dismantle the social welfare state are having the unintended effect of removing government oversight. Workplace conditions, environmental controls, hiring practices, housing codes, health regulation, and other areas of an expanded social welfare state that limited the power of economic elites have all come under scrutiny. For sociological work on economic elites and public policy in the United States, see Mills (1959) and Domhoff (1990).

14. In response to her public silencing, Guinier collected her writings in an edited

volume and went on the lecture circuit. The ideas that she expresses in her 1994 volume and in her 1992 article on voting rights are simple yet threaten the current organization of democratic processes in the United States. Guinier was a threat not because her ideas were "wild" but because they could be implemented. For an overview of her views on democracy, see Guinier (1992; 1994). Also, for an analysis of Guinier's public silencing, see Patricia Williams's essay "A Hearing of One's Own" (1995, 137–49).

2. Coming to Voice, Coming to Power

1. I use the terms *self-definition* and *self-determination* because they directly refer-ence the social movements of the 1960s and 1970s that were central to the emergence of contemporary Black feminist thought. Iris Marion Young describes oppression as a structural condition experienced by groups, with injustice defined as group disadvan-tage within a given social system. Studying the social movements of the 1960s and 1970s, Young observes that such movements shifted the concept of oppression from that of a tyrannical power that coerces a group's subordination to that of "the everyday practices of a well-intentioned liberal society" (1990, 41). As applied to race, this changing view of oppression works with notions of institutionalized racism. See also Young's distinction between oppression and domination (33–38).

2. Scott (1990) points out that groups in power also generate "hidden transcripts," things that they would rather oppressed groups not know about them. To me, uncover-ing the hidden transcripts of groups in power constitutes an important area of research. For example, studies of the social construction of White identity that "air the dirty laundry" of White people represent important challenges to racial oppression (see, e.g., McIntosh 1992; Frankenberg 1993; and Pratt 1993).

3. My use of *breaking silence* contrasts with other uses that stress individual con-sciousness. Specifically, notions of breaking silence, coming out, becoming visible, and speaking out are themes common to much contemporary lesbian writing (see, e.g., Stanley and Wise 1993). As Minnie Bruce Pratt observes, "Certainly this emphasis is to be expected in a literature springing from our experience: in order to live fully as les-bians we have to be able to *find* each other" (1993, 10). African-American women owe much to lesbian writing, especially to work that uses an intersectional framework (see, e.g., Segrest 1994). However, because of differences in overall group location, themes in lesbian literature also differ from those in African-American women's writings. In lesbian writing, breaking silence remains necessary in identifying and discovering group-based, institutional dimensions of heterosexism that precede political resistance. In contrast, regardless of how they evaluate them, Black women as a collectivity have differential access to resistance traditions from Black civil society. Breaking silence con-stitutes a way of coming to terms with this preexisting, albeit nascent or subjugated, consciousness. Black lesbians participate in both groups and therefore are better posi-tioned to see both the contributions and the limitations of each group's standpoint (see, e.g., Smith 1983; and Lorde 1984). Other lesbians of color also describe the coming out process as one linked to group-based experiences associated with their racial or ethnic groups (Anzaldúa 1987). In brief, the social location of a group will frame its use of any strategy, in this case, of breaking silence.

4. Noteworthy examples of important works from the 1980s include Angela Davis's book on African-American women's political economy, *Women, Race, and Class* (1981); the groundbreaking essay by the Combahee River Collective "A Black Feminist Statement," published in 1982; Alice Walker's *In Search of Our Mothers' Gardens* (1983); Barbara Smith's anthology of Black women's writings *Home Girls: A Black*

Feminist Anthology (1983), which dealt with the overlooked issue of Black lesbianism; Audre Lorde's important collection of essays *Sister Outsider,* published in 1984; works of Black feminist literary critics such as Barbara Christian's *Black Feminist Criticism: Perspectives on Black Women Writers* (1985), and Hazel Carby's *Reconstructing Womanhood: The Emergence of the Afro-American Woman Novelist* (1987); June Jordan's collections of political essays *Civil Wars* (1981) and *On Call* (1985); and Filomina Chioma Steady's essay "African Feminism: A Worldwide Perspective" (1987). These works and many others during the decade spoke to the actions of Black women in and out of academia in developing Black feminist thought.

5. For example, Jhally and Lewis's study of the "enlightened racism" of American television viewers who avidly watched the Huxtable family on the hugely popular *Cosby Show* in the 1980s yet staunchly resisted efforts to racially integrate their neighborhoods, schools, and workplaces (1992) speaks to this seeming contradiction. White viewers honestly felt that they were more enlightened about racial matters because they would welcome Black families like the Huxtables into their living rooms. In this case, even when such images were unaccompanied by real structural shifts in power, symbolic inclusion masked continued discriminatory practices. Many Black women writers also investigate this theme of symbolic inclusion. For example, see bell hooks's essays critiquing how cultural production constructs blackness (1990).

6. Standpoint theory posits a distinctive relationship among a group's position in hierarchical power relations, the experiences attached to differential group position, and the standpoint that a group constructs in interpreting these experiences (Hartsock 1983; Harding 1986). For example, African-Americans living in Mississippi in the 1960s saw a connection between their common oppression as Black people, their similar experiences with poverty and political disenfranchisement, the shared understanding that most Blacks grappled with similar issues, and the nature of political activism needed to democratize Mississippi schools, workplaces, government agencies, and public facilities. In this chapter, I invoke standpoint theory without subjecting it to a critical eye. My goal here is to introduce some of the internal controversies that frame current uses of this theory. See chapter 6 for an analysis of standpoint theory and its influences on varying models of group construction.

7. Choosing a term to describe these relationships remains difficult. In *Black Feminist Thought* (1990), I introduced the term *matrix of domination* as a heuristic device for describing structural power relations that house individuals and groups. But although this usage accounts for social structures, it underemphasizes human agency. The matrix of domination could be seen as one pole of a continuum of power relations. On the other end could be placed Stuart Hall's more fluid term *articulation.* Hall describes a similar phenomenon yet maintains the fluidity associated with social constructionism and postmodern theory. See Grossberg (1996) and Slack (1996) for discussions of Hall's definition of articulation. At this point, I find both of these poles limited and have chosen to use Kimberle Crenshaw's *intersectionality* (1991) as a term that stands between these alternatives.

8. Black feminism has a different meaning in Britain and elsewhere. For an analysis of alternative meanings of *Black* not attached to essentialist identities, see Nain (1991) and Anthias and Yuval-Davis (1992).

9. I recognize that a considerable portion of Black women's intellectual production in academia comes from women who are in the humanities. In these areas, individual narratives and subjective elements of the human experience are typically elevated above the types of social structural concerns that I argue for here. However, the best work within the humanities manages to do both—one can read Toni Morrison, for example,

on multiple levels. Take *Beloved* (1987), a novel that is considered one of her greatest works. The narrative is highly subjective and is often read as a universal story about motherhood, love, and other human concerns. At the same time, however, Morrison situates these themes within a context of injustice. In brief, although it is extremely difficult, I think it is possible to develop recursive analyses within Black feminist thought that keep issues of agency and social structure in play.

On Fighting Words with "Fighting Words"

1. For example, scholarship in Europe and the United States has long demonstrated a fascination for studying racial differences, especially those distinguishing Blacks and Whites. Even when such differences proved elusive or when science itself had to be manipulated to prove them, the interest remained (Gould 1981; Stepan 1982; Tucker 1994). This scholarly search for the meaning of race reflected political and social conditions in which finding such meanings was essential to relations of rule (Gossett 1963; Jordan 1968). A similar situation existed in evaluating gender differences (Harding 1986, 1991; Hubbard 1990), generating a body of scholarship that occupied a similar place in justifying women's continued subordination (Jones 1985; Amott and Matthaei 1991).

2. Racism against Blacks is not the only form of racism. But in the United States, it is one of the most virulent forms and becomes the benchmark against which racism targeted toward other groups is measured. For theoretical analyses of race and racism that address their philosophical foundations, see Balibar and Wallerstein (1991), Anthias and Yuval-Davis (1992), and Goldberg (1993). British scholars and activists, in particular, have problematized the notion of "Black," because the term carries a different meaning in the context of British colonial history and European nationalism. See, for example, Poliakov (1974), Gilroy (1987), and Hall (1992). The social construction of Jewishness in terms of race provides insights into the racialization process. See, for example, Gilman (1985) and Proctor (1988).

3. I use quotation marks around "fighting words" to indicate the legal doctrine. For a social-historical overview of hate speech generally, especially the legal history of the "fighting words" construct, see Walker (1994). A similar concept exists in Germany, a country also experiencing considerable hate speech. There, the colloquial and commonly used term *Schriebtischtater*, translated to mean "writing-desk assailants," is used to describe those responsible for inciting racial violence through political speeches, the media, and other comparable outlets. I am indebted to Melinda Spong Guenes for this insight.

3. On Race, Gender, and Science

1. Discussions of the effects of social location or positionality have a distinguished history in the sociology of knowledge. For example, see analyses of the role of the stranger in generating knowledge (Simmel 1921; Schutz 1944), as well as Merton's exploration of insiders and outsiders (1972). For discussions specific to insider knowledges of race and gender in sociology, see William J. Wilson's interpretation of insider knowledge, "The New Black Sociology" (1974); Dorothy Smith's examination of the gendered dimensions of insider knowledge in sociology (1990a); and my analysis of insiderism and sociological theory (1992b). For a discussion of the concept of individuals in outsider-within locations, namely, individuals whose degrees and other qualifications afford them legal rights of belonging but whose historical exclusion predisposes insiders

to question their presence, see Collins (1986). Myerson and Scully's analysis of "tempered radicalism" in organizational settings (1995) parallels some of the ideas explored here. Current literacy criticism also explores this theme of positionality (see, e.g., Awkward 1995), as does emerging work in queer theory (see, e.g., Fuss 1991).

2. Several sources provided information on African-American women sociologists. Jacqueline Johnson Jackson's foundational essay (1974) suggested an initial list of names of Black women earning doctorates prior to 1970. This listing was supplemented by the National Science Foundation's Survey of Earned Doctorates between 1978 and 1995, a listing of participants in the Minority Fellowship Program of the American Sociological Association, and my personal knowledge. To determine whether each woman actually received a doctorate in sociology, dissertation abstracts were consulted. Those Black women who both received doctorates in related fields and are thought of as sociologists were included if they published. The greatest difficulty consisted in verifying whether an individual woman was African-American. These methods yielded a sample of an estimated 272 African-American women with earned doctorates in sociology, with names found for 140 women. Despite great care, I am sure that some women have been included in error, other women would object to being racially categorized as Black, and still others were inadvertently omitted from this preliminary list. For more information on the sample, see Patrice L. Dickerson's unpublished manuscript (1997).

3. My use of the term *postmodernity* references a range of intellectual debates situated across diverse academic disciplines. Philosophers tend to speak of "modernity" as arising during the 1600s, whereas cultural critics apply the term *modernism* to literary and artistic tendencies of the early twentieth century. Development theorists refer to the "modernization" of different societies moving toward industrialization, capitalist market economies, and political democracy. Across these varying uses, little agreement exists concerning the contours of postmodernity as a distinctive mode of social organization, with postmodernism as an intellectual crystallization of its meaning. For sociological treatments of these themes, see Rosenau's summary of the implications of postmodernism for the social sciences (1992), Bauman's discussion of how sociology might shed light on postmodernity (1992), and Lash's sociology of postmodernity (1990).

4. Although in this chapter I treat sociology as a fairly homogeneous enterprise, I recognize the diverse traditions within the field. Specifically, my comments about sociological empiricism and its influence by positivist science are more applicable to American sociology and the empiricist tradition in Britain than to sociology in France and Germany. For overviews of diverse traditions within sociology, see Ross (1991) and Levine (1995). Moreover, some argue that postmodern social theory is not especially new; instead, it can be seen as a continuation of long-standing constructionist traditions within sociology. Postmodern challenges within a range of disciplines have garnered considerable attention. For discussions of the implications of postmodernism for sociology and social science, see the introduction to Seidman and Wagner's edited volume (1992), as well as essays within the volume. Two additional useful sources are Rosenau's accessible overview (1992) and Best and Kellner's analysis (1991).

5. Although sociologist William E. B. Du Bois certainly tried to internalize scientific norms that encouraged him to view himself as a raceless, genderless man of science, the virulent racism of the turn of the century militated against African-American professionals actually functioning in this fashion. For example, although armed with a doctorate from Harvard University, Du Bois could not get a full-time job at the University of Pennsylvania, because he was Black. Even those Black scientists employed by historically Black institutions routinely encountered de jure and de facto racial discrimination that influenced housing, transportation, job opportunities, education, and virtually all

aspects of their daily lives. Following Du Bois, several other Black male sociologists did earn doctorates and, in the case of E. Franklin Frazier, managed to receive considerable professional recognition (Blackwell and Janowitz 1974; Platt 1991).

6. Examining Black women's participation in the American Sociological Association (ASA), the primary professional association of sociologists in the United States, illustrates these exclusionary practices of race and gender. Prior to 1968–1970, when the Caucus of Black Sociologists and the Women's Sociology Caucus presented resolutions to the ASA concerning the status of Blacks and women in the discipline, Black women participated only sporadically in sociology as a profession (Wilkinson 1981; Roby 1992). For example, before World War II, no Black person or woman served as president of the ASA or held any leadership position on the ASA Council. From the inception of the organization in 1906 through 1997, only two Black men served as president of the ASA—E. Franklin Frazier and William Julius Wilson. During this same period, seven White women held the position of president—Dorothy Swaine Thomas (1952), Mirra Komarovsky (1973), Alice Rossi (1983), Mathilda White Riley (1986), Joan Huber (1989), Maureen Hallinan (1995), and Jill Quadagno (1997). Four of these women had spouses who were active in the field—two were also ASA presidents, and a third was ASA secretary (see Roby 1992, 40 n. 56). Elected as ASA vice president in 1991, Doris Wilkinson was the first African-American woman and woman of color to sit on the ASA Council.

7. The *AJS* was selected because it represents the journal with the most longevity in the field and thus serves as a historical record of the types of themes within the discipline. As the journal associated with the Department of Sociology at the University of Chicago, widely accepted as the department essential to the success of American sociology, the *AJS* contains a wide range of material. During the period of closest scrutiny for this study, 1895–1920, the journal published a range of articles reflecting the diverse perspectives extant during the formation of the field.

8. Michel Foucault's discussion of the Panopticon as a form of surveillance that supplanted earlier forms of power relations seems apt here. Foucault describes the workings of the prison and its new form of organization: "Each individual, in his place, is securely confined to a cell from which he is seen from the front by the supervisor; but the side walls prevent him from coming into contact with his companions. He is seen, but he does not see; he is the object of information, never a subject in communication" (1979, 200). This passage eerily describes the classification and organization of Dorothy Smith's objectified knowledge (1990a), one in which the scientist replaces the prison guard as seeing all relevant knowledge, and the observed are reduced to biological data amenable to quantification and statistical manipulation. It also reflects the isolation experienced by African-American women professionals who find themselves increasingly placed under surveillance, discussed in chapter 1.

9. Trinh Minh-ha points out how important to this entire process were academic disciplines in general, and anthropology in particular: "Science is Truth, and what anthropology seeks first and foremost through its noble defense of the native's cause (whose cause? you may ask) is its own elevation to the rank of Science." In this sense, anthropology is not the "bastard of colonialism but the legitimate offspring of the Enlightenment" (1989, 57). A similar phenomenon was observed in the discipline of history; as it became more professionalized, the role of the historian as ethical and moral teacher gave way to the historian as a rational interpreter of empirical facts. Black women appeared in this increasingly positivistic history in old, familiar roles, as slave women and mammies (Morton 1991).

10. Dorothy Smith suggests that the very practice of doing sociology is one of

changing lived experience into forms of objectified knowledge necessary for relations of ruling. Smith explores sociological practices of writing as ideologies that "convert what people experience directly . . . into forms of knowledge in which people as subjects disappear and in which their perspectives or their own experience are transposed and subdued by the magisterial forms of objectifying discourse" (1990a, 4). Smith's ethnographic work on how science constructs mental illness from lived experiences (chaps. 5 and 6) illustrates this process.

11. Despite these impressive gains, the approximately 272 Black women identified so far as receiving doctorates in sociology remain a modest percentage of sociologists overall. I focus on Black women doctorates because this group typically possess the credentials to move into research and teaching positions in higher education that allow them the opportunity to publish. I view the ability to publish in sociology journals as an indicator of impact on the field of sociology. Despite these proportional increases, the number of Black women earning doctorates in all fields remains small. For example, in 1977, 432 Black women earned doctorates, as compared to 684 Black men. After a decade of increase for Black women followed by a decrease, 448 Black women earned doctorates in 1987, whereas Black men experienced a continual decrease during this decade, to a low of 317 earned doctorates in 1987 (Magner 1989).

12. I used several criteria in identifying these three periods. Depending on the opportunities and constraints provided by the timing of their years of graduate training, earning the doctorate, and seeking to enter the job market as professional sociologists, Black women faced markedly different opportunity structures to work as professional sociologists. Political, economic, and social conditions in the United States also shaped what was possible within sociology for those fortunate enough to work as professional sociologists.

13. Mary Jo Deegan (1991) uses five criteria to develop her list of fifty-one "founding sisters" in sociology. Ida Wells Barnett remains the only African-American woman who met Deegan's criteria. The case of Barnett raises the question of the combination of behavior—in this case, Barnett's sociological actions—and the significance of a community of practitioners having the power to define those actions as legitimate. In a similar effort to redefine the participation of Black women as sociological, Charles Lemert distinguishes between "professional" and "practical" sociologists and claims that "Anna Julia Cooper's work represented, in effect, an ideal type of practical sociology" (1995, 190). Despite Deegan's and Lemert's well-intentioned wishes to rewrite sociological history, I question their inclusions. In my assessment, sociology defined itself via the *absence* of women such as Cooper and Barnett. Thus, to claim them now seems somewhat self-serving.

14. Verification of the list of Black women in sociology remains difficult. The citation of the source for Anna Johnson Julian is from Harry Washington Greene. In a section called "First Doctorates in the Social Sciences," Greene notes, "Anna Johnson Julian is the first and only woman in the field of sociology, having taken the degree from the University of Pennsylvania in 1937" (1946, 47). I have not been able to corroborate this claim.

15. One core feature of this legitimation is knowing and using scientific language. As James Scott observes, "The conflict will accordingly take a dialogic form in which the language of the dialogue will invariably borrow heavily from the terms of the dominant ideology prevailing in the public transcript" (1990, 102). More recently, Black women in the social sciences have rejected extreme postmodern claims that structural truths cannot exist. Recent research in antiracist, feminist cultural studies scholarship has challenged both the practices of positivist science and the feasibility of its goal of

uncovering structural truths. A long-standing body of research has demonstrated that positivist science has been used to dominate and control people of color. For example, numerous African-American intellectuals, including William E. B. Du Bois, Anna Julia Cooper, E. Franklin Frazier, Mary McLeod Bethune, Oliver Cox, Joyce Ladner, and others, have contested some of the major tenets about Black people that have been forwarded in sociology, history, psychology, education, and the law. More recently, feminist scholars have pointed out the use of positivist science in structuring and controlling women across a range of societies. Moreover, much of the critique has moved beyond the issue of how a basically good positivist science has been perverted by political and economic ends, to a critique of the racism framing scientific methodology, constructs, and theories of the science itself (Gould 1981; Proctor 1988; Duster 1990). Feminist philosophers have actively challenged the seeming objectivity of positivist science and have explored its gendered nature (Keller 1985; Harding 1986, 1991; Jaggar 1983). More recent scholarship has begun to explore the interconnectedness of racism and sexism within positivist science (Stepan 1990; Harding 1991). In large part, Black women in social science eschew these approaches.

16. The works of La Frances Rodgers-Rose and Gloria Joseph, two Black women sociologists, further illustrate the increasing attention to race and gender intersectionality characterizing this period. Although Rodgers-Rose gained a doctorate from the University of Iowa in 1964, her dissertation topic differed from that of her edited volume *The Black Woman* (1980). Joseph's 1967 dissertation from Cornell University was followed by a coedited volume on Black and White women's relationship to feminism. Collectively, women like Ladner, Rodgers-Rose, and Joseph continue to work within sociological frameworks, but they combine these frameworks in innovative ways to recontextualize Black women's experiences. They also demonstrate the increasing significance given to investigating intersections of race and gender in sociological treatments of Black women's experiences.

17. Particularly innovative work managed to combine the critique of the Black matriarchy with this heightened sensitivity to identifying the structural causes of Black women's disadvantage. For example, Gloria Jones-Johnson (1988) explores what she calls the "victim-bind dilemma" of Black women sociologists in academia, one wherein Black women are viewed either as inferiors (the legacy of viewing Black women as doubly victimized by racism and sexism) or as superwomen (superstrong Black matriarchs). Caught between these two sets of expectations, Black women sociologists face being viewed either as inadequate and thereby unworthy of mentoring and other academic services or as so exceptional that they are asked to perform duties beyond those of everyone else—the Black-woman-on-every-committee phenomenon. Jones-Johnson's analysis parallels Wahneema Lubiano's discussion of the inadequate "welfare queen" and the superstrong Black Lady Overachiever (1992), discussed in chapter 1.

18. Prior to Joyce Ladner's dissertation, Black women in sociology did not write doctoral dissertations on Black women. Although it is beyond the scope of this study, a content analysis of the work of early Black women sociologists might reveal a nascent paradigm of intersectionality shaping their work. Consider, for example, the title of Joan Louise Gordon's 1955 dissertation written at the University of Pennsylvania, "Some Socio-Economic Aspects of Selected Negro Families in Savannah, Georgia: With Special Reference to the Effects of Occupational Stratification on Child Rearing." This title taps three categories: The focus on Negroes places the work within a race-based scholarship aiming to refute historical claims of Black deviance. The focus on family responds to gender-based sociological traditions. And what is even more unusual is the linking of both of these with two issues not typically seen in literature on Blacks,

namely, class analysis of occupational stratification and child rearing from the literature on women. Although more study is needed, examples such as this might reveal a much earlier exploration of intersections of race, gender, and class than I suggest here.

4. What's Going On?

1. Little agreement exists in classifying postmodern social theories. For example, whereas McGowan (1991) identifies poststructuralism, contemporary Marxism, neo-pragmatism, and feminism as four prominent variants of postmodern theory, Best and Kellner (1991) concentrate primarily on French poststructuralist theory as foundational for all postmodernist discourse. Despite clear differences among these areas, I discuss postmodernism as if it had a coherency that it neither seeks nor possesses. For discussions of poststructuralism, primarily as a theory of literature, see Weedon (1987), Harding (1991), and McGowan (1991). For discussions of postmodernism that reflect its use as a more general theory of culture, see Lash (1990). For analyses of postmodernism and the social sciences, see Rabinow and Sullivan's edited volume on interpretive social science (1987), Rosenau's analysis of postmodernism and the social sciences (1992), Bauman's approach to sociology and postmodernity (1992), and Lash's sociology of postmodernity (1990). Nicholson's introduction analyzing postmodernism and feminism (1990) raises concerns similar to those in this chapter, as does Best and Kellner's analysis of the politics of a range of postmodern social theories (1991, chapters 7 and 8).

2. Sociologist Nicos Mouzelis (1995) makes a similar distinction. He notes that sociological theory can be divided into one of two types. Substantive theories constitute a set of interrelated statements trying to explain something that is new. Substantive theories can be proven true or false via empirical investigation. In contrast, a second approach defines theory as a conceptual framework—a paradigm, metatheory, or heuristic device—that provides guiding principles for exploring other social phenomena. In this chapter, my analysis of postmodernism evaluates its use under this second meaning. My initial outline of intersectionality in chapter 3 presents it as a conceptual framework.

3. Hartsock speculates that the social locations of two types of academics might influence the types of social theory they produce: "If, as a group, modernist theories represent the views of the colonizer who accepts, postmodernist ideas can be divided between those who, like [Richard] Rorty, ignore the power relations involved, and those, like [Michel] Foucault, who resist these relations" (1990, 164). Pierre Bourdieu makes a similar point about a group he calls the "dominated among the dominant" (1990, 145).

4. In answering the question why such a relativist discourse exists now, Hartsock speculates, "I contend that these intellectual moves are no accident (but no conspiracy either). They represent the transcendental voice of the Enlightenment attempting to come to grips with the social and historical changes of the middle-to-late twentieth century" (1990, 164). Henry Louis Gates Jr. also questions why the colonial paradigm seems to be returning as a metaphor when the field of studying colonialism has gotten more specific. Gates notes that "the sovereign-colony relation is simply another instance of the spatial topography of center and margin on which oppositional criticism subsists. And it is just this model that . . . has started to exhaust its usefulness in describing our own modernity" (1992b, 189). I suspect that the increasing attractiveness of colonial metaphors may stem from their attention to group-based, structural sources of power as compared to current emphases on individual sources of empowerment. For

another view of the attractiveness of colonial metaphors, see the discussion of stand-point theory in chapter 6.

5. I find it fascinating that Michel Foucault, Jean Baudrillard, Jacques Derrida, Julia Kristeva, Roland Barthes, Jean-François Lyotard, and other French thinkers associated with the origins of postmodernism seem to have direct connections to the period of French decolonization, especially the Algerian Revolution. Despite these links, analyses of French poststructuralism and the emergence of postmodernism in the 1960s routinely allude to the changing *intellectual* climate in France stimulated by student movements of 1968 and other social movements, leaving French colonial policy alone. Both Albert Memmi and Frantz Fanon write as colonial subjects dealing with the dismantling of old colonial centers that oppressed them. In contrast, the majority of thinkers viewed as important to postmodernism wrote from within the center of French colonial power, either as colonizers who accepted or as those who refused.

6. Pierre Bourdieu makes a similar point. He notes that the ambiguity of the positions adopted by the dominated among the dominant is linked to their "precariously balanced position. Despite their revolt against those they call the 'bourgeois,' they remain loyal to the bourgeois order, as can be seen in all periods of crisis in which their specific capital and their position in the social order are really threatened" (1990, 145). My analysis emphasizes the structural conditions that frame the emergence of post-modernism at this time. It is not meant to be read as a discussion of the psychological makeup of individuals engaged in research from within postmodernist assumptions. This is where I part ways with Memmi, a theorist who wrote in a time when psychological models were more prominent in social theory and when the tendency to frame larger social conditions such as racism in the language of psychology (i.e., as prejudice and bias) was more prevalent.

7. In pointing out the problematic dimensions of postmodern views of power in the American academy, I am not arguing that local politics is irrelevant or is not growing. My argument addresses my concern with the absence of a structural analysis of power. I also recognize that many thinkers classified as postmodern, for example, Fredric Jameson, do write of large, global trends. One interesting issue is how thinkers are being reclassified. Jameson is more often identified with Marxism and linked to the Frankfurt school of critical theory, itself increasingly distinguished from the seemingly true postmodernists of France.

8. For a similar argument, see Dorothy Smith's recommendations concerning a sociology for women (1987). Theories of power for women build on the "capacities, abilities, and strengths" of women and use these features as "guides for a potential transformation of power relationships" (Hartsock 1990, 158). Postmodern theorists typically have no such agenda.

9. Many summaries of postmodernism allude to this continuum. Rosenau (1992) makes a distinction between skeptical and affirmative postmodernists, whereas Fuchs and Ward (1994) see DECONSTRUCTION and "deconstruction" as ends of a continuum. Best and Kellner's distinction (1991) between extreme postmodern theories (those of Baudrillard and parts of Lyotard, Foucault, Deleuze, and Guattari) and reconstructive postmodern theories (those of Jameson, Laclau and Mouffe, Flax, and postmodernist feminists) explores these relationships among variations of postmodernism most fully.

5. When Fighting Words Are Not Enough

1. Molefi Asante's volume *The Afrocentric Idea* (1987) is most often credited with introducing the term *Afrocentrism*. Both Asante's *Kemet, Afrocentricity, and Knowledge*

(1990) and Maulana Karenga's *Introduction to Black Studies* (1982) are considered "instructional and model texts that focus on theory, methods, and disciplinary location of Africology" (Conyers 1995, 15). For an overview of Afrocentrism written by an insider, see Kershaw (1992). For an outsider's overview that succinctly summarizes its scope and practices, see Marable (1993), especially pp. 119–22. Marable makes a distinction between "scholarly" and "vulgar" Afrocentrism, viewing thinkers such as Asante as "scholarly" and media figures associated with political issues as "vulgar." Marable does not simply juxtapose "scholarly" and "vulgar" as positive and negative variations but also critiques inconsistencies in "scholarly" Afrocentrism. Ransby and Matthews (1993) also discuss the resurgence of Black cultural nationalism in African-American communities. They link Afrocentrism to interest in Malcolm X and rap music within hip-hop culture.

2. Darlene Clark Hine (1992) classifies Black studies scholarship in three paradigmatic orientations, namely, the traditionalist, feminist, and Afrocentrist. Individual scholars often cannot be easily classified within one orientation and may move among all three. Hine argues that Black studies practitioners reflect diverse racial backgrounds and can be found across a range of academic disciplines. However, although Black studies units house practitioners of all three paradigms, the Afrocentrist paradigm is found almost exclusively within Black studies programs and departments. Hine's view differs from other taxonomies. For examples, see essays in Talmadge Anderson's volume (1990), especially the introductory essay "Black Studies: Overview and Theoretical Perspective."

3. For contrasting interpretations of the history of Black studies programs in higher education, see Huggins (1985), especially his discussion "Separatism—Black Cultural Nationalism" (45–46), and Conyers (1995). Former Black Panther Elaine Brown (1992) provides a political analysis of Maulana Karenga's Black cultural nationalism and its impact on Black studies formation at UCLA. Henry Louis Gates Jr. (1992b) offers an interesting comparison between the different paths taken by Black studies and women's studies and their impact on Black women's studies. Gates notes that the Black Arts movement of the 1960s generated Black studies but did not have an impact on the traditional university curriculum. In contrast, White women in the academy and the women's studies programs they created have influenced the general curriculum and in turn are part of the revitalization of Black women's studies.

Accounting for the appeal of Afrocentrism to some Black academics in higher education is another issue. Describing the relationship of British Black social workers to their clients, Paul Gilroy speculates about how the contradictory location of Blacks working on behalf of Black issues in White-supported institutional settings heightens the appeal of Black consciousness approaches such as Afrocentrism to this constituency: "It is possible to see the invocation of racial identity and culture in the mystic forms of kinship and blood characteristic of cultural nationalism as the means with which black professionals in these institutions have sought to justify the special quality of their relationship with their black clients. These ideas provide a superficially coherent ideological reply to the contradictory position black professionals occupy" (1987, 66–67). In short, Afrocentrism may provide a mechanism for remaining ideologically connected to Black civil society when practitioners find themselves distanced by being in White-controlled institutions.

4. In this effort, Black cultural nationalism is not an aberration but instead shows parallels to other groups expressing comparable nationalist aspirations. Analyzing Chicano nationalism, theorist Genero M. Padilla observes, "What we see repeated again and again, whether it be in nineteenth-century Hungary or Czechoslovakia, the Irish

nationalist movement, the African anti-colonial uprisings, or even the French Canadian autonomy drive . . . is a close relationship between a people's desire to determine their own political fortunes and their passion to report their own cultural myths, a vital psychic component of national identity which gives energy and purpose to their political struggle" (1989, 113). Black cultural nationalism aims to give a similar purpose to Black political struggle, namely, the purpose of self-definition and self-determination. As Padilla points out, "Without heroic dreams and cultural symbols of mythic proportion . . . the material aims of a nationalist movement may lack the spiritual center which sustains struggle" (114).

5. For an analysis and a historical context for this approach and its ties to prior racial analyses, see Appiah (1992). The chapter "Ethnophilosophy and Its Critics" is especially useful, particularly Appiah's critique of Diop (101) and the links between Pan-Africanism and Black cultural nationalism.

6. Invoking African-derived frameworks to explain and interpret Black life and culture originated much earlier (Herskovits 1990). For example, William E. B. Du Bois's work on the Negro-American family (1969) explicitly addressed the African origins of such family life. Du Bois's situation illustrates how political factors have shaped the contours of Afrocentrism. Du Bois could not find a position as an academician and turned to political activism as the primary orientation for his intellectual production. As a result, although he may have pursued Afrocentric scholarship had he been able to find the resources to do so, he turned to political activism outside academia (Broderick 1974; Green and Driver 1978). Thus, the issue is less the longevity of Afrocentrism as a theoretical orientation guiding scholarship and more the lack of institutional resources available for the development of Afrocentrism.

7. For representative scholarship in Black psychology, see articles by Wade Nobles, Na'im Akbar, and William E. Cross, among others, in the special issue "Psychological Nigrescence" of the *Consulting Psychologist* (1989). Also, the *Journal of Black Psychology* routinely examines issues of Black identity.

8. Baraka has since gone through substantial changes of political philosophy. Smitherman reports that Baraka had the following reaction to the 1995 Million Man March on Washington: "Some Blacks, such as 1960s activist and writer Amiri Baraka, took issue with the March because it did not include women. Baraka remarked that if he were going to war, he wouldn't leave half the army at home" (1996, 105).

6. Some Group Matters

1. Standpoint theory alone cannot explain Black women's experiences. Instead, it constitutes one of many conceptual frameworks that I use in analyzing Black feminist thought. Despite the overtly claimed and clearly stated eclecticism of my own work, I remain amazed at repeated efforts to categorize my ideas in one theoretical framework or another, generally without full knowledge of the scope of my work. I interpret this pressure to classify works in this fashion as a shortcut way of analyzing social phenomena. Grounded in circular reasoning, one identifies what one perceives as the essence of one approach, classifies thinkers and/or their works in those categories, and then accepts or rejects their ideas based on one's initial classification. Intellectual work typically reflects much more complexity than this, and Black women's intellectual traditions in the United States certainly cannot be adequately addressed by any one approach (standpoint theory or any other).

2. Although bodies receive race and gender classifications, people routinely try to escape from, blur, or challenge the legitimacy of the boundaries between their assigned

category and others. The history of racial and gender "passing" (when Blacks "pass" as White and women "pass" as men) speaks to one way of transgressing boundaries. The strength of these performances reveals how classifications are rooted not in nature but in power relations. Similarly, the current attention to racially mixed individuals (as evidenced by the ongoing debate to change the racial categories of the U.S. census) and to intersexed individuals (those whose sex cannot easily be assigned at birth) also speaks to the permeability of racial and sexual borders. Although these cases are transgressive, installing these specific acts as a new transgressive politics writ large seems shortsighted. It's like chipping away at the edges of a giant mountain, claiming that each chip weakens the structure while failing to realize that the mountain of race and gender classification is far from crumbling.

3. Iris Marion Young contends that the New Left social movements of the 1960s and 1970s introduced new meanings of oppression by stressing group location in social institutions: "In its new usage, oppression designated the disadvantage and injustice some people suffer not because a tyrannical power coerces them, but because of the everyday practices of a well-intentioned liberal society" (1990, 41). Oppression became less associated with individual intentionality and more with the everyday workings of social structures that manufactured groups in hierarchies. In my brief analysis of intergenerational transfer of group privilege later in this chapter, I build on Young's notion of group-based oppression carried out by social institutions. As Young continues, "We cannot eliminate this structural oppression by getting rid of the rulers or making some new laws, because oppressions are systematically reproduced" (41).

4. This slippage between the individual and the group as units of analysis also fosters a reductive and problematic reading of "voice" as symbolic of group consciousness. Individual "voice" is not the same as group "voice" or standpoint. Typically, this reduction operates by imagining how *individuals* negotiate self-definitions and then claiming that through a "family resemblance," *collectivities* undergo a similar process. Because collectivities certainly do construct stories in framing their identity, this approach appears plausible. However, can the individual stand as proxy for the group and the group for the individual? Moreover, can this particular version of the individual serve as the exemplar for collective group identity? If an individual reasons from his or her own personal experiences that "since *we* are all the same under the skin, therefore, what *I* experience must be the same as what *everybody else* experiences," a certain perception of group narrative structure emerges. If an individual believes that his or her personal experiences in coming to voice—especially the inner voices within his or her individual consciousness, which are hidden from hierarchal power relations—not only reflect a common human experience but, more to the point, serve as an exemplar for how *group* consciousness and decision making operate, then individual experience becomes the model for comprehending group processes. This approach minimizes the significance of conflict between groups in generating group narratives. In the model wherein individuals conduct inner dialogues among various parts of their "selves," the process of mediating conflicting identities occurs within each individual. The individual always holds complete power or agency over the consciousness that he or she constructs in his or her own mind and over the voice that she or he uses to express that consciousness.

5. For the moment, I am deliberately choosing to use the term *intersectionality* instead of its related term *articulation,* even though articulation approximates my understanding of intersectionality. In her essay "The Theory and Method of Articulation in Cultural Studies," Jennifer Daryl Slack examines the meaning of articulation in the work of British sociologist Stuart Hall. Recognizing the difficulty of developing a precise definition of articulation, Slack notes that articulation "isn't *exactly* anything"

(1996, 117; emphasis in original). Although articulation is obviously a very powerful concept that closely parallels what I am calling intersectionality, there may be a difference between them. Slack describes the relationship between ideas and social structure that she sees emerging in cultural studies and that is captured by articulation: "The context is not something *out there, within which practices occur or which influence the development of practices. Rather, identities, practices, and effects generally, constitute the very context in which they are practices, identities or effects*" (125; emphasis in original). Although I value the effort to infuse a more dynamic dimension into analyses of social phenomena, this definition seems too much of a closed loop for me. I prefer, at least analytically, to retain the distinction between context and ideas that Slack collapses into one. Thus, the notion of intersectionality seems more closely wedded to notions of articulation that assume an independent existence for social structure. For additional insight into Hall's use of the term *articulation,* see Grossberg (1996).

6. Many thinkers have worked within a sociology-of-knowledge framework. At first glance, the links between a sociology of knowledge associated with Robert Merton and a standpoint theory associated with Karl Marx may seem surprising. Merton is typically associated with a structural-functionalism that omits questions of power. Although Merton is known for his contributions to the sociology of science, he treats science as one knowledge among many. Merton has been central in bringing ideas of the sociology of knowledge, historically associated more with theoretical and historicist traditions of Europe than with empiricist traditions in American sociology, to American sociology. As Merton suggests in his important essay "Paradigm for the Sociology of Knowledge," originally published in 1945, "The perennial problem of the implications of existential influences upon knowledge for the epistemological status of knowledge has been hotly debated from the very outset" (Merton 1973, 13).

In contrast, Marx's entire focus seems to be hierarchy. The fundamental questions that link diverse thinkers in this field are flexible enough to accommodate a considerable variability on the connections between knowledge and social structure. Merton places far less emphasis than Marx on the hierarchical or power dimensions of social structure. In contrast, Marx focuses on the power dimensions of social structure; his ideas that are now known as standpoint theory are designed to explore the connections between hierarchical power relations and ensuing knowledges or standpoints. Moreover, thinking through the connections between knowledge and power is an especially sociological concern, because sociology examines social structures. French philosopher Michel Foucault (1977) points out that it is not a question of emancipating truth from systems of power. Rather, the issue lies in detaching the power of truth from its hegemonic institutional contexts. Foucault suggests that rather than being outside power or deprived of power, truth remains grounded in real-world politics. Each society has its own "regime of truth" or "general politics" of truth. These regimes consist of the types of discourses harbored by a particular society that it causes to function as true; epistemological criteria that distinguish truth from falsehoods; and legitimating mechanisms that determine the status of those charged with constructing truth (Foucault 1977). Using a more general definition of class as group leads one in a different direction. Like Robert Merton (1973), I see Karl Mannheim's work (1954) as extending the idea of class as a group with a connection to knowledge, to broader types of social groups. Thus, although the language of standpoint remains affiliated with Marxist social theory, the idea of knowledge emerging from groups differentially placed in social conditions transcends its origins in Marxism.

7. The literature on economic class is vast, and I make no attempt to review it here. Both Grimes (1991) and Vanneman and Cannon (1987) provide useful resources for

summarizing and critiquing American scholarship on economic class. In brief, within American social science, economic class is routinely associated with either Karl Marx (social class) or Max Weber (status). The status-attainment perspective has garnered the most attention in American social science. Sacks (1989) takes the position that economic class should be conceptualized as group relationships and that efforts to assign a class category to individuals in order to examine economic class consciousness overlook the more significant features of economic class analysis. Thus, the approach that I use in developing a context for standpoint theory is already a minority position. For a discussion of the origins of feminist standpoint epistemology in a Marxist standpoint theory of labor, see Smith (1987), especially pp. 78–81.

8. Bourdieu makes a similar point about the differences between the ideas in Marxist social theory and the use to which those ideas are put: "Marxism, in the reality of its social use, ends up by being a mode of thought completely immune to historical criticism, which is a paradox, given the potentialities and indeed, the demands inherent in Marx's thought" (1990, 17).

9. Current debates that juxtapose class and culture as if these were two oppositional and distinct processes may create artificial boundaries where none exist. Economic class is typically theorized on the level of macrosociological structures—labor markets, industrial sectors, and the like. In contrast, historically, studies of group culture have emphasized ethnic and tribal cultures emerging from small-group interactions. This seeming division of the themes of economics, political science, and sociology as being best suited for one type of issue, namely, economic class, and the humanities of history, literary studies, English, and literature as dealing with another, reflects the problems inherent in relying too heavily on disciplinary approaches to each concept. Sociology claimed the concept of social class and, from its inception, has studied economic class as a structural phenomenon largely divorced from culture. In contrast, until the advent of British cultural studies and its subsequent impetus on communications studies generally to take on the theme of mass culture, culture remained largely the province of anthropologists who carried out studies of culture in other societies.

7. Searching for Sojourner Truth

1. For example, by denouncing the war in Vietnam, Martin Luther King Jr. saw the connections between racism and imperialism. Moving outside the confines of Black civil society allowed him to gain additional insights concerning the connections among systems of oppression. King's stance was unpopular with African-Americans, who counseled him to stick to the issue of race. Yet King was also unpopular with White Americans, because of his position on race. The biographies and work of many prominent Third World intellectuals also reflect these themes. Many cannot return to their nations, because the social distance is too great or their ideas are too dangerous. See, for example, Minh-ha (1989), Said (1990), and Spivak (1993).

2. In his study of the philosophical foundations of racism, David Goldberg offers a comparable analysis of the connections between contained space and relations of ruling: "Racial categories have been variously spatialized . . . since their inception into continental divides, national localities, and geographic regions. Racisms become institutionally normalized in and through spatial configuration, just as social space is made to seem natural, a given, by being conceived and defined in racial terms . . . *apartheid* space . . . the logical implication of racialized space" (1993, 185).

3. Although I rely on Henderson's insightful analysis, my use of the testimonial tradition differs from hers. Henderson describes a both/and positionality expressed by

Black women writers, one wherein African-American women are simultaneously opposed to and in solidarity with other groups: "These writers enter simultaneously into
familial, or *testimonial* and public, or *competitive* discourses—discourses that both
affirm and challenge the values and expectations of the reader. As such, black women
writers enter into testimonial discourse with black men as blacks, with White women as
women, and with black women as black women. At the same time, they enter into competitive discourse with black men as women, with White women as blacks, and with
White men as black women" (1989, 20; emphasis in original). Within this meaning, one
testifies to those with whom one has shared commonalities, and engages in competitive
discourse with those who have competing interests. The fixity of categories of assumed
common interests created by race and gender may not be as clear-cut. I prefer to see
Black women engaging in simultaneous testimonial and competitive discourse with all
other groups and with each other.

4. A definition of freedom varies depending on who controls the definition. Certainly
for slaves, formal emancipation constituted freedom. For other generations of African-
Americans, freedom was associated with gaining political rights and protections in the
public sphere that were associated with formal citizenship. The civil rights movement
demonstrated, however, that freedom would be accomplished only when substantive
rights of citizenship became available to African-Americans. Richard King's study of the
civil rights movement and the meaning of freedom (1992) explores how freedom operates as a deep root in African-American social and political thought. Currently, freedom
may mean protection from surveillance and disciplinary control, a move out of the public sphere. These understandings of freedom all require self-determination or group empowerment. According to philosopher Iris Marion Young, notions of freedom, justice,
and self-determination are connected: "If justice is defined negatively as the elimination
of structures of domination, then justice implies democratic decision-making. Democracy is a condition of freedom in the sense of self-determination" (1990, 91).

5. Pierre Bourdieu's notion of habitus (1990) speaks to the use of multiple strategies
developed here. Bourdieu defines strategy as the "product of the practical sense as the
feel for the game, for a particular, historically determined game—a feel which is acquired in childhood, by taking part in social activities" (1990, 62–63). According to
this definition, individuals who have experienced similar situations develop a common
arsenal of responses or strategies in response to the "game" or social situation that constitutes their specific history. Bourdieu continues: "The good player, who is so to speak
the game incarnate, does at every moment what the game requires. That presupposes a
permanent capacity for invention, indispensable if one is to be able to adapt to indefi-
nitely varied and never completely identical situations. This is not ensured by mechani-
cal obedience to the explicit, codified rule (when it exists)" (63). From this perspective,
a good Black woman game player would fit into her role as Black woman and would
survive in subordination. What Black women need to know is how to resist the *rules* of
the game. The goal is not to excel at coping with injustice, but to eliminate it altogether.

6. Similar themes have been expressed in certain interpretations of postmodernism.
According to one source, "Postmodernists tend to favor forms of social inquiry which
incorporate an explicitly practical and moral intent, that are contextual and restricted
in their focus (local stories are preferred over general ones), and that are narratively
structured, rather than articulating a general theory" (Seidman and Wagner 1992, 7).
Although the focus on local stories and local strategies for resistance is refreshing, this
focus in no way guarantees that the local will have an explicitly practical and moral intent. Social theorist Steven Seidman suggests that theorists shift their roles from "building general theory or providing epistemic warrants for sociology to serving as moral

and political analysts, narrators of stories of social development, producers of genealogies and social critics" (1992, 48). In describing interpretive social science, another source claims that it "seeks to replace the standing distinction between the social sciences as descriptive disciplines and the humanities as normative studies with the realization that all human inquiry is necessarily engaged in understanding the human world from within a specific situation. This situation is always and at once historical, moral, and political" (Rabinow and Sullivan 1987, 20–21).

7. The term *critical mass* has multiple meanings across quite diverse fields of study. For example, as used in nuclear physics, the term refers to a catalytic function, the amount of fuel needed for a fission chain reaction to occur. Another meaning of *critical mass* emerges from its use in business. Although the term is widely used and does not have a uniform meaning, it often refers to a threshold of some sort. Examples of the meaning of *critical mass* as approximating a pressure or protest group come from many sources. The power of pressure groups acting as a critical mass has long been recognized by formal governments that often aim to diffuse the power of such groups. For example, tactics of gerrymandering congressional districts, forbidden by the 1965 Voting Rights Act, were designed to dilute the voting strength of African-Americans and other racial and ethnic minority groups to prevent the action of voting as a pressure group. In other cases, a well-organized critical mass acting as a pressure or protest group is difficult to stop. For example, a critical mass in traffic is a group of riders large enough to hold up opposing traffic at an intersection. When cyclists use the term, it usually refers to a group large enough to take all lanes of a street. For a New York City group that organizes what it calls Critical Mass rides, a critical mass is the minimum number of cyclists needed to bike safely on crowded urban streets. Group members say that the rides operate as a "xerocracy"—rule by the copy machine and without leaders. New York's Critical Mass is part of a larger movement-without-borders, with rides taking place in cities around the United States, as well as overseas. Cities such as Montreal, Seattle, Boston, Washington, D.C, Rio de Janeiro, and many others have regular Critical Mass rides. One of the unique aspects to a Critical Mass ride is its "organized coincidence." When skaters find out about it, they just show up and travel with the cyclists. In this example, although the notion of a catalyst for a larger movement is maintained, the vision of the larger movement consists of explicitly shutting down business-as-usual. The field of electronic communications provides a final meaning of the term *critical mass*. The critical mass of a software product describes a condition whereby fixing one bug introduces additional bugs. When software achieves critical mass, it can never be fixed—it can only be discarded and rewritten. This meaning of *critical mass* references a condition in which reform no longer seems feasible. Continuing to try to fix social systems may yield a critical mass that needs to be discarded.

8. I have deliberately avoided defining justice, because I think that it is difficult to do so within assumptions of individualism. Iris Marion Young, however, sees social justice as the degree to which a society maintains social institutions necessary to oppose oppression and domination (1990, 37). What I like about Young's analysis is that she aims to build a theory of justice from the group-based traditions of the new social movements. The issue of justice, especially the significance of having an ethical foundation to scholarship, emerges in the work of other scholars of color, especially those in legal studies. Critical race theorists Richard Delgado, Kimberle Crenshaw, Charles Lawrence, and Mari Matsuda oppose hate speech by invoking ethical as well as rational criteria (Matsuda et al. 1993). Matsuda, for example, claims that hate speech is wrong because it violates human rights protections. In a carefully argued case that distinguishes

between protected and unprotected speech, Matsuda contends that a challenge to certain types of hate speech can be made on moral, ethical grounds.

9. The growing literature by womanist theorists and theologians examines spirituality broadly defined. For an anthology of works in this tradition, see Townes (1993). Groups with different histories may rely on divergent themes and ways of moving their membership. For example, the issues of equality, justice, liberation, and freedom emerge from groups with histories of oppression. African-Americans routinely stress these issues, and they are part of the moral and ethical systems of African-American culture (Mitchell and Lewter 1986; Cannon 1988). In contrast, beliefs in traditional cultures that have had minimal contact with the West and/or with systems of domination imported from the West reflect a concern with other issues that give life meaning. For example, traditional African cosmologies stress issues of humanity and community (Mbiti 1969; Serequeberhan 1991).

Black women writers explore and build on a spiritual tradition articulated in the tradition of Black women's literature. Finding meaning through a spiritually infused Black women's tradition permeates Black women's cultural production and political activism. Many African-American women writers invoke variations of Black women's spirituality in constructing their fiction. For example, Toni Morrison's *Beloved* (1987), Alice Walker's *The Temple of My Familiar* (1989), and Gloria Naylor's *Mama Day* (1988) all rely on images and metaphors of a spiritual world that transcends the natural or physical world. Accessing this spiritual dimension can be central to Black women's healing and survival in harsh environments structured by intersecting oppressions. For example, the women in Toni Cade Bambara's *The Salt Eaters* (1980) and in Paule Marshall's novel *Praisesong for the Widow* (1983) move toward wholeness and healing when they embrace their spirituality. Recall these controversial lines from Ntosake Shange's choreopoem *for colored girls who have considered suicide / when the rainbow is enuf:* "i found god in myself / & i loved her / i loved her fiercely" (1975, 67).

10. It is important to distinguish between Black women's embeddedness in sacred and secular traditions of spirituality and the regulation of this spirituality by organized religions and other social institutions. Some scholars see Black Christian traditions as problematic and as fostering the social control of Black women through their general practices and patriarchal structures (Grant 1982; Marable 1983). In contrast, others view these same traditions as highly sustaining for African-American women, claiming that churches provide African-American women with a community that not only offers interpretations other than those put forth by dominant society, but also provides safe spaces in which to develop leadership skills (Grant 1989, 1992; Sanders 1995; Sobel 1979; Gilkes 1985).

Glossary

binary thinking: An either/or way of thinking about concepts or realities that divides them into two mutually exclusive categories, for example, white/black, man/woman, reason/emotion, and heterosexual/homosexual.

Black civil society: A set of institutions, communication networks, and practices that help African-Americans respond to economic and political challenges confronting them. Also known as the *Black public sphere* or the *Black community.*

Black nationalism: A political philosophy based on the belief that Black people constitute a people or nation with a common history and destiny.

canon: A body of knowledge and/or scholarly works meant to represent the traditions of a particular academic discipline or area of inquiry.

capitalism: An economic system based on the private ownership of the means of production. Typically characterized by extreme distributions of wealth and large differences between the rich and the poor.

center/margin metaphor: A literary metaphor that describes core/periphery power relations. The center/margin metaphor was an important precursor to the emergence of decentering as one rubric of postmodernism.

class: In its most general sense, a group or collective of persons differentiated from other social groups by cultural forms, practices, or ways of life. *Economic class* refers to a group of people who share a common placement in a political economy. This meaning of *economic class* parallels that of the term *social class,* which typically refers to group location in capitalist political economies.

colonialism: A situation in which one group of people rules another in an exploitive relationship with political, economic, social, and cultural dimensions.

commodification: In capitalist political economies, the act of assigning economic values to land, products, services, and ideas that are bought and sold in marketplaces as commodities.

consciousness-raising: Exercises designed to help individuals or groups become more aware of the workings of political, social, economic, and/or cultural issues in their everyday lives.

containment strategies: Strategies that aim to silence those who speak out against or in other ways resist oppression. The two major containment strategies used against Blacks in the United States are racial segregation (e.g., racial discrimination meant to exclude Blacks from good schools, jobs, housing, health care, and other social benefits) and surveillance.

context of discovery: An area in science in which hypotheses are selected and refined. Refers to the process used to select problems worth studying.

context of justification: The part of science in which hypotheses are tested and evidence gathered. Includes shared assumptions concerning empiricism and rationality.

core/periphery relationships: A variety of unequal, exploitive political and economic relationships in which one group at the center of power exploits groups on the periphery of power. Classical colonialism, neocolonialism, internal colonialism, segmented industrial sectors within capitalist political economies, and segmented labor markets have all been described as core/periphery relationships.

critical social theory: Theorizing about the social in defense of economic and social justice. Stated differently, critical social theory encompasses bodies of knowledge and sets of institutional practices that actively grapple with the central questions facing groups of people differently placed in specific political, social, and historic contexts characterized by injustice. What makes critical social theory "critical" is its commitment to justice, for one's own group and/or for other groups.

decentering: The unseating of those who occupy centers of power, as well as the knowledge that defends their power. Typically applied to elite White male power, the concept of decentering can apply to any type of group-based power.

deconstruction: In its most general sense, a constellation of methodologies used to dismantle truths or perceived norms. Deconstructive methodologies generally use three steps: identifying the binaries or oppositions that structure an argument; revealing how the dependent, negative term creates conditions for the existence of the positive term; and replacing binaries with more fluid concepts. The goal is to transcend binary logic by simultaneously being both and neither of the binary terms.

distributive paradigm of justice: A theory of justice that focuses on allocating material goods, such as resources, income, wealth, or the distribution of social positions, especially jobs. This emphasis ignores the social structures and institutional contexts that often determine distributive patterns. Distributive paradigms view social justice as rights or bundles of static things, often in scarce supply, that are distributed to the most worthy.

domain assumptions: Guiding principles or beliefs that distinguish bodies of knowledge from one another.

elite discourses: Bodies of knowledge representing the interests of any group that dominates or rules other groups.

epistemology: Standards used to assess what we know or why we believe what we believe.

essentialism: The belief that individuals or groups have inherent, unchanging characteristics rooted in biology or in a self-contained culture that explains their status. When linked to oppressions of race, gender, and sexuality, binary thinking constructs "essential" group differences.

everyday racism: Practices of everyday lived experience that discriminate against people of color but that, because they are so routine, typically go unnoticed or remain unidentified as racism.

false universalism: Closely linked to power relations, false universal perspectives reflect the worldview of a small group of people who define themselves not only as the inclusive kind of human but also as both the norm for humanity and the ideal human.

"fighting words" doctrine: "Fighting words" consist of insults of such dimension that they either urge people to violence or inflict harm. In the United States, although the First Amendment to the Constitution is designed to protect political speech of all types, bomb

threats, incitements to riot, obscene phone calls, "fighting words," and all speech that infringes on public order can be prohibited in the interests of the common good.

hegemony: A form or mode of social organization wherein the dissent of oppressed groups is absorbed and thereby depoliticized. Alternately, the diffusion of power throughout the social system such that multiple groups police one another and suppress each other's dissent.

heuristic device: A conceptual framework describing what kinds of things to consider rather than describing actual patterns of social organization. Heuristic devices aim neither to prove things right or wrong nor to gather empirical data to test the existence of social phenomena.

hierarchical power relations: A constellation of organized practices in employment, government, education, law, business, and housing that work to maintain an unequal and unjust distribution of social resources. Race, economic class, gender, sexuality, citizenship status, ethnicity, and age constitute major dimensions of hierarchical power relations in the United States.

identity politics: A form of political resistance in which an oppressed group rejects its devalued status and claims its difference as positive. Also, a way of knowing that sees concrete, lived experiences as important to creating knowledge and crafting political strategies.

institutionalized racism: The combination of practices whereby Blacks and other people of color as a group or class receive differential treatment within schools, housing, employment, health care, and other social institutions. Unlike bias and prejudice, which are characteristics of individuals, institutionalized racism operates through the everyday rules and customs of social institutions.

intersectionality: An analysis claiming that systems of race, economic class, gender, sexuality, ethnicity, nation, and age form mutually constructing features of social organization.

metaphor: In everyday use, an interpretive framework that guides social meaning and serves as a mental map for understanding the world. Metaphors work by showing how a set of relations that seems evident in one sphere might illuminate thinking and action in other spheres.

modernity: A generally accepted new form of global social organization that developed when science and reason became important principles in European societies. Philosophers tend to speak of "modernity" as arising during the 1600s, whereas cultural critics apply the term *modernism* to literary and artistic tendencies of the early twentieth century. Development theorists refer to the "modernization" of different societies that move toward industrialization with capitalist market economies and political democracy.

oppositional knowledge: A type of knowledge developed by, for, and/or in defense of an oppressed group's interests. Ideally, it fosters the group's self-definition and self-determination.

organic intellectual: A thinker who emerges from an oppressed group and reflects its concerns and interests.

orienting strategies: A conceptual framework or set of guiding principles that identify how to approach social reality, not what is true about the world. Heuristic devices provide orienting strategies.

outsider-within locations: Social locations or border spaces marking the boundaries between groups of unequal power. Individuals acquire identities as "outsiders within" by their placement in these social locations.

positivist science: A discourse that emerged in conditions of modernity that assumes that the tools of science can represent reality and discover universal truth.

postmodernism: A conceptual framework applied to the social world based on decentering power relations, deconstructing universal truths about the world, and recognizing multiplicity or differences of experiences and perspectives on the world.

praxis: Simultaneously, ideas that inform practice and practice that shapes ideas. The struggle of Black feminist thought for self-definition and self-determination constitutes a Black feminist praxis.

primitive: A foundational descriptor applied to people of African descent that emerged in conjunction with colonialism. Black people were characterized as more natural, more sexually uninhibited, and more violent than Whites.

private transcripts: The secret knowledge generated by a group on either side of power that is shared in private when the surveillance of the group on the other side seems absent. For oppressed groups, such knowledge typically remains "hidden" because revealing it weakens its purpose of assisting oppressed groups in dealing with oppression. Also known as hidden transcripts or *subjugated knowledge.*

public and private spheres: Two areas of social organization, with the public sphere of work and government usually juxtaposed to the private sphere of home and family. Typically, federal, state, and local governmental units constitute the state segment of the public sphere, with the franchise being used to determine formal citizenship rights.

Corporations, the media, civic associations, and all social institutions not attached to the state constitute civil society, the other segment of the public sphere.

public transcripts: The public discourses or knowledges of academia, government bureaucracies, the press, the courts, and popular culture. Controlled by elite groups, this public discourse typically counts as legitimated knowledge and often is grounded in false universals.

racial etiquette: Patterned race relations of domination and subordination.

racialization: The assignment of a racial meaning to a previously racially neutral event.

racially coded language: Language without an explicit reference to race but embedded with racial meaning nonetheless.

racial segregation: The division of racial groups into separate physical and symbolic spaces based on the belief that proximity to the group deemed inferior will harm the allegedly superior group. Though currently forbidden by law in the United States, racially segregated neighborhoods, schools, occupational categories, and access to public facilities persist.

racial solidarity: The belief that members of a racial group have common interests and should support those interests above the interests of members of other racial groups.

racism: A system of unequal power and privilege in which human beings are divided into groups or races, with social rewards being unevenly distributed to groups based on their racial classification. Variations of racism include institutionalized racism, scientific racism, and everyday racism. In the United States, racial segregation constitutes a fundamental organizing principle of racism.

recontextualization: The act of changing the meaning of existing knowledge by establishing a new interpretive framework for it.

rhetoric of color blindness: A view of the world that resists talking of race because to do so is believed to perpetuate racism. This rhetoric is necessary for tolerance to emerge as the way people should treat one another across differences.

scientific racism: A specific body of knowledge about Blacks, Asians, Native Americans, Whites, and Latinos produced within biology, anthropology, psychology, sociology, and other academic disciplines. Designed to prove the inferiority of people of color.

self-definition: The power to name one's own reality.

self-determination: The power to decide one's own destiny.

social theory: A body of knowledge and a set of institutional practices that actively grapple with the central questions facing a group of people in a specific political, social, and historic context. Instead of circulating exclusively as a body of decontextualized ideas among privileged intellectuals, social theory emerges from, is legitimated by, and reflects the concerns of actual groups of people in particular institutional settings.

standpoint theory: A social theory arguing that group location in hierarchical power relations produces shared experiences for individuals in those groups, and that these common experiences can foster similar angles of vision leading to a group knowledge or standpoint deemed essential for informed political action.

subjugated knowledge: The secret knowledge generated by oppressed groups. Such knowledge typically remains "hidden" because revealing it weakens its purpose of assisting oppressed groups in dealing with oppression. Subjugated knowledges that resist oppression become oppositional knowledges.

surveillance: A strategy of control whereby people's words and actions are constantly watched and recorded.

transvaluation: The act of accepting guiding principles, ideas, or rules while changing the meanings or valuations attached to them.

Works Cited

Addams, Jane. 1895–1896. "A Belated Industry." *American Journal of Sociology* 1:536–50.

Adler, Jerry, et al. 1991."African Dreams." *Newsweek*, September 23, 42–50.

Adler, Karen S. 1992. "'Always Leading Our Men in Service and Sacrifice': Amy Jacques Garvey, Feminist Black Nationalist." *Gender and Society* 6 (3): 346–75.

Akbar, Na'im. 1989. "Nigrescence and Identity: Some Limitations." *Counseling Psychologist* 17 (2): 258–63.

———. 1991. "The Challenge of Implementation." *Black Collegian* 22 (1): 36–38.

Amott, Teresa L. 1990. "Black Women and AFDC: Making Entitlement out of Necessity." In *Women, the State, and Welfare*, edited by Linda Gordon, 280–98. Madison: University of Wisconsin Press.

Amott, Teresa L., and Julie Matthaei. 1991. *Race, Gender, and Work: A Multicultural Economic History of Women in the United States*. Boston: South End.

Andersen, Margaret. 1991. "Feminism and the American Family Ideal." *Journal of Comparative Family Studies* 22 (2), summer: 235–46.

Anderson, Benedict. 1983. *Imagined Communities: Reflections on the Origin and Spread of Nationalism*. London: Verso.

Anderson, Margo J. 1988. *The American Census: A Social History*. New Haven: Yale University Press.

Anderson, Talmadge, ed. 1990. *Black Studies: Theory, Method, and Cultural Perspectives*. Pullman: Washington State University Press.

Anthias, Floya, and Nira Yuval-Davis. 1992. *Racialized Boundaries: Race, Nation, Gender, Colour, and Class in the Anti-racist Struggle*. New York: Routledge.

Anzaldúa, Gloria. 1987. *Borderlands/La Frontera*. San Francisco: Spinsters/Aunt Lute.

Appiah, Kwame Anthony. 1992. *In My Father's House: Africa in the Philosophy of Culture*. New York: Oxford University Press.

Arnold, Regina. 1993. "Black Women in Prison: The Price of Resistance." In *Women of Color in U.S. Society,* edited by Maxine Baca Zinn and Bonnie Thornton Dill, 171–84. Philadelphia: Temple University Press.

Asante, Molefi Kete. 1987. *The Afrocentric Idea.* Philadelphia: Temple University Press.

———. 1990. *Kemet, Afrocentricity, and Knowledge.* Trenton, N.J.: Africa World Press.

Asante, Molefi Kete, and Karaimu Welsh Asante, eds. 1990. *African Culture: The Rhythms of Unity.* Trenton, N.J.: Africa World Press.

Avery, Byllye Y. 1994. "Breathing Life into Ourselves: The Evolution of the National Black Women's Health Project." In *The Black Women's Health Book: Speaking for Ourselves,* edited by Evelyn C. White, 4–10. Seattle: Seal.

Awkward, Michael. 1995. *Negotiating Difference: Race, Gender, and the Politics of Positionality.* Chicago: University of Chicago Press.

Baldwin, James, and Margaret Mead. 1971. *A Rap on Race.* New York: Laurel.

Baldwin, Joseph. 1980. "The Psychology of Oppression." In *Contemporary Black Thought: Alternative Analyses in Social and Behavioral Sciences,* edited by Molefi Kete Asante and Abdulai S. Vandi, 95–110. Beverly Hills: Sage.

Balibar, Etienne, and Immanuel Wallerstein. 1991. *Race, Nation, Class: Ambiguous Identities.* New York: Verso.

Bambara, Toni Cade, ed. 1970. *The Black Woman: An Anthology.* New York: Signet.

———. 1980. *The Salt Eaters.* New York: Vintage.

Bannerji, Himani. 1995. *Thinking Through: Essays on Feminism, Marxism, and Anti-racism.* Toronto: Women's Press.

Baraka, Imamu Amiri. 1970. "Black Woman." *Black World* 19 (9): 7–11.

Baran, Paul, and Paul Sweezy. 1966. *Monopoly Capital.* New York: Monthly Review Press.

Barkan, Elazar. 1992. *The Retreat of Scientific Racism: Changing Concepts of Race in Britain and the United States between the World Wars.* Cambridge: Cambridge University Press.

Barker, Martin. 1990. "Biology and the New Racism." In *Anatomy of Racism,* edited by David Theo Goldberg, 18–37. Minneapolis: University of Minnesota Press.

Barnett, Bernice McNair. 1993. "Invisible Southern Black Women Leaders in the Civil Rights Movement: The Triple Constraints of Gender, Race, and Class." *Gender and Society* 7 (2): 162–82.

Bash, Harry. 1979. *Sociology, Race, and Ethnicity: A Critique of American Ideological Intrusions upon Sociological Theory.* New York: Gordon & Breach.

Bauman, Zygmunt. 1992. *Intimations of Postmodernity.* New York: Routledge.

Beale, Frances. 1995 [1970]. "Double Jeopardy: To Be Black and Female." In *Words of Fire: An Anthology of African American Feminist Thought,* edited by Beverly Guy-Sheftall, 146–55. New York: New Press.

Belenky, Mary Field, Blythe McVicker Clinchy, Nancy Rule Goldberger, and Jill Mattuck Tarule. 1986. *Women's Ways of Knowing.* New York: Basic Books.

Bell, Derrick. 1987. *And We Are Not Saved: The Elusive Quest for Racial Justice.* New York: Basic Books.

Ben-Jochannan, Yosef. 1972. *Black Man of the Nile and His Family (African Foundations of European Civilization and Thought).* New York: Alkebu-lan Books.

Bernal, Martin. 1987. *Black Athena: The Afroasiatic Roots of Classical Civilization.* Vol. 1. New Brunswick, N.J.: Rutgers University Press.

Berry, Mary Frances. 1994 [1971]. *Black Resistance, White Law: A History of Constitutional Racism in America.* New York: Penguin.

Berry, Mary Frances, and John Blassingame. 1982. *Long Memory: The Black Experience in America*. New York: Oxford University Press.

Best, Steven, and Douglas Kellner. 1991. *Postmodern Theory: Critical Interrogations*. New York: Guilford.

Blackwell, James, and Morris Janowitz, eds. 1974. *Black Sociologists: Historical and Contemporary Perspectives*. Chicago: University of Chicago Press.

Blauner, Bob. 1972. *Racial Oppression in America*. New York: Harper & Row.

———. 1989. *Black Lives, White Lives: Three Decades of Race Relations in America*. Berkeley: University of California Press.

Blauvelt, Mary Taylor. 1900–1901. "The Race Problem as Discussed by Negro Women." *American Journal of Sociology* 6: 662–72.

Bobo, Jacqueline. 1995. *Black Women as Cultural Readers*. New York: Columbia University Press.

Bonacich, Edna. 1989. "Inequality in America: The Failure of the American System for People of Color." *Sociological Spectrum* 9 (11): 77–101.

Boulton, Guy. 1996. "Walnut Hills Graduate Took on Texaco." *Cincinnati Enquirer,* December 8: I1–I2.

Bourdieu, Pierre. 1990. *In Other Words: Essays towards a Reflexive Sociology*. Stanford: Stanford University Press.

Braxton, Joanne M. 1989. *Black Women Writing Autobiography: A Tradition within a Tradition*. Philadelphia: Temple University Press.

Breitman, George, ed. 1965. *Malcolm X Speaks*. New York: Grove.

Brewer, Rose. 1988. "Black Women in Poverty: Some Comments on Female-Headed Families." *Signs* 13 (2): 331–39.

———. 1989. "Black Women and Feminist Sociology: The Emerging Perspective." *American Sociologist* 20 (1): 57–70.

Broderick, Francis L. 1974. "W. E. B. Du Bois: History of an Intellectual." In *Black Sociologists: Historical and Contemporary Perspectives*, edited by James E. Blackwell and Morris Janowitz, 3–24. Chicago: University of Chicago Press.

Brodhead, Frank. 1987. "The African Origins of Western Civilization." *Radical America,* May 21, 29–37.

Brown, Elaine. 1992. *A Taste of Power: A Black Woman's Story*. New York: Pantheon.

Brown, Elsa Barkley. 1989. "African-American Women's Quilting: A Framework for Conceptualizing and Teaching African-American Women's History." *Signs* 14 (4): 921–29.

———. 1994. "Negotiating and Transforming the Public Sphere: African American Political Life in the Transition from Slavery to Freedom." *Public Culture* 7 (1): 107–46.

Cabral, Amilcar. 1973. "National Liberation and Culture." In *Return to the Source: Selected Speeches of Amilcar Cabral*, 39–56. New York: Monthly Review Press.

Caldwell, Paulette M. 1991. "A Hair Piece: Perspectives on the Intersection of Race and Gender." *Duke Law Journal* 365: 365–96.

Calhoun, Craig. 1993. "Nationalism and Ethnicity." *Annual Review of Sociology* 19: 211–39.

———. 1995. *Critical Social Theory: Culture, History, and the Challenge of Difference*. Cambridge, Mass.: Blackwell.

Cannon, Katie G. 1988. *Black Womanist Ethics*. Atlanta: Scholars Press.

Caraway, Nancie. 1991. *Segregated Sisterhood: Racism and the Politics of American Feminism*. Knoxville: University of Tennessee Press.

Carby, Hazel. 1987. *Reconstructing Womanhood: The Emergence of the Afro-American Woman Novelist*. New York: Oxford University Press.

————. 1992. "The Multicultural Wars." In *Black Popular Culture,* edited by Michele Wallace and Gina Dent, 187–99. Seattle: Bay Press.

Chandler, Zala. 1990. "Voices beyond the Veil: An Interview of Toni Cade Bambara and Sonia Sanchez." In *Wild Women in the Whirlwind,* edited by Joanne Braxton and Andree Nicola McLaughlin, 342–62. New Brunswick, N.J.: Rutgers University Press.

Chisholm, Shirley. 1970. *Unbought and Unbossed.* New York: Avon.

Chow, Esther Ngan-Ling, Doris Wilkinson, and Maxine Baca Zinn, eds. 1996. *Race, Class, and Gender: Common Bonds, Different Voices.* Thousand Oaks, Calif.: Sage.

Chow, Rey. 1993. *Writing Diaspora: Tactics of Intervention in Contemporary Cultural Studies.* Bloomington: Indiana University Press.

Chrisman, Robert. 1992. Introduction to *Court of Appeal: The Black Community Speaks Out on the Racial and Sexual Politics of Thomas vs. Hill,* edited by Robert Chrisman and Robert L. Allen. New York: Ballantine.

Christian, Barbara. 1985. *Black Feminist Criticism: Perspectives on Black Women Writers.* New York: Pergamon.

————. 1988. "The Race for Theory." *Feminist Studies* 14 (1): 67–79.

————. 1989a. "But What Do We Think We're Doing Anyway: The State of Black Feminist Criticism(s) or My Version of a Little Bit of History." In *Changing Our Own Words: Essays on Criticism, Theory, and Writing by Black Women,* edited by Cheryl A. Wall, 58–74. New Brunswick, N.J.: Rutgers University Press.

————. 1989b. "But Who Do You Really Belong To—Black Studies or Women's Studies?" *Women's Studies* 17 (1–2): 17–23.

Cleage, Pearl. 1993. *Deals with the Devil and Other Reasons to Riot.* New York: Ballantine.

Cleaver, Eldridge. 1968. *Soul on Ice.* New York: McGraw-Hill.

Cliff, Michelle. 1988. "A Journey into Speech." *The Graywolf Annual 5: Multicultural Literacy,* edited by Rick Simonson and Scott Walker, 57–62. St. Paul: Graywolf.

Cohen, Anthony P. 1985. *The Symbolic Construction of Community.* New York: Tavistock.

Cole, Johnetta B. 1993. *Conversations: Straight Talk with America's Sister President.* New York: Anchor.

Collins, Patricia Hill. 1986. "Learning from the Outsider Within: The Sociological Significance of Black Feminist Thought." *Social Problems* 33 (6): 14–32.

————. 1989. "A Comparison of Two Works on Black Family Life." *Signs* 14 (4): 875–84.

————. 1990. *Black Feminist Thought: Knowledge, Consciousness, and the Politics of Empowerment.* New York: Routledge, Chapman & Hall.

————. 1992a. "Learning to Think for Ourselves: Malcolm X's Black Nationalism Reconsidered." In *Malcolm X: In Our Own Image,* edited by Joe Wood, 59–85. New York: St. Martin's.

————. 1992b. "Transforming the Inner Circle: Dorothy Smith's Challenge to Sociological Theory." *Sociological Theory* 10 (1): 73–80.

————. 1993. "Black Feminism in the Twentieth Century." In *Black Women in the United States: An Historical Encyclopedia,* edited by Darlene Clark Hine, Elsa Barkley Brown, and Rosalyn Terborg-Penn, 418–25. New York: Carlson.

————. 1997. "African-American Women and Economic Justice: A Preliminary Analysis of Wealth, Family, and Black Social Class." *University of Cincinnati Law Review* 65(3): 825–52.

———. 1998a. "Intersections of Race, Class, Gender, and Nation: Some Implications for Black Family Studies." *Journal of Comparative Family Studies* 29 (1): 27–36.

———. Forthcoming, 1998b. "It's All in the Family: Intersections of Gender, Race, Class, and Nation." *Hypatia.*

The Combahee River Collective. 1982. "A Black Feminist Statement." In *All the Women Are White, All the Blacks Are Men, But Some of Us Are Brave: Black Women's Studies,* edited by Gloria T. Hull, Patricia Bell Scott, and Barbara Smith, 13–22. Old Westbury, N.Y.: Feminist Press.

Commander, Lydia K. 1908–1909. "The Self-Supporting Woman and the Family." *American Journal of Sociology* 14: 752–57.

Cone, James H. 1972. *The Spirituals and the Blues: An Interpretation.* New York: Seabury.

Conyers, James L., Jr. 1995. *The Evolution of African American Studies.* Lantham, Md.: University Press of America.

Coontz, Stephanie. 1992. *The Way We Never Were: American Families and the Nostalgia Trap.* New York: Basic Books.

Cooper, Anna Julia. 1892. *A Voice from the South; by a Black Woman of the South.* Xenia, Ohio: Aldine Printing House.

Cose, Ellis. 1993. *The Rage of the Privileged Class.* New York: HarperCollins.

Cox, Oliver. 1948. *Caste, Class, and Race.* New York: Modern Reader.

Crawford, Vicki. 1990. "Beyond the Human Self: Grassroots Activists in the Mississippi Civil Rights Movement." In *Women in the Civil Rights Movement: Trailblazers and Torchbearers, 1941–1965,* edited by Vicki L. Crawford, Jacqueline Anne Rouse, and Barbara Woods, 13–26. Bloomington: Indiana University Press.

Crawford, Vicki L., Jacqueline Anne Rouse, and Barbara Woods, eds. 1990. *Women in the Civil Rights Movement: Trailblazers and Torchbearers, 1941–1965.* Bloomington: Indiana University Press.

Crenshaw, Kimberle Williams. 1991. "Mapping the Margins: Intersectionality, Identity Politics, and Violence against Women of Color." *Stanford Law Review* 43 (6): 1241–99.

———. 1992. "Whose Story Is It Anyway? Feminist and Antiracist Appropriations of Anita Hill." In *Race-ing Justice, En-gendering Power,* edited by Toni Morrison, 402–40. New York: Pantheon.

———. 1993. "Beyond Racism and Misogyny: Black Feminism and 2 Live Crew." In *Words That Wound: Critical Race Theory, Assaultive Speech, and the First Amendment,* edited by Mari J. Matsuda, Charles R. Lawrence III, Richard Delgado, and Kimberle Crenshaw, 111–32. Boulder: Westview.

Cross, William. 1971. "The Negro to Black Conversion Experience: Toward a Psychology of Black Liberation." *Black World* 20 (9): 13–27.

Daniels, Jessie. 1997. *White Lies.* New York: Routledge.

Davies, Carole Boyce. 1994. *Black Women, Writing, and Identity: Migrations of the Subject.* New York: Routledge.

Davis, Angela Y. 1974. *Angela Davis: An Autobiography.* New York: Bantam.

———. 1981. *Women, Race, and Class.* New York: Random House.

———. 1989. *Women, Culture, and Politics.* New York: Random House.

———. 1994. "Afro Images; Politics, Fashion, and Nostalgia." *Critical Inquiry* 21 (2): 37–45.

———. 1995 [1971]. "Reflections on the Black Woman's Role in the Community of Slaves." In *Words of Fire: An Anthology of African American Feminist Thought,* edited by Beverly Guy-Sheftall, 200–218. New York: New Press.

Dawson, Michael C. 1994. "A Black Counterpublic? Economic Earthquakes, Racial Agenda(s), and Black Politics." *Public Culture* 7 (1): 195–224.

Deegan, Mary Jo. 1991. Introduction to *Women in Sociology: A Bio-bibliographical Sourcebook*, edited by Mary Jo Deegan, 1–28. New York: Greenwood.

Delgado, Richard. 1984. "The Imperial Scholar: Reflections on a Review of Civil Rights Literature." *University of Pennsylvania Law Review* 132: 561–78.

Dent, Gina. 1992. "Black Pleasure, Black Joy: An Introduction." In *Black Popular Culture,* edited by Michele Wallace and Gina Dent, 1–19. Seattle: Bay Press.

Diawara, Manthia. 1992. "Afro-kitch." In *Black Popular Culture,* edited by Michele Wallace and Gina Dent, 285–91. Seattle: Bay Press.

Dickerson, Bette J., ed. 1995. *African American Single Mothers: Understanding Their Lives and Families.* Thousand Oaks, Calif.: Sage.

Dickerson, Patrice L. 1997. "African-American Female Sociologists: Historical Doctorate Production Trends, Dissertations, and Publications." Unpublished manuscript, Department of Sociology, University of Michigan at Ann Arbor.

Dill, Bonnie Thornton. 1983. "Race, Class, and Gender: Prospects for an All-Inclusive Sisterhood." *Feminist Studies* 9 (1): 131–50.

———. 1988a. "'Making Your Job Good Yourself': Domestic Service and the Construction of Personal Dignity." In *Women and the Politics of Empowerment,* edited by Ann Bookman and Sandra Morgen, 33–52. Philadelphia: Temple University Press.

———. 1988b. "Our Mothers' Grief: Racial Ethnic Women and the Maintenance of Families." *Journal of Family History* 13 (4): 415–31.

Diop, Cheikh Anta. 1974. *The African Origin of Civilization: Myth or Reality.* Edited and translated by Mercer Cook. Westport, Conn.: Lawrence Hill.

Domhoff, G. William. 1990. *The Power Elite and the State: How Policy Is Made in America.* New York: de Gruyter.

Dubey, Madhu. 1994. *Black Women Novelists and the Nationalist Aesthetic.* Bloomington: Indiana University Press.

Du Bois, William E. B. 1961 [1903]. *The Souls of Black Folk.* New York: Dodd, Mead.

———. 1967 [1899]. *The Philadelphia Negro: A Social Study.* New York: Schocken.

———. 1969 [1908]. *The Negro American Family.* Westport, Conn.: Negro Universities Press, Greenwood Press.

DuCille, Ann. 1994. "The Occult of True Black Womanhood: Critical Demeanor and Black Feminist Studies." *Signs* 19 (3): 591–629.

Duster, Troy. 1990. *Backdoor to Eugenics.* New York: Routledge, Chapman & Hall.

Dyson, Michael Eric. 1992. "Melanin Madness: A Struggle for the Black Mind." *Emerge,* February, 32–37.

———. 1993. *Reflecting Black: African-American Cultural Criticism.* Minneapolis: University of Minnesota Press.

Edwards, Richard. 1979. *Contested Terrain: The Transformation of the Workplace in the Twentieth Century.* New York: Basic Books.

Epstein, Cynthia Fuchs. 1973. "Positive Effects of the Multiple Negative: Explaining the Success of Black Professional Women." *American Journal of Sociology* 78 (4): 912–35.

Essed, Philomena. 1991. *Understanding Everyday Racism: An Interdisciplinary Theory.* Newbury Park, Calif.: Sage.

Estell, Kenneth. 1994. *The African-American Almanac.* 6th ed. Detroit: Gale Research.

"Excerpts from Tapes in Discrimination Lawsuit." 1996. *New York Times,* November 4, D4.

Ezorsky, Gertrude. 1991. *Racism and Justice: The Case for Affirmative Action*. Ithaca: Cornell University Press.

Fanon, Frantz. 1963. *The Wretched of the Earth*. New York: Grove.

———. 1967. *Black Skin, White Masks*. New York: Grove.

Fausto-Sterling, Anne. 1992. *Myths of Gender: Biological Theories about Women and Men*. 2d ed. New York: Basic Books.

Feagin, Joe R., and Melvin P. Sikes. 1994. *Living with Racism: The Black Middle-Class Experience*. Boston: Beacon.

Flax, Jane. 1990. "Postmodernism and Gender Relations in Feminist Theory." In *Feminism/Postmodernism*, edited by Linda J. Nicholson, 39–62. New York: Routledge.

Fordham, Signithia. 1993. "'Those Loud Black Girls': (Black) Women, Silence, and Gender 'Passing' in the Academy." *Anthropology and Education Quarterly* 24 (1): 3–32.

Forgacs, David, ed. 1988. *An Antonio Gramsci Reader: Selected Writings, 1916–1935*. New York: Schocken.

Foucault, Michel. 1977. "The Political Function of the Intellectual." *Radical Philosophy*. 17 (summer): 12–14.

———. 1979. *Discipline and Punish: The Birth of the Prison*. Translated by Alan Sheridan. New York: Schocken.

———. 1980a. *The History of Sexuality*. Vol. 1, *An Introduction*. Translated by Robert Hurley. New York: Vintage.

———. 1980b. *Power/Knowledge: Selected Interviews and Other Writings, 1972–1977*. Edited by Colin Gordon. New York: Pantheon.

Frankenberg, Ruth. 1993. *White Women, Race Matters: The Social Construction of Whiteness*. Minneapolis: University of Minnesota Press.

Franklin, V. P. 1992. *Black Self-Determination: A Cultural History of African-American Resistance*. Chicago: Lawrence Hill.

———. 1995. *Living Our Stories, Telling Our Truths: Autobiography and the Making of the African-American Intellectual Tradition*. New York: Scribner.

Fraser, Nancy. 1989. *Unruly Practices: Power, Discourse, and Gender in Contemporary Social Theory*. Minneapolis: University of Minnesota Press.

Fraser, Nancy, and Linda Nicholson. 1990. "Social Criticism without Philosophy: An Encounter between Feminism and Postmodernism." In *Feminism/Postmodernism*, edited by Linda J. Nicholson, 19–38. New York: Routledge.

Freire, Paulo. 1970. *The Pedagogy of the Oppressed*. New York: Herder & Herder.

Fuchs, Stephan, and Steven Ward. 1994. "Deconstruction: Making Facts in Science, Building Cases in Law." *American Sociological Review* 59 (4): 481–500.

Fusco, Coco. 1992. "Pan-American Postnationalism: Another World Order." In *Black Popular Culture*, edited by Michele Wallace and Gina Dent, 279–84. Seattle: Bay Press.

Fuss, Diana. 1989. *Essentially Speaking: Feminism, Nature, and Difference*. New York: Routledge, Chapman & Hall.

———. 1991. "Inside/Out." In *Inside/Out: Lesbian Theories, Gay Theories*, edited by Diana Fuss, 1–10. New York: Routledge.

Galton, Francis 1904–1905. "Eugenics: Its Definition, Scope, and Aims." *American Journal of Sociology* 10: 1–6.

———. 1905–1906. "Studies in Eugenics." *American Journal of Sociology* 11: 11–25.

Gates, Henry Louis, Jr. 1992a. "Black Demagogues and Pseudo-Scholars." *New York Times,* July 20, Op-Ed section.

————. 1992b. *Loose Canons: Notes on the Culture Wars.* New York: Oxford University Press.

Gayle, Addison. 1971. *The Black Aesthetic.* Garden City, N.Y.: Doubleday.

Geschwender, James A., and Rita Caroll-Seguin. 1990. "Exploding the Myth of African-American Progress." *Signs* 15 (2): 285–99.

Giddings, Paula. 1984. *When and Where I Enter: The Impact of Black Women on Race and Sex in America.* New York: Morrow.

Gilkes, Cheryl Townsend. 1980. "'Holding Back the Ocean with a Broom': Black Women and Community Work." In *The Black Woman,* edited by La Frances Rodgers-Rose, 217–32. Beverly Hills: Sage.

————. 1983a. "From Slavery to Social Welfare: Racism and the Control of Black Women." In *Class, Race, and Sex: The Dynamics of Control,* edited by Amy Swerdlow and Hanna Lessinger, 288–300. Boston: Hall.

————. 1983b. "Going Up for the Oppressed: The Career Mobility of Black Women Community Workers." *Journal of Social Issues* 39 (3): 115–39.

————. 1985. "'Together and in Harness': Women's Traditions in the Sanctified Church." *Signs* 10 (4): 678–99.

————. 1988. "Building in Many Places: Multiple Commitments and Ideologies in Black Women's Community Work." In *Women and the Politics of Empowerment,* edited by Ann Bookman and Sandra Morgen, 53–76. Philadelphia: Temple University Press.

————. 1994. "'If It Wasn't for the Women . . .': African American Women, Community Work, and Social Change." In *Women of Color in U.S. Society,* edited by Maxine Baca Zinn and Bonnie Thornton Dill, 229–46. Philadelphia: Temple University Press.

Gilman, Charlotte Perkins. 1908–1909. "How Home Conditions React upon the Family." *American Journal of Sociology* 14: 592–95.

Gilman, Sander L. 1985. *Difference and Pathology: Stereotypes of Sexuality, Race, and Madness.* Ithaca, N.Y.: Cornell University Press.

Gilroy, Paul. 1987. *"There Ain't No Black in the Union Jack": The Cultural Politics of Race and Nation.* Chicago: University of Chicago Press.

————. 1992. "It's a Family Affair." In *Black Popular Culture,* edited by Michele Wallace and Gina Dent, 303–16. Seattle: Bay Press.

————. 1993. *The Black Atlantic: Modernity and Double Consciousness.* Cambridge: Harvard University Press.

Giovanni, Nikki. 1970. *Black Feeling, Black Talk, Black Judgement.* New York: Morrow.

Glenn, Evelyn Nakano. 1985. "Racial Ethnic Women's Labor: The Intersection of Race, Gender, and Class Oppression." *Review of Radical Political Economics* 17 (3): 86–108.

Goldberg, David Theo. 1993. *Racist Culture: Philosophy and the Politics of Meaning.* Cambridge, Mass.: Blackwell.

Golden, Marita. 1995. *Saving Our Sons: Raising Black Children in a Turbulent World.* New York: Anchor.

Goldsmith, William W., and Edward J. Blakely. 1992. *Separate Societies: Poverty and Inequality in U.S. Cities.* Philadelphia: Temple University Press.

Gordon, David, Richard Edwards, and Michael Reich. 1982. *Segmented Work, Divided Workers: The Historical Transformation of Labor in the United States.* New York: Cambridge University Press.

Gordon, Joan Louise. 1955. "Some Socio-economic Aspects of Selected Negro Families in Savannah, Georgia: With Special Reference to the Effects of Occupational Stratification on Child Rearing." Ph.D. diss., University of Pennsylvania.

Gossett, Thomas F. 1963. *Race: The History of an Idea in America*. Dallas: Southern Methodist University Press.

Gould, Stephen Jay. 1981. *The Mismeasure of Man*. New York: Norton.

Grant, Jacqueline. 1982. "Black Women and the Church." In *All the Women Are White, All the Blacks Are Men, But Some of Us Are Brave: Black Women's Studies*, edited by Gloria T. Hull, Patricia Bell Scott, and Barbara Smith, 141–52. Old Westbury, Conn.: Feminist Press.

———. 1989. *White Women's Christ and Black Women's Jesus: Feminist Christology and Womanist Response*. Atlanta: Scholars Press.

———. 1992. "Jesus and the Task of Redemption." In *We Belong Together: Churches in Solidarity with Women*, edited by Sarah Cunningham, 30–42. New York: Friendship.

Grant, Linda. 1994. "Helpers, Enforcers, and Go-Betweens: Black Females in Elementary School Classrooms." In *Women of Color in U.S. Society*, edited by Maxine Baca Zinn and Bonnie Thornton Dill, 43–63. Philadelphia: Temple University Press.

Green, Dan. S., and Edwin Driver, eds. 1978. *W. E. B. Du Bois: On Sociology and the Black Community*. Chicago: University of Chicago Press.

Greenberg, Stanley B. 1980. *Race and State in Capitalist Development*. New Haven: Yale University Press.

Greene, Harry Washington. 1946. *Holders of Doctorates among American Negroes: An Educational and Social Study of Negroes Who Have Earned Doctoral Degrees in Course, 1876–1943*. Boston: Meador.

Gregory, Steven. 1994. "Race, Identity, and Political Activism: The Shifting Contours of the African American Public Sphere." *Public Culture* 7 (1): 147–64.

Grimes, Michael D. 1991. *Class in Twentieth-Century American Sociology*. New York: Praeger.

Grossberg, Lawrence. 1996. "On Postmodernism and Articulation: An Interview with Stuart Hall." In *Stuart Hall: Critical Dialogues in Cultural Studies*, edited by David Morley and Kuan-Hsing Chen, 131–50. New York: Routledge.

Guillaumin, Colette. 1995. *Racism, Sexism, Power, and Ideology*. New York: Routledge.

Guinier, Lani. 1992. "Voting Rights and Democratic Theory: Where Do We Go From Here?" In *Controversies in Minority Voting: The Voting Rights Act in Perspective*, edited by Bernard Grofman and Chandler Davidson, 283–92. Washington: Brookings Institution.

———. 1994. *The Tyranny of the Majority: Fundamental Fairness in Representative Democracy*. New York: Free Press.

Guy-Sheftall, Beverly. 1986. "Remembering Sojourner Truth: On Black Feminism." *Catalyst*, fall, 54–57.

———. 1995. "The Evolution of Feminist Consciousness among African American Women." In *Words of Fire: An Anthology of African American Feminist Thought*, edited by Beverly Guy-Sheftall, 1–22. New York: New Press.

Habermas, Jürgen. 1989. *The Structural Transformation of the Public Sphere*. Cambridge: MIT Press.

Hacker, Andrew. 1992. *Two Nations: Black and White, Separate, Hostile, Unequal*. New York: Ballantine.

Hage, Jerald, Michael Aiken, and Cora Marrett. 1971. "Organization Structure and Communications." *American Sociological Review* 36: 860–71.

Hall, Jacqueline Dowd. 1983. "The Mind That Burns in Each Body: Women, Rape, and Racial Violence." In *Powers of Desire: The Politics of Sexuality*, edited by Ann Snitow, Christine Stansell, and Sharon Thompson, 329–49. New York: Monthly Review Press.

Hall, Stuart. 1992. "What Is This 'Black' in Black Popular Culture?" In *Black Popular Culture*, edited by Michele Wallace and Gina Dent, 21–33 . Seattle: Bay Press.

Haller, Mark H. 1984 [1963]. *Eugenics: Hereditarian Attitudes in American Thought*. New Brunswick, N.J.: Rutgers University Press.

Halpin, Zuleyma Tang. 1989. "Scientific Objectivity and the Concept of 'the Other.'" *Women's Studies International Forum* 12 (3): 575–99.

Haraway, Donna. 1988. "Situated Knowledges: The Science Question in Feminism and the Privilege of Partial Perspective." *Feminist Studies* 14 (3): 575–99.

———. 1989. *Primate Visions: Gender, Race, and Nature in the World of Modern Science*. New York: Routledge, Chapman & Hall.

Harding, Sandra. 1986. *The Science Question in Feminism*. Ithaca, N.Y.: Cornell University Press.

———. 1991. *Whose Science? Whose Knowledge? Thinking from Women's Lives*. Ithaca, N.Y.: Cornell University Press.

———, ed. 1993. *The "Racial" Economy of Science: Toward a Democratic Future*. Bloomington: Indiana University Press.

Hartsock, Nancy. 1983. "The Feminist Standpoint: Developing the Grounds for a Specifically Feminist Historical Materialism." In *Discovering Reality*, edited by Sandra Harding and Merrill B. Hintikka, 283–310. Boston: Reidel.

———. 1987. "Rethinking Modernism: Minority vs. Majority Theories." *Cultural Critique* 7: 187–206.

———. 1990. "Foucault on Power: A Theory for Women?" In *Feminism/Postmodernism*, edited by Linda Nicholson, 157–75. New York: Routledge.

Hekman, Susan. 1997. "Truth and Method: Feminist Standpoint Theory Revisited." *Signs* 22 (2): 341–65.

Held, David. 1980. *Introduction to Critical Theory: Horkheimer to Habermas*. Berkeley: University of California Press.

Henderson, Mae Gwendolyn. 1989. "Speaking in Tongues: Dialogics, Dialectics, and the Black Woman Writer's Literary Tradition." In *Changing Our Own Words: Essays on Criticism, Theory, and Writing by Black Women*, edited by Cheryl A. Wall, 16–37. New Brunswick, N.J.: Rutgers University Press.

Herskovits, Melville. 1990 [1941]. *The Myth of the Negro Past*. Boston: Beacon.

Higginbotham, Elizabeth. 1983. "Laid Bare by the System: Work and Survival for Black and Hispanic Women." In *Class, Race, and Sex: The Dynamics of Control*, edited by Amy Smerdlow and Hanna Lessinger. Boston: Hall.

———. 1994. "Black Professional Women: Job Ceilings and Employment Sectors." In *Women of Color in U.S. Society*, edited by Maxine Baca Zinn and Bonnie Thornton Dill, 113–31. Philadelphia: Temple University Press.

Higginbotham, Elizabeth, and Lynn Weber. 1992. "Moving Up with Kin and Community: Upward Social Mobility for Black and White Women." *Gender and Society* 6 (3): 416–40.

Higginbotham, Evelyn Brooks. 1992. "African-American Women's History and the Metalanguage of Race." *Signs* 17 (winter): 251–74.

———. 1993. *Righteous Discontent: The Women's Movement in the Black Baptist Church, 1880–1920*. Cambridge: Harvard University Press.

Hill, Adelaide Cromwell. 1952. "The Negro Upper Class in Boston—Its Development and Present Social Structure." Ph.D. diss., University of Pittsburgh.

Hine, Darlene Clark. 1992. "The Black Studies Movement: Afrocentric-Traditionalist-Feminist Paradigms for the Next Stage." *Black Scholar* 22 (3): 11–18.

————. 1993. " 'In the Kingdom of Culture': Black Women and the Intersection of Race, Gender, and Class." In *Lure and Loathing: Essays on Race, Identity, and the Ambivalence of Assimilation,* edited by Gerald Early, 337–51. New York: Penguin.

Holloway, Joseph, ed. 1990. *Africanisms in American Culture.* Bloomington: Indiana University Press.

Holmes, Stevan A. 1995. "Retail Incident Incenses Washington." *New York Times,* December 10, Sec. 1, p. 1.

Hood, Robert E. 1994. *Begrimed and Black: Christian Traditions on Blacks and Blackness.* Minneapolis: Fortress.

hooks, bell. 1990. *Yearning: Race, Gender, and Cultural Politics.* Boston: South End.

hooks, bell, and Cornel West. 1991. *Breaking Bread: Insurgent Black Intellectual Life.* Boston: South End.

Hord, Fred Lee (Mzee Lasana Okpara), and Jonathan Scott Lee. 1995. " 'I Am Because We Are': An Introduction to Black Philosophy." In *I Am Because We Are: Readings in Black Philosophy,* edited by Fred Lee Hord and Jonathan Scott Lee, 1–16. Amherst: University of Massachusetts Press.

Hubbard, Ruth. 1990. *The Politics of Women's Biology.* New Brunswick, N.J.: Rutgers University Press.

Huber, Joan. 1995. "Institutional Perspectives on Sociology." *American Journal of Sociology* 101 (1): 194–216.

Huggins, Nathan. 1985. *Afro-American Studies.* New York: Ford Foundation.

Hull, Gloria T., Patricia Bell Scott, and Barbara Smith, eds. 1982. *All the Women Are White, All the Blacks Are Men, But Some of Us Are Brave: Black Women's Studies.* Old Westbury, N.Y.: Feminist Press.

Hurston, Zora Neale. 1978 [1937]. *Their Eyes Were Watching God.* Urbana: University of Illinois Press.

Jackson, Jacqueline Johnson Clarke. 1960. "Goals and Techniques in Three Negro Civil-Rights Organizations in Alabama." Ph.D. diss., Ohio State University.

————. 1974. "Black Female Sociologists." In *Black Sociologists: Historical and Contemporary Perspectives,* edited by James E. Blackwell and Morris Janowitz, 267–95. Chicago: University of Chicago Press.

Jaggar, Alison M. 1983. *Feminist Politics and Human Nature.* Totowa, N.J.: Rowman & Allanheld.

————. 1989. "Love and Knowledge: Emotion in Feminist Epistemology." In *Gender/Body/Knowledge: Feminist Reconstructions of Being and Knowing,* edited by Alison M. Jaggar and Susan R. Bordo, 145–71. New Brunswick, N.J.: Rutgers University Press.

James, Stanlie, and Abena Busia, eds. 1994. *Theorizing Black Feminisms.* New York: Routledge.

Jameson, Fredric. 1984. "Postmodernism, or the Cultural Logic of Late Capitalism." *New Left Review* 146: 53–92.

Jarrett, Robin. 1994. "Living Poor: Family Life among Single Parent, African American Women." *Social Problems* 41 (February): 30–49.

Jewell, K. Sue. 1993. *From Mammy to Miss America and Beyond: Cultural Images and the Shaping of U.S. Social Policy.* New York: Routledge.

Jhally, Sut, and Justin Lewis. 1992. *Enlightened Racism.* Boulder: Westview.

John, Mary E. 1996. *Discrepant Dislocations: Feminism, Theory, and Postcolonial Histories.* Berkeley: University of California Press.

Jones, Jacqueline. 1985. *Labor of Love, Labor of Sorrow: Black Women, Work, and the Family from Slavery to the Present*. New York: Basic Books.

Jones, James H. 1993. *Bad Blood: The Tuskegee Syphilis Experiment*. New York: Free Press.

Jones, Rhett S. 1973. "Proving Blacks Inferior: The Sociology of Knowledge." In *The Death of White Sociology*, edited by Joyce Ladner, 114–35. New York: Vintage.

Jones-Johnson, Gloria. 1988. "The Victim-Bind Dilemma of Black Female Sociologists in Academe." *American Sociologist* 19 (4): 312–22.

Jordan, June. 1981. *Civil Wars*. Boston: Beacon.

———. 1985. *On Call*. Boston: South End.

———. 1992. *Technical Difficulties: African-American Notes on the State of the Union*. New York: Pantheon.

Jordan, Winthrop D. 1968. *White over Black: American Attitudes toward the Negro, 1550–1812*. New York: Norton.

Joseph, Gloria I. 1990. "Sojourner Truth: Archetypal Black Feminist." In *Wild Women in the Whirlwind*, edited by Joanne Braxton and Andree Nicola McLaughlin, 35–47. New Brunswick, N.J.: Rutgers University Press.

Julian, Anna Johnson. 1937. "Standards of Relief: An Analysis of One Hundred Family Case Records." Ph.D. diss., University of Pennsylvania.

Kaplan, Elaine Bell. 1997. *Not Our Kind of Girl: Unraveling the Myths of Black Teenage Motherhood*. Berkeley: University of California Press.

Karenga, Maulana Ron. 1978. "Afro-American Nationalism: Beyond Mystification and Misconception." *Black Books Bulletin*, spring, 7–12.

———. 1982. *Introduction to Black Studies*. Los Angeles: University of Sankore Press.

———. 1988. "Black Studies and the Problematic of Paradigm: The Philosophical Dimension." *Journal of Black Studies* 18 (4): 395–414.

———, ed. 1990. *Reconstructing Kemetic Culture: Papers, Perspectives, Projects*. Los Angeles: University of Sankore Press.

Katz, Michael B. 1989. *The Undeserving Poor: From the War on Poverty to the War on Welfare*. New York: Pantheon.

Keith, Michael, and Malcolm Cross. 1993. "Racism and the Postmodern City." In *Racism, the City, and the State*, edited by Malcolm Cross and Michael Keith, 1–30. New York: Routledge.

Keller, Evelyn Fox. 1985. *Reflections on Gender and Science*. New Haven: Yale University Press.

Kershaw, Terry. 1992. "Afrocentrism and the Afrocentric Method." *Western Journal of Black Studies* 16 (3): 160–68.

Kevles, Daniel J. 1985. *In the Name of Eugenics: Genetics and the Uses of Human Heredity*. Berkeley: University of California Press.

King, Deborah. 1988. "Multiple Jeopardy, Multiple Consciousness: The Context of Black Feminist Ideology." *Signs* 14 (autumn): 42–72.

King, Richard H. 1992. *Civil Rights and the Idea of Freedom*. Athens: University of Georgia Press.

Ladner, Joyce. 1968. "On Becoming a Woman in the Ghetto: Modes of Adaptation." Ph.D. diss., Washington University.

———. 1972. *Tomorrow's Tomorrow*. Garden City, N.Y.: Doubleday.

Lash, Scott. 1990. *Sociology of Postmodernism*. New York: Routledge.

Lather, Patti. 1991. *Getting Smart: Feminist Research and Pedagogy with/in the Postmodern*. New York: Routledge.

Lawrence, Charles R., III. 1993. "If He Hollers Let Him Go: Regulating Racist Speech on Campus," In *Words That Wound: Critical Race Theory, Assaultive Speech, and the First Amendment,* edited by Mari J. Matsuda, Charles R. Lawrence III, Richard Delgado, and Kimberle Crenshaw, 53–88. Boulder: Westview.

Lawrence, Charles R., III, Mari J. Matsuda, Richard Delgado, and Kimberle Crenshaw. 1993. Introduction to *Words That Wound: Critical Race Theory, Assaultive Speech, and the First Amendment,* edited by Mari J. Matsuda, Charles R. Lawrence III, Richard Delgado, and Kimberle Crenshaw, 1–16. Boulder: Westview.

Lemert, Charles. 1992. "General Social Theory, Irony, Postmodernism." In *Postmodernism and Social Theory,* edited by Steven Seidman and David Wagner, 17–46. Cambridge, Mass.: Blackwell.

———, ed. 1993. *Social Theory: The Multicultural and Classic Readings.* Boulder: Westview.

———. 1995. *Sociology after the Crisis.* Boulder: Westview Press.

Lerner, Gerda, ed. 1972. *Black Women in White America: A Documentary History.* New York: Vintage.

Levine, Donald L. 1995. *Visions of the Sociological Tradition.* Chicago: University of Chicago Press.

Liu, Tessie. 1991. "Teaching the Differences among Women from a Historical Perspective." *Women's Studies International Forum* 14 (4): 265–76.

Lorde, Audre. 1984. *Sister Outsider.* Trumansburg, N.Y.: Crossing Press.

Lubiano, Wahneema. 1992. "Black Ladies, Welfare Queens, and State Minstrels: Ideological War by Narrative Means." In *Race-ing Justice, En-gendering Power,* edited by Toni Morrison, 323–63. New York: Pantheon.

Lugones, Maria C. 1994. "Purity, Impurity, and Separation." *Signs* 19 (2): 458.

Lusane, Clarence. 1993. "Rap, Race, and Politics." *Race and Class* 35 (1): 41–55.

Lyman, Stanford. 1972. *The Black American in Sociological Thought: A Failure of Perspective.* New York: Capricorn.

Madhubuti, Haki R. 1990a. *Black Men: Obsolete, Single, Dangerous?* Chicago: Third World Press.

———, ed. 1990b. *Confusion by Any Other Name: Essays Exploring the Negative Impact of the Blackman's Guide to Understanding the Blackwoman.* Chicago: Third World Press.

Madrid, Arturo. 1988. "Missing People and Others: Joining Together to Expand the Circle." In *The Graywolf Annual 5: Multicultural Literacy,* edited by Rick Simonson and Scott Walker. St. Paul: Graywolf.

Madriz, Esther. 1997. *Nothing Bad Happens to Good Girls: Fear of Crime in Women's Lives.* Berkeley: University of California Press.

Magner, Denise K. 1989. "Decline in Doctorates Earned by Black and White Men Persists, Study Finds; Foreign Students and U.S. Women Fill Gaps." *Chronicle of Higher Education,* March 1, A11–A15.

Mannheim, Karl. 1954 [1936]. *Ideology and Utopia: An Introduction to the Sociology of Knowledge.* New York: Harcourt, Brace & World.

Marable, Manning. 1983. *How Capitalism Underdeveloped Black America.* Boston: South End.

———. 1991. *Race, Reform, and Rebellion.* 2d ed. Jackson: University Press of Mississippi.

———. 1993. "Beyond Identity Politics: Towards a Liberation Theory for Multicultural Democracy." *Race and Class* 35 (1): 113–30.

Marrett, Cora Bagley. 1968. "Consensus and Organizational Effectiveness." Ph.D. diss., University of Wisconsin at Madison.

Marshall, Paule. 1983. *Praisesong for the Widow.* New York: Putnam.

Martínez, Rubén. 1992. *The Other Side: Notes from the New L.A., Mexico City, and Beyond.* New York: Vintage.

Marx, Karl. 1963 [1852]. *The Eighteenth Brumaire of Louis Bonaparte.* New York: International.

Massey, Douglas S., and Nancy A. Denton. 1993. *American Apartheid: Segregation and the Making of the Underclass.* Cambridge: Harvard University Press.

Matthews, Nancy A. 1989. "Surmounting a Legacy: The Expansion of Racial Diversity in an Anti-rape Movement." *Gender and Society* 3 (4): 518–32.

Matsuda, Mari J. 1989. "Public Response to Racist Speech: Considering the Victim's Story." *Michigan Law Review* 87 (August): 2320–81.

Matsuda, Mari J., Charles Lawrence 111, Richard Delgado, and Kimberle Crenshaw, eds. 1993. *Words That Wound: Critical Race Theory, Assaultive Speech, and the First Amendment.* Boulder: Westview.

Mbiti, John S. 1969. *African Religions and Philosophy.* London: Heinemann.

McClintock, Anne. 1995. *Imperial Leather: Race, Gender, and Sexuality in the Colonial Conquest.* New York: Routledge.

McGowan, John. 1991. *Postmodernism and Its Critics.* Ithaca, N.Y.: Cornell University Press.

McIntosh, Peggy. 1992. "White Privilege and Male Privilege: A Personal Account of Coming to See Correspondences through Work in Women's Studies." In *Race, Class, and Gender: An Anthology,* edited by Margaret Andersen and Patricia Hill Collins, 76–86. Belmont, Calif.: Wadsworth.

McKay, Nellie. 1992. "Remembering Anita Hill and Clarence Thomas: What Really Happened When One Black Woman Spoke Out." In *Race-ing Justice, En-gendering Power,* edited by Toni Morrison, 269–89. New York: Pantheon.

McKay, Nellie, Patricia Hill Collins, Mae Henderson, and June Jordan. 1991. "The State of the Art." *Women's Review of Books* 8 (5), February: 23–26.

McKee, James B. 1993. *Sociology and the Race Problem: The Failure of a Perspective.* Urbana: University of Illinois Press.

Memmi, Albert. 1965. *The Colonizer and the Colonized.* Boston: Beacon.

Mercer, Kobena. 1994. *Welcome to the Jungle: New Positions in Black Cultural Studies.* New York: Routledge.

Merton, Robert K. 1972. "Insiders and Outsiders: A Chapter in the Sociology of Knowledge." *American Journal of Sociology* 78: 9–47.

———. 1973. *The Sociology of Science: Theoretical and Empirical Investigations.* Chicago: University of Chicago Press.

Miles, Robert. 1987. "Recent Marxist Theories of Nationalism and the Issue of Racism." *British Journal of Sociology* 38 (1): 24–43.

———. 1989. *Racism.* New York: Routledge.

Mills, C. Wright. 1959. *The Power Elite.* New York: Oxford University Press.

Minh-ha, Trinh T. 1989. *Woman, Native, Other: Writing Postcoloniality and Feminism.* Bloomington: Indiana University Press.

Minnich, Elizabeth Kamarck. 1990. *Transforming Knowledge.* Philadelphia: Temple University Press.

Mirza, Heidi Safia, ed. 1997. *Black British Feminism: A Reader.* New York: Routledge.

Mitchell, Henry H., and Nicholas Cooper Lewter. 1986. *Soul Theology: The Heart of American Black Culture.* San Francisco: Harper & Row.

Mohanty, Chandra Talpade. 1989–90. "On Race and Voice: Challenges for Liberal Education in the 1990s." *Cultural Critique* (winter): 179–208.

Morris, Aldon D. 1984. *The Origins of the Civil Rights Movement: Black Communities Organizing for Change.* New York: Free Press.

Morrison, Toni. 1970. *The Bluest Eye.* New York: Pocket.

———. 1987. *Beloved.* New York: Knopf.

Morton, Patricia. 1991. *Disfigured Images: The Historical Assault on Afro-American Women.* New York: Praeger.

Moses, Wilson Jeremiah. 1978. *The Golden Age of Black Nationalism, 1850–1925.* New York: Oxford University Press.

Moses, Yolanda T. 1989. *Black Women in Academe: Issues and Strategies.* Project on the Status and Education of Women. Washington: Association of American Colleges.

Mouzelis, Nicos. 1995. *Sociological Theory: What Went Wrong? Diagnosis and Remedies.* New York: Routledge.

Mueller, Carol. 1990. "Ella Baker and the Origins of 'Participatory Democracy.'" In *Women in the Civil Rights Movement: Trailblazers and Torchbearers, 1941–1965,* edited by Vicki L. Crawford, Jacqueline Anne Rouse, and Barbara Woods, 51–70. Bloomington: Indiana University Press.

Mullings, Leith. 1994. "Images, Ideology, and Women of Color." In *Women of Color in the United States,* edited by Maxine Baca Zinn and Bonnie Thornton Dill, 265–90. Philadelphia: Temple University Press.

Murray, Pauli. 1995 [1970]. "The Liberation of Black Women." In *Words of Fire: An Anthology of African American Feminist Thought,* edited by Beverly Guy-Sheftall, 186–97. New York: New Press.

Myers, Linda Jane. 1988. *Understanding an Afrocentric World View: Introduction to an Optimal Psychology.* Dubuque: Kendall/Hunt.

Myerson, Debra, and Maureen Scully. 1995. "Crossroads: Tempered Radicalism and the Politics of Ambivalence and Change." *Organization Science* 6 (5): 585.

Nain, Gemma Tang. 1991. "Black Women, Sexism, and Racism: Black or Antiracist Feminism?" *Feminist Review* 37 (spring): 1–22.

Naples, Nancy A. 1991. "'Just What Needed to be Done': The Political Practice of Women Community Workers in Low-Income Neighborhoods." *Gender and Society* 5 (4): 478–94.

Naylor, Gloria. 1988. *Mama Day.* New York: Ticknor & Fields.

Neely, Barbara. 1992. *Blanche on the Lam.* New York: Penguin.

Nicholson, Linda J. 1990. Introduction to *Feminism/Postmodernism,* edited by Linda Nicholson, 1–18. New York: Routledge.

Nobles, Wade. 1972. "African Philosophy: Foundations for Black Psychology." In *Black Psychology,* edited by Reginald L. Jones, 18–32. New York: Harper & Row.

Nsiah-Jefferson, Laurie. 1989. "Reproductive Laws, Women of Color, and Low-Income Women." In *Reproductive Laws for the 1990s,* edited by Sherrill Cohen and Nadine Taub, 23–67. Clifton, N.J.: Humana.

Oliver, Melvin L., and Thomas M. Shapiro. 1995. *Black Wealth/White Wealth: A New Perspective on Racial Inequality.* New York: Routledge.

Omi, Michael, and Howard Winant. 1994. *Racial Formation in the United States: From the 1960s to the 1990s.* 2d ed. New York: Routledge.

Omolade, Barbara. 1994. *The Rising Song of African American Women.* New York: Routledge.

Orfield, Gary, and Carole Ashkinaze. 1991. *The Closing Door: Conservative Policy and Black Opportunity.* Chicago: University of Chicago Press.

Padilla, Genero M. 1989. "Myth and Comparative Cultural Nationalism: The Ideological Uses of Aztlan." In *Aztlan: Essays on the Chicano Homeland,* edited by

Rudolfo A. Anaya and Francisco A. Lomeli, 111–34. Albuquerque: Academia/ El Norte.

Painter, Nell. 1992. "Hill, Thomas, and the Use of Racial Stereotype." In *Race-ing Justice, En-gendering Power,* edited by Toni Morrison, 200–214. New York: Pantheon.

———. 1993. "Sojourner Truth." In *Black Women in the United States: An Historical Encyclopedia,* edited by Darlene Clark Hine, Elsa Barkley Brown, and Rosalyn Terborg-Penn, 1172–76. New York: Carlson.

Park, Robert Ezra. 1950. *Race and Culture.* Glencoe, Ill.: Free Press.

Petrie, Phil, et al. 1991. "Afrocentrism in a Multicultural Democracy." *American Visions,* August, 20–26.

Pinkney, Alphonso. 1976. *Red, Black, and Green: Black Nationalism in the United States.* London: Cambridge University Press.

Platt, Anthony M. 1991. *E. Franklin Frazier Reconsidered.* New Brunswick, N.J.: Rutgers University Press.

Poliakov, Leon. 1974. *The Aryan Myth: A History of Racist and Nationalist Ideas in Europe.* London: Heinemann.

Poster, Winifred R. 1995. "The Challenges and Promises of Class and Racial Diversity in the Women's Movement: A Study of Two Women's Organizations." *Gender and Society* 9 (6): 659–79.

Pratt, Minnie Bruce. 1993. "Books in the Closet, in the Attic, Boxes, Secrets." In *Daily Fare: Essays from the Multicultural Experience,* edited by Kathleen Aguero, 1–19. Athens: University of Georgia Press.

Proctor, Robert N. 1988. *Racial Hygiene: Medicine under the Nazis.* Cambridge: Harvard University Press.

"Psychological Nigrescence." 1989. *Consulting Psychologist* 12 (2), April (special issue).

Quadagno, Jill. 1994. *The Color of Welfare: How Racism Undermined the War on Poverty.* New York: Oxford University Press.

Rabinow, Paul, and William M. Sullivan. 1987. "The Interpretive Turn: A Second Look." In *Interpretive Social Science: A Second Look,* edited by Paul Rabinow and William Sullivan, 1–30. Berkeley: University of California Press.

Rainwater, Lee, ed. 1970. *Soul.* New York: Aldine.

Ransby, Barbara, and Tracye Matthews. 1993. "Black Popular Culture and the Transcendence of Patriarchial Illusions." *Race and Class* 35 (1): 57–68.

Reagon, Bernice Johnson. 1987. "African Diaspora Women: The Making of Cultural Workers." In *Women in Africa and the African Diaspora,* edited by Rosalyn Terborg-Penn, Sharon Harley, and Andrea Benton Rushing, 167–80. Washington: Howard University Press.

Richards, Dona. 1980. "European Mythology: The Ideology of 'Progress.'" In *Contemporary Black Thought,* edited by Molefi Kete Asante and Abdulai S. Vandi, 59–79. Beverly Hills: Sage.

———. 1990. "The Implications of African-American Spirituality." In *African Culture: The Rhythms of Unity,* edited by Molefi Kete Asante and Kariamu Welsh Asante, 207–31. Trenton, N.J.: Africa World Press.

Richie, Beth E. 1996. *Compelled to Crime: The Gender Entrapment of Battered Black Women.* New York: Routledge.

Riggs, Marlon. 1992. "Unleash the Queen." In *Black Popular Culture,* edited by Michele Wallace and Gina Dent, 99–105. Seattle: Bay Press.

Roby, Pamela. 1992. "Women and the ASA: Degendering Organizational Structures and Processes, 1964–1974." *American Sociologist* 23 (1): 18–48.

Rodgers-Rose, La Frances, ed. 1980. *The Black Woman*. Beverly Hills: Sage.

Rollins, Judith. 1985. *Between Women: Domestics and Their Employers*. Philadelphia: Temple University Press.

Rose, Tricia. 1994. *Black Noise: Rap Music and Black Culture in Contemporary America*. Hanover, N.H.: Wesleyan University Press.

Rosenau, Pauline Marie. 1992. *Post-modernism and the Social Sciences*. Princeton: Princeton University Press.

Ross, Dorothy. 1991. *The Origins of American Social Science*. New York: Cambridge University Press.

Ross, Edward A. 1906–1907. "Western Civilization and the Birth Rate." *American Journal of Sociology* 12: 609–17.

Sacks, Karen Brodkin. 1988. "Gender and Grassroots Leadership." In *Women and the Politics of Empowerment*, edited by Ann Bookman and Sandra Morgen, 77–96. Philadelphia: Temple University Press.

———. 1989. "Toward a Unified Theory of Class, Race, and Gender." *American Ethnologist* 16 (3): 534–50.

Saegert, Susan. 1989. "Unlikely Leaders, Extreme Circumstances: Older Black Women Building Community Households." *American Journal of Community Psychology* 17 (3): 295–317.

Said, Edward W. 1978. *Orientalism*. New York: Vintage.

———. 1990. "Zionism from the Standpoint of Its Victims." In *Anatomy of Racism*, edited by David Goldberg, 210–46. Minneapolis: University of Minnesota Press.

———. 1993. *Culture and Imperialism*. New York: Knopf.

Sanders, Cheryl J. 1995. *Empowerment Ethics for a Liberated People: A Path to African American Social Transformation*. Minneapolis: Fortress.

Sands, Aimee. 1993. "Never Meant to Survive: A Black Woman's Journey—An Interview with Evelynn Hammonds." In *The "Racial" Economy of Science: Toward a Democratic Future*, edited by Sandra Harding, 239–48. Bloomington: Indiana University Press.

San Juan, E., Jr. 1992. *Racial Formations/Critical Transformations: Articulations of Power in Ethnic and Racial Studies in the United States*. Atlantic Highlands, N.J.: Humanities.

Sarachild, Kathie. 1978 [1973]. "Consciousness-Raising: A Radical Weapon." In *Feminist Revolution*. 2d ed. Edited by Redstockings, 144–50. New York: Random House.

Scales-Trent, Judy. 1989. "Black Women and the Constitution: Finding Our Place, Asserting Our Rights." *Harvard Civil Rights–Civil Liberties Law Review* 24 (1), winter: 9–43.

Schutz, Alfred. 1944. "The Stranger: An Essay in Social Psychology." *American Journal of Sociology* 49: 499–507.

Scott, James C. 1990. *Domination and the Arts of Resistance: The Hidden Transcripts*. New Haven: Yale University Press.

Scott, Joseph W. 1984. "1984: The Public and Private Governance of Race Relations." *Sociological Focus* 17 (3): 175–87.

Scott, Patricia Bell. 1982. "Debunking Sapphire: Toward a Non-racist and Non-sexist Social Science." In *All the Women Are White, All the Blacks Are Men, But Some of Us Are Brave: Black Women's Studies*, edited by Gloria T. Hull, Patricia Bell Scott, and Barbara Smith, 85–92. Old Westbury, N.Y.: Feminist Press.

Segrest, Mab. 1994. *Memoir of a Race Traitor*. Boston: South End.

Seidman, Steven. 1992. "Postmodern Social Theory as Narrative with a Moral Intent."

In *Postmodernism and Social Theory,* edited by Steven Seidman and David Wagner, 47–81. Cambridge, Mass.: Blackwell.

Seidman, Steven, and David G. Wagner. 1992. Introduction to *Postmodernism and Social Theory,* edited by Steven Seidman and David Wagner, 1–14. Cambridge, Mass.: Blackwell.

Serequeberhan, Tsenay. 1991. *African Philosophy: The Essential Readings.* New York: Paragon.

Shange, Ntozake. 1975. *for colored girls who have considered suicide / when the rainbow is enuf.* New York: Macmillan.

Simmel, Georg. 1921. "The Sociological Significance of the Stranger." In *Introduction to the Science of Sociology,* edited by Robert E. Park and Ernest W. Burgess, 322–27. Chicago: University of Chicago Press.

Slack, Jennifer Daryl. 1996. "The Theory and Method of Articulation in Cultural Studies." In *Stuart Hall: Critical Dialogues in Cultural Studies,* edited by David Morley and Kuan-Hsing Chen, 112–27. New York: Routledge.

Smith, Barbara. 1983. *Home Girls: A Black Feminist Anthology.* New York: Kitchen Table.

———. 1990. "The Truth That Never Hurts: Black Lesbians in Fiction in the 1980s." In *Wild Women in the Whirlwind,* edited by Joanne Braxton and Andree Nicola McLaughlin, 213–45. New Brunswick, N.J.: Rutgers University Press.

Smith, Barbara Ellen. 1995. "Crossing the Great Divides: Race, Class, and Gender in Southern Women's Organizing, 1979–1991." *Gender and Society* 9 (6): 680–96.

Smith, Dorothy E. 1987. *The Everyday World as Problematic: A Feminist Sociology.* Boston: Northeastern University Press.

———. 1990a. *The Conceptual Practices of Power: A Feminist Sociology of Knowledge.* Boston: Northeastern University Press.

———. 1990b. *Texts, Facts, and Femininity: Exploring the Relations of Ruling.* New York: Routledge, Chapman & Hall.

Smith, Valerie. 1989. "Black Feminist Theory and the Representation of the 'Other.'" In *Changing Our Own Words: Essays on Criticism, Theory, and Writing by Black Women,* edited by Cheryl A. Wall, 38–57. New Brunswick, N.J.: Rutgers University Press.

Smitherman, Geneva. 1977. *Talkin and Testifyin: The Language of Black America.* Boston: Houghton Mifflin.

———. 1996. "A Womanist Looks at the Million Man March." In *Million Man March/Day of Absence,* edited by Haki R. Madhubuti and Maulana Karenga, 104–7. Chicago: Third World Press.

Sobel, Mechal. 1979. *Trabelin' On: The Slave Journey to an Afro-Baptist Faith.* Princeton: Princeton University Press.

Souljah, Sister. 1994. *No Disrespect.* New York: Random House.

Spelman, Elizabeth V. 1988. *Inessential Woman: Problems of Exclusion in Feminist Thought.* Boston: Beacon.

Spivak, Gayatri Chakravorty. 1993. *Outside in the Teaching Machine.* New York: Routledge.

Sprague, Joey, and Mary K. Zimmerman. 1989. "Quality and Quantity: Reconstructing Feminist Methodology." *American Sociologist* 20 (1): 71–86.

Squires, Gregory D. 1994. *Capital and Communities in Black and White: The Intersections of Race, Class, and Uneven Development.* Albany: State University of New York Press.

Stanley, Liz, and Sue Wise. 1993 [1983]. *Breaking Out Again: Feminist Ontology and Epistemology.* New York: Routledge.

Stauder, Jack. 1993. "The 'Relevance' of Anthropology to Colonialism and Imperialism." In *The "Racial" Economy of Science: Toward a Democratic Future,* edited by Sandra Harding, 408–27. Bloomington: Indiana University Press.

Steady, Filomina Chioma. 1987. "African Feminism: A Worldwide Perspective." In *Women in Africa and the African Diaspora,* edited by Rosalyn Terborg-Penn, Sharon Harley, and Andrea Benton, 3–24. Washington: Howard University Press.

Stepan, Nancy. 1982. *The Idea of Race in Science: Great Britain, 1800–1960.* Hamden, Conn.: Archon.

———. 1990. "Race and Gender: The Role of Analogy in Science." In *Anatomy of Racism,* edited by David Goldberg, 38–57. Minneapolis: University of Minnesota Press.

Stepan, Nancy, and Sander L. Gilman. 1993. "Appropriating the Idioms of Science: The Rejection of Scientific Racism." In *The "Racial" Economy of Science: Toward a Democratic Future,* edited by Sandra Harding, 170–93. Bloomington: Indiana University Press.

Sterling, Dorothy, ed. 1984. *We Are Your Sisters: Black Women in the Nineteenth Century.* New York: Norton.

Sudarkasa, Niara. 1981. "Interpreting the African Heritage in Afro-American Family Organization." In *Black Families,* edited by Harriet Pipes McAdoo, 37–53. Beverly Hills: Sage.

Takaki, Ronald. 1993. *A Different Mirror: A History of Multicultural America.* Boston: Little, Brown.

Tate, Claudia, ed. 1983. *Black Women Writers at Work.* New York: Continuum.

Terborg-Penn, Rosalyn. 1986. "Black Women in Resistance: A Cross-Cultural Perspective." In *In Resistance: Studies in African, Caribbean, and Afro-American History,* edited by Gary Y. Okhiro. Amherst: University of Massachusetts Press.

Terborg-Penn, Rosalyn, Sharon Harley, and Andrea Benton Rushing, eds. 1987. *Women in Africa and the African Diaspora.* Washington: Howard University Press.

Terrelonge, Pauline. 1984. "Feminist Consciousness and Black Women." In *Women: A Feminist Perspective.* 3d ed. Edited by Jo Freeman, 557–67. Palo Alto, Calif.: Mayfield.

Thompson, Robert Farris. 1983. *Flash of the Spirit: African and Afro-American Art and Philosophy.* New York: Vintage.

Thorne, Barrie. 1992. "Feminism and the Family: Two Decades of Thought." In *Rethinking the Family: Some Feminist Questions,* edited by Barrie Thorne and Marilyn Yalom, 3–30. Boston: Northeastern University Press.

Torgovnick, Marianna. 1990. *Gone Primitive: Savage Intellects, Modern Lives.* Chicago: University of Chicago Press.

Townes, Emilie M. ed. 1993. *A Troubling in My Soul: Womanist Perspectives on Evil and Suffering.* Maryknoll, N.Y.: Orbis.

Tucker, William H. 1994. *The Science and Politics of Racial Research.* Urbana: University of Illinois Press.

Turner, James E. 1984. "Foreword: Africana Studies and Epistemology: A Discourse in the Sociology of Knowledge." In *The Next Decade: Theoretical and Research Issues in Africana Studies,* edited by James E. Turner, v–xxv. Ithaca, N.Y.: Cornell University Africana Studies and Research Center.

U.S. Bureau of the Census. 1968 [1918]. *Negro Population, 1790–1915.* Reprint, New York: Arno.

———. 1979. *Twenty Censuses: Population and Housing Questions, 1790–1980.* Prepared by the Data User Services Division. Washington, D.C.: Government Printing Office.

Van Deburg, William L. 1992. *New Day in Babylon: The Black Power Movement and American Culture, 1965–1975.* Chicago: University of Chicago Press.

Van Dijk, Teun A. 1993. *Elite Discourse and Racism.* Newbury Park, Calif.: Sage.

Vanneman, Reeve, and Lynn Weber Cannon. 1987. *The American Perception of Class.* Philadelphia: Temple University Press.

Wagner, David G. 1992. "Daring Modesty: On Metatheory, Observation, and Theory Growth." In *Postmodernism and Social Theory,* edited by Steven Seidman and David Wagner, 199–220. Cambridge, Mass.: Blackwell.

Walker, Alice. 1982. *The Color Purple.* New York: Washington Square Press.

———. 1983. *In Search of Our Mothers' Gardens.* New York: Harcourt Brace Jovanovich.

———. 1989. *The Temple of My Familiar.* New York: Harcourt Brace Jovanovich.

———. 1992. *Possessing the Secret of Joy.* New York: Harcourt Brace Jovanovich.

Walker, Samuel. 1994. *Hate Speech: The History of an American Controversy.* Lincoln: University of Nebraska Press.

Wall, Cheryl A. 1989. *Changing Our Own Words: Essays on Criticism, Theory, and Writing by Black Women.* New Brunswick, N.J.: Rutgers University Press.

Wallace, Michele. 1990. *Invisibility Blues: From Pop to Theory.* New York: Verso.

Walters, Ronald W. 1993. *Pan Africanism in the African Diaspora: An Analysis of Modern Afrocentric Political Movements.* Detroit: Wayne State University Press.

Washington, Margaret, ed. 1993. *Narrative of Sojourner Truth.* New York: Vintage.

Weber, Lynn, Elizabeth Higginbotham, and Bonnie Thornton Dill. Forthcoming. "Sisterhood as Collaboration: Building the Center for Research on Women at the University of Memphis." In *Feminist Sociology,* edited by Barbara Laslett and Barrie Thorne. New Brunswick, N.J.: Rutgers University Press.

Weber, Max. 1968 [1921]. *Economy and Society.* Totowa, N.J.: Bedminster.

Weedon, Chris. 1987. *Feminist Practice and Poststructuralist Theory.* New York: Blackwell.

Welsing, Frances Cress. 1991. *The Isis Papers: The Keys to the Colors.* Chicago: Third World Press.

West, Candace, and Sarah Fenstermaker. 1995. "Doing Difference." *Gender and Society* 9(1): 8–37.

West, Cornel. 1990. "The New Politics of Difference." In *Out There: Marginalization and Contemporary Cultures,* edited by Russell Ferguson, Martha Gever, Trinh T. Minh-ha, and Cornel West, 19–38. Cambridge: MIT Press.

———. 1992. "The Postmodern Crisis of the Black Intellectuals." In *Cultural Studies,* edited by Lawrence Grossberg, Cary Nelson, and Paula A. Treichler, 689–96. New York: Routledge, Chapman & Hall.

———. 1993. *Race Matters.* Boston: Beacon.

White, E. Frances. 1987. "Civilization Denied: Questions on *Black Athena.*" *Radical America,* May 21, 38–40.

———. 1990. "Africa on My Mind: Gender, Counter Discourse, and African-American Nationalism." *Journal of Women's History* 2 (1), spring: 73–97.

White, Jack. 1996a. "Texaco's High-Octane Racism Problems." *Time,* November 25, 33–34.

———. 1996b. "Texaco's White-Collar Bigots." *Time,* November 18, 104.

White, Joseph L., and Thomas A. Parham. 1990. *The Psychology of Blacks: An African-American Perspective.* 2d ed. Englewood Cliffs, N.J.: Prentice Hall.

Wilkinson, Doris. 1981. "Evolution of the Participation of Women and Minorities in the ASA." *American Sociologist* 16 (May): 101–2.

Williams, Patricia J. 1991. *The Alchemy of Race and Rights: Diary of a Law Professor.* Cambridge: Harvard University Press.

———. 1995. *The Rooster's Egg: On the Persistence of Prejudice.* Cambridge: Harvard University Press.

Williams, Shirley. 1990. "Some Implications of Womanist Theory." In *Reading Black, Reading Feminist: A Critical Anthology,* edited by Henry Louis Gates Jr., 68–75. New York: Meridian.

Wilson, Melba. 1993. *Crossing the Boundary: Black Women Survive Incest.* Seattle: Seal.

Wilson, William Julius. 1974. "The New Black Sociology: Reflections on the 'Insiders and Outsiders' Controversy." In *Black Sociologists: Historical and Contemporary Perspectives,* edited by James E. Blackwell and Morris Janowitz, 322–38. Chicago: University of Chicago Press.

———. 1978. *The Declining Significance of Race.* Chicago: University of Chicago Press.

———. 1987. *The Truly Disadvantaged.* Chicago: University of Chicago Press.

Winant, Howard. 1993. "Difference and Inequality: Postmodern Racial Politics in the United States." In *Racism, the City, and the State,* edited by Malcolm Cross and Michael Keith, 108–27. New York: Routledge.

———. 1994. *Racial Conditions: Politics, Theory, Comparisons.* Minneapolis: University of Minnesota Press.

Work, Monroe. 1900–1901. "Crime among the Negroes of Chicago: A Social Study." *American Journal of Sociology* 6: 204–23.

Wyche, Karen Fraser, and Sherryl Browne Graves. 1992. "Minority Women in Academia: Access and Barriers to Professional Participation." *Psychology of Women Quarterly* 16: 429–37.

Young, Iris Marion. 1990. *Justice and the Politics of Difference.* Princeton: Princeton University Press.

Yuval-Davis, Nira. 1997. *Gender and Nation.* Thousand Oaks, Calif.: Sage.

Zahan, Dominique. 1979. *The Religion, Spirituality, and Thought of Traditional Africa.* Chicago: University of Chicago Press.

Zinn, Maxine Baca. 1989. "Family, Race, and Poverty in the Eighties." *Signs* 14 (4): 856–74.

Zinn, Maxine Baca, and Bonnie Thornton Dill, eds. 1994. *Women of Color in U.S. Society.* Philadelphia: Temple University Press.

Index

Addams, Jane, 100
Africa: in Afrocentrism, 155–56; Egypt (Kemet), 156, 163, 180; as imagined past, 177; as "Mother," 173; philosophy and cosmology of, 162, 163, 274 n.9; in primitivist discourse, 99
African-Americans. *See* Blacks in the United States
African-American women. *See* Black women in the United States
Afrocentrism, 88–94, 156, 158, 163, 266–67 n.1; and Black consciousness, 156–57; Black cultural nationalism as precursor of, 159–67; contradictions within, 155–56; as critical social theory, 90, 158, 194; and "fighting words" paradigm, 158, 180–83; media coverage of, 156, 158; similarities to religion, 167; and "soul" as essential Blackness, 160, 162; treatment of Black culture in, 174, 176; treatment of gender in, 174–80; treatment of truth in, 165, 236. *See also* Black cultural nationalism
Akbar, Na'im, 164
Anthias, Floya, 52, 206
Anzaldúa, Gloria, 236

Appiah, Kwame Anthony, xix, 87, 91, 235
Arnold, Regina, 117
articulation, 209, 228, 259 n.7, 269–70 n.5
Asante, Molefi, 162, 166, 178, 257 n.10; *The Afrocentric Idea,* 266–67 n.1; *Kemet, Afrocentricity, and Knowledge,* 266–67 n.1
Awkward, Michael, 55, 235

Baker, Ella, 26–27, 249–50
Baldwin, James, 180
Bambara, Toni Cade, 56, 59, 178; *The Black Woman,* 73, 179; *The Salt Eaters,* 274 n.9
Bannerji, Himani, 13
Baraka, Imamu Amiri, 168–74, 268 n.8
Barnett, Ida Wells, 75, 107–8, 109, 263 n.13
Barthes, Roland, 266 n.5
Baudrillard, Jean, 266 nn.5, 9
Beale, Frances, 226
Bell, Derrick, 57–58, 218
Ben-Jochannan, Yosef: *Black Man of the Nile and His Family,* 161
Berger, Peter, xix

levels of social organization within, 226–28; naming, 56–70, 73; and postmodernism, 68, 143; reliance of, on testimonial tradition, 237; significance of dialogue to, 72–76; significance of groups to, 203–11, 223; significance of voice to, 50, 58, 119, 236–39; social location and, 201–3, 211, 231–36

Bobo, Jacqueline, 227

boundaries and boundary maintenance: of academic disciplines, 107; between Black women and Black men, 63, 69–70, 226; of discourses, 89–92, 268 n.2; intersectionality and, 206; role of language in, 143; significance of symbolism in, 105; transgression of, 121, 231, 269 n.2

Bourdieu, Pierre, 237, 253 n.3, 265 n.3, 266 n.6, 271 n.8, 272 n.5

breaking silence, 47–56, 86–87, 258 n.3

Brewer, Rose, 116

Brown, Elaine, 168

Brown, Elsa Barkley, 25, 60, 88, 248–50

Brown, James, 43

Brown v. Board of Education (1954), 5, 255 n.2

Cabral, Amilcar, 163, 167

Calhoun, Craig, 254 n.4

Cannon, Katie, 246

capitalism, 57–58, 104, 133, 188, 214, 216; defined, 275

Carby, Hazel, 55, 73, 149, 150, 152; *Reconstructing Womanhood,* 259 n.4

Center for Research on Women (Memphis State University), 117–18

Chisholm, Shirley, 59; *Unbought and Unbossed,* 48

Chow, Rey, 133, 136

Chrisman, Robert, xxii

Christian, Barbara, 143; *Black Feminist Criticism,* 259 n.4

Civil Rights Act (1964), 255 n.2

civil rights movement, 13, 113, 201, 247

class, 209; defined, 254 n.6, 255–56 n.4, 276; economic class, 101, 107–8, 212–16, 256 n.4, 276; race-class, concept of, 209–10

Cleage, Pearl, 65–66, 67

Cliff, Michelle, xiii

Clinton, Bill, 41

Clinton, George, and the Funkadelics of Parliament, 34

Cole, Johnetta, xxii, 188

Collins, Patricia Hill: *Black Feminist Thought,* xvii, xxi, 6, 8, 254–55, n.3, 259 n.7; "Learning from the Outsider Within," 6

colonialism, 128–31; defined, 276

Combahee River Collective, 59; "A Black Feminist Statement," 258 n.4

Commander, Lydia Kingmill, 100

commodification, xxi, 54, 141, 235; of Black women's writing, 57, 73–74; and cultural capital, 141, 216–17; defined, 276; of difference, 56, 147–48; and intellectual property, 57–58; of postcoloniality, 235

community: alternative views of, 248–49; as feature of class formation, 217–18; treatment of, in Black nationalism, 161, 167

consciousness: Black, 43, 156, 157; consciousness-raising, 28, 46, 276; and internalized oppression, 161; significance of group culture for, 217–18; voice as symbolic of, 46–47, 269 n.4

Cooper, Anna Julia, 46–47, 75, 263 n.13, 264 n.15

core/periphery relationships: defined, 276

Cosby Show (television show), 39–40, 42, 43, 259 n.5

Cose, Ellis, 11–12

Cox, Oliver, 264 n.15

Crenshaw, Kimberle, 88, 206, 259 n.7, 273 n.8

critical mass, 51, 242–43, 273 n.7; Black women in sociology as, 114–20

Cross, Malcolm, 127

Daniels, Jessie, 118, 257 n.12

Davies, Carole Boyce, 126–27, 233–34

Davis, Angela, 56, 59–60, 168, 175, 231–32; "Reflections on the Black Woman's Role in the Community of Slaves," 59; *Women, Race, and Class,* 258 n.4

decentering: defined, 126–37, 277

Patricia Hill Collins is the Charles Phelps Taft Professor of Sociology in the Department of African-American Studies at the University of Cincinnati. Her scholarship examines issues of gender, race, social class, and nation, specifically relating to African-American women. Her first book, *Black Feminist Thought: Knowledge, Consciousness, and the Politics of Empowerment* (1990), has won many awards. Edited with Margaret L. Andersen, her second book, *Race, Class, and Gender: An Anthology* (1992), now in its third edition, is widely used in undergraduate classrooms throughout the United States.